T5-ARD-315

RELATED TITLES FOR COLLEGE-BOUND STUDENTS

Test Preparation

AP Biology

AP Calculus AB

AP Chemistry

AP English Language & Composition

AP English Literature & Composition

AP Macroeconomics/Microeconomics

AP Physics B

AP Psychology

AP Statistics

AP U.S. Government & Politics

AP World History

SAT II: Biology

SAT II: Chemistry

SAT II: Mathematics

SAT II: Physics

SAT II: Spanish

SAT II: U.S. History

SAT II: World History

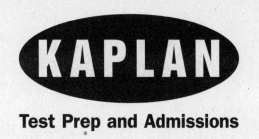

Test Prep and Admissions

AP® U.S. History

An Apex Learning Guide

2005 Edition

By Mark Bach and Betsy Fitzgerald

Simon & Schuster

NEW YORK · LONDON · SYDNEY · TORONTO

AP® is a registered trademark of the College Entrance Examination Board, which neither sponsors nor endorses this product.

Kaplan Publishing
Published by Simon & Schuster
1230 Avenue of the Americas
New York, NY 10020

Copyright © 2005 by Apex Learning Inc.

All rights reserved. No part of this book may be reproduced or transmitted in any form or by any means, electronic
or mechanical, including photocopying, recording, or by any information storage and retrieval system, without the
written permission of the Publisher, except where permitted by law.

Kaplan® is a registered trademark of Kaplan, Inc.

For all references in this book, AP is a registered trademark of the College Entrance Examination Board which is not
affiliated with this book.

For bulk sales to schools, colleges, and universities, please contact: Order Department, Simon and Schuster,
100 Front Street, Riverside, NJ 08075. Phone: (800) 223-2336. Fax: (800) 943-9831.

Contributing Editors: Seppy Basili and Jon Zeitlin
Executive Editor: Jennifer Farthing
Project Editor: Sandy Gade
Production Manager: Michael Shevlin
Interior Page Layout: Jan Gladish and Renée Mitchell
Cover Design: Cheung Tai

Manufactured in the United States of America
Published simultaneously in Canada

January 2005
10 9 8 7 6 5 4 3 2 1

ISBN 0-7432-6061-9

Table of Contents

About the Authors

Mark Bach

Bach is a faculty consultant for the College Board and helps to score the AP History exam every June with many other history teachers. He is also an examiner for the International Baccalaureate in History. He taught overseas for 20 years in Taipei, Osaka, and New Delhi. He currently lives in Seattle and teaches AP U.S. History online for APEX Learning. At other times he is an avid skier, wine maker, and flyer.

Betsy Fitzgerald

Fitzgerald is a 32-year veteran history teacher at Erskine Academy, a private high school in South China, ME. She teaches Advanced Placement United States History and a wide range of other subjects. She also serves as the history department chair and was instrumental in creating the School and Local Government Project, a statewide program that offers lesson plans for the teaching of local government in Maine. Educated at the University of Maine—Machias, she holds a Masters from the Edmund S. Muskie School of Public Policy and is currently a doctoral student in public policy. She is a member of the Board of Directors of the National Council for Social Studies and the Maine Council for the Social Studies. Fitzgerald has presented at conferences and workshops across the state of Maine and at national conferences in San Antonio and Phoenix. Outside the world of education, Fitzgerald has served as an interim town manager, and currently serves as a town selectman and a code enforcement officer.

kaptest.com/publishing

The material in this book is up-to-date at the time of publication. For any important late-breaking developments—or changes or corrections to the Kaplan test preparation materials in this book—we will post that information online at **kaptest.com/publishing.** Check to see if there is any information posted there regarding this book.

kaplansurveys.com/books

What did you think of this book? We'd love to hear your comments and suggestions. We invite you to fill out our online survey form at **kaplansurveys.com/books**. Your feedback is extremely helpful as we continue to develop high-quality resources to meet your needs.

| SECTION ONE |

The Basics

Chapter One: **Inside the AP U.S. History Exam**

Congratulations! You should be proud of yourself for deciding to take the Advanced Placement U.S. History exam. If you have taken Advanced Placement U.S. History in high school or have a good foundation in American history, taking the AP exam can help you earn college credit and/or placement into advanced coursework. In addition to getting a head start on your college coursework, you can improve your chances of acceptance to competitive schools since colleges know that AP students are better prepared for the demands of college courses.

This book is designed to help you prepare for the AP exam in U.S. History. We've included information about the format of the exam, test-taking strategies, and an extensive review of essential topics. Each chapter includes review questions, which will help you identify your strengths and weaknesses and help you to establish a plan for preparing for the exam. Also included are two practice tests with answers and explanations. With Kaplan's proven test-taken strategies, hundreds of practice questions, and guidelines for writing your essay responses, you will be able to take the exam with confidence.

AN OVERVIEW OF THE TEST STRUCTURE

The Advanced Placement U.S. History exam is designed yearly by the AP Test Development Committee. The exam is an opportunity for you to demonstrate that you have mastered skills equivalent to those typically found in introductory college U.S. History classes.

The AP United States History Exam is three hours and five minutes long and has two sections: a 55-minute, multiple-choice section and a 130-minute, free-response essay section.

Section	Number of Questions	Time
I	80 multiple choice questions	55 minutes
II	3 free-response questions including:	130 minutes
	one document-based essay question	(60 minutes recommended) and
	two standard essay questions	(70 minutes recommended)

Total 3 hours, 5 minutes

Section I consists of 80 multiple-choice questions. The majority of the questions are on the 19th and 20th centuries. Approximately one-sixth of the questions will deal with the period through 1789, one-half with the period from 1790 to 1914, and one-third with the period from 1915 to the present.

Section II consists of the document-based essay question (DBQ) and two standard essays. Although the multiple-choice section may include a few questions on the period since 1980, none of the free-response questions will deal specifically with this period. Test-takers must answer two standard essay questions; usually they can select two questions from a total of four questions provided.

The free-response section begins with a required 15-minute reading period. Students are encouraged to spend most of the 15 minutes analyzing the documents and outlining their response to the document-based essay question (DBQ). The required DBQ is different from the standard essays because it emphasizes that the student both analyzes and synthesizes historical information. The DBQ will require students to relate documents as well as verbal, quantitative, or pictorial materials to a historical theme or period of time. It is important to remember to incorporate outside knowledge into the writing of the DBQ.

The multiple-choice and free-response sections cover a wide range of topics, including social and economic change, political institutions, behavior, and public policy. In the multiple-choice section these topics account for approximately 35 percent of the questions; social change accounts for another 35 percent. The remaining questions are spread over such topics as diplomacy and international relations, economic developments, and cultural developments. A number of the social and economic history questions deal with such traditional topics as the impact of legislation on social groups and the economy, or pressures created by the political process.

Exam Topics

The AP U.S. History exam covers the major topical areas of a standard college level United States history course. The following outline is only to be used as a guide. As the AP exam covers the time period from discovery and the first European explorations to the present day, the student is reminded that questions can come from any time period. The following topical outline does not mention the personalities without whom our nation would not have made the jump from colony to world power.

Topic I:
Foundations of U.S. History (1492–1764)

This topic covers the initial explorations of the Americas, the motivation for colonization, the growth of the colonies and the forms of government that were used.

Topic II:
Defining Democracy (1764–1848)

This topic covers the period from 1764 (the end of the French and Indian War) to the American Revolution. Students are introduced to the concept of salutary neglect, the Articles of Confederation and the constitutional conventions that produced the U.S. Constitution. The Federalists and Antifederalists marched across the country, moved into Louisiana, and elected Andrew Jackson. By the time he entered the White House, the people of this nation knew what it meant to be Americans.

Topic III:
The Civil War Era (1844–1865)

Slavery, ignored during the writing of the Constitution, would rear its ugly head on several occasions before the Civil War. The Missouri Compromise and the Compromise of 1850 served only to put off the confrontation. The sectional pressure was relentless, with the West working for equal treatment, the South to maintain its way of life, and the North to continue its expansion.

Topic IV:
Reconstruction (1865–1877)

After the Civil War ended at Appomattox Court House, the country had just a few days before John Wilkes Booth fired the fateful bullets into Abraham Lincoln. Andrew Johnson faced a hostile Congress bent on exacting tribute from the South. He would fire a hostile Secretary of War, Edwin Stanton, to test a new law passed by Congress requiring Congress to approve the dismissal of members of the president's cabinet. One vote short of the two-thirds majority needed, Johnson finished his term and slipped away. General Grant found running the country more difficult than running an army.

Topic V:
Industrialization (1875–1900)

The United States was changing from an agrarian to industrial society. The millions of immigrants, the abundant natural resources, the available investors, and the entrepreneurs all came together to force expansion in all directions. Standing in direct opposition to the unregulated expansion of business were the Progressives. These reformers worked for reforms across society: slums, education, hospitals, meat packing plants, and working conditions.

Topic VI:
Expansion and World War I (1895–1919)

Countries around the world were flexing their imperialistic muscles. European countries took control of the African continent. Theodore Roosevelt issued the Roosevelt Corollary to the Monroe Doctrine. The Spanish-American-Cuban War, fought against a reluctant opponent, took four months. The Panama Canal began to become a reality. World War I shook the foundations of the monarchial structures in Europe. The United States entered the fray and provided the men and means for an Allied victory. The Treaty of Versailles would spawn a second war and push an American president to a breakdown.

Topic VII:
Roaring Twenties and Economic Decline (1920–1939)

The isolationists wanted to turn their backs on Europe, "making the world safe for democracy" (Wilson's pledge). This was not glamorous; the trenches were always wet and the weapons of war were deadly. The newest weapon was the airplane. The scandals of the Harding presidency yielded to the Coolidge administration and the phenomenal growth of big business, often at the expense of the workers. When the economy began to slide, Herbert Hoover maintained that government should not interfere, and when it did, it was too little too late. Franklin Roosevelt was elected on the promise to put people to work. Congress passed more legislation in the first one hundred days of the Roosevelt administration than had ever been passed before.

Topic VIII:
World War II and its Aftermath (1930–1950)

Appeasement in Europe did not stop Hitler and the Nazis from taking over the continent in a series of quick strikes; only Great Britain stood in the way. Roosevelt and Churchill, negotiating the Atlantic Charter, pledged to work towards peace. Creative funding of the war effort kept the Americans out of the war until the Japanese changed the perspective by bombing Pearl Harbor on Dec. 7, 1941. Two days later the United States was fighting a war on two fronts. The watershed year was 1945. Franklin Roosevelt died in his sleep and Harry Truman was president, the wars were over, two atomic bombs had been exploded, and the Soviets had not de-mobilized in Europe. In 1949 the North Koreans invaded and the United States was again involved in an armed conflict. The policy of containment was implemented.

Topic IX:
The Modern Age (1950–2003)

President Eisenhower negotiated the end of the Korean conflict; Eisenhower was president during the decade when Americans were more interested in home and hearth than in continuing to be players on the world stage. Although there was the move to ignore world events, the United States' status as the only legitimate challenge to the Soviet Union made that impossible. Several times the two superpowers stood face-to-face (Bay of Pigs, Cuban Missile Crisis) and several times they stepped back. It would take visionary leader Mikhail Gorbachev to step forward and negotiate with the American Ronald Reagan. As a result, the Berlin Wall was torn down, the Soviet Union's satellite states became independent, and the world watched the leading Communist country remake itself into a capitalistic state.

Currently, the world watches as the United States and 28 other nations declare war on terrorism after the attacks on the Twin Towers in New York City. Whether or not the United States likes the role, it is the only world superpower today. With that designation comes both glory and criticism.

You might be tempted to skip some sections from your AP course, such as civil rights or public policy. Perhaps you're short on time, or you assume you won't be tested on these topics. This is a mistake! All course topics are covered in the multiple-choice portion of the test. If you lack substantive knowledge about certain topics covered in the course, your score will suffer.

KAPLAN
Test Prep and Admissions

HOW THE EXAM IS SCORED

The AP exam is graded on a scale of 1–5.

AP Grades

5:	Extremely well qualified
4:	Well qualified
3:	Qualified
2:	Possibly qualified
1:	No recommendation

The score distribution among test takers on a recent test was as follows:

AP Grade	Percentage of Test Takers
5	11.2
4	21.1
3	23.6
2	32.4
1	11.6

Each college and university sets its own policy regarding granting of college credit based on an AP grade; some colleges require a 5 while others may only require a grade of 3. Check with the colleges you are applying to in order to find out their policies regarding granting of credit based on the AP test.

To arrive at an AP grade of 1–5, raw scores on both the multiple-choice section and the free-response section are first computed. The two scores are combined to provide a composite score between 0 and 170 points. Your composite score is not reported to you or to institutions; you will only receive your score on a 1–5 scale so you will not know how many questions you missed or how you did on the essays.

Scoring the Multiple-Choice Section

The multiple-choice section generally accounts for one half of the total test score. It is graded by computer. The level of difficulty is deliberately set so that the student has to answer about 60 percent of the questions correctly to receive a grade of 3 (if the essay questions are not factored into the score).

KAPLAN
Test Prep and Admissions

Random guessing on the multiple-choice questions is unlikely to improve your score because one-fourth of a point is subtracted from your score for each incorrect answer, while no points are subtracted for a blank answer. However, it would be to your advantage to answer a question if you can eliminate one or more of the answer choices.

Scoring the Free-Response Section

The free-response section of the AP U.S. History exam is scored by college professors and AP teachers known as "faculty consultants." During the annual AP Reading, which takes place during the two weeks in June, hundreds of faculty consultants converge at a location to grade the essays of the thousands of students that take the AP U.S. History test. A different faculty consultant reads each of the students three essays and grades the essay based on detailed scoring standards for that question. Each free-response question is scored on a scale of 0–9, with 9 standing for excellent.

As you know, the free-response section of the tests consists of a DBQ and two standard essay questions. The free-response section (Section II) of the test accounts for about half of your AP U.S. History raw score. Within that section, the DBQ is the most important question since it is weighted to account for about half of the points possible on Section II. Each of the other two essay questions accounts for about a quarter of the points possible. The precise scoring formula varies slightly for each test; on a recent exam; for example, the DBQ accounted for 24 percent of the raw score, the two standard essay questions together accounted for 29 percent, and the multiple-choice section accounted for 47 percent.

The practice tests in this book are followed by formulas that will allow you to compute your estimated AP score. However, remember that it is impossible to provide a completely accurate score on the practice tests largely because it is difficult for you to grade your own essay questions.

REGISTRATION AND FEES

To register for the exam, contact your school guidance counselor or AP Coordinator. If your school does not administer the exam, contact AP Services for a listing of schools in your area that do.

The fee for each AP Exam is $82. The College Board offers a $22 credit to qualified students with acute financial need. A portion of the exam fee may be refunded if a student does not take the test. There may be a late fee for late exam orders. Check with AP Services for applicable deadlines.

You should bring the following items to the test center on test day:

- Photo I.D.
- Your secondary school code number (see your Guidance Counselor or AP Coordinator)
- Your social security number
- Several sharpened No. 2 pencils
- Eraser
- A watch, in case your exam room doesn't have a clock you can see easily

Here are items you should NOT bring:

- Scratch paper (you will make your notes in the test booklet)
- Books, dictionaries, notes, or correction fluid
- Beepers or cell phones, or anything that has a beeper function
- Food or drink

ADDITIONAL RESOURCES

For more information on the AP Program and the U.S. History Exam, please contact AP Services at:

AP Services
P.O. Box 6671
Princeton, NJ 08541-6671
(609) 771-7300
Toll-free: (888) CALL-4-AP (888-225-5427)
Fax: (609) 530-0482
TTY: (609) 882-4118
Email: apexgrams@info.collegeboard.org
Website: www.collegeboard.com/ap/students/index.html

Chapter Two: **Strategies for Success: It's Not Always How Much You Know**

Now that you've got some idea of the kind of adversary you face in the AP, it's time to start developing your strategy mindset.

The AP is a unique test. While it requires prior knowledge of facts, it goes one step further: You will be expected to draw links and analyze relationships among historical actors and institutions, and your score will depend on your ability to do so. Nobody expects you to know which political party will win in a policy battle in the Congress, but you will be expected to analyze the relevant factors and relationships in such a contest. In other words, you must be able to apply the facts that you have learned in school. If you cannot, you will be at a decided disadvantage.

The goal of the AP exam is to assess your conceptual knowledge and your ability to analyze and understand relationships. Try to master all the material from your AP course, with special emphasis on how the main components of history—things like personalities, events, political parties, the Constitution, and states—are related.

Before test day, review the table of contents in your textbook, and visit www.collegeboard.com/ap/students/index.html for more tips and information about the test.

HOW TO APPROACH MULTIPLE-CHOICE QUESTIONS

The test contains 80 multiple-choice questions which you are given 55 minutes to answer. An understanding of the test and of the best strategies to use in attacking the test will allow you to do your best on this section.

1. Answer the easy questions first.

Easy questions are worth just as many points as hard questions. To maximize your score, you need to answer as many questions correctly as possible—but it doesn't matter if they are easy or hard. And if you run out of time, you'll want to be sure you have gotten to all the questions that would earn you points. So on your first pass through the multiple-choice section, answer all the easy questions. Circle the harder questions and come back to them later. Don't waste valuable time on consuming questions early in the exam. You're better off spending those extra few minutes answering three or four easier questions.

As a point of interest, each test question has been refined five or six times, and must pass a stringent pretest phase. Key criteria used are (a) that the question is not ambiguous, (b) that there is only one correct answer, and (c) that the question asks about an important concept, relationship, or definition.

2. Guess intelligently and with caution.

Random guessing will not help your score and it may very well hurt it. There is a one-fourth of a point deduction for a wrong answer but no deduction for a blank answer. This is known as a "guessing penalty." If you can rule out a few answer choices first, your odds of guessing correctly will improve. But if you know virtually nothing about a topic and are totally stumped on a question, you are better off leaving it blank.

3. Be careful with your answer grid.

Your AP score is based on the answers you indicate on your answer grid. So even if you have aced every question, you'll get a low score if you make a mistake when you grid your answers. Be careful! Keep track of the spaces in relation to the questions—particularly if you skip around. Otherwise, you may spend valuable time erasing and regridding your answers. Also, if you do change an answer, be sure to erase your previous answer cleanly. The answer sheets are scored by machines that might misinterpret stray pencil marks.

4. Keep track of time

In Section I, you'll have 55 minutes to complete 80 questions. That means about 40 seconds per question.

KAPLAN
Test Prep and Admissions

HOW TO APPROACH FREE-RESPONSE QUESTIONS

Half of your score is determined by how well you do on the free-response section. In this section you'll have to answer three questions—two standard essay questions and one DBQ (document-based question). Taking advantage of proven strategies for attacking these questions will help you maximize your score. Read this list carefully and remember these suggestions—they will give you a competitive advantage over test takers who haven't a clue how to approach the test.

Read the question twice before you begin to organize your answer.

Misreading the question is a common error. Doing all the right work but then getting the wrong answer can be seriously depressing. So make sure you are answering the right question.

If you are asked to list things, use an itemized list with numbers or with the words "first," "second," and "third." This will help keep you on track as you enumerate each item, and it will clarify your list for the grader.

Sometimes questions will include a caution against using a certain approach in your answer. For example, a statement that says, "Your answer should not include a discussion of presidential primary elections." This is a clear prohibition and you should make sure you abide by it.

Understand the structure of the question.

Be sure you're clear on what you're being asked to do: compare, describe, explain, identify, list, and select mean different things, and if your answers take this into account, your free-response answers will be stronger. Your goal is to have a clear, directed response rather than a general, undirected essay. It's tempting to change the question a little to one that might be more to your liking. This won't work on this test and you won't get points for knowing something else or answering a question that was not asked. In the free-response portion, make sure you answer the question that is asked.

Many questions provide a general thesis or framework in the lead sentence. Not long ago, AP questions allowed students to articulate their own theses about a general subject. Now, in order to guide you more, the Test Development Committee has redesigned the questions so that you'll be given a thesis from which to work. As you formulate your answer, don't lose focus on the given thesis. But don't simply restate it either; make sure to present a thoughtful and well-elaborated answer.

Before you begin to write, consider the following questions:

a. What subject(s) compose the focus of the question?

b. What tasks are you being asked to perform?

c. What specific information is called for?

d. How can you develop a clear and complete answer without being vague or writing filler?

Answer free-response questions directly and explicitly.

You don't want to write everything you know about a subject, though you might be tempted to do this in hopes of "hitting" the target. That reasoning won't work here (and your score will suffer), so do not beat around the bush or write a vague essay with filler. The question will guide you; if you're asked to link institutional processes with public policy, write a focused essay that presents explicit links.

Questions asking for a list usually want narrow, specific items. Do not list items that you would use in a general essay about the subject. If the remainder of the question asks for links, that would be an appropriate place to elaborate.

Prioritize the free-response questions according to difficulty.

Again, your goal is to score as many points in this section as possible. Read all the questions first, then decide which one you will be able to answer most easily and most effectively. Do that one first, and then go back to the ones that are harder for you.

Be careful with the factual statements you make.

As a general rule, minor factual errors in an essay won't necessarily harm your essay score. In other circumstances, they can be quite fatal.

Let's say you can't remember the exact dates of Ronald Reagan's presidency (1981–1989). Your essay incorrectly says 1984–1992. That alone will not be fatal to your score unless the remainder of your essay turns on those incorrect years.

A more serious error would be one in which you began an essay with, "Reagan and his national security advisor Henry Kissinger interacted repeatedly during the Gulf War of 1989 to foil attempts by the secretary of defense to prosecute the war successfully." This statement contains several errors that would most certainly hurt your score. First, Kissinger was not Reagan's national security advisor. Second, Reagan was not president during the Gulf War. And third, the national security advisor during the Gulf War did not intrude on the execution of the military operations by the secretary of defense, or even interfere with the chairman of the joint chiefs or field commander. This answer would convey that you have no grasp of facts or relationships, which could be very detrimental to your score.

Prepare an outline and a list of key terms.

Graders are looking for main ideas, supporting details, and key terms. Think about what you'll write, and organize the ideas into outline form before you begin writing. Make a list of key terms to include in each paragraph.

Mark up your test booklet.

You may be used to having teachers tell you not to write in your books. But when taking the AP exam, it is to your advantage to mark up your test booklet. Label diagrams, cross out incorrect answer choices, write down key acronyms in the margins (for example, NIMBY can help you remember the concept behind "Not in My Backyard.") But always spell out the concept the first time you use an acronym.

KAPLAN
Test Prep and Admissions

Write neatly.

Penmanship is not graded when the free-responses are read. However, a reader who must struggle to make out sentences is bound to have a harder time evaluating the essay. Write carefully, and if your handwriting tends to be hard to read, make an effort to write more legibly than usual.

If your handwriting is hard to read because you feel pressured for time, try writing fewer sentences. A concise, neater essay may be stronger than a long, messier one. Try to resist the temptation to write long answers just to fill up the page.

Keep track of time.

It's important to keep track of time as you work through the test. You will have to pace yourself, or else you'll run out of time. In Section II, you'll have 130 minutes to answer a DBQ and two standard essays. For the DBQ, students are advised to spend 15 minutes analyzing the documents and 45 minutes writing the response. For the two standard essays, students are advised to spend five minutes planning and 30 minutes writing each response.

No cheating.

It is hardly necessary to indicate that such behavior is unacceptable, but you should know that cheating on the AP Exam is dealt with quite severely. The effort it takes to cheat is much greater than the effort required to learn the material. Furthermore, the consequences of such behavior are very serious and long term.

And apart from the illegal component of cheating, you would be shortchanging yourself; if you were placed in an advanced course for which you weren't fully prepared, you would find yourself at a disadvantage.

HOW TO APPROACH THE STANDARD ESSAY QUESTIONS

Focus on the Question

As you probably realized from reading the first three strategies above, focusing on the question is probably the most important key to a successful essay. When you prepare to write an essay, you must focus all your concentration on the question that is being asked. This seems so obvious but is the most common mistake made by students. They read the question quickly, think they know what it means, and start dashing off the essay. Instead you must zoom in on the question and pick it apart. After you have understood exactly what needs to be done, then—and only then—should you start writing. Let's try a question from an AP exam.

> *Analyze the ways in which the Great Depression altered the American social fabric in the 1930s.*

First, find the key words in the question that will help you write a good essay in response. There are four of them:

> *Analyze the ways in which the **Great Depression altered** the American **social fabric** in the 1930s.*

> **Analyze.** This is your job; to analyze the social impact of the Depression upon America. To analyze means to observe and draw conclusions. This is different from narrating what has happened in history so you will NOT be describing the Great Depression but rather telling of its impact on a society. You must also know the difference between analysis and narration. Many students think if they retell the history they are doing well. Historical analysis is an active intellectual activity which tries to find meaning out of human experience, while narrating is just a repetition of what has happened.

> **The Great Depression.** An event of great importance in the 20th century. If you know it well, you will be able to say something of its legacy in American history.

> **Altered.** This question demands that you tell how the Depression changed America. Again, if you talk about what caused the Depression or about the political impact it had you will be missing the point.

> **Social fabric.** This is a bit tricky as we have a metaphor here to talk about the complex nature of a society. But you must have a sense of how the Depression changed social norms after 1930. Since most textbooks highlight the New Deal, you may feel more able to talk about the political or economic impact of the Depression. If you do, however, your essay will not receive even a middling grade. So stick to the question and write about what the Great Depression did to marriages, families and birthrates. Then, you will be on the right track.

Common Pitfalls

Besides the dangers of not understanding the question, there are two other common mistakes made by students: (1) mismanaging time and (2) trying to say too much in a short essay.

You have 35 minutes for each of the standard essays in the free-response section of the test. A good rule of thumb is to spend at least five minutes picking apart the question and making a quick outline. You need to have a watch with you during the exam and you should put it right next to the exam paper. Refer to it every so often so you know when you must wrap the essay up and move on. If you look at the time and find you have ten minutes to write your last essay, you'll know that you have failed in managing the time available.

Another pitfall, especially for students who have studied hard, is trying to say too much about the subject. If you had an hour to write an essay this would not be a problem as you could write 1,000 words, but in 30 minutes you barely have time to create a thesis with two or so subtopics and write five paragraphs. So do not be tempted to tell about the details you know about the Treaty of Versailles or Jacksonian democracy; just create a straightforward thesis and stick to it. Often in a short essay, less is more.

HOW TO APPROACH THE DOCUMENT-BASED QUESTION (DBQ)

The DBQ that you will write is a special kind of essay that is unique to the history class. It tries to put you in the role of an historian using primary documents to understand the past. As you do with the standard essay questions, you should pick the question apart and underline the key terms and verbs that tell you what must be done. Look at the following example.

> *Although the **New England and Chesapeake regions** were both settled largely by people from England, **by 1700** they had evolved **into two distinct societies**. **Why** did this development occur?*
>
> *Use the documents AND your knowledge of the colonial period **up to 1700** to develop your answer.*
>
> You had better know your geography for this one. You would be surprised how many students are not sure where the Chesapeake is. Keep your answer focused on the two geographical regions specified in the question. Discussing how this compared to Georgia will bring your score down, not give you extra points.
>
> Also keep in mind that these questions are often **time specific** so you must only discuss the time period specified, in this case, the pre-1700 period. Start discussing the French and Indian War (which began in 1763) and you are in trouble.
>
> Finally, note that this is a "why" question so you must discuss reasons why these two areas of British America became different over time. But in order to answer "why" you also need to know what those differences were. This is early colonial history so you have only about a hundred years to dig into.

The DBQ differs from the standard essay questions since, with the DBQ, you are required to analyze and synthesize the historical data provided in the documents. Usually there are six to eight documents provided that relate to the era being examined. These documents could include a letter written long ago, a ship's manifest, a campaign speech, or a political cartoon. Examine them to determine what information they give and try to incorporate something from each of these in your essay. The essay will be judged on its thesis, argument, and supporting evidence.

Each document comes with its own letter designator (A-H for example). When you refer to one of these items in your essay, you are required to cite it by its letter name at the end of the sentence like this: "(Doc. D)."

Unfortunately the College Board is no longer announcing the time periods that the document-based questions come from so the question could be from any era. However, remember that no DBQs will deal specifically with the period since 1980.

How the Free-Response Questions Are Scored

AP examiners get together a month after the exam is given and read all the essays from students all over the world. In 2002, over 800 history teachers from high schools and colleges read over 400,000 essays in one week at Trinity University. Essays are graded on a scale of 0–9 which is broken down as shown below. As an example, let's look at another essay question that could appear on the AP exam.

> *Analyze the contributions of TWO of the following in helping to frame the Constitution of the United States in 1787: James Madison, Alexander Hamilton, or George Washington.*

The 8–9 Essay
- Contains a clear, well developed thesis that analyzes the contributions of two individuals in helping write the new Constitution
- Supports the thesis with substantial, specific, relevant information
- Presents a reasonably balanced treatment of both persons
- Is well organized
- May contain minor errors

The 5–7 Essay
- Presents a thesis, which may be partially developed, that analyzes the ways in which two individuals helped write the new Constitution
- Supports the thesis with some relevant and specific information
- Has some analysis of the impact of the contributions of both persons
- May be unbalanced in the treatment of the two persons
- Has acceptable organization
- May contain errors that do not seriously detract from the quality of the essay

The 2–4 Essay
- Simply restates the question or lacks a thesis, or contains a confused or unfocused thesis
- Provides few relevant facts, or lists facts with little application to the thesis
- Has little or no analysis; may contain only generalizations
- May deal with only one person, or two in a limited manner
- May be poorly organized
- May contain major errors that detract from the essay

The 0–1 Essay
- Contains no thesis or a thesis that does not address the question
- Exhibits inadequate or inaccurate understanding of the question
- Contains no analysis
- Is poorly organized and/or poorly written

STRESS MANAGEMENT

The countdown has begun. Your date with the test is looming on the horizon. Anxiety is on the rise. The butterflies in your stomach have gone ballistic. Your thinking is getting cloudy. Maybe you think you won't be ready. Maybe you already know your stuff, but you're going into panic mode anyway. Don't freak! It's possible to tame that anxiety and stress—before and during the test.

Remember, a little stress is good. Anxiety is a motivation to study. The adrenaline that gets pumped into your bloodstream when you're stressed helps you stay alert and think more clearly. But if you feel that the tension is so great that it's preventing you from using your study time effectively, here are some things you can do to get it under control.

Take control.

Lack of control is a prime cause of stress. Research shows that if you don't have a sense of control over what's happening in your life, you can easily end up feeling helpless and hopeless. Try to identify the sources of the stress you feel. Which ones can you do something about? Can you find ways to reduce the stress you're feeling about any of these sources?

Focus on your strengths.

Make a list of areas of strength you have that will help you do well on the test. We all have strengths, and recognizing your own is like having reserves of solid gold at Fort Knox. You'll be able to draw on your reserves as you need them, helping you solve difficult questions, maintain confidence, and keep test stress and anxiety at a distance. And every time you recognize a new area of strength, solve a challenging problem, or score well on a practice test, you'll increase your reserves.

Imagine yourself succeeding.

Close your eyes and imagine yourself in a relaxing situation. Breathe easily and naturally. Now, think of a real-life situation in which you scored well on a test or did well on an assignment. Focus on this success. Now turn your thoughts to the test, and keep your thoughts and feelings in line with that successful experience. Don't make comparisons between them; just imagine yourself taking the upcoming test with the same feelings of confidence and relaxed control.

Set realistic goals.

Facing your problem areas gives you some distinct advantages. What do you want to accomplish in the time remaining? Make a list of realistic goals. You can't help feeling more confident when you know you're actively improving your chances of earning a higher test score.

Exercise your frustrations away.

Whether it's jogging, biking, pushups, or a pickup basketball game, physical exercise will stimulate your mind and body, and improve your ability to think and concentrate. A surprising number of students fall out of the habit of regular exercise, ironically because they're spending so much time prepping for exams. A little physical exertion will help to keep your mind and body in sync and will help you sleep better at night.

Avoid drugs.

Using drugs (prescription or recreational) specifically to prepare for and take a big test is definitely self-defeating. (And if they're illegal drugs, you may end up with a bigger problem on your hands than the AP U.S. History test). Mild stimulants, such as coffee or cola, can sometimes help as you study since they keep you alert. On the down side, too much of these can also lead to agitation, restlessness, and insomnia. It all depends on your tolerance for caffeine.

Eat well.

Good nutrition will help you focus and think clearly. Eat plenty of fruits and vegetables, low-fat protein such as fish, skinless poultry, beans, and legumes, and whole grains such as brown rice, whole wheat bread, and pastas. Don't eat a lot of sugar and high-fat snacks, or salty foods.

Work at your own pace.

Don't be thrown if other test takers seem to be working more furiously than you during the exam. Continue to spend your time patiently thinking through your answers; it will lead to better results. Don't mistake the other people's sheer activity as signs of progress and higher scores.

Keep breathing.

Conscious attention to breathing is an excellent way to manage stress while you're taking the test. Most of the people who get into trouble during tests take shallow breaths: They breathe using only their upper chests and shoulder muscles, and may even hold their breath for long periods of time. Conversely, those test takers who breathe deeply in a slow, relaxed manner are likely to be in better control during the session.

Stretch.

If you find yourself getting spaced out or burned out as you're taking the test, stop for a brief moment and stretch. Even though you'll be pausing on the test for a moment, it's a moment well spent. Stretching will help to refresh you and refocus your thoughts.

KAPLAN
Test Prep and Admissions

AP U.S. History Review

Chapter Three: **Foundations of U.S. History**

- Timeline: Beginnings to 1763
- Introducing U.S. History
- The Colonial Experience
- Governing the Colonies
- Multiple-Choice Questions
- Essay Question
- Answer Key
- Answers and Explanations
- Analysis of the Free-Response Essay

TIMELINE: BEGINNINGS TO 1763

800 B.C.	Rise of Adena-Hopewell agricultural civilization in northeastern North America.
400 B.C.	Arrival of Pueblo-Hohokam culture in Southwest.
A.D. 600	Rise of Mississippian agricultural groups in Southeast.
c. 985–c. 1010	Norse settlements in Newfoundland.
1492–1565	Spanish and Portuguese exploration, conquest, and colonization in Americas, mainly Mexico, Central and South America, and Caribbean.
1520	Expulsion of Martin Luther from church; beginning of Reformation conflicts in northern Europe.
1536	Publication of John Calvin's *Institute*.
Early 1600s	Establishment of Iroquois League.
1603–1608	Champlain's explorations in eastern Canada; establishment of New France.
1607	Establishment of Jamestown colony.

1619	First documented arrival of Africans in British North American mainland colonies.
1620	Establishment of Plymouth colony.
1630s–1660s	First wave of large-scale English migration to North American colonies.
1636	Roger Williams banished to what becomes Rhode Island.
1642–1646	English Civil War.
1651–1673	Passage of Navigation Acts.
1660	Restoration of English monarchy; establishment of Carolina colony.
1664	British take New Amsterdam from Dutch, rename colony New York.
1675	King Philip's War in New England.
1676	Bacon's Rebellion in Virginia.
1680	Pueblo Revolt in New Mexico.
1681	Beginning of Pennsylvania colony.
1688	Glorious Revolution in England.
1689–1748	European wars (King William's War, Queen Anne's War, King George's War) spill over to North America.
1696	Establishment of Board of Trade to oversee and regulate colonial trade.
1700–1750	First major expansion of African chattel slavery in southern colonies.
1717–1775	Mass migration from North Britain to inland and backcountry.
1720s–1740s	Era of Salutary Neglect.
1732	Establishment of Georgia colony.
1740s	Great Awakening.
1754	French and Indian War/Seven Years' War begins.
1763	Treaty of Paris signed, ceding Canada to Britain.

INTRODUCING U.S. HISTORY

When looking at the development of the North American continent, one is struck by the relative newness of the countries that are located there. The discovery of the land masses that have become Canada, the United States, and Central America were not known to the Europeans, beyond a few stories, until Columbus made his historic voyages. The Asian, Norsemen, and Portuguese fishermen's tales did not make it to "prime time."

The Europeans finally did make it to the "New World" and began a legacy that is evident even today. The "great biological exchange" brought on the unification of the plant and animal systems of the European and American continents. The animals of Europe, such as horses, cattle, pigs, sheep, and goats were unknown in the Americas. The Europeans had never seen the iguana, flying squirrels, bison, toucans, or hummingbirds. The plant exchange was even more radical because it resulted in a change in the diets of people in both hemispheres. The white potato actually originated in South America, while rice, wheat, barley, oats and coffee came from Europe. The advantage of the plant exchange was that the food plants complemented each other; there was little, if any, competition. There was a major negative exchange, however, of disease. Europeans brought with them diseases such as measles, typhus, and smallpox, to which the Native Americans had no natural immunity. Millions died as a result.

After Columbus, the forces of exploration and imperialism motivated men to travel into the unknown. The race was on. Each country was motivated by its own interests. For example, the Spanish were motivated by their search for gold; the French by their desire to exploit the resources of this new area; and the English needed space, as they were searching for a foothold on the world.

Adena-Hopewell

This was the culture of Northeast North America from 800 B.C. to A.D. 600. Remains found have shown a developed social structure and evidence of division of labor. Earthworks and burial mounds (some shaped like snakes, birds, and other animals) have been discovered. Hopewellians established a trade network that spanned the continent.

Aztecs

This native American people were settlers of present-day Mexico. They founded Tenochtitlán (now Mexico City) in 1325 and extended their control over central Mexico. Montezuma II ruled over 5 million by the time of the Spanish arrival in 1519.

biological exchange

The plants and animals of Europe and the New World were distinct biological systems. The diffusion of the two systems (animal and plant) was rapid. Native Americans knew nothing of horses, cattle, pigs, sheep, and goats. Europeans had never seen iguana, flying squirrels, bison, cougars, or hummingbirds. The plant exchange resulted in a revolution in diets of both hemispheres. Maize, potatoes, and beans were unknown in Europe; rice wheat, barley, oats, and bananas soon were introduced in return.

John Calvin

Calvin was a French scholar who was forced to flee from France because of his religious beliefs. He was welcomed in Geneva, Switzerland, where he developed a large following and became one of the most influential leaders in the Reformation. The Puritans and Huguenot settlers to the New World carried his doctrine.

Calvinism

This was the Christian religious doctrine that described all people as damned, but Christ's sacrifice made their redemption possible. Predestination was part of Calvin's doctrine, along with strict morality and hard work. Lay members could share in church governance through elders and ministers called presbytery. His doctrines became the basis for Congregationalists, Presbyterians, Puritans, and Huguenots.

Elizabeth I (1558–1603)

This queen of England oversaw Church of England's shift to Protestantism. The Latin liturgy became *The Book of Common Prayer*, and clergy could marry. Some who wished to "purify" the church left England as the Puritans or Separatists.

KAPLAN
Test Prep and Admissions

Henry VIII (1509–1547)

This English King established the Church of England (Anglican) after the Pope refused to grant his annulment. His second wife produced not the son he sought but his daughter, Elizabeth I.

Martin Luther

This German monk posted his "Ninety-Five Theses" in protest of church abuses, especially the sale of "indulgences," a process in which priests would forgive sins in exchange for goods and money. Luther said salvation could be won only through faith in Christ and a direct relationship with God.

Plymouth

The settlement of the Pilgrims (Separatists), who cut off all ties to the Church of England. They initially headed for Virginia and lost their way, landing instead on Cape Cod. In 1620, 101 sailed on the Mayflower. Before disembarking, the Pilgrims signed the Mayflower Compact, an agreement of the group to follow the rules adopted by majority vote. Some argue this was the first example of a constitution signed in the colonies.

Reformation

The serious challenges to the Catholic Church began in 1517 with Martin Luther. Lutheranism, Calvinism, and other Christian doctrines spread through Europe and would later arrive in America. In England, a disagreement between Henry VIII and the Catholic pope led to the founding of the Church of England.

Captain John Smith

An adventurer, Smith was appointed to manage Jamestown. He was a strict disciplinarian and said, "he that will not work shall not eat." He bargained with the Native Americans and explored (mapped) the Chesapeake area. He returned to England in 1609 after suffering a gunpowder burn and never returned to the colonies.

Virginia Company

The London Group of the Virginia Company established the first permanent colony in Virginia in 1607 on the James River. Reorganized Jamestown governance was completed in 1609 to interest new investors. In 1618, Sir Edwin Sandys instituted reforms such as the headright policy and the first Representative Assembly in 1619.

THE COLONIAL EXPERIENCE

Beginning in the late 15th century, European nations took a strong interest in exploring and colonizing the Americas. For Spain, France, England, and the Netherlands, the Americas represented an opportunity to make money, spread religion, and gain political supremacy over the rival nations. The Spanish focused their attentions on Central and South America, where the precious metals were found. The French laid claim to much of North America, became allies of the Native Americans, and established a trading empire. The English laid claim to North America as well, but focused their attentions particularly on the east coast of the United States. The Dutch would establish themselves in New Amsterdam, but would be the first European nation to leave the area, when the English forced them out.

Bacon's Rebellion

Nathaniel Bacon led frontier servants, small farmers, and slaves against Virginia's wealthy planters and political leaders that resulted in the burning of Jamestown in 1676. Bacon also conducted assaults against peaceful Native Americans (he claimed they were "all alike").

William Bradford

Bradford was the leader of the Pilgrims and Governor of Plymouth. Bradford kept a tight rein on the settlement, allowing very little latitude to the colonists. He intuitively understood that their safety lay in their numbers.

The Carolinas

Founded in 1670 and named for Charles I, king of England, Carolina became prosperous from the production of rice and indigo. Its first settlement, Charleston, was the leading city of the South at the time of the American Revolution. Smaller farmers predominated in the settlement of the northern part of Carolina and in 1712 this region officially separated, creating two colonies, North and South Carolina.

Connecticut

The 1633 Plymouth-based group settled in the Connecticut River Valley and founded settlements three years later. Thomas Hooker led three church congregations to Wethersfield, Windsor, and Hartford. In 1639 the Connecticut General Court adopted Fundamental Orders of Connecticut, a series of laws that provided a government that did not limit suffrage to church members.

Delaware

Once a part of Pennsylvania, a 1701 grant gave it the right to choose its own assembly. It had the same governor as Pennsylvania until the American Revolution.

Jonathan Edwards

Edwards's most famous sermon, "Sinners in the Hands of an Angry God," was an appeal to parishioners to repent. He did not reduce religion to an entirely emotional level, but sought to describe the glory, beauty, and love of God. He was the most important leader of the First Great Awakening (see separate entry).

Enlightenment

A new direction in the world of ideas climaxed by Newton's *Principia*, which described the theory of gravity. This was an investigation into natural law that could be understood through reason and explained though mathematics. Newton speculated that natural laws governed all things and reason could make people aware of natural laws.

First Great Awakening

A revival of religious zeal heralded by Jonathan Edwards that spread through the colonies. The Great Awakening brought religion to a prominent position in society. Begun in 1734, it reached its peak in 1741.

Benjamin Franklin

Referred to as the epitome of the Enlightenment, he was truly a Renaissance man. He owned a print shop, published "Poor Richard's Almanac," invented the lightning rod, the Franklin stove, and helped start an Academy that was the beginning of the University of Pennsylvania. Taking an early retirement, he devoted himself to public service and was present at the signing of the Declaration of Independence and the Constitution.

General Assembly of Virginia

On July 30, 1619 the settlers organized a representative assembly. The first meeting included the governor, six counselors, and 22 burgesses. They met for five days in Jamestown.

Georgia

The last of British colonies to be established in North America; it was unique in that it was set up as a philanthropic experiment and a military buffer against Spanish Florida. General James Oglethorpe was the soldier who designed the defenses. He also supported the establishment of Georgia as colonial refuge for the poor and for those suffering religious persecution.

headright system

A system established by the Virginia Company as an incentive to settlement, each settler received a "headright" of land for paying his own way or bringing others.

Anne Hutchinson

Hutchinson challenged Puritan leaders and beliefs by advocating a belief in the sanctity of one's faith and God's grace. After a two-day trial before judges and ministers, Hutchinson was banished in 1638 to an island south of Providence, Rhode Island. She died in 1644, massacred in a Native American attack.

indentured servitude

Indenture was a contract by which a person agreed to work for a specific number of years in return for the cost of transportation across the Atlantic to the colonies. Usually set for a term of four to seven years, when the indenture ended the servant could claim his freedom. Many servants died before completing their term of indenture.

Iroquois League

The Iroquois League was an alliance of five Native American tribes in central New York State who spoke related languages. In the 1600s, sachems (chiefs) made decisions for the 12,000 members. A patriarchal society by nature, women nonetheless had the power to nominate candidates to the tribal council and remove corrupt leaders.

Jamestown

This settlement, the first permanent colony in Virginia, was established 40 miles up the James River (to hide it from the Spanish) in 1607. The colonists had difficulty building the settlement, as they were more motivated to find gold than prepare for winter weather.

John Locke

Locke was a British political philosopher and a leading figure of Enlightenment. He believed that governments derived their authority from the people. He argued that humans were created equal and had certain inalienable rights, including life, health, liberty, and possessions. Locke's political thought greatly influenced Thomas Jefferson and the writing of the Declaration of Independence.

Maryland

Maryland was a proprietary colony founded by Lord Baltimore in 1634 as a haven for Catholics. Baltimore was the first settlement. In 1649, the colony granted religious liberty to all Christians. At the time of the American Revolution, it had a larger percentage of Catholics than any other colony but it attracted settlers of many different denominations. See also: Maryland Toleration Act.

Maryland Toleration Act

This law, adopted in 1649, guaranteed that Christians would not be persecuted for their religious beliefs. It serves as a landmark for religious tolerance even though it was limited to those who expressed belief in the Holy Trinity.

Massachusetts Bay Company

Chartered by Puritans in England, the Massachusetts Bay Company established the Massachusetts Bay Colony on a grant of land between the Charles and Merrimack Rivers in 1630. The company served as the government of the colony until 1684. It had America's first bicameral (two-house) assembly: the House of Assistants (modeled after the House of Lords) and the House of Deputies (modeled after the House of Commons).

Mayflower Compact

This document was written and signed by Pilgrims on the Mayflower in 1620 because they had arrived in Massachusetts and would settle beyond the jurisdiction of any organized government. They agreed to majority rule and to abide by laws made by their own, chosen leaders.

New Hampshire

Puritans from the Massachusetts Bay Colony began settling New Hampshire during the 1620s and it became a separate royal colony in 1679.

New Jersey

The lands between the Hudson and Delaware Rivers were granted by the Duke of York to Sir George Carteret and Lord John Berkley. Settled by the Dutch and Puritans, Newark was the first settlement. Originally divided into East and West, the two sections were united as a single royal colony in 1702.

New York

The Dutch founded New Amsterdam (now New York City) at the mouth of the Hudson River in 1624. The British took control of the region in the Second Dutch War (1664–1667) and converted it into a British proprietary colony.

William Penn

Penn received rights in 1681 to a tract stretching from Delaware River westward. He encouraged the settlement of the area by writing glowing descriptions and offering religious liberty and aid to immigrants. Philadelphia (City of Brotherly Love) grew as a result of his efforts. Penn learned the language of the Delaware Native Americans, and the settlers lived among the tribe peacefully for over fifty years. Penn, a Quaker, lived in the colony for only four years before returning to England.

Pennsylvania

Founded by William Penn, the colony was established on a tract of land granted to William Penn that stretched westward from Delaware River. The first settlement was Philadelphia. The government included freemen (tax payers and property owners), and the governor had no veto power. The colony became a refuge for Quakers and other religious dissenters.

Pilgrims

Established the Plymouth Colony. As the strictest group of Puritans, these Separatists cut all ties with the Church of England. Originally leaving England for Holland in 1607 to escape persecution, they moved to the New World after concerns for their way of life and worship were raised.

Plymouth

The 101 Pilgrims on the Mayflower first landed on December 26, 1619 at Cape Cod, where rough weather forced them to remain over the winter. The following spring they moved on to found the colony of Plymouth, which is now part of Massachusetts.

Puritans

This religious group wanted to "purify" the Church of England, which, although it had split off from the Catholic Church, had not changed much in religious doctrine. The Puritans followed the doctrines of John Calvin and were known for their strict religious beliefs. They embraced hard work and strict laws enforcing Puritan morality. Persecuted in England, over 70,000 Puritans crossed the Atlantic to the Massachusetts Bay Colony in the Great Migration of the 1630s.

Quakers

Founded in 1647 by George Fox, the group favored individual inspiration and interpretation. They gave up formal ceremonies and a formal ministry, refused to offer any social ranking, and advocated a peaceful coexistence with all. They were often subjected to intense persecution but did not retaliate. Religious tolerance, equality of the sexes, and full participation of women in religious affairs were also part of their tolerance for others.

Rhode Island

Founded by separate groups of Puritans led by Roger Williams and Anne Hutchinson, the colony became a haven for those who found Massachusetts Bay too restrictive.

rice and indigo

These two crops served to advance the economies of South Carolina. Indigo was a blue dye stuff that grew to be in great demand in the British woolens industry. Rice grew well in South Carolina, where tide water rivers flooded and drained.

KAPLAN
Test Prep and Admissions

John Rolfe

He experimented with growing varieties of tobacco. He married Pocahontas in part to divert a crisis after her capture in 1613. Her father, Powhatan, agreed to the union.

Salem Witch Trials

The hysteria began in 1691 when adolescent girls accused a number of women of being witches, resulting in the deaths of several residents. Explanations of the hysteria include longtime feuds and property disputes or just relief from everyday life. New thinking suggests the accused, all women, had defied the roles of society and were perceived as a threat to the conventional traditions.

Captain John Smith

As the leader of the Jamestown settlement he imposed strict discipline in the colony and said anyone who did not work did not eat. He also negotiated with the Native Americans and mapped the Chesapeake Bay area. He suffered a powder burn and returned to England in 1609.

tobacco

In 1612 John Rolfe experimented with growing the plant, which was deemed harsh. He experimented with some "more palatable" Spanish hybrids and by 1616, the tobacco "weed" was exported in great quantities for European consumption.

George Whitefield

Whitefield was the 27-year-old minister who worked to restore religious fervor to American congregations through his dramatic sermonizing. He arrived in 1739 in Philadelphia and soon had everyone talking of his eloquence.

Roger Williams

Williams arrived in Massachusetts in 1631. A literal separatist, he would ultimately leave for Rhode Island after banishment in 1635. Allowed to escape by Governor Winthrop, Williams established Providence, the first permanent Rhode Island settlement in 1636 and the first settlement in the New World to legislate freedom of religion. His work created a society that lived up to his principles of religious freedom and government based on the consent of the people.

John Winthrop

Winthrop served as the first governor of Massachusetts Bay Colony, establishing a theocracy (government by the Puritan religious leaders). Winthrop took advantage of a charter loophole that allowed him to transfer the governing power to Massachusetts, rather than London. Winthrop landed first at Salem (1630) but then eventually made Boston (then called Charlestown after King Charles I of England) the colonial seat of government.

KAPLAN
Test Prep and Admissions

GOVERNING THE COLONIES

The colonists came to the New World for many reasons and their motivations influenced the types of colonies that grew. There were joint stock companies that funded some colonies; these were investments of men, and money, all with the potential to make their investors millions. That kind of a return was rarely seen. There were proprietary colonies, those established by royal decree and those whose existence was testimony to a charter. There were the church-related colonies that were governed by the men of the cloth.

The economies of the colonies differed. The climatory and geographical differences served to create colonies that maximized their advantages and minimized their liabilities. The New World was not a forgiving place, the colonists discovered. The winters in New England were long and cold. If food were not stockpiled, people would starve. The southern colonies had their own problems; mosquitoes and diseases had run rampant and whole settlements disappeared almost overnight.

Some colonies recognized religious freedom; others expelled those who would seek to worship differently. There was a colony established as a buffer between the English and Spanish and a home for the debtors—the layers of society that had few options. The settlers were not restricted to the coastline; soon settlements were established up and down the many rivers.

The opportunities seemed without end. The Native Americans, however, saw this flood of white Europeans in less than a positive light. The Europeans brought with them the concept of land ownership, an idea in direct opposition to the Native American idea of collective land ownership. This philosophical difference was the first of many that the Native Americans would experience, and most of these differences would be resolved at the expense of the tribes.

Albany Plan of Union

The Albany Congress (1754) enlisted Iroquois support. The Plan of Union (conceived by Benjamin Franklin) described a chief executive (President-General of the United Colonies), a Grand Council of 48 chosen by colonial assemblies. This body would oversee colonial interests of defense, Native American relations, trade, and settlement of the West. Colonials rejected the plan.

Sir Edmund Andros

He was the first royal governor of the Dominion of New England (1686–1688). A former soldier, Andros was efficient and loyal to the crown, but tactless when facing resentment in Massachusetts over taxation. Andros suppressed town governments and enforced trade laws. He also took over one of the Puritan churches. After the Glorious Revolution, Andros was arrested and Massachusetts was returned to its former governor.

Board of Trade

Created in 1696 to take the place of the Lords of Trade, this group supervised the enforcement of the Navigation Acts, and recommended ways to increase the production of raw materials and limit the manufacture of products.

KAPLAN
Test Prep and Admissions

Dominion of New England

After revocation of Massachusetts' charter, a plan to create a Dominion of New England for all colonies from New England south through New Jersey was put forth. The Dominion's governor was named by royal authority and had no assembly. It lasted until the Glorious Revolution suspended James II's authority.

Enlightenment

A new direction in the world of ideas climaxed by Newton's *Principia*, which described the theory of gravity. This was an investigation into natural law that could be understood through reason and explained though mathematics. Newton speculated that natural laws governed all things and reason could make people aware of natural laws.

Benjamin Franklin

Franklin, who became a civic leader in Philadelphia, epitomized the Enlightenment in the eyes of the Americans and Europeans. He opened a printing shop and published the *Pennsylvania Gazette* and *Poor Richard's Almanac.* He would found a library, set up a fire company, invent the lightening rod and Franklin stove, and help establish the University of Pennsylvania. Franklin's *Experiments and Observations on Electricity* would establish his reputation as a thinker. He would serve as the voice of reason and caution during the debates at the Continental Congresses.

French and Indian War

This conflict (1754–1763) pitted the British against the French and their allies, the Native Americans. In 1755, the British captured Nova Scotia and sent most of its French population across the continent. Many of the Acadians found their way to French Louisiana where they became the "Cajuns" (a corruption of Acadians). The war was waged on the frontiers of North America, but coincided with the Seven Years' War in Europe. British sea power began to cut off French reinforcements and supplies to the New World. In 1759 a three-pronged British attack ended French power in North America. The war dragged on until 1763 ending with the Peace of Paris.

fur trade

The first trading relationship between Europeans and Native Americans was in furs. The French worked much harder at maintaining a good relationship with the Native Americans than did the British. This was a reflection of the motivations for settlement: the French saw North America as a resource, the British saw it as an opportunity for expansion and settlement.

Glorious Revolution

In 1688 King James II was deposed, and William and Mary ascended to the throne. The Glorious Revolution established the principle of Parliamentary power over royal power.

Hudson's Bay Company

A British company that maintained outposts in the interior of Canada, for the purchase of furs.

KAPLAN

Test Prep and Admissions

Leisler's Rebellion

A local rebellion in New York by Jacob Leisler, a German immigrant who kept New York under his control for two years (supported by militia). In 1691, a new governor was appointed; Leisler was slow to turn over authority. He and his son-in-law were charged with treason and hanged; Parliament later exonerated them. The factions would affect New York politics for years afterwards.

mercantilism

An economic system in which economic activity is closely regulated by the government to maximize profits for the king and ruling class. Under this system the colony existed for the good of the mother country. Generally the colony's role was to provide raw materials (especially products that the mother country could produce itself) and serve as a market for goods produced in the mother country.

Navigation Acts

The 1633 Navigation Act required that all goods going to the British colonies had to be routed through England. Parliament passed a restriction in 1651 that all goods imported into either England or the colonies had to be on English ships. European goods were excluded. In 1660 new requirements were added: ships crews had to be three-quarters English and certain goods were to go only to England or the colonies. These included tobacco, cotton, indigo, ginger, sugar, and later rice, hemp, masts/spars, and furs.

New France

Permanent French settlements, the first in Quebec City in 1608, were established as a result of the Champlain-led explorations of the St. Lawrence valley. New France stretched from Nova Scotia across the Quebec area to the Great Lakes.

Peace of Paris of 1763

The Treaty of Paris ended the French and Indian War and France's power in North America. Britain acquired all France's possessions east of the Mississippi River (except New Orleans) and took control of Spanish Florida. As compensation for Florida, Spain received Louisiana from France.

salutary neglect

Salutary neglect was the English colonial policy that allowed the colonies to grow and develop relatively unsupervised. As England was focused on fighting wars with France, colonial assemblies expanded their power and influence, graduating to self-government.

Whigs (Great Britain)

The British political party that opposed James II, led the Glorious Revolution of 1688. They were also supporters of parliamentary supremacy over royal authority.

MULTIPLE-CHOICE QUESTIONS

1. The most famous Enlightenment figure living in colonial America was:

   (A) John Locke.

   (B) Voltaire.

   (C) John Winthrop.

   (D) Alexander Hamilton.

   (E) Benjamin Franklin.

2. The Dutch settled New Amsterdam primarily to:

   (A) secure naval stores for their military.

   (B) expand their commercial and mercantile network.

   (C) gain colonies to produce agricultural goods.

   (D) check the growth of the Spanish empire.

   (E) find a religious haven for the persecuted.

3. Which of the following best describes the Virginia colony?

   (A) The government of the Virginia colony received no charter of government from any English authority.

   (B) Captain John Smith was chosen to lead the Virginia colony during its early years.

   (C) The Separatists who established Virginia colony were members of the Church of England.

   (D) The colony was a commercial success from the start.

   (E) None of the above correctly best describes the Virginia colony.

4. What best describes the economic differences between the colonies of Massachusetts and Virginia?

   (A) Virginian farms were small while Massachusetts was dominated by plantations

   (B) The cattle trade was most important in Virginia while the slave trade was commercially important in Massachusetts

   (C) Tobacco was the primary cash crop of Virginia while Massachusetts depended on marine trade and commerce

   (D) Rice and indigo were staple crops at Jamestown while cotton was grown around Boston

   (E) Massachusetts depended on mining while Virginia was primarily a commercial trading center

5. The North American colonies took advantage of Great Britain's policy of salutary neglect to:

   (A) spread slavery to the 13 colonies.

   (B) make alliances with Native Americans.

   (C) establish religious freedom.

   (D) work out trade agreements to acquire products from other countries.

   (E) establish a stronger militia.

6. Of the following, which colony was the most tolerant of religious diversity?

   (A) Plymouth

   (B) New Hampshire

   (C) Massachusetts Bay

   (D) Pennsylvania

   (E) Virginia

7. Which of the following was true of the Great Awakening:

   (A) It reinforced the power of the Church of England in the South.

   (B) The Puritan congregations became more pious.

   (C) It undermined the position of the traditional clergy.

   (D) Congregationalists and Presbyterians merged to create one denomination.

   (E) All of the above were true of the Great Awakening.

8. French, Spanish, and English colonies were all similar in that they:

   (A) provided a haven for the persecuted in Europe.

   (B) were the extension of mercantile policies.

   (C) were permitted to have representative legislatures.

   (D) were founded by private enterprise.

   (E) were all founded by the conquistadors.

9. The largest and oldest settlement in New France was:

   (A) Albany.

   (B) Quebec.

   (C) Ottawa.

   (D) Toronto.

   (E) Halifax.

10. Which factor was most important in bringing about the Albany Congress of 1754?

    (A) The formal declaration of war against France

    (B) The renewed growth of churches after the Great Awakening

    (C) Benjamin Franklin's opposition to the king

    (D) The need for better defense against the French and their native allies

    (E) A desire for an alliance between the colonies and the Spanish

11. Who of the following was not associated with the Massachusetts Bay colony?

    (A) Edmund Andros

    (B) John Smith

    (C) Cotton Mather

    (D) John Winthrop

    (E) Ann Hutchinson

12. The theology of Calvinism was most prevalent in the colony of:

    (A) Massachusetts.

    (B) Maryland.

    (C) South Carolina.

    (D) Georgia.

    (E) New York.

13. The largest city in the English colonies by the mid-18th century:

    (A) had a population of about 2,000.

    (B) had a population of about 1,000,000.

    (C) was Philadelphia.

    (D) was New York.

    (E) was Charleston, South Carolina.

14. The Proclamation Line of 1763 was created to:

    (A) allow the expansion of British colonies to the Mississippi River.

    (B) unify the colonies during the French and Indian War.

    (C) discourage land speculation in New England.

    (D) better defend settlers against the attacks of the French.

    (E) stop westward settlement beyond the Alleghenies.

15. The colony of Georgia was:

    (A) a buffer between the British and Spanish empires.

    (B) founded as a proprietary colony.

    (C) led by James Oglethorpe.

    (D) in part a penal colony with many debtors and other unfortunates as original settlers.

    (E) all of the above.

16. Which of the following was true of most Anglicans who emigrated to 17th century British America:

    (A) they rejected the authority of the king.

    (B) they considered themselves Separatists.

    (C) they were loyal to the king and members of the Church of England.

    (D) they wished to settle in the North.

    (E) they intended to return to England.

17. Unlike New France and the Spanish settlements, the English colonies were:

    (A) all founded without royal initiative.

    (B) all successful from the very beginning.

    (C) dependent upon slave labor.

    (D) kept under strict royal control.

    (E) intolerant of other national groups who wanted to settle in America.

18. The prescribed role for women in colonial America was to:

    (A) enter public service when they came of age.

    (B) handle the business of farming.

    (C) take leadership roles in church congregations.

    (D) obey their fathers and husbands and nurture the children.

    (E) work alongside the men in the fields.

19. African slavery brought which of the following to British America?

    (A) Profits for the ships that brought the slaves from West Africa

    (B) Cheap labor for the large plantations

    (C) New musical influences to European-American culture

    (D) New words borrowed into the English language

    (E) All of the above

20. In general, the colonial wars were an American sideshow to larger conflicts in Europe between:

    (A) England and Spain.

    (B) England and Holland.

    (C) Spain and Holland.

    (D) France and Spain.

    (E) England and France.

KAPLAN
Test Prep and Admissions

ESSAY QUESTION

1. Compare and contrast the New World colonial policies of England and France during the 17th and 18th centuries.

_____

_____

_____

_____

_____

_____

_____

_____

_____

_____

_____

_____

_____

_____

_____

_____

_____

_____

_____

_____

_____

ANSWER KEY

Multiple-Choice Questions

1. E
2. B
3. B
4. C
5. D
6. D
7. C
8. B
9. B
10. D
11. B
12. A
13. C
14. E
15. E
16. C
17. A
18. D
19. E
20. E

KAPLAN
Test Prep and Admissions

Answers and Explanations

1. E

As an inventor, writer and publisher, Franklin was the best known American during the Enlightenment. He personified the interests in science and learning associated with his day. He also helped found libraries and promoted philosophical debate in the British America.

2. B

The Dutch like the French and English believed in mercantilist theory which suggests that nations which gather territory and resources will maintain their wealth. The Dutch explored the eastern coast of North America and built a fort at what is now New York City. This was a small outpost for trading furs and other commercial ventures.

3. B

Virginia started out as a vain attempt to find a passage to Asia through the New World. English gentlemen ill suited for life in the wilderness signed on but many did not survive the first year. John Smith took a leadership role and had to oversee food gathering and production so the early settlement would not be wiped out entirely by starvation and disease.

4. C

Tobacco was introduced from the West Indies and established the economy of Virginia after 1610. The dependence on this cash crop was a hallmark of the early South. Poor farmland in New England led Massachusetts to develop its fishing industry and Boston was established as a busy trading port by 1640.

5. D

England allowed considerable freedom in regards to trade and commerce in the early colonial period. Trade laws were not enforced and there was some corruption and graft that took place. British Americans took advantage of this to engage in 'illegal' trade with the Spanish and French which allowed them access to more goods and products.

6. D

One of the features of 'Quakerism' which was transplanted in Pennsylvania was absolute freedom of conscience. This meant individuals could seek God's will by themselves and would not impose their beliefs on others. Pennsylvania thus had many settlers whose beliefs were not tolerated in other colonies.

7. C

The Great Awakening was a religious revival that impacted the growing frontier of British America. It was in part anti-materialistic and criticized the established congregations for caring too much about money. The authority of the pastors and clergy of these churches was undermined by this new revival and many new congregations were organized in response to the movement.

8. B

All European exploration and colonization was inspired by the theory of mercantilism. This stated that nations should gather as much wealth and natural resources so they could be as self-sufficient as possible. The kingdoms of Europe hoped to benefit from their New World colonies, which is why they sought precious metals at first and later goods they could sell for money.

9. B

The French used the St. Lawrence River to penetrate the North American wilderness. Settlements were built along this river reaching from the ocean to the Great Lakes. The foremost settlement was Quebec, founded in 1608, several hundred miles up river from the mouth of the St. Lawrence.

10. D

Brought about by French-sponsored raids on the frontier of British America, the Albany Congress debated a plan by Franklin to organize colonial defense. They also invited native groups loyal to Britain to help with the French threat.

11. B

John Smith was an early leader of the Jamestown colony which became a part of the larger Virginia colony. He never visited Massachusetts and was famous for his relationship with Pocahontas, a Native woman who later actually traveled to England.

KAPLAN
Test Prep and Admissions

12. A

The Separatists and the Puritans who helped settle Massachusetts were both Calvinistic groups that left England dissatisfied with the official Church of England. They followed the teachings of John Calvin, one of the great Reformation leaders who believed that the established church needed to be purified and simplified. Calvin's belief in a hard-working and pious life had great influence on the American work ethic.

13. C

As British America grew, various urban ports sprang up. Boston, New York and Philadelphia were all examples of this. By 1750, Philadelphia was the largest prosperous trading and urban center with about 30,000 people.

14. E

The Proclamation Line of 1763 was a vain attempt to stop colonials from crossing the mountains to the west. The crown hoped that this would lessen tensions with the Natives. The king wished to placate the tribes who had helped fight the French in the recent war and assure them that the whites would stay in the coastal areas.

15. E

Georgia was one of the last colonies founded on what is now the east coast of America. It was proprietary because the king granted the charter to an individual, James Oglethorpe. The attempt to take petty criminals and have them settle in the South was a mixed success but the English did want some outposts in the region to discourage the expansion of Spanish Florida.

16. C

The Church of England was the official church of the kingdom and most English were members. They are called Anglicans. This church was transplanted when the British settled in North America and existed in most colonies. Some colonies like Virginia made it the official denomination. Unlike the minority Puritans who saw the Church of England as corrupt, Anglicans were part of the British establishment and generally loyal to the crown.

17. A

British colonies were chartered by different groups who wanted to seek wealth and religious freedom in the New World. Expeditions were privately funded and allowed by the crown as a beneficial expansion of British territories. In contrast, Spanish expeditions were paid for by the royal family in the early years of exploration.

18. D

Women were extensions of their fathers and husbands during the colonial era. Generally considered inferior to men, women had to take their place in the home as mothers and caretakers. The role of wife at that time meant that it was a woman's duty to follow and support her husband in whatever he did.

19. E

The slave trade caused a cultural transference from Africa to North America that is considerable. African language, musical forms, religion and other customs melted into the fabric of the American experience. Africans performed all manners of services as slaves and freepersons that impacted the new culture in British America.

20. E

England and France were the two rival powers in Europe from the 1600s until the mid 1700s. Various wars were fought in Europe while settlements were founded in New France and in British America. While larger scale battles were fought on the continent, smaller scale fighting took place in what is now Pennsylvania, New York, Michigan and Canada.

KAPLAN
Test Prep and Admissions

ANALYSIS OF THE FREE-RESPONSE ESSAY

Question:

Compare and contrast the New World colonial policies of England and France during the 17th and 18th centuries.

Basic Background

- Quebec founded by French in 1608 on the St. Lawrence Seaway
- Jamestown founded in 1607 along the Virginia coast.

Key Points

British Colonies

- Strong navy and merchant marine fleet
- Joint stock companies defined groups that would settle in North America
- Men came first and then later whole families
- Very diverse groups from within England came to settle
- Non-English such as Dutch and Swedes also absorbed into colonies

French Colonies

- Smaller population and more dispersed than British
- Focused on the fur trade in the North
- Founded outposts rather than settlements
- Formed cooperative relationships with Natives; often intermarried
- Smaller male population integrated itself into Native culture
- Served as mediators between some Great Lakes tribes
- Spread Catholicism through missionary work
- Promoted hatred for the British

KAPLAN
Test Prep and Admissions

Similarities	Dissimilarities
Both were ruled by Christian European monarchies	England was Protestant France was Catholic
Both traded with the natives, had alliances with various tribes	British colonies were more independent
Products were shipped back to Europe to be sold (tobacco and fur)	Many British came to settle permanently in the New World
Both adhered to the mercantilistic theory of the time period	British America grew into a much larger group of colonies

Scoring Rubric

There are five scoring ranges:

Excellent

The answer must have a strong, clear thesis that states at least two similarities and two dissimilarities between British and French colonial practices. The quality of the writing should be excellent, the answer must show logical patterns, and the student should include many of the major points in the above list (though they may go beyond the list). The organization should be clear. The answer may contain minor errors.

Very Good

The answer must have a thesis that makes a comparison between British and French colonial policies. Organization of the answer must show logical patterns, and the student should include many of the specific points from the above list.

Adequate

The answer must try to make some argument and must include at least some of the points listed above. There may be flaws in the thesis argument.

Flawed

The answer will demonstrate serious weaknesses. It may have no thesis argument at all, and it will include few of the points listed above. The answer may show little understanding of the colonial period or its economic backdrop.

Severely Flawed

The answer will demonstrate almost no attempt to answer the question, and will include very few, if any, of the points listed above.

Chapter Four: **The American Revolution**

- Timeline: 1763–1790

- The Road to Revolution

- The Revolutionary War

- From Confederation to Constitution

- Multiple-Choice Questions

- Essay Questions

- Answer Key

- Answers and Explanations

- Analyses of the Free-Response Essays

TIMELINE: 1763–1790

1763	End of Seven Years' War; British Empire much expanded in North America.
1763	Pontiac's Rebellion.
1763	Proclamation Line of 1763 forbids English settlement west of the Appalachians.
1763–1765	Grenville's first colonial trade regulations passed.
1765	Protests against regulations, especially Stamp Act.
1766	Stamp Act repealed.
1767	Townshend Acts.
1768	Protest against Townshend Acts, including activism by Sons of Liberty.
1770	Boston Massacre.
1773	Tea Act.
1773	Boston Tea Party.
1774	Coercive Acts (Intolerable Acts).
1774	First Continental Congress meets, passes Declaration of American Rights, calls for organized boycott of British goods.

KAPLAN
Test Prep and Admissions

1775	British attempt to seize arms stored at Concord (Massachusetts) leads to beginning of war.
1775	George Washington named commander-in-chief of Continental Army; fighting spreads beyond New England.
1776	Publication of Thomas Paine's *Common Sense*.
1776	Congress adopts Declaration of Independence.
1777	Americans win battle of Saratoga (New York).
1778	Americans sign treaties of alliance with France.
1779	Americans defeat Iroquois in upstate New York.
1781	American-French combined forces force Cornwallis to surrender at Yorktown (Virginia).
1781	Articles of Confederation ratified by all the former colonies.
1783	Peace of Paris signed; Americans gain independence and territory to the Mississippi.
1785	Land Ordinance passed, dividing western land where Native American titles had been extinguished into a rectangular grid of 36-square-mile townships and 640-acre lots.
1786–1787	Shay's Rebellion (Massachusetts).
1786	Annapolis Convention.
1787	Northwest Ordinance passed, specifying process by which territories could become states.
1787	Constitutional Convention.
1787–1790	States ratify new Constitution.

THE ROAD TO REVOLUTION

The story of the development of the United States of America continues with the ever increasing number of settlements and pressure on Native Americans to move back out of the way. The Proclamation Line of 1763 was signed by Great Britain in order to appease the Native Americans and the French. It stipulated that settlers were to be restricted from going beyond the crest of the Appalachian Mountains. Furthermore, the colonial governors were not to authorize surveys or issue land grants for any territory beyond the line. It should be noted here that while this Proclamation Line of 1763 was designed to protect lands from encroachment, the settlers moved over the ridges and continued to spread out over the terrain nonetheless.

On another front and almost simultaneously, Lord George Grenville was looking at ways to replenish the treasury. He believed that the British Army was needed to protect the colonies, despite the fact that the colonies had been left almost alone while Great Britain was involved with fighting in other corners of the world. This period of "salutary neglect" would lead to colonial disagreement with Grenville's policies. The basis of the argument was that Grenville's view of the "cash cow" of colonies was in direct opposition to the colonies' view of their own existence and their relationship with Great Britain.

Although the story of the deteriorating relationship between Great Britain and the colonies lasts a very short time before war, it is important to remember some of the logistical problems. Ships had to cross the Atlantic Ocean, and that was not a passage that happened flawlessly. Messages were delayed, lost, and sometimes changed in transit. Representatives had to wait for instructions, ministers had to make decisions without the benefit of counsel. Having the historical advantage of hindsight, the student of today can easily point to the crucial mistakes; keep that viewpoint on the horizon.

British common law, although not actually written, has been followed for centuries and Parliament had control of the British purse strings. The colonists questioned Parliament's right to levy taxes. The colonists thought of themselves as good Englishmen and felt that Parliament did not accurately represent them, for there was no representative from the colonies seated in Parliament. The colonies petitioned for representation through the Declaration of the Rights and Grievances of the Colonies. The King adamantly refused to discuss the problem, and Grenville denounced the colonists as "ungrateful."

Enforcement of the new legislation continued. Diverse groups of colonists found themselves agreeing, some for the first time. Acts of frustration turned into acts of violence. The Boston Massacre occurred after a crowd gathered before the Custom House and began to aggravate the troops there. A British soldier was knocked down; when he arose and fired into the crowd, a volley of gunfire resulted. When it was said and done, five lay dead, and eight more were wounded. Reaction was swift up and down the eastern seaboard, but remember the underlying belief of the colonists: they were good English subjects, and rebellion was too radical a step to take.

The next two years saw a slow growth of the idea of a union of the states. The First Continental Congress met in 1774 in Philadelphia, to consider that very idea. The Congress instead endorsed the Suffolk Resolves, which declared actions of Parliament null and void, and advocated for economic sanctions against British commerce. Events were quickly moving beyond the point of reconciliation.

The armed conflict that became known as the American Revolution began with an attempt by the British army to seize the Boston militia's stores. When local patriots were warned, the Minutemen responded at Lexington Green. After a skirmish left eight Americans dead and ten wounded, the British faced a gauntlet of colonists in order to return to the safety of Boston. The drastic step of armed conflict had been taken; the colonies were at war.

Samuel Adams

Adams's passion was politics. He was convinced that Parliament had no right to legislate for the colonies. He organized of the Sons of Liberty, and orchestrated the Boston Tea Party. His description of the shooting incident in Boston as a "massacre" would be used to incite anti-British feeling. A distant cousin of John Adams (the second President), Sam Adams is buried on Boston Common.

Ethan Allen

Fort Ticonderoga fell to the Green Mountain Boys led by Ethan Allen of Vermont on May 10, 1775.

KAPLAN
Test Prep and Admissions

Crispus Attucks

The story goes that Attucks was a runaway mulatto slave who had worked around Boston. At the Boston Massacre, he was at the front of the crowd into which British soldiers fired. Five died including Attucks, the first martyr of the colonial resistance.

Battle of Bunker Hill

In June 1775 a colonial militia of Massachusetts built fortifications on Breed's Hill, next to Bunker Hill in Boston. The British force attacked and managed to take the hill, but suffered over a thousand casualties. Americans claimed a victory of sorts, based on the heavy casualties they inflicted. The battle had two effects: the large number of casualties made English generals more cautious, and the Congress recommended that all able-bodied men enlist in the militia. There was no longer a middle ground between Patriot and Loyalist.

Battle of Lexington

In April 1775, General Thomas Gage sent out a large force to seize military supplies in Concord, Massachusetts. Warned by Paul Revere and William Dawes, the militia of Lexington (Minutemen) faced the British. The Americans had to retreat, eight were killed. This was the first battle of the American Revolution.

Boston Massacre

In March 1770, a group of colonists harassed guards near the Custom House. Guards fired into the crowd, killing five and wounding many more. The guards were tried for murder, defended by John Adams, and acquitted.

Boston Tea Party

The 1773 action of throwing 342 chests of tea, valued at £15,000, into Boston Harbor served to illuminate the growing conflict between the colonies and Parliament. The colonists refused to buy cheaper tea (British East India Company), as they did not agree that Parliament had the right to tax the colonies. The reaction to the dumping of the tea was mixed; some considered it to be a justifiable defense of their liberty, others thought it too radical an action.

Coercive Acts

These four acts of 1774 were directed mainly at the people of Boston and Massachusetts. The Port Bill closed the port of Boston and prohibited trade in and out of the harbor until compensation was received for the tea. The Massachusetts Government Act reduced the power of the Massachusetts legislature. The Administration of Justice Act allowed royal officials accused of crimes to be tried in England. The expansion of the Quartering Act enabled British troops to be quartered in private homes, and it applied to all the colonies.

Common Sense

Thomas Paine's pamphlet was first published anonymously in Philadelphia. He attacked the allegiance to the monarchy and refocused the anger of the colonists. The common sense of the matter, said Paine, was that the king of England and his friends were responsible for the ill will toward the colonies. Americans should look out for their own interests, abandon the king, and declare their independence. Within three months, more than 150,000 copies had been published and distributed.

Continental Congress

The first Continental Congress assembled in Philadelphia in 1774. The delegates acted to adopt and issue a series of resolutions and protests. The Congress also heard a plan of union devised by Joseph Galloway of Pennsylvania. The second Continental Congress convened in Philadelphia in 1775 and assumed the role of a "de facto" government and named George Washington as commander-in-chief of the Continental Army.

Currency Act

In 1764, the colonies faced a shortage of hard money, which was sent to pay debts in England. To address the problem, the colonies began issuing their own paper money. British creditors feared a depreciated currency, so Parliament passed the Currency Act, which forbid the colonies (first New England, though eventually extended to all the colonies) to make their currency legal tender. The action had a deflationary impact on the colonies.

Declaration of Independence

The document, drafted by Thomas Jefferson, declared the independence of the colonies. The Continental Congress made eighty-six changes to the original draft, shortening it and making minor revisions to the wording. The document was a combination of Jefferson's draft of the pre-amble to the Virginia Constitution (written a few weeks earlier) and George Mason's draft of Virginia Declaration of Rights. The end result was based, in part, on John Locke's contract theory of government that argued that governments derive their power from the consent of the people. The document listed "repeated injuries and usurpations" and declared the thirteen "United Colonies" to be free and independent.

Declaratory Act

This 1766 act was passed and said that Parliament had the right to tax and make laws for the colonies "in all cases whatsoever." This statement by Parliament made no concession to the colonies with regard to taxes, and made no mention of them either. This would soon lead to more conflict within a year.

John Dickinson

Dickinson was the Pennsylvania colonial leader who wrote *Letters from a Pennsylvania Farmer*. These publications argued against the indirect taxes of the Townshend Acts.

Gaspee

This British customs ship ran aground off the coast of Rhode Island in 1772. A group of colonists seized the opportunity to get rid of the ship. They disguised themselves as Native Americans, ordered the British crew off, and then set fire to the ship. The British ordered an investigation.

George III

George III was the King of Great Britain during the colonial resistance.

George Grenville

First Lord of the Treasury, he took for granted the need for soldiers in the colonies to defend the frontier. He took this position in part to offset a rapid demobilization that would retire a large number of British officers and provoke political criticism. He argued that the Americans were obligated to share the costs of their own defense because he needed to find new sources of revenue to support the troops. Other regulatory measures included the Sugar Act and the Currency Act of 1764.

Thomas Hutchinson

Hutchinson was the Governor of Massachusetts who moved soldiers out of town after the Boston Massacre to prevent further bloodshed. He would later face off against Sam Adams over three ships filled with tea in Boston Harbor. The ships were boarded in the night and 342 chests of tea were dumped by the disguised Americans.

Thomas Jefferson

Jefferson was the author of *Summary View of the Rights of British America*, a pamphlet arguing that the colonies were not subject to Parliament, but to the crown, making it a separate realm. In 1776, Jefferson was designated the draftsman of the Declaration of Independence.

Letters from a Pennsylvania Farmer

John Dickinson of Pennsylvania made his argument that duties were a form of taxation and could not be assessed against the colonies without the consent of their assemblies. He argued that the principle of no taxation without representation was an essential principle of English law.

James Otis

In 1768, Otis and Sam Adams wrote the Massachusetts Circular Letter urging colonies to petition Parliament to repeal the Townshend Acts. British officials ordered the men to retract the letter, and the colonists boycotted British goods in return. Smuggling activities increased again.

Thomas Paine

He arrived in the colonies in 1775. He came from a Quaker background and had yet to succeed. His marriage had failed, as had his business. At 37, he came to the colonies with a letter of introduction to Benjamin Franklin. As the author of *Common Sense*, he proved he was able to move many with his words.

Proclamation of 1763

The British, in an effort to stabilize the western frontier, ruled that colonists were to be prohibited from settling west of the Appalachian Mountains. Although designed to prevent hostilities between the Native Americans and the colonists, the measure was met with anger and defiance and thousands went west in spite of the boundary.

Paul Revere

A silversmith of Boston, Revere brought word to the first Continental Congress of the Suffolk Resolves, which declared the Intolerable Acts null and void, urged Massachusetts to arm itself, and called for a boycott against British commerce. Revere would later distinguish himself by warning the Minutemen of the approaching British troops at the Battle of Lexington.

KAPLAN

Test Prep and Admissions

Sons of Liberty

This was the radical group of colonists, led by Sam Adams, who carried out the Boston Tea Party. Disguised as Mohawk Native Americans, they dumped 342 chests of tea into the harbor to protest the East Indian Tea Company's monopoly on the importation of tea into the colonies.

Stamp Act

In an effort to raise funds to support British troops in the colonies, this action was passed in 1765. It placed a stamp requirement on all legal documents, newspapers, pamphlets, and ads. This was a direct tax, paid by the people in the colonies. The Act was repealed in 1766 and the Declaratory Act was passed at the same time.

Sugar Act

This legislation, also known as the Revenue Act of 1764, cut duties on molasses from sixpence to threepence a gallon. In addition, the Sugar Act levied new duties on imports of foreign textiles, wines, coffee, indigo and sugar. This was the first example of legislation designed to raise revenue and not to regulate trade.

Townshend Acts

Parliament enacted new duties on imports of tea, glass, and paper. The law required that the revenues raised were to pay officials of the crown, making those officials independent of the colonial assemblies. The act also provided for searches of private homes for smuggled goods and suspended New York's assembly for their defiant stand on the Quartering Act.

Virginia Resolves

These were the 1765 objections to the Stamp Act, a series of resolutions sponsored by Patrick Henry. Virginians, said Henry, were entitled to the rights of Englishmen and Englishmen could be taxed only by their own representatives. In 1769, a new set of resolves were passed by Virginia. These restated the rights to tax Virginians belonged to Virginia, challenged the removal of a person to England for trial, and called upon the colonies to unite.

THE REVOLUTIONARY WAR

The American Revolution was the war that no one wanted to fight. The colonists thought they had made it clear to the English that were Parliament to include a representative from the colonies, then their objections to the new taxes would by nil, or at least no greater than any other Englishman with respect to taxes. But the king did not see things that way. He was equally clear that no representative from the colonies would be tolerated.

Reluctantly, the colonists prepared themselves for the confrontation. At the start of the war there was not even widespread support within the colonies for the fight. Radicals were at work, the Loyalists said. As the war progressed, however, more and more colonists began to see that independence was the only option left to them.

KAPLAN
Test Prep and Admissions

52 Section Two: AP U.S. History Review
Chapter Four

George Washington, the commander-in-chief of the military forces, was not an experienced commander. He spent as much time writing to Congress for support as he did preparing military strategy. His own commanders were plotting behind his back to take over the military. The winters were cold and the supplies were few. Sometimes marching was used as a method to keep the troops warm as much as to accomplish a military objective.

Help would come from some unusual sources. The Baron von Steuben arrived and was taken with General Washington and the goal of the American troops. He pushed and cajoled and trained the men into coherent fighting units. The Marquis de Lafayette came, stayed on to become Washington's chief-of-staff and would bring French support to the colonials. Then the military began to win some of the battles. Sneaking up on the Hessians Christmas night in Trenton may have been a small victory, but its importance was that the Americans saw they could win a strategic battle.

By the waning days of the war, some of the British commanders were thinking about reaching some sort of compromise with the Americans because they feared a war that would go on forever. Only through a stroke of luck in a delayed message and cooperating weather did Washington bottle General Cornwallis on the Yorktown peninsula. Cornwallis had sent a message to have British ships meet them and pick up the troops. Instead, the French ships came around the corner and Cornwallis knew he was defeated.

After the war, the Americans were somewhat dumbfounded. Subsequent history has shown that the Americans were not at all sure they would win and when they did, the next steps were unclear. But forward they moved, into an organizational plan for the new nation.

Abigail Adams

The wife of John Adams, Abigail Adams maintained the home while Adams served his country. A devoted patriot and a prolific letter writer, she served as her husband's confidante throughout their lifetimes.

John Adams

Adams was the ardent patriot from Massachusetts. He was a member of the committee that drafted the Declaration of Independence. He also served as a delegate to the Continental Congresses and as an ambassador. He would become the second president of the United States and father to the sixth president, John Quincy Adams.

Benedict Arnold

Arnold was the American commander whose legacy is one of a turncoat. He made plans to allow the British to take West Point, but the plan was foiled. Arnold escaped to England where he lived out the remainder of the war. History suggests that his wife's Loyalist leanings were influential in reversing Arnold's allegiances.

Articles of Confederation

John Dickinson provided the first draft of a constitution that Congress modified to protect the powers of the states. The Articles were adopted in 1777 but not ratified until 1781, as there were some disagreements over western lands. The Articles created a unicameral (one-house) government to be called Congress. Each state would have one vote, and at least 9 of 13 states were needed to approve important laws. The Articles gave Congress the power to wage war, make treaties, send diplomats, and borrow money. Conversely, Congress did not have the power to regulate commerce, collect taxes, or enforce its own laws. Congress, under the Articles did accomplish winning the war, establishing a policy for western lands (Land Ordinance of 1785) and for the large territory between the Great Lakes and the Ohio River (Northwest Ordinance of 1787).

Cherokees

The Cherokee were the primary Native American tribe of the western Carolinas. They were persuaded to strike at frontier settlements in Virginia and the Carolinas as early as 1776. Retaliation came as South Carolina forces burned their towns and supplies of corn. In 1780 a Virginia-North Carolina force attacked, killing 29 and burning over 1,000 towns and 50,000 bushels of corn and other supplies, in part to prevent the Cherokee from aiding General Cornwallis. After the Revolution, the way was clear for rapid settlement of their lands.

Continental Army

These troops were citizen-soldiers, mostly poor native-born Americans or immigrants who had come as indentured servants or convicts. The Congress appointed Washington commander-in-chief. The number of troops fluctuated constantly, from a high of 20,000 to a low point of 5,000. Regiments were organized by each state, and the states were supposed to keep them filled with volunteers.

Lord Cornwallis

Cornwallis was the British commander at the final confrontation of the Revolution. Cornwallis surrendered four years to the day after the Battle of Saratoga. His force of 7,000 was contained by American and French forces in 1781.

Declaration of Independence

The document, drafted by Thomas Jefferson, set forth the notion of independence of the colonies. The Continental Congress made 86 changes to the original draft, shortened it and made minor revisions to the wording. The document was a combination of Jefferson's draft of the preamble to the Virginia Constitution (written a few weeks earlier) and George Mason's draft of Virginia Declaration of Rights. The end result was based, in part, on John Locke's contract theory of government that argued that governments derive their power from the consent of the people. The document listed "repeated injuries and usurpations" and declared the thirteen "United Colonies" to be free and independent.

Horatio Gates

He was an American commander, and a favorite of New Englanders. He led American troops against "Gentleman Johnny" Burgoyne and captured his army at Saratoga.

William Howe

Howe was the commander-in-chief of the King's forces in America. His cautionary moves allowed Washington's troops to escape more than once; he stayed in Philadelphia while Washington wintered at Valley Forge. Based in New York, Howe did force the evacuation of the city by the Patriots, but missed several opportunities to bring the war to a speedy conclusion.

Loyalists

They were the pro-British Tories, the defenders and supporters of British rule over the American colonies.

militia

These troops served two purposes. They represented a home guard, defending their communities and they helped to supplement the numbers in the Continental army. To repel an attack, they would appear and once the danger was past, they would return home. This exasperated commanders, who could not count on their numbers.

Peace of Paris (1783)

This peace treaty officially ending the war of independence against Britain was finally signed in 1783. It provided that Britain would recognize the United States as an independent nation; that the Mississippi River would be the western boundary; that Americans would have fishing rights off the coast of Canada; and that the Americans would pay the debts owed to British merchants and honor Loyalists claims for property taken during the war.

republicanism

This concept of government was radically different from the monarchies which prevailed in Europe. The American government would derive its authority from the consent of the people rather than the divine right of kings. As citizens of a free republic, it was hoped, Americans would embody the civic virtues necessary for the success of their government.

Saratoga

Burgoyne's attempt to bisect the colonies. He headed toward Lake Champlain in 1777. After capturing Fort Ticonderoga, his delayed movements allowed American forces to arrive from the south. American forces fought back at Oriskay, NY and gave General Benedict Arnold time to arrive in relief. Colonel John Stark and New England militia forced Burgoyne to retreat to Saratoga, where General Gates surrounded him. Word of this American victory made it a decisive turning point, the French began to supply the Americans by sending fourteen ships, and the Spanish government also sent supplies.

Treaty of Alliance

The second treaty signed with France. In it, France agreed that if it entered the war, both countries would fight until American independence was attained and neither country would agree to a treaty or peace without the formal consent of the other. The third requirement stated that each guaranteed the other's possessions in America. France also stated that it would not seek Canadian or other British possessions on the North American mainland.

Treaty of Amity and Commerce

After the British defeat at Saratoga, the French signed with the Americans in 1778 this treaty in which France recognized the United States as a nation and offered trade concessions including shipping privileges.

Yorktown

This was the last major battle of the American Revolution. In 1781, British troops were surrounded on a peninsula near Yorktown, Virginia. With strong support from the French naval and military forces, Washington's army of almost 16,000 forced the surrender of 7,000 British troops under the command of General Charles Cornwallis.

FROM CONFEDERATION TO CONSTITUTION

After the American Revolution was over, the colonies needed to find a form of organization that would fit the colonies now calling themselves states. The complaints and fears that had driven them to revolution now drove them to a loose organization. There was no question that the states would stay together. The question was, under what form of political organization?

The Articles of Confederation would be the model. Each state would remain autonomous and make its own decisions. The loose confederation would apply to the national issues. The Articles specified that any agreement had to be unanimous, that a state could choose to stay away from the meetings, and that each state would tax its own residents. Off the United States lurched into history.

It would not be long before the states began to see the problems that were inherent in the Articles. First, there was no power to tax; secondly, there were no controls over interstate commerce; and thirdly, there was no way to make the states enforce the laws. Each state was trying to maximize its trade at the expense of the other states. The whole organization was not working. Rumors began to fly that some colonists were thinking of approaching the British Parliament as asking for acceptance into the British Empire once again.

That could not happen. The founding fathers knew that such a course would negate all the sacrifice of those who had died during the war and that any sort of deal would never benefit the colonists in any way. The Continental Congress met in Philadelphia to begin to write a new document that would become the law of the land. It would take two summers behind closed windows to formulate the Constitution of the United States of America. No written record exists of those deliberations.

When the Constitution was ready to be ratified by the states, the first reaction was confusion. Where, the colonists wanted to know, were the guarantees of personal freedoms, where were the protections against double jeopardy, writs of assistance, and bills of attainder? The Constitution went back for revisions. When it reappeared, the Constitution came with the attached Bill of Rights. These first ten amendments contained the personal freedoms and protections we don't even think about anymore, we just know we have them.

In order to persuade colonists to ratify the Constitution, the *Federalist Papers* were published, one at a time. These letters were written under the pen name of Publius. Three Federalists, Alexander Hamilton, John Jay, and James Madison, were the authors. They wrote with great persuasion, fearing chaos if the Constitution were not approved. The Antifederalists were unsuccessful and the Constitution was ratified in 1791.

The Constitution of the United States of America was unusual, bred in part through the unusual circumstances, and remains to this day a model document. In three pages it spells out the powers and duties of government. The first three articles describe the three branches of the government: the legislative, executive, and judicial. In the remaining articles, the processes for amending and ratifying are described, and the promise that all states ratifying will accept the Constitution and the federal government as the supreme law of the land are spelled out. Attached to the document were the first ten amendments, the Bill of Rights. Within that framework, the United States got off to another start.

Imbedded within the Constitution is a unique relationship for the three branches of the government. The colonists were still reluctant to cede their authority to a higher power for they feared that one branch might gain more power and take over the entire government. To allay those fears, the framers built into the Constitution a system of "checks and balances" for the national government. Each branch had certain powers and every other branch had some check on those powers. For example, the executive branch (headed by the president) had the power to appoint ministers and ambassadors. The confirmation of those appointments was to be voted by one half of the Legislative Branch, the Senate. The executive branch nominates Supreme Court justices; the Senate had the responsibility of confirmation. The laws of the country are passed by the Legislative branch (the Congress); the Executive branch can agree or veto those laws and the Supreme Court has the power and responsibility to evaluate those laws as to their constitutionality. The Legislative branch can override a veto by a majority of two-thirds of each house, in spite of the Chief Executive's vote.

Also built into the document was the process by which law was to be made. The course of legislation was to be parallel in each house. After the bill was introduced, it was assigned to a committee. The committees were necessary because each member of the Congress could not possibly become knowledgeable about every proposal. The committee process, which consisted of members of Congress as committee members, was instituted to provide a network of members who knew a lot about a certain subject matter. There were committees for financial matters, committees for foreign relations matters, and so forth. The committees would hold public hearings so that the members of the public had the opportunity to voice their opinions on what ever matter was under discussion. After the public hearing part of the process was completed, the committee would meet and discuss the matter. Their committee report would become the next step. When the legislation came back to the body for a full discussion (back on the floor), the committee report would be part of the record. The members would debate and vote their support or denial on the matter. If the legislation was approved, it went to a conference committee made up of members of both houses so that the final document was the same from both the houses. If the legislation was not approved, the sponsors had another opportunity to gather support and get the votes. Pending that activity, the legislation might "die" for that session.

Before the legislation could become law, however, it needed the signature of the Chief Executive. Signing was the easy part. If the president vetoed legislation, the Congress could either accept the rejection or try and override the veto by gathering votes of a two-thirds majority in both houses. There was also a device known as a pocket veto. By this method, the president, who has ten days to sign, holds onto the legislation when the Congress is within ten days of adjournment, and the bill dies anyways.

The role of the Supreme Court was unclear until the appointment of John Marshall as Chief Justice. Serving for 34 years, Marshall established the right of the judiciary for judicial review. The Court had the right, indeed, the responsibility, to review each action of Congress to its constitutionality. The Court also defined the cases they would hear. Those of original jurisdiction, when the case came directly to the Supreme Court, such as disputes between two states; and appellate jurisdiction, when the case was being heard on appeal. The United States Supreme Court was the final step in the process; from that court there was no appeal.

Written by design to be relatively simple, the United States Constitution has been used as the model for most of the U.S. state constitutions and for a number of countries around the world. It is necessary to note that as the first ten amendments were ratified as a part of the original document, the remaining 17 amendments means the Constitution has been changed only 17 times since 1791. That seems remarkable in light of the fact that the founding fathers knew nothing of the intricacies of modern life.

Antifederalists

The Antifederalists opposed ratification of the Constitution and warned of the dangers of a strong central government that had been the cause of the long struggle with England. They also noted the absence of a bill of rights protecting individuals and the states.

Articles of Confederation

This was the document agreed to by the colonies after the American Revolution. It provided for a loose organization of states. Each state was to be autonomous. The weaknesses of the Articles were to become apparent soon.

Charles A. Beard

Published in 1913, *An Economic Interpretation of the Constitution*, authored by Beard, criticized the founders in Philadelphia as having selfish economic interests in the outcome of the ratification of the Constitution. His thesis did bring a sense of proportion to the beliefs of the founders, but subsequent documentation refuted many of his charges.

Constitution of the United States

The document serves as the plan for the government of the United States. It outlines the powers and duties of the government and has served, with few changes, for the entire history of these United States.

Constitutional Convention

Circumstances warranted a reassessment of the Articles of Confederation. In 1787, states named delegates and began meeting in late May. The vision during those meetings is testimony to the men there. They came from all walks of life, and eight had signed the Declaration of Independence. Experience had by now persuaded the delegates that an effective central government needed the power to tax, regulate commerce, provide for the defense and make laws binding on citizens. Experience also suggested that states ought not to be able to issue money, make contracts and treaties, wage war, and establish tariffs.

KAPLAN

Test Prep and Admissions

Federalist Papers

This collection of essays was authored and published in New York between 1787 and 1788 under the name of Publius. The authors were, in reality, Alexander Hamilton (who wrote 50), James Madison (wrote 30), and John Jay (wrote 5). The essays defended the principle of a single national government, but also tried to reassure readers that there was nothing to fear regarding government takeovers or tyrannical behavior. Madison's Number 10 is perhaps the most famous; in it he argues that the very size of the country would make it impossible for any single faction to form a majority and take over the government.

Federalist Party

These supporters of ratification of the Constitution saw only opportunities with the new governmental structure. They insisted that the new government would contribute to the prosperity of the country.

Great Compromise

This was the first real division of the Constitutional Convention; it involved the issue of representation. Roger Sherman of Connecticut suggested a compromise. It gave the more populous states representation in the House of Representatives based on their population. Representation in the Senate was to be on an equal basis for all states.

Alexander Hamilton

Hamilton was one of the primary authors of the *Federalist Papers*. He served as the aide-de-camp to Washington during the Revolution, became the first Secretary of the Treasury, conceived the monetary policy of the United States, and died in a duel.

Land Ordinance of 1785

This law, passed by Congress under the Articles of Confederation, outlined a rectangular plan of land surveys and sales for the territories. Each township would be six miles square, divided into 36 lots (or sections) one mile square (640 acres). Each acre was to be auctioned at no less that $1.00 an acre, or $640 in total. The terms favored land speculators as few people had that much cash. The ordinance did set aside the income from one sixteenth of a section for support of schools, which was exceptional at a time when public support of education was a rarity.

James Madison

Madison was the central figure at the Constitutional Convention, the man who knew the most about the historic forms of government. He assumed the role of the major author of the Constitution.

Newburgh Conspiracy

During the last year of the war, a delegation of officers traveled to Philadelphia with a petition for redress. There, they were drawn in to a scheme to force states to yield more power to Congress. Hamilton asked Washington to lend his support to the plan. Although Washington sympathized with the officers, he was not supportive of a military coup. The conspiracy ended there.

Northwest Ordinance

This 1787 plan was a specific description of government for the territories. It required a waiting period before statehood as Congress was concerned about squatters and demands for free land. The Ordinance did provide for statehood requests when the population reached 60,000, guarantees of a Bill of Rights, and the prohibition of slavery. The great significance of the Ordinance was that it provided that new states were to be admitted as equals with all the other states.

separation of powers

Another description of the system of checks and balances imbedded in the Constitution that kept any one branch of the national government from assuming more power than any other. Each branch had powers that were checked in some fashion by another branch, for example, the Executive Branch nominated Supreme Court justices, but the nominations were subject to the approval of the Senate (Legislative branch).

Shay's Rebellion

This was the first real challenge to the new organization of states. Daniel Shay, a war veteran, led a group of Massachusetts farmers in revolt. They wanted a more flexible monetary policy, laws that would allow them to use products as money, and the right to postpone the payment of taxes. The men were disbursed after a broadside from the militia. The rebellion had some success in that it motivated Congress to reassess the Articles.

Adam Smith

Smith was the author of *The Wealth of Nations*. This Scot wrote the classic argument against mercantilism in 1776.

KAPLAN
Test Prep and Admissions

MULTIPLE-CHOICE QUESTIONS

1. Which statement was NOT used by the British to justify colonial taxation after 1763?

    (A) There were heavy administrative expenses maintaining the empire.

    (B) The war debt was considerable and colonists should help pay it.

    (C) Taxes were uniform throughout the Empire.

    (D) The colonies had representation in Parliament.

    (E) American colonists were not taxed as heavily as people in England.

2. During the American Revolution, the main reason the American government sought recognition from foreign nations was to:

    (A) improve relations with Spanish settlers.

    (B) make taxation easier on the frontier.

    (C) facilitate arms purchases and the borrowing of money to fund the war.

    (D) make a negotiated peace with England.

    (E) expand existing settlements along the coast.

3. According to the Constitution, which people in the new government would be elected directly by the people?

    (A) Senators

    (B) Members of the House of Representatives

    (C) Judges in federal courts

    (D) The president

    (E) All of the above

4. The anti-slavery language was stricken from the first draft of the Declaration of Independence in 1776 because:

    (A) the Constitution was going to handle the issue later.

    (B) the Continental Congress feared the British reaction to it.

    (C) Benjamin Franklin objected to it.

    (D) slaves were about to be freed anyway.

    (E) the southern colonies were dependent upon slave labor.

5. What characterizes the violence witnessed at the Boston Tea Party, Bacon's Rebellion, and Shay's Rebellion?

    (A) The participants were all arrested and punished.

    (B) All took place in the cities.

    (C) Violence was directed towards representatives of distant authority.

    (D) Many lives were lost in each incident.

    (E) All of the above are true.

6. Which of the following sums up the attitude of the Founding Fathers towards political parties?

    (A) A multi-party system is essential for stable democracy.

    (B) In a republic, parties are useful devices for organizing the people.

    (C) Parties are dangerous expressions of political ambition and selfishness.

    (D) Parties are engines of democracy and essential to the republic.

    (E) All political organizations need to be regulated by the government.

7. Which of the following statements about the Peace of Paris (1783) is true?

   (A) Spain regained control of Gibraltar.

   (B) Florida was given back to France.

   (C) Britain recognized the United States and agreed to the Mississippi River as the western boundary.

   (D) France regained fishing rights in the Gulf of Mexico.

   (E) Britain had to pay American war debts.

8. The Federalists allowed the addition of the Bill of Rights to the Constitution because they:

   (A) needed support from the Antifederalists to ratify the Constitution.

   (B) wanted to highlight the slavery issue.

   (C) wanted to strengthen the power of the new government.

   (D) wanted to assure Washington's election as president.

   (E) thought the Bill of Rights would weaken the powers of the judicial system.

9. One of the greatest achievements of the U.S. government under the Articles of Confederation was:

   (A) the pacification of the Native Americans in Ohio.

   (B) a strong president to run the government.

   (C) a parliament modeled after English government.

   (D) an effective unicameral legislature.

   (E) the Land Ordinance of 1785 to settle land disputes in the West.

10. The Townshend Acts:

    (A) were supported by a majority of colonists.

    (B) led to Shay's Rebellion.

    (C) was intended to raise revenue to support British troops in the colonies.

    (D) were import taxes on glass, tea, and paper to help pay for imperial administration.

    (E) were designed to regulate trade rather than raise revenue.

11. England refused to leave military forts in U.S. territory after the Revolutionary War because:

    (A) Napoleon threatened to expand his American empire.

    (B) the forts were needed for Canadian defense.

    (C) France would not give up New Orleans as promised.

    (D) the United States had not honored the debts to Loyalists.

    (E) Loyalists were not allowed to emigrate to Canada.

12. The Proclamation of 1763:

    (A) was designed to keep Native Americans from settling on colonists' land.

    (B) remained intact for more than 10 years.

    (C) forbade colonists to settle west of the Appalachians.

    (D) was designed to protect English manufacturing.

    (E) introduced a tax on sugar.

KAPLAN
Test Prep and Admissions

13. The Northwest Ordinance of 1787 allowed for:

    (A) taxation of frontier outposts.

    (B) a system whereby territories can become states.

    (C) land speculation in the Northwest region.

    (D) peaceful negotiation with the native tribes in regards land transfers.

    (E) stronger communities on the western frontier.

14. Which of the following was a colonial objection to the Stamp Act?

    (A) Taxes were on exported goods.

    (B) Colonial assemblies had no say in the decision to levy the tax.

    (C) The taxes meant the movement of scarce colonial resources to Britain.

    (D) Revenue would pay for the expenses of Parliament in London.

    (E) Taxes did not raise enough revenue to pay the debts of the war.

15. What booklet was seen as the most persuasive argument for American independence from England?

    (A) *A Treatise on the People by Samuel Adams*

    (B) *The Liberator* by William Garrison

    (C) *The Star Spangled Banner* by Francis Scott Keye

    (D) *Common Sense* by Thomas Paine

    (E) *The Declaration of Independence* by Thomas Jefferson

16. During the Confederation period, the most prominent Federalists who argued for a strong central government were:

    (A) George Mason and Patrick Henry.

    (B) Nathan Hale and General Gage.

    (C) John Adams and Henry Clay.

    (D) Thomas Jefferson and John Hancock.

    (E) Alexander Hamilton and James Madison.

17. The New Jersey Plan at the Constitutional Convention advocated:

    (A) a republican form of government that would have a strong executive.

    (B) that a strong judicial branch be established.

    (C) that a Bill of Rights was necessary to protect individual liberties.

    (D) that the Constitution would promote control of the government by one party.

    (E) equal representation in the legislature to safeguard the power of the small states.

18. After many military defeats during the Revolutionary War, what proved crucial to the eventual success of the Continental Army?

    (A) The waning resistance of the Loyalists in the colonies

    (B) The king's desire for peace

    (C) Congress' ability to raise money for the war

    (D) The tenacious leadership of George Washington

    (E) The Continental Army always being well supplied

19. Which of the following enabled the Americans to defeat the British in 1781?

    (A) The capture of Benedict Arnold that same year

    (B) Wellington's victory at Saratoga

    (C) French military assistance

    (D) Loans from Austria

    (E) Parliament gave up trying to win a war in North America

20. The ratification of the Constitution was accomplished when:

    (A) all states voted to accept the new government.

    (B) over half the states voted to ratify the new government.

    (C) at least nine states out of thirteen ratified the document.

    (D) the Federalists gained control of all the state assemblies.

    (E) George Washington agreed to become the first president.

ESSAY QUESTIONS

1. What was the greatest single factor that led to the American victory in her War of Independence against Great Britain?

_____

_____

_____

_____

_____

_____

_____

_____

_____

_____

2. Why did many colonists remain loyal to the king during the American Revolution?

_____

_____

_____

_____

_____

_____

_____

_____

_____

_____

ANSWER KEY

Multiple-Choice Questions

1. C
2. C
3. B
4. E
5. C
6. C
7. C
8. A
9. E
10. D
11. D
12. C
13. B
14. B
15. D
16. E
17. E
18. D
19. C
20. C

Answers and Explanations

1. C

Britain did not have uniform taxation throughout the empire; thus the British could not use this argument to justify colonial taxation. In fact, the tax burden on the American colonists was less than that faced by the British people themselves. The British argued that taxation in their colonies in America after the French War in the 1760s was needed to pay the debts from the war and the costs of colonial administration. The British claimed the colonists had "virtual" representation in Parliament—their interests were represented although they didn't actually elect any members.

2. C

The Americans were desperate for money to pay for the war and foreign relations were conducted to help pay for arms and supplies. War is always expensive and every participant must come up with funding to finance the fighting. This often means borrowing money from the citizenry or other nations.

3. B

When the Constitution was written in 1788 only the members of the House of Representatives were directly elected by the people in each congressional district. The president is chosen indirectly by the Electoral College, judges are appointed, and senators were originally chosen by the state assemblies.

4. E

Even though Thomas Jefferson was a southerner and a slave owner he believed that slavery should be abolished. Other delegates from colonies such as South Carolina did not agree and threatened to walk out of the Continental Congress unless the anti-slavery language in the Declaration of Independence was taken out. Later, at the Constitutional Convention, it was agreed that the importation of slaves would be ended 20 years after the Constitution was ratified. Slavery would continue to exist, however, for another 50 years after that.

5. C

Americans have demonstrated a clear pattern of rebelling against perceived injustice and taxes in particular. Various rebellions during and after the colonial period saw uprisings against royal governors, tax laws, and local courts. All showed an anti-authoritarian impulse that has always existed in the American culture.

6. C

The Founding Fathers did not imagine the political evolution that would take place within one decade of the writing of the Constitution. By 1800, there was a two party system which vied for power in the federal and local governments. Washington was critical of this development and believed that nothing good would come of such bitter competition. He watched this in his own cabinet as Jefferson and Hamilton became the two leading figures in the two parties, the Federalists and the Republicans.

7. C

The Peace of Paris (1783) was a complex negotiation to settle the issues of the American war of independence. While France and Spain tried to gain some advantage from Great Britain, the newly created United States needed to firm up its new borders and settle financial issues. Britain's recognition of the independence of the United States and its western boundary at the Mississippi River was the most important feature of the Treaty.

8. A

Some Americans were concerned that individual freedoms were left undefined by the new Constitution. They wanted these spelled out in the form of 10 amendments, or additions, made to the document that created the new U.S. government. In order to gain the support needed to ratify the Constitution, the Federalists promised that basic freedoms would be defined after its ratification. This happened as promised.

9. E

The Land Ordinance of 1785 was a systematic plan for land survey in the West. It created townships and allowed the buying of land at set rates. This created a plan for land development and helped organize new settlements in what was then the northwestern part of the country.

10. D

The Townshend Acts were named after Lord Townshend and were a group of laws passed by Parliament to raise revenue for England. They targeted common items such as glass and paper. These revenues paid the salaries of the royal officials, making them more independent of the colonial assemblies that used to pay them.

11. D

The British insisted that those colonists who had been loyal to the king should be paid for any loss of property resulting from the war. When that happened, the British would surrender the forts in the Northwest (present-day Ohio and Michigan).

12. C

After the French and Indian War, Britain took possession of vast territories in North America. Some native tribes who had helped the British in the war wanted assurances that white settlers would not encroach beyond the Appalachian Mountains. The king issued the proclamation but it angered the colonists who resented being kept from land in the West.

13. B

There were conflicting land claims in the West by states after the Revolutionary War. These claims were finally given up and new territorial boundaries were set. According to the Northwest Ordinance, a territory could apply for statehood in Congress when the population reached 60,000 people. This allowed new states to be added to the Union as settlers continued west after 1787.

14. B

In the 1760s Parliament enacted tax laws to help pay for the recent war and other imperial expenses. Because colonists in British America did not vote in parliamentary elections they had no power to influence the passing of these laws. Their own colonial assemblies had no power to influence Parliament in faraway London, so this seemed undemocratic and arbitrary.

15. D

Thomas Paine had been called the great propagandist of the American Revolution. His pamphlet, Common Sense, was first printed in Philadelphia. It said that the king was no longer to be obeyed and that Americans should seek their own independence. Thousands of copies were eventually printed and it convinced many Americans that it might be worth the fight to be free from the crown.

16. E

A small group of the Founding Fathers were convinced that the Articles of Confederation needed to be replaced with a stronger blueprint for American government. Among these were Hamilton and Madison who helped write the new Constitution in Philadelphia in 1787. They later wrote the Federalist Papers to help convince the states to accept the new design for government.

17. E

During the Constitutional Convention in Philadelphia in 1787, the large and small states debated how power should be allocated in the new government. Small states such as New Jersey were afraid that they would be eclipsed by the larger states of Virginia and Massachusetts. They argued that all states should have equal representation in the new federal Congress.

18. D

At the beginning of the war with Britain, there were many who assumed that the colonists could not stand up against one of the best armies in the world at that time. Short of money and supplies, the Continental Army was at a great disadvantage. Washington proved adept at keeping his army together and escaping to fight another day, even when the battles were lost.

19. C

Certainly the assistance of the French was a great military and psychological benefit to the American cause after Saratoga. French ground troops joined Washington in the final campaigns of the war and the French naval blockade sealed up Cornwallis at Yorktown. The French Marquis de Lafayette served loyally with Washington throughout the war.

20. C

Nine states of the original thirteen were needed to ratify the Constitution for it to be accepted by the new United States. Smaller states were the first to ratify the document, but its acceptance wasn't certain until Virginia and New York voted for ratification.

KAPLAN

Test Prep and Admissions

ANALYSES OF THE FREE-RESPONSE ESSAYS

Question 1:

What was the greatest single factor that led to the American victory in her War of Independence against Great Britain?

Key Points

American Advantages

- A clear grievance with the crown
- Steadfast and determined leadership: Adams, Washington, Jefferson, Franklin
- French assistance after Saratoga (1777)
- Knowledge of the terrain and tactics learned from earlier battles with Natives and the French
- Loans from Spanish and Dutch

British Disadvantages

- Arrogant and mediocre military leadership
- Supply problems
- Faced with hostile colonials
- Opposition within Parliament to the American campaign
- Continuing cost of fighting so far from home
- Need for the use of mercenaries
- French and Spanish antipathy

Comparison of British and American military strength

American	British
Fluctuating Continental army that grew and shrank over the years	Well-equipped and trained regular army
Some foreign officers to help with training: von Steuben	Some German troops supplemented the British forces
Intelligent officer corps that learned quickly in battle	Some Loyalist support in the colonies
Resourceful: Made use of captured cannon and other materials	Had the support of a first rate navy
Learned to fight in adverse conditions and did not give up	Assumed that the war would be quickly won

Scoring Rubric

There are five scoring ranges:

Excellent

The answer must have a strong, clear thesis that states ONE compelling reason why the American cause prevailed between 1775 and 1781. The quality of the writing should be excellent, the answer must show logical patterns, and the student can include one of the major points in the above list (though they may go beyond the list). The organization should be clear. The answer may contain minor errors.

Very Good

The answer must have a thesis that makes an argument about how the Americans won their independence. Organization of the answer must show logical patterns, and the student should include many of the specific points from the above list.

Adequate

The answer must try to make some argument and must include at least some of the points listed above. There may be flaws in the thesis argument.

Flawed

The answer will demonstrate serious weaknesses. It may have no thesis argument at all, and it will include few of the points listed above. The answer may show little understanding of American strengths or British disadvantages during the war.

Severely Flawed

The answer will demonstrate almost no attempt to answer the question, and will include very few, if any, of the points listed above.

Question 2:

Why did many colonists remain loyal to the king during the American Revolution?

Key Points

- Most colonials had been raised to respect the crown
- Many considered themselves more British and not 'American'
- Some were suspicious of 'radicals' and their ideas
- Many believed that England could not be defeated

Revolutionary Geography and Background

- Boston was the hotspot of the Revolution
- Many Loyalists lived in the South and in seaport towns and cities
- In every colony, advocates for independence were in the minority
- The Anglican church was usually pro-British
- Back country people in the Carolinas and New York were often loyal to the king
- Loyalists tended to show themselves when the British army appeared nearby

Scoring Rubric

There are five scoring ranges:

Excellent

The answer must have a strong, clear thesis that gives a profile of the Loyalist during the War of Independence. The essay should focus on reasons why many colonists did not support the movement for Independence even after the war had broken out. The quality of the writing should be excellent, the answer must show logical patterns, and the student should include many of the major points in the above list (though they may go beyond these points). The organization should be clear. The answer may contain minor errors.

Very Good

The answer must have a thesis that explains clearly the divided loyalties that many British Americans felt before and after 1775. The answer must be logically organized, and the student should include many of the specific points from the above list.

Adequate

The answer must try to make some argument and must include at least some of the points listed above. There may be flaws in the thesis argument.

Flawed

The answer will demonstrate serious weaknesses. It may have no thesis argument at all, and it will include few of the points listed above. The answer may show little understanding of colonial society and why the Loyalists did not support independence.

Severely Flawed

The answer will demonstrate almost no attempt to answer the question, and will include very few, if any, of the points listed above.

Chapter Five: **The Early Republic**

TIMELINE: 1789–1824

1789	Constitution goes into effect; George Washington elected president.
1790	Alexander Hamilton's First Report on the Public Credit submitted to House of Representatives.
1791	Bill of Rights (first 10 amendments to Constitution) ratified.
1792	National bank established.
1793	French-British wars continue almost uninterrupted until 1815.
1793	Citizen Genêt.
1794	Battle of Fallen Timbers; coalition of northwestern Native Americans defeated.
1794	Whiskey Rebellion in Pennsylvania.
1795	Jay's Treaty with Britain ratified.
1795	Pinckney's Treaty with Spain ratified.
1796	Election of John Adams.
1797	XYZ Affair; increased tensions with France.
1798	Alien and Sedition Acts passed.

1798	Kentucky and Virginia Resolutions passed in response to Alien and Sedition Acts.
1800	Republicans come to power; Thomas Jefferson elected president.
1803	Supreme Court establishes power of judicial review in *Marbury v. Madison.*
1803	Louisiana Purchase.
1804	Lewis and Clark expedition leaves from St. Louis.
1804	Jefferson reelected president.
1807	Embargo Act forbidding American trade passed.
1808	U.S. participation in international slave trade abolished.
1808	James Madison elected president.
1811	Tecumseh and allies defeated at battle of Tippecanoe.
1811	Charter of national bank lapses, is not renewed by Congress.
1812	Madison re-elected president.
1812–1814	War with Britain.
1812–1813	American efforts to invade Canada fail.
1814	Andrew Jackson defeats Creeks at Battle of Horseshoe Bend.
1814	British occupy Washington, D.C., attack Baltimore.
1814	Treaty of Ghent signed, restoring prewar territorial boundaries.
1814	New Englanders consider secession at Hartford Convention.
1815	Americans commanded by Andrew Jackson win Battle of New Orleans.
1816	James Monroe elected president.
1816	National bank re-established.
1818	Jackson defeats Spanish and Seminoles in Florida.
1818	United States and Britain agree to joint occupation of Oregon country.
1819	Panic of 1819 ends postwar boom.
1819	*McCulloch v. Maryland* and *Dartmouth College v. Woodward* establish supremacy of national government over states and limit states' power over contracts, respectively.
1820	Missouri Compromise admits Maine to union as a free state, Missouri as a slave state, and sets northern boundary of 36°30′ for expansion of slavery into Louisiana Purchase.
1823	Monroe Doctrine.
1824	*Gibbons v. Ogden* clarifies Congress' power to regulate interstate commerce.

THE FEDERALISTS

The story of the Americans continues after the fighting of the Revolution with the uneasy establishment of a government weak on power and beholden to the individual states. Remember the objections to British rule, the loss of individual freedoms, and the power to determine a destiny free of oppressive tax policies. Cooler heads would ultimately prevail, and the Constitutional Convention was called together to work out a better political arrangement than was offered under the Articles of Confederation. The weaknesses of the Articles were plain to see, and the fears of the individual states were equally plain.

The contributions of the founding fathers to a document that has survived relatively unchanged until today is a testimony to their foresight and faith in a governmental process. George Washington would serve as the country's first president. The esteem in which he was held served to establish many traditions of the presidency, including the tradition of serving only two consecutive terms (which was observed until Franklin Roosevelt held office and the passing of the 22nd Amendment). After Washington left office, John Adams, who served one term, succeeded him. The Federalists, however, were losing political power; the change was completed when Thomas Jefferson became the third president in 1800. The House of Representatives elected Jefferson as no clear majority was achieved in the Electoral College; he and Aaron Burr each received 73 votes.

The Constitution was working; the Federalists were right to support the passage of the document. A peaceful passage of the reins of power had been accomplished, and the intentions of the founding fathers were clear. The experiment was a success.

John Adams

As the second president of the United States, Adams would be faced with several foreign relations problems. The most prominent question was whether to support the revolution in France, France's enemies, or neither side. Taxation, the Alien and Sedition Acts, the suppression of the Whiskey Rebellion, and Jay's Treaty did not serve to make him a popular man. He would serve only one term.

Alien and Sedition Acts

These were actually four separate pieces of legislation that limited the freedom of speech and press and the liberty of aliens. They did not originate with Adams, but he agreed to them. The Naturalization Act changed the length of time of residency for citizenship purposes from five to fourteen years. The Alien Act allowed the president to deport dangerous "aliens" or face imprisonment. The Alien Enemy Act allowed the president, in time of war, to expel or imprison enemy aliens, and the Sedition Act defined as a crime any conspiracy against the government.

Bank of the United States

This was a significant part of Alexander Hamilton's vision of a program of government finances and economic development for the United States. The bank would issue bank notes (paper money) to provide a uniform currency. Government bonds would be held by the bank to back up the value of the currency.

Bill of Rights

The first ten amendments were ratified along with the Constitution; in fact, states reported they would not ratify with out the specific protections of free speech, freedom of the press, and the other civil rights and liberties of today.

Daniel Boone

Boone blazed the trail through the Appalachian Mountains to Kentucky through the Cumberland Gap. He led settlers in 1773 through the Gap in southwestern Virginia but was repulsed by Native Americans. Two years later he and other woodsmen widened the Wilderness Road through which more than 300,000 would travel to the Kentucky River. The settlement of Boonesborough (Lexington, KY) was the first in the interior.

Aaron Burr

Burr's was the checkered career. His duel with Alexander Hamilton resulted in Hamilton's death. He was a vice president who tied with Jefferson in 1800 in the Electoral College, and lost. He would attempt to orchestrate a secession of Louisiana and a separate republic. He was betrayed and tried for treason. He escaped to France but returned in 1812. He lived out his days in New York practicing law.

Cabinet system

Washington's task as chief executive was to organize the new department of the executive branch. The four initial advisors (T. Jefferson—Secretary of State; A. Hamilton—Secretary of Treasury; H. Knox—Secretary of War; and E. Randolph—Attorney General) became known as the Cabinet. To this day, the President calls Cabinet meetings in order to obtain advice and information from the various departments of the government.

elastic clause

The last of the powers of Congress as enumerated in Article I, Section 8 of the Constitution. In it, Congress has the power to enact "all laws necessary and proper" to carry out the forgoing powers of that list in Section 8. The authors of the Constitution knew they could not envision the United States one hundred years hence, and had to create a mechanism to adapt to the changing circumstances.

excise tax

Hamilton persuaded Congress to pass these taxes, especially on whiskey, to raise some of the needed funds to pay off war debts after Congress did not set tariff rates high enough.

Federalist Party

Those who supported the Constitution and a strong federal government were the foundation of this, the first of the political parties. They did, however, argue against the addition of the Bill of Rights to the Constitution. They said that since members of Congress were to be elected by the people, they did not need to be protected against themselves. Additionally, they suggested, it was better to assume all rights were protected than to create a list that might be limiting in some way. They also supported Alexander Hamilton and his financial program.

Genêt Affair

Genêt, the French minister to the United States, broke the rules of diplomacy by appealing directly to the American people regarding support of the French Revolution. He was removed by the French government, but stayed in the United States as a private citizen.

Alexander Hamilton

The first Secretary of the Treasury, Hamilton proposed to pay off the national debt at face value and have the federal government assume the war debts of the states. He also wanted to protect the new industries through high tariffs and create a national bank for depositing government funds and printing paper money.

John Jay

The first Chief Justice of the Supreme Court, Jay had much prior political experience. He had served as a Continental Congress president, ambassador to England, and as the American minister to Spain. He served with John Adams and Benjamin Franklin in negotiating the Peace of Paris in 1783. He became a supporter of the Constitution through his co-authorship of *The Federalist* and would negotiate the treaty that bears his name.

Jay's Treaty

Washington's envoy to Great Britain was charged with the task of talking Britain out of its practice of searching and seizing American ships and impressing seamen into the British Navy. After negotiations, Jay brought back a treaty that said Great Britain would give up its posts on the western frontier, but said nothing about the seizure of ships and impressments. The treaty was ratified by a slim margin. It was not popular but kept the United States at peace with the both France and Great Britain.

Thomas Jefferson

Jefferson was the third president of the United States who would see the purchase of the Louisiana Territory and the doubling of the size of the United States, the submission of the Barbary pirates, the ill effects of the Embargo Act, and the movement toward the War of 1812 during his two administrations.

Jeffersonian Republicans (Democratic Republicans)

The first time in American history that one political party had given over power to the opposition party occurred when the new political party headed by Jefferson came into power in 1801.

Judiciary Act

Passed in 1801 just before the Republican Thomas Jefferson took office as president, it was intended to keep control of the judiciary in the hands of the Federalists. It provided that the next vacancy on the Supreme Court should not be filled, it created 16 circuit courts and increased the number of attorneys, clerks, and marshals. The Act was repealed later in 1801, so the circuit judgeships were eliminated as well as other offices.

KAPLAN
Test Prep and Admissions

John Marshall

He was appointed by John Adams to serve as Chief Justice. His years on the Court (34 total) saw decisions affirming judicial review, the right to take appeals from state courts, checking the power of states in terms of contracts, and building the power of the central government. His last great decision was in regards to interstate commerce.

Pinckney's Treaty

This treaty was negotiated with Spain and involved the opening of the lower Mississippi River and New Orleans to American trade. Americans also got the right to transfer cargoes in New Orleans without paying duties to the Spanish government. This treaty also settled the northern boundary of Florida.

protective tariff

A tariff is a tax on an imported good. Protective tariffs serve to do exactly that: protect the good made in the United States. Protective tariffs have been instituted and repealed on goods depending upon the world markets and the manufacturers in the United States.

Report on the Manufactures

This was Alexander Hamilton's report to Congress that outlined a program of protective tariffs and other governmental supports of businesses.

Report on the Public Credit

Hamilton's first report made two key recommendations to Congress. It advocated funding the federal debt at face value and assuming the debts of the states from the Revolution. This second installment came as a report to Congress that included a proposal for an excise tax on liquor as a way to aid the raising of revenue to cover the public debt. Hamilton also advocated the establishment of a national bank and national mint.

strict versus loose interpretation of the Constitution

Those who favored a strict interpretation of the Constitution said that they could do only what was listed in the document. Those who favored a loose interpretation thought they were limited only if the Constitution specifically stated that something could not be done. Jefferson was a strict constructionist; but when faced with the obvious advantages of purchasing Louisiana, found a loose interpretation could justify the purchase.

Treaty of Greenville

This treaty, signed in 1795, said the United States would buy, for an annuity of $10,000, the rights to the southeastern quarter of the Northwest Territory (now Ohio and Indiana). The high Native American losses at the Battle of Fallen Timbers precipitated the treaty.

Virginia and Kentucky Resolutions

The Alien and Sedition Acts generated responses from the Republicans. The Supreme Court had not yet established the principle of judicial review. The Kentucky and Virginia legislatures adopted a resolution that said the two states had entered into a compact and that if any federal action broke the compact, they could nullify federal law. This nullification controversy would reappear in the 1830s.

George Washington

Washington was the first president of the United States and the man to whom subsequent presidents were compared. Future presidents would follow his advice regarding alliances, but his advice regarding political parties was already moot. One consequence of his presidency was the two-term practice.

Washington's Farewell Address

He warned against the policies and practices he considered unwise. This message, with significant help from Hamilton, warned Americans not to get involved in European affairs, or make permanent alliances with other countries. He also warned against sectionalism and political parties.

Whiskey Rebellion

From western Pennsylvania came the challenge to the federal government. A group of farmers refused to pay the excise tax on whiskey. Washington sent 15,000 state militiamen, under the command of Alexander Hamilton, to the scene. The show of force deflated the rebellion without bloodshed.

XYZ Affair

This was the first major challenge to President John Adams. French warships were reportedly seizing American ships. Adams sent a delegation to Paris to negotiate a peaceful settlement. Certain French ministers, identified as "X, Y, and Z" requested bribes as the cost of entering into negotiations. The American delegates refused. There were demands for war, but Adams knew the American Army and Navy were not strong enough for a war against a major world power. He avoided war and sent new ministers to France.

THE JEFFERSONIAN REPUBLICANS

Jefferson, as the first Republican, took pains to eliminate partisan bitterness in his first term. He gave up the coach and six horses used to travel about the city by the two previous presidents. His messages to Congress were written to avoid the appearance of a "speech from the throne," but one might suspect that other motives were at play here; Jefferson was a poor public speaker and a fine writer. He held dinners at the White House at a round table so all would be equal. Jefferson appointed men of his own party to policy-making positions. His cabinet was filled with men from all parts of the country.

His first administration faced two great tests; the Supreme Court's decision in *Marbury v. Madison* was the first. In its decision, the Supreme Court declared a federal law unconstitutional. John Marshall wrote the opinion for a unanimous Court. William Marbury deserved his commission (Adams' midnight appointment), but the Court could not require its deliverance. The implications of the ruling were clear in Marshall's words. The precedent that the court could declare a federal law invalid on the grounds that it violated provisions of the Constitution was established.

Jefferson's second great test came with the opportunity to buy the area owned by France called Louisiana. Jefferson had sent ministers to Napoleon with an offer to buy the area around New Orleans. In response, Napoleon offered the entire territory to the ministers. They accepted the

KAPLAN
Test Prep and Admissions

offer. These events presented Jefferson with a dilemma. A strict interpreter of the Constitution, Jefferson had no power to buy property. However, the power to purchase the territory was included within the confines of treaty-making powers. Congress approved the purchase 26–6. Implied power interpretation was accepted. With the purchase, the size of the United States doubled and Jefferson's vision of a nation of "yeoman farmers" could become a reality.

John Adams

Adams, the second president of the United States, won the presidency by three electoral votes. His administration saw the XYZ Affair, the passing of the Alien and Sedition Acts, and the impact of the Kentucky and Virginia Resolutions (which declared that the states had entered into a "compact" in forming the national government and therefore if any act of the federal government broke the compact, a state could nullify the federal law). After one term, Adams was beaten by Jefferson.

John Quincy Adams

John Quincy Adams was the sixth president of the United States, son of a president and former Secretary of State under Monroe. Adams became president after the House of Representatives decided the contest as not one of the four candidates had a majority in the Electoral College (Jackson had won the popular vote; with four candidates, there was no majority). Henry Clay used his influence to get Adams enough votes, and President Adams then appointed Clay as Secretary of State. Adams asked Congress for money for internal improvements, aid to manufacturing, and a national university. In 1828, Congress passed a new tariff law that pleased the northern manufacturers and displeased the southern planters.

Barbary pirates

These pirates lived and operated in the Mediterranean Sea. Washington and Adams had paid tribute to the Barbary governments. When the Pasha of Tripoli demanded a higher sum in tribute, Jefferson sent a small fleet. Fighting lasted for four years. Although the United States Navy did not achieve a decisive victory, it did gain the respect of nations in and around the Mediterranean and offered some protections to American shipping. Lieutenant Stephen Decatur slipped into Tripoli Harbor at night and set fire to the frigate *Philadelphia*, which had been captured along with its crew. The pasha settled for $60,000 and released the crew. It was still tribute, but much less than the $300,000 originally demanded.

Battle of New Orleans

This last confrontation of the War of 1812, stopping the British effort to control the Mississippi River, was led by Andrew Jackson in conjunction with Native Americans, frontiersmen, free African Americans, and Creoles. The victory was impressive but almost meaningless as it was fought on January 8, 1815—two weeks after the peace had been signed in Ghent, Belgium.

Battle of Tippecanoe

In 1811, Governor William Henry Harrison attacked Tecumseh's capital, Prophet's Town, while their leader was away. The Shawnees lost a bloody battle that left about a quarter of Harrison's men dead or wounded. Only later did Harrison realize the extent of the damage inflicted on the Shawnee, as many fled to Canada. The battle reinforced suspicions that the British were inciting the Native Americans. His success at the battle would later become a slogan for Harrison's campaign for president: "Tippicanoe and Tyler, too."

Berlin and Milan Decrees

Napoleon's retaliation for the Orders of Council of 1806 and 1807 that Britain issued barring all trade between England and Europe. In addition, any ship going to a continental port was to get a license and would be subject to British inspection. Napoleon instituted his Berlin Decree in 1806 and the Milan Decree in 1807, which barred British ships from French ports and neutral ships that complied with British rules would be subject to seizure. American ships were caught in the middle; either way they would be in violation of one of the country's regulations.

Aaron Burr

Burr served as Jefferson's vice president and, had he not gotten caught up in some political schemes, he might have succeeded in becoming president. His political future died at the duel where Hamilton died. He was indicted for murder in New York and New Jersey. He did return to preside over the Senate, safe so long as he stayed out of those two states. Burr did attempt to establish a personal empire for himself in the West. The conspiracy folded and the participants were tried; Burr came before Chief Justice John Marshall. Two major constitutional precedents were established as a result of the case. Jefferson refused a subpoena requiring him to appear in court with certain papers (claiming executive privilege and the importance of the independence of the executive branch). The second result was a definition of treason.

Chesapeake-Leopard Affair

In 1807, the British warship *Leopard* fired upon the American *Chesapeake*. Three Americans were killed and four others were taken and impressed into the British navy. Anti-British feeling ran high and there were demands for war. Jefferson instead used economic pressure and diplomatic means to avoid a confrontation.

Embargo Act

Passed in 1807, this legislation was an alternative to war. It prevented American ships from sailing into any foreign ports. Jefferson hoped that since the Americans were Britain's largest trading partner, that the embargo would stop them from violating the rights of neutral nations. It backfired and brought great economic stress to the United States. The British were willing to do anything to control the seas, and had little trouble in substituting South American goods for those from the U.S. The embargo devastated the American economy, especially New England. Jefferson called for a repeal of the Embargo Act in 1809. Even after the repeal, U.S. ships could legally trade with all nations except Britain and France.

Alexander Hamilton

The first Secretary of the Treasury, Hamilton had served as Washington's aide-de-camp during the Revolution. He would outline a program for economic development of the United States that passed with little change. He advocated for a program of protective tariffs, which would become policy. His First Report to the House of Representatives made two recommendations: funding of the federal debt at face value, and the assumption of all state debts from the revolution (to the tune of $21 million). He also organized the National Bank. The resulting debate was the first regarding the interpretation of the Constitution. Hamilton wanted a country with a strong central government that actively encouraged capitalism. He would die as a result of wounds suffered at the hands of Aaron Burr in a duel.

KAPLAN
Test Prep and Admissions

Hartford Convention

This meeting represented the climax of New England's disapproval of "Mr. Madison's War." Although the New Englanders had managed to keep out of the war and profit from illegal trading and privateering, they had monopolized the import trade and engaged in active trading with the enemy. After Napoleon's fall, the British blockaded New England, occupied Maine and conducted raids along the coastline. Federalists in Massachusetts voted for a convention of New England states to plan for an independent action. The result of the Hartford Convention was the downfall of the Federalist party, as the call for succession had been lost in the celebration of the New Orleans action and the Ghent treaty.

Andrew Jackson

Jackson was the seventh president of the United States and the first to come from the "frontier." During his administrations universal male suffrage was attained, and the two-party system came into being, which led to the party nominating conventions and the popular election of the president. On the other hand, the administrations were also notorious for the perpetuation of the spoils system, and Jackson's "Kitchen Cabinet."

Thomas Jefferson

Jefferson was the third president of the United States who envisioned the country as an agrarian-based society. His vision prompted his expansion of the U.S. through the Louisiana Purchase and his change in stance concerning the interpretation of the Constitution from that of a strict interpretation to a looser position. His first term was relatively calm as he maintained the national bank, Hamilton's debt-repayment plan, and the neutrality policies of Washington and Adams. He also retained the support of Republicans by supporting a limited central government. He reduced the size of the military, eliminated a number of federal jobs, repealed the excise tax (especially on whiskey) and lowered the national debt.

Toussaint L'Overture

He was the leader of the rebellion in Santo Domingo against the French. His rebellion resulted in heavy losses for the French and served to suggest to Napoleon that a presence in the area would be a costly stance to maintain.

Lewis and Clark expedition

Jefferson persuaded Congress to fund a scientific exploration of the West, to be led by Captain Meriwether Lewis and William Clark. The expedition continued for over two years, but returned intact. The benefits of the expedition included increased geographic and scientific knowledge of the previously unexplored country, stronger claims to the Oregon Territory, and improved relations with Native American tribes.

Louisiana Purchase

President Jefferson sent ministers to France to negotiate for the purchase of New Orleans and a strip of land extending from that port eastward to Florida. Napoleon's ministers countered with an offer of $15 million for the entire Louisiana territory, and the Americans accepted. The constitutional question of buying land was not addressed specifically but Jefferson was persuaded to set aside his strict interpretation of the Constitution for the good of the country. He submitted the purchase to the Senate as an example of the President's power to make treaties, with consent of the Senate. The Purchase more than doubled the size of the country, removed a foreign nation from the border, and guaranteed the expansion of the United States beyond the Mississippi River.

Macon's Bill Number 2

The economic problems continued into 1810. Nathaniel Macon introduced legislation to restore trade with Britain and France. His bill also provided that if either Britain or France agreed to U.S. neutral rights at sea, then the U.S. would prohibit trade with that nation's foe.

James Madison

Jefferson's vice president, Madison was viewed as a brilliant thinker and statesman. He had worked with Jefferson to establish the Democratic-Republican party. He did not have the political skills of Jefferson, but was supported by a caucus of congressional Republicans, and so defeated the Federalist challenge. His presidency was confronted with the same international problems as Jefferson's second term, but he was finally persuaded to go to war.

Marbury v. Madison

This was the first major case decided by the Supreme Court with John Marshall as chief justice. William Marbury had sued for his federal appointment as a judge, made in the last few hours of the Adams administration and not delivered by order of the new president, Jefferson. Marshall ruled that it would be unconstitutional for the Court to award him a writ of mandamus (an order to force Madison to deliver the commission), so ultimately the commission was not delivered to Marbury. By ruling a law of Congress to be unconstitutional, Marshall established the doctrine of *judicial review*.

John Marshall

The Federalist judge had been appointed chief justice by John Adams. He would serve for 34 years and exert as much influence on the Supreme Court as Washington did on the presidency. His decisions in several landmark cases had the effect of strengthening the national government, sometimes at the expense of states' rights. He set the precedent for the Supreme Court: It would have the power to decide whether an act of Congress or of the President was or was not allowed by the Constitution.

midnight judges

The last-minute appointments of Federalists to judgeships by John Adams, just before Thomas Jefferson became president. Jefferson held up the appointment papers, not delivering them to the recipients. William Marbury sued, the *Marbury v. Madison* decision resulted.

James Monroe

Monroe was the fifth president and the fourth from Virginia. His eight-year administration would be noted for the acquisition of Florida, the Missouri Compromise, and the Monroe Doctrine. The Monroe years were somewhat remarkable for their surface spirit of nationalism, optimism, and goodwill. This positive outlook can be attributed to the Republicans' domination of politics in every area of the country. Though oversimplified, the era saw a host of problems: debates over tariffs, the national bank, internal improvements, and public land sales. Sectionalism concerns were rising into the national consciousness and the apparent peaceful political landscape would dissolve two years later. The actual time of "good feelings" was from the election of 1816 to the Panic of 1819.

KAPLAN
Test Prep and Admissions

Non-Intercourse Act of 1809

After the repeal of the Embargo Act, President Madison hoped to end the economic problems while maintaining rights as a neutral nation. The legislation allowed for trade with all nations except Britain and France.

Revolution of 1800

This refers to the nonviolent transfer of political power from the Federalists of Washington and Adams to Jefferson and the Democratic-Republicans.

Second Bank of the United States

This was part of Henry Clay's American System, his plan to promote economic growth. The plan consisted of three parts: protective tariffs, a national bank, and internal improvements. The national bank, argued Clay, would keep the system running smoothly by providing a national currency. Congress chartered the Second Bank in 1816 as the charter on the First Bank, Alexander Hamilton's creation, had been allowed to expire in 1811.

Tariff of 1816

After the War of 1812, Congress raised the tariff on certain goods for the express purpose of protecting American manufacturers. It was the first protective tariff, passed to protect against the dumping of British goods on American markets after American manufacturers had built factories to supply goods that had been previously imported from Britain.

Tecumseh

The Shawnee leader who tried to form a confederation of the tribes to defend their lands as he believed they held their lands in common. He died in the Battle of the Thames in 1813.

Treaty of Ghent

The peace treaty ending the War of 1812. The treaty was negotiated after stalling on both sides. After news of the American win on Lake Champlain, the British began to weaken their stance. One by one, both sides dropped their demands. The negotiators agreed to end the war, return the prisoners, restore the previous boundaries, and settle nothing else. The treaty was signed Christmas Eve, 1814.

war hawks

This term described the members of Congress from the southern and western districts who began to campaign for a war in defense of "national honor." They included Henry Clay, Richard Johnson, Felix Grundy, and John C. Calhoun. The "new boys" were dubbed "war hawks."

THE RISE OF NATIONALISM

Following Jefferson into the presidency was James Madison, whose administration focused on foreign affairs almost from the beginning. By continuing to insist on neutral rights and freedom of the seas, he continued Jefferson's policy of "peaceable coercion." Affairs continued to deteriorate. The War of 1812, the main cause of which was the demand for neutral rights, was the result. Two years later the Treaty of Ghent would be signed, ending the conflict.

The War of 1812 changed American-British relations forever. It had generated a spirit of nationalism in America. It also pushed the United States toward economic independence, as the trade interruptions had given American manufacturers the opportunity to grow and develop. Lastly, it was apparent that this new nation was here to stay and that it was not to be considered as part of the European power struggles any longer.

On the other side of the nation, in the lands of the Louisiana Purchase, there was constant pressure to open new lands. This forced Native Americans to move, sign treaties they did not understand, and lose control over their lands. Two Shawnee leaders, Tecumseh and his brother Tenskwatawa (The Prophet), decided to take action. Tecumseh traveled throughout the territory urging the tribes to form a "confederation" to defend the land and arguing that no land cession was valid without the consent of all the tribes, since they held the lands in common. His brother traveled and called upon Native Americans to resist the "white man's whiskey" and lead a simple life within their means. Their end came at the Battle of Tippecanoe.

The lessons of the past 40 years were not lost on the Federalists and the Republicans. A peacetime army and navy were needed. New industries wanted tariffs. Internal improvements, especially roads to the interior, were a necessity. President Madison embraced nationalism and a broad interpretation of the Constitution. The Federalists took up Jefferson's strict interpretation and states' rights. This reversal of roles would occur again.

Dartmouth v. Woodward

This landmark Supreme Court decision involved an attempt by the New Hampshire legislature to change a provision in Dartmouth College's charter. The state placed Dartmouth under a new board named by the governor, while the original charter called for a self-perpetuating board. Daniel Webster represented Dartmouth and won the case. The charter, said Chief Justice John Marshall, was a valid contract in which the legislature had unconstitutionally interfered.

Era of Good Feelings

According to the more traditional view of the period, the Monroe presidency was a time of nationalism, optimism, and goodwill. This was accomplished by the dominance of one political party, the Republicans, over all three sections (North, South, and West) of the country. It is an oversimplification.

Gibbons v. Ogden

This decision would establish national supremacy in regulating interstate commerce. Aaron Ogden received the exclusive right to operate a ferry between New York and New Jersey. Thomas Gibbons came into competition with him. The Court ruled that the monopoly granted by the state conflicted with federal law, and that the exclusive right was null and void.

Jeffersonian Republicans (Democratic-Republicans)

The political party of the Adams presidency was the first to become a true political party. The democratic leanings of Thomas Jefferson served to inspire the "farmers" to oppose the Federalists. It was with Jefferson's election in 1800 that the transition of power would be accomplished without violence. They would enjoy true political domination at times.

KAPLAN
Test Prep and Admissions

John Marshall

Marshall was appointed by John Adams as Chief Justice. His 34 years on the Court saw decisions affirming judicial review, the right to take appeals from state courts, checking the power of states in terms of contracts, and building the power of the central government. His last great decision was in regards to interstate commerce.

McCulloch v. Maryland

This is probably the single most important decision of the Marshall Court. In it, Marshall established the supremacy of federal law. He wrote that Maryland's effort to tax the national bank was in conflict with federal law and was thus unconstitutional.

Missouri Compromise

So long as the balance between slave and free states was maintained, southern states could block legislation that threatened their interests. When Missouri petitioned for statehood, the North felt threatened, because slavery was firmly established there. Missouri was the first part of the Louisiana Purchase territory to apply for statehood; northerners and southerners both worried about the precedent that would be set.

Monroe Doctrine

This statement of American policy was issued to ward off any moves by the European nations in Central and South America. First contained in Monroe's Message to Congress in 1823, the doctrine later came to be named after its originator. It said, in part, that the American continents were not "…subjects for future colonization"; that the European political systems were different and any attempt to extend their systems was dangerous; that the United States would not interfere with existing European colonies; and that the United States would keep out of the internal affairs of European nations.

Panic of 1819

The Era of Good Feelings lasted until this panic, which was instigated by the Second Bank of the United States. The Bank had tightened credit in an effort to control inflation. Many state banks closed as a result, the value of money fell, and there was widespread unemployment. The depression was most severe in the West.

Tallmadge Amendment

John Tallmadge of New York proposed, during the Missouri statehood debate, a two-pronged amendment. He suggested prohibiting the further introduction of slaves in Missouri and requiring the children of slaves to be emancipated at age 25. Southern senators were outraged and saw it as the first step towards eliminating slavery in all states.

Transcontinental Treaty (1819)

Secretary of State John Quincy Adams negotiated the extension of a U.S. boundary to the Pacific coast. Spain would cede all of Florida to the United States in return for American assumption of claims against Spain up to $5 million. The western boundary of the Louisiana Purchase would run to the Pacific. The treaty was considered a triumph in foreign policy.

MULTIPLE-CHOICE QUESTIONS

1. Which policy was advocated by Alexander Hamilton as the Secretary of the Treasury?

    (A) That all coins should be minted in gold

    (B) There should be no national bank

    (C) Tariffs should be lowered to protect manufacturers

    (D) The federal government should assume the war debts of the states

    (E) An export tax be levied on wood products

2. Which of the following statements correctly characterizes the 10th Amendment to the U.S. Constitution?

    (A) It guaranteed freedom of speech and the right of assembly.

    (B) It guaranteed some civil rights for African Americans.

    (C) It prohibited the national government from interfering in the religious beliefs or practices of any citizen.

    (D) It said that powers not specifically given to the national government by the Constitution remained with the states or the people.

    (E) It guaranteed the right of trial by a jury of one's peers.

3. The Kentucky and Virginia Resolutions took the position that:

    (A) the 'supremacy clause' of the Constitution applied only to foreign powers.

    (B) Congress was responsible for maintaining the vitality of an opposition party.

    (C) only fiscal measures enacted by the state could be approved by Congress.

    (D) the authority of the state government included the power to decide constitutional issues.

    (E) only the Supreme Court had the power to restrict freedom of speech.

4. Which feature of the Washington administration is NOT derived from the Constitution?

    (A) The Chief Justice was appointed by the president.

    (B) The president shall appoint his cabinet.

    (C) The vice president shall preside over the Senate.

    (D) The president is commander in chief of the military.

    (E) The president could stay in office as long as the people elected him.

5. The principle motivation for drafting the Bill of Rights was the desire to:

    (A) protect individual rights not specified in the articles of the Constitution.

    (B) ensure that all laws in the future would be constitutional.

    (C) restore the power of the states.

    (D) clarify the relationship of the states to the federal government.

    (E) increase the power of the Executive branch.

6. The Treaty of Ghent, which ended the War of 1812, stated that:

    (A) the crest of the Rocky Mountains would be the new national border.

    (B) the United States reestablished close and friendly relations with France.

    (C) boundaries from before the war would remain unchanged.

    (D) Britain would retain fishing rights off Newfoundland.

    (E) Texas became part of the United States.

7. Which of the following was the most compelling cause of the War of 1812?

    (A) British restriction of American neutral shipping rights at sea

    (B) French intrusion along the Mississippi

    (C) British efforts to invade and regain control of the Ohio Valley area

    (D) An American desire to conquer Canada

    (E) Napoleon's military success in the Caribbean

8. The election of Thomas Jefferson was called the 'Revolution of 1800' because:

    (A) Aaron Burr was a radical Republican.

    (B) the government was completely changed by the new party.

    (C) all the Federalist policies were sure to be undone.

    (D) power had peacefully transferred to another party for the first time.

    (E) some thought a military takeover was likely.

9. President Washington's Neutrality Proclamation of 1793 was issued because:

    (A) Jefferson was clearly in favor of an alliance with Great Britain.

    (B) the French were invoking the Franco-American alliance in their fight with Britain.

    (C) the Dutch wanted revenge for military defeats in Austria.

    (D) Canadians were allying with northern tribes on the border.

    (E) Spanish pirates were creating trouble in Florida.

10. The Hartford Convention was called because:

    (A) of attacks on the frontier by tribes allied with Britain.

    (B) the war hawks were impatient with President Madison.

    (C) the embargo was popular in the north.

    (D) the South feared a British invasion during the war.

    (E) New England did not support the war with Britain in 1812.

11. Jefferson's Embargo of 1807 backfired because:

    (A) farmers could not sell their produce to other states.

    (B) illegal trading continued with Spain.

    (C) it hurt American business interests and shut down exports.

    (D) it led to a significant increase in American manufacturing.

    (E) it helped perpetuate slavery.

12. Which of the following would have been most likely to support Jefferson in 1800?

    (A) A New York merchant

    (B) A southern plantation owner

    (C) A Boston ship owner

    (D) An urban banker

    (E) An Anglican priest

13. The United States was able to buy Louisiana because:

    (A) the United States allied with other nations to oppose both Britain and France.

    (B) Napoleon needed money for his military expenses in Europe.

    (C) the United States was very wealthy after the Revolutionary War.

    (D) Spain forced the French to sell its North American territory.

    (E) Napoleon was threatened by his generals in Paris.

14. In his farewell address, Washington:

    (A) criticized the growing spirit of sectionalism in the country.

    (B) discouraged the idea of political parties.

    (C) urged Americans not to become involved in permanent alliances with foreign nations.

    (D) said that it was acceptable for the United States to make temporary alliances with countries in the cases of emergencies only.

    (E) took all of the above positions

15. Which is the NOT in the preamble of the Constitution?

    (A) To form a more perfect union

    (B) To protect life, liberty, and the pursuit of happiness

    (C) To promote the general welfare

    (D) To secure the blessings of liberty

    (E) To provide for the common defense

16. Marshall established the doctrine of judicial review by ruling in:

    (A) *Northern Securities v. the United States.*

    (B) *Adams v. Dickenson.*

    (C) *Fletcher v. Peck.*

    (D) *Dartmouth v. Woodward.*

    (E) *Marbury v. Madison.*

17. What was the Federalist rationalization for the Alien and Sedition Acts?

    (A) The XYZ affair revealed that the French were threatening the United States.

    (B) Party factionalism was creating tensions among the Federalists.

    (C) Jefferson was too outspoken against the Bank of the United States.

    (D) War could be avoided.

    (E) Freedom of speech had to be protected by the government.

18. The American System promoted by Henry Clay sought to:

    (A) protect American manufacturers using a tariff.

    (B) reestablish the national bank.

    (C) foster nationalism and unity.

    (D) improve the roads and canals of the nation.

    (E) All of the above

KAPLAN
Test Prep and Admissions

19. Jefferson, a strict constructionist in most cases, found it necessary to interpret the Constitution broadly when he:

    (A) negotiated the Louisiana Purchase.

    (B) vetoed the charter of the Bank of the United States.

    (C) sought to balance the national budget.

    (D) sought to impeach John Marshall.

    (E) pushed for the Embargo of 1807.

20. The Shawnee leader who rallied the tribes against white intrusion in 1811 was:

    (A) Ticonderoga.

    (B) Chief Pequot.

    (C) Tecumseh.

    (D) Winnemuka.

    (E) Geronimo.

ESSAY QUESTIONS

1. Contrast the Hamiltonian and Jeffersonian philosophies that helped frame the Early Republic.

_____

_____

_____

_____

_____

_____

_____

_____

_____

2. What challenges did the young United States face in its relations with nations in Europe?

_____

_____

_____

_____

_____

_____

_____

_____

_____

ANSWER KEY

Multiple-Choice Questions

1. D
2. D
3. D
4. B
5. A
6. C
7. A
8. D
9. B
10. E
11. C
12. B
13. B
14. E
15. B
16. E
17. A
18. E
19. A
20. C

Answers and Explanations

1. D

After the Revolutionary War, the states had large debts and the economy of the young nation was unstable. Hamilton wanted to bind the nation together financially and assert the power of the federal government. Thus, he urged that the country deal with the debts collectively. This helped establish the fiscal foundation of the new government.

2. D

Some of the Founding Fathers were concerned that the states were going to be subordinated to the Federal government. Because of this some pushed for a clause that would give all unspecified powers in the Constitution to the states. This is why each state still passes its own laws in regards to issues such as the drinking age or when a person can drive a car.

3. D

Before the Supreme Court had established the power to decide the constitutionality of American laws, the Republicans tried to assert that the states could decide this. It was largely a response to the Alien and Sedition Acts that the Federalists had passed. This idea that states could 'nullify' a law remained a strong belief of some people (especially southerners) for a half century after Jefferson.

4. B

One of the great precedents in government set by Washington was the organization of the Executive branch. Since this was not specified in the Constitution, Washington created departments headed by secretaries. This formed the first cabinet with the newly created departments of War, Justice, State, and the Treasury. While the Constitution during Washington's time permitted the president to stay in office as long as the people continued to elect him, George Washington established the precedent that presidents would leave office after two terms.

5. A

Antifederalists who feared a strong central government that would threaten personal liberties wanted a Bill of Rights. Virginia had included such a Bill in its state constitution so there was already precedent for this. The Bill of Rights lists freedoms that had been denied the colonists under British rule, such as speech, the press, and assembly.

6. C

The War of 1812 was ended without resolving any of the issues that started the war. Tired of fighting in Europe, the British agreed to an armistice which was negotiated in Ghent. The basic principle was a return to conditions that existed before the war with neither side gaining anything. In other words, *status quo antebellum*.

7. A

Of all the causes of the War of 1812, British interference in American shipping was the most galling. The British boarded U.S. ships and searched them arbitrarily. Sometimes they even took crew and forced them into the Royal Navy.

8. D

When the Republicans were victorious over the Federalists in the election of 1800, it was the first time in U.S. history that there was a political transfer of power from one group to another. That this occurred without violence or resistance was seen as evidence of democratic stability. Adams and the Federalists were not happy to lose but handed over the government without incident.

9. B

One of the great dangers facing the very young and weak United States was that it might be drawn into a European war. The French Revolution had created great tension in Europe and the French hoped for American support. They had helped with the American Revolution so it was hoped that the U.S. would return the favor. Washington resisted this and declared that America would remain neutral in European affairs.

10. E

The greatest opposition to war with Britain was centered in New England. Shipping and trading interests in the Northeast had the most to lose when commerce with Britain was disrupted. As the war went on, there was a

KAPLAN
Test Prep and Admissions

meeting in Hartford, Connecticut to discuss whether New England might even secede from the Union and create a new nation. The discussion came to nothing as the war ended and trade was resumed.

11. C

Jefferson was bedeviled with an undeclared war on the high seas so he thought ending all foreign trade would solve the problem. Instead, it crippled the economy and made the business interests cry for relief. Jefferson himself realized it was a failure and requested that the embargo be repealed as his presidency ended.

12. B

The Federalists led by Hamilton were supported by the business and merchant class in the early years of American history. The Republicans led by Jefferson were supported by the agrarian, or farmer, class. The plantation owner would have tended to vote for Jefferson, who was also a plantation owner.

13. B

In 1803 the United States made an offer to buy New Orleans due to the importance to American shipping of this port city strategically located at the mouth of the Mississippi River. At the same time the Napoleonic wars were getting under way in Europe and Napoleon was concerned about his military expenses. He was also having trouble in the Caribbean with a slave revolt and realized he could not handle his European and American problems at the same time. He surprised the American emissaries by offering to sell all of Louisiana to the U.S.

14. E

Washington was gravely concerned for the future of the nation when he stepped down as president. He was dismayed by the political infighting among his own cabinet members, a situation that was helping create political parties. He also worried that America would be drawn into the fighting in Europe, and advised a neutral policy with few binding connections with other nations.

15. B

All of the above statements are taken from the Preamble of the U.S. Constitution except the reference to "life, liberty and the pursuit of happiness." This is a quote from the Declaration of Independence written by Jefferson in 1776.

16. E

John Marshall was Chief Justice on the Supreme Court and made important contributions to the young American legal system. The most important was a clever precedent he set in *Marbury v. Madison* when he declared an act of Congress void by declaring it unconstitutional. This meant that any law could be challenged in the courts. Many of the most important developments in American law have resulted when the Supreme Court has exercised this right to review laws that may conflict with the Constitution.

17. A

The Federalists were appalled by the violence associated with the French Revolution and the corruption of the post-revolutionary regime in Paris. The XYZ scandal created further controversy in America and stirred up much criticism against the Adams administration. The Alien and Sedition Acts made such criticism punishable and also targeted immigrants, who Federalists feared were importing radical ideas into the country.

18. E

After the War of 1812, Henry Clay from Kentucky believed that the new nationalism should inspire a program to improve and develop the nation. This included the encouragement of factory production, improving transportation, and reviving the Bank of the United States.

19. A

Jefferson had criticized the Federalists when they used powers not stipulated in the Constitution. But when he became president he found that this was sometimes necessary. The offer to double the size of the nation in 1803 was irresistible and even Jefferson could not remain a strict interpreter of the Constitution in this case. He remained a proponent of small government and states' rights but used his executive power when it was needed to benefit the nation.

20. C

Right before the War of 1812, natives tribes were gathering their forces against Americans on the frontier. Combining their strength under a great leader, Tecumseh, they posed a considerable threat to white settlement in what is now Indiana and Illinois. The confederation of tribes was defeated at the Tippecanoe River while Tecumseh was away. An important figure in that battle, William Henry Harrison, later became president.

ANALYSES OF THE FREE-RESPONSE ESSAYS

Question 1:

Contrast the Hamiltonian and Jeffersonian philosophies that helped frame the Early Republic.

Key Points

Hamiltonian positions

- Strong American economy built upon the urban merchant class
- Established tariff and other tax mechanisms
- Preference for Britain over France
- Well-defined central government with power over the states
- Feared the 'mob mentality' of the lower classes

Jeffersonian positions

- Decentralized government with the states having more power
- Had a revolutionary view of history and saw violent change as necessary
- Saw the yeoman farmer as the true American
- Favored France over England
- Believed in an 'egalitarian' ideal where all are equal to one another
- Once he was president, basically isolationist

Scoring Rubric

There are five scoring ranges:

Excellent

The answer must have a strong, clear thesis that shows the differences between the political views of Hamilton and Jefferson. The quality of the writing should be excellent, the answer must show logical patterns, and the student should include many of the major points in the above list (though they may go beyond the list). The organization should be clear. The answer may contain minor errors.

Very Good

The answer must have a thesis that makes an argument about the differences between the political views of Hamilton and Jefferson. Organization of the answer must show logical patterns, and the student should include many of the specific points from the above list.

Adequate

The answer must try to make some argument and must include at least some of the points listed above. There may be flaws in the thesis argument.

Flawed

The answer will demonstrate serious weaknesses. It may have no thesis argument at all, and it will include few of the points listed above. The answer may show little understanding of Hamiltonian or Jeffersonian policies and goals.

Severely Flawed

The answer will demonstrate almost no attempt to answer the question, and will include very few, if any, of the points listed above.

Question 2:

What challenges did the young United States face in its relations with nations in Europe?

Key Points

European History 1789–1815

- The French Revolution and its aftermath dominated European history after 1789
- The United States had complex relationships with both France and England
- The first four presidents after 1788 tried to steer the U.S. in a neutral position between Britain and France

Washington, Adams, Jefferson, Madison—main foreign problems they faced

- French military activity in Caribbean, Haiti
- French control of the Mississippi River through ownership of New Orleans
- XYZ Affair during Adams administration
- Britain and France at war from 1803
- Both Britain and France interfering with U.S. shipping
- In 1807, the Jay Treaty commercial provisions expire, not renewed by Britain
- British ship *Leopard* fires on American ship *Chesapeake*
- Increasing interference by Britain with American shipping, impressment of American sailors

Jefferson and Madison—foreign policy actions

- Both tried to keep U.S. neutral, and out of European affairs
- Jefferson: against all "entangling alliances" and any kind of foreign "entanglements"—thus, different from Washington, who said "temporary" ones were acceptable at times
- Jefferson's Embargo of 1807
- Non-Intercourse Act of 1809: against Britain and France but would allow trade with whichever one agreed to support American neutrality
- Declared war on Britain in 1812

Assessment of early American foreign policies—trying to avoid "entanglements"

- Reaction to Jay's Treaty after 1795
- Adams and Jefferson able to resist "war fever" in 1797 and 1807; the public wanted war
- The Embargo of 1807 failed to achieve its goals—was repealed in 1809 by Congress (Jefferson signed the repeal)
- The Non-Intercourse Act also failed to achieve goals; Napoleon proved to be a more clever diplomat than his American counterparts
- The Americans and British fought to a "standstill" in the War of 1812; Americans, focused on neutrality, had left their army small and poorly equipped
- The Treaty of Ghent ended the war with no American gains

Scoring Rubric

There are five scoring ranges:

Excellent

The answer must have a strong, clear thesis that gives an assessment of the basic American foreign policy dilemmas from 1789 to 1815. The essay should focus on efforts to stay out of European affairs. The quality of the writing should be excellent, the answer must show logical patterns, and the student should include many of the major points in the above list (though they may go beyond these points). The organization should be clear. The answer may contain minor errors.

Very Good

The answer must have a thesis that focuses on the foreign policy challenges experienced by Washington, Adams, Jefferson and Madison. The answer must be logically organized, and the student should include many of the specific points from the above list.

Adequate

The answer must try to make some argument and must include at least some of the points listed above. There may be flaws in the thesis argument.

Flawed

The answer will demonstrate serious weaknesses. It may have no thesis argument at all, and it will include few of the points listed above. The answer may show little understanding of early American foreign policy decisions and impacts.

Severely Flawed

The answer will demonstrate almost no attempt to answer the question, and will include very few, if any, of the points listed above.

Chapter Six: **The Age of Jackson**

- Timeline: 1824–1849
- Jacksonian Democracy
- The Emergence of Reform Movements
- Sectionalism
- Multiple-Choice Questions
- Essay Questions
- Answer Key
- Answers and Explanations
- Analyses of the Free-Response Essays

TIMELINE: 1824–1849

1824	John Quincy Adams elected president; election decided in the House of Representatives. Andrew Jackson accuses Adams of making a "corrupt bargain" with Henry Clay to win Clay's support and the presidency.
1825	Erie Canal opens from Albany to Buffalo.
1828	High protective tariff passed.
1828	John C. Calhoun's *South Carolina Exposition and Protest*, explaining the ideas of nullification and interposition, published.
1828	Baltimore and Ohio Railroad opens.
1828	Andrew Jackson elected.
1829	Gold discovered in Georgia; pressure on Cherokee lands increases.
1830	Webster-Hayne debates clarify states' rights and nationalist arguments.
1830	Indian Removal Act passed.
1830	Joseph Smith begins forming Mormon Church.
1831	John Marshall rules in *Cherokee Nation v. Georgia* that the Cherokee tribe is a "domestic dependent nation."

1831	Nat Turner rebellion in Virginia.
1831	William Lloyd Garrison begins publishing *The Liberator*.
1832	Jackson vetoes extension of the Bank of the United States' charter.
1832	Jackson reelected.
1832	Marshall upholds Cherokee autonomy and independence from Georgia law in *Worcester v. Georgia*; Jackson tacitly refuses to enforce decision.
1832–1833	Nullification crisis in South Carolina; compromise brokered by Henry Clay.
1833	Federal deposits withdrawn from Bank of the United States and put into state banks.
1833	American Temperance Union formed.
1833	American Anti-Slavery Society formed.
1834	Anti-Jackson Whig coalition begins to form.
1835	Cherokee sign treaty ceding lands in Georgia for territory in Oklahoma.
1835	Seminole War, which lasts seven years, begins in Florida.
1836	Martin Van Buren elected president.
1837	Nationwide economic crisis.
1837	Ralph Waldo Emerson delivers "American Scholar" lecture.
1837	Anti-slavery editor Elijah Lovejoy killed in Illinois.
1838	Cherokee nation departs the southeast for Oklahoma on Trail of Tears.
1839	Charles Finney preaches for six months in Rochester, New York.
1840	William Henry Harrison elected president after "log cabin and hard cider" campaign.
1844	Joseph Smith murdered in Illinois.
1845	Frederick Douglass publishes autobiography.
1847	Mormons arrive in Utah, found Salt Lake City.
1848	Seneca Falls Convention.
1849	Henry David Thoreau publishes "Civil Disobedience."

JACKSONIAN DEMOCRACY

The no-nonsense president was in the White House. Andrew Jackson called a spade a spade; he neither minced words nor ran a popularity contest as president. Jackson was slightly defensive about his upbringing, and therefore compensated for it by being direct. He did not agree with the concept of a Bank of the United States; he thought it gave control of the money to the "rich" back east. He vetoed it. He did not agree with the Supreme Court decision giving the Cherokee Nation the status of a sovereign nation; he forced the Cherokee to move west. In defiance he suggested that Chief Justice John Marshall try to enforce his decision.

KAPLAN
Test Prep and Admissions

Perhaps a man like Jackson was what the country wanted and needed at the time. Certainly there have been other examples of such a relationship later in our history. Jackson was the right man at the time. The country was moving westward, and here was a president who not only came from the West but also understood and would speak for the needs of that region. People knew he would try and get that region some of the same benefits the other parts of the country were enjoying, such as roads and shipped goods and representative government.

Jackson did not disappoint the voters. He took on some of the issues and the big politicians. He understood the ramifications of nullification. He appreciated people who helped him get elected, and he certainly used the spoils system. And Jackson left the presidency ready for Martin Van Buren to take over effortlessly, another example of the seamless transition of power.

Jackson also brought to the White House a new concept of democracy. His was the democracy of the "common man." After Jackson was sworn in as president, the party at the White House was so rowdy that the building needed extensive repairs after the crowds had left. Everyone wanted to touch him; Jackson was "their" man. The new concept of democracy was not lost on the experienced politicians. Some of them shook their heads and wagered the demise of the country now that the Westerners had come to town. Thomas Jefferson's "yeoman farmers" had given way to the West.

John Quincy Adams

Adams eked out a victory in the House of Representatives with the help of Henry Clay in 1824. A former Secretary of State, Adams was the son of President John Adams. His administration asked for money for internal improvements and aid to manufacturing. He was probably the most intelligent man ever to serve as president. He served only one term as president and then returned to the House of Representatives as a representative from Massachusetts.

"American System"

This was Henry Clay's Whig party platform supporting a national bank, federal funding for internal improvements, and a protective tariff.

Anti-Masons

Founded in opposition to the fraternal order, this new political party entered the 1832 campaign. The Anti-Masons were the first to hold a national nominating convention and the first to announce a platform.

Bank War (Jackson's)

Henry Clay took on the issue in 1832, an election year. Jackson believed the national bank to be unconstitutional. Clay got Congress to pass a bill renewing the charter of the national bank. Jackson vetoed the bill and withdrew all federal funds from the bank, claiming it a private monopoly created at the expense of the common people. The issue created such a backlash for Clay that Jackson was re-elected by a large margin.

KAPLAN
Test Prep and Admissions

Nicholas Biddle

Biddle was the President of the Bank of the United States. Although he managed to soften the ups and downs in the economy through federal deposits, Jackson suspected him of abuses of power and serving the interests of the wealthy. Biddle's arrogance was a factor in the confrontation.

John C. Calhoun

Calhoun's career as a South Carolina senator and Jackson's first vice president followed a shift in his political philosophy from an early war hawk nationalist to a states' rights sectionalist.

Cherokee Nation v. Georgia

The State of Georgia passed a law requiring the Cherokee to migrate to the West; however, the Cherokees challenged the law. The 1831 Supreme Court decision ruled that the Cherokees in Georgia had the right to sue in federal court. This case was followed by the Court's ruling the following year in *Worcester v. Georgia* (see separate listing).

Henry Clay

Clay had an important influence on politics for many years. Clay, as Jackson's chief political opponent, favored the national bank and his "American System," and tried a bank re-chartering bill. It backfired and Jackson won re-election by a wide majority. As the Speaker of the House, he engineered Adams' election in 1824.

"corrupt bargain"

This accusation of a secret political deal was hurled at Henry Clay and John Quincy Adams after Adams won election as President in the House of Representatives. After Adams was elected, he appointed Clay as his secretary of state.

Cumberland Road

The National, or Cumberland, Road was the first federally funded interstate road network. By 1818, it was open from Cumberland, Maryland to Wheeling, West Virginia and by 1838 it had been extended to Vandalia, Illinois. It reduced transportation costs and helped the commercialization of agriculture.

Democrats (Jacksonian)

Supporters of Andrew Jackson favored a limited government, free trade, and equal economic opportunities for white males. They did not support monopolies, high tariffs, or a national bank. Their voter base was to be found mostly in the south and west.

Era of Good Feelings

This term was used to describe James Monroe's presidency, in part because there was only one political party. Rivals for the presidency would begin to flock during the beginning of Monroe's second term.

William Henry Harrison

Harrison became president in 1840. Nominated by the Whigs, he had an impressive record of service: victor at the Battle of Tippecanoe against the Shawnee in 1811, former governor of the Indiana Territory, congressman and senator from Ohio, and Minister to Columbia. His running mate was John Tyler. The Whigs had no platform and ran a campaign called "Log Cabin and Hard Cider," depicting Harrison as a simple man of the people. The campaign also had as its slogan: "Tippecanoe and Tyler, too." He died 31 days after giving a 90-minute acceptance speech in the rain.

Indian removal

Although Jackson professed a respect for Native Americans, his policies did not match his rhetoric. He signed into law the Indian Removal Act in 1830, which provided for the resettlement of thousands. The Bureau of Indian Affairs was created to assist the tribes. Jackson argued he wanted to protect Native American culture from assimilation by the white settlers. The most celebrated case involved Native Americans in Georgia (see *Cherokee Nation v. Georgia*).

internal improvements

President Jackson had some of the same reluctance to use federal funds for local projects as had Madison and Monroe. In 1830, the Maysville Road Bill was passed. The road was entirely within Henry Clay's home state of Kentucky, and although it was part of a larger project to link the National Road through to Cincinnati, it was still a local project, and Jackson vetoed the bill. Jackson supported interstate projects such as the National Road, but not all the pork barrel projects every congressman tried to bring home to his district. Jackson's attitude set the precedent that there were definite limits to federal funds; railroads would be built with state and private capital until the 1850s.

Maysville Road Bill

One of the internal improvements using federal funds vetoed by Jackson, because it lay completely within Henry Clay's home state of Kentucky. See also: internal improvements.

Missouri Compromise

A balance of free and slave states (giving both sides equal representation in the Senate) had been maintained since the turn of the century. Missouri petitioned for statehood, but with its well-established slave-holding status, it would have upset the balance. Henry Clay won support for three bills, which, taken together, became known as the Missouri Compromise. Missouri would be admitted as a slave-holding state; Maine would be admitted as a free state; and in the rest of the Louisiana Purchase north of 36° 30', slavery would be prohibited.

nullification

John C. Calhoun's theory that each state had the right to decide for itself whether to obey a federal law or to declare it null and void (having no effect within its boundaries).

Panic of 1837

The economic depression, caused in part by the failure to renew the charter of the Bank of the United States, occurred just as Martin Van Buren took office. Banks began closing their doors. The Whigs blamed the Democrats for poor economic strategies that allowed for little federal input into the economy.

KAPLAN
Test Prep and Admissions

South Carolina Exposition and Protest (1828)

John C. Calhoun wrote this document in opposition to the tariff of 1828, but it was a disguised effort to check the most extreme states' rights supporters with a theory that stopped nullification short of secession. The unsigned statement was sent along with the South Carolina objections to the tariff. Calhoun wanted to preserve the Union by protecting the planters and slaveholders of the South.

Specie Circular

In 1837, President Jackson determined that the government would accept only hard currency in payment for government lands. The purpose of the order was to prevent opportunities to commit fraud connected with the use of bank notes and credit. This would follow Jackson since finding actual hard currency was difficult, and therefore many farmers attempting to buy government land were at the mercy of speculators.

spoils system

Winning government jobs was a major goal of the political parties. Jackson believed in appointing people to federal jobs if they actively campaigned for him and the Democratic Party. This policy of dispensing government jobs as a reward for party loyalty was called the spoils system. Many argued that it promoted government corruption.

Tariff of 1816

The tariff was first intended to protect industry in the U.S., not to generate revenue. Some viewed the tariff as an incentive to develop industry and the South did have some plans to establish some textile mills. However, after a while, the tariff became a sectional issue, with manufacturers and processors of the North favoring higher tariffs, and planters of the South favoring a lower duty.

Trail of Tears

This was the name given to the trek of the Cherokee from Georgia to Oklahoma. Fifteen thousand Cherokee were forced to move in 1838 by the U.S. Army after Jackson had left office. The trip, taken under harsh conditions, saw the deaths of over 4,000 Native Americans.

Martin Van Buren

As Jackson's secretary of state he rivaled John C. Calhoun for the position of successor to President Jackson. He was a skilled politician, the one who advised Jackson through political crises such as the use of federal funds for local projects (the Maysville Road) and nullification. Van Buren became president after Jackson.

Daniel Webster

He was an accomplished orator and lawyer who, as a Senator from Massachusetts, would take the floor against Robert Hayne of South Carolina. Webster defended the federal government and said that a state could neither nullify a federal law nor secede from the Union. His closing words became classic: "Liberty and union, one and inseparable, now and forever."

Webster-Hayne debate

In the Senate in 1830 Robert Hayne argued that the government endangered the Union by imposing a policy that would cause hardship on one section to the benefit of another. Hayne explained his concept of the federal government as the "agent" of the states, saying that the states could judge whether the "agent" had overstepped its bounds. Daniel Webster countered with a nationalistic view of the Constitution. See also: Daniel Webster.

Whig Party

The political party led by Henry Clay favored his American System (a national bank, federal funding for internal improvements, and a protective tariff). The party leaders spoke out against the "social ills," such as immorality, vice, and crime which they blamed on immigrants. Their support was drawn from New England, the Northeast, and the West.

Worcester v. Georgia

This was the second Supreme Court decision (1832) that involved the Cherokees and the State of Georgia (see *Cherokee Nation v. Georgia*). The Court ruled that the Cherokee were a sovereign nation and that the laws passed by the Georgia Legislature requiring them to leave Georgia had no bearing on the Cherokee Nation. President Jackson repudiated John Marshall's ruling: "John Marshall has made his decision, now let him enforce it." The Native Americans were forced by the U.S. Army to move to Oklahoma (see Trail of Tears) in spite of the Court's decisions in their favor.

THE EMERGENCE OF REFORM MOVEMENTS

The United States was an infant nation on the world stage; it had no long history of political development. Without the baggage of a long history, the country could provide a landscape where social activism, religious movements, and the ideas of the Enlightenment could quickly take root and grow.

The Second Great Awakening began slowly but quickly spread across the country. At Yale, the Reverend Timothy Dwight inspired young men to become evangelical preachers of the gospels. This new breed allowed free will, or "free agency," to play a role in salvation thereby placing much greater importance on the individual and his decisions. In New York, Charles Finney started an even more radical form of revivalism. Finney and his followers differed from the more traditional religious leaders in their perception of the role of the individual in his own salvation. Traditionalists argued that people could not earn or choose salvation. Finney said the only thing preventing conversion was the individual. He appealed to people's emotions and fear of damnation and got thousands to declare a renewed faith. In the South, preachers traveled from one location to another and attracted thousands to hear dramatic preaching at outdoor revivals. However, the Second Great Awakening caused new layers in society. Sandwiched between the newer evangelical sects and the older Protestant churches, the romanticists and idealists strove to change society.

Mormonism took a different tactic, but is still considered a part of the Second Great Awakening. In 1830 Joseph Smith began forming his own church, the Church of Jesus Christ of Latter-Day Saints. His followers found in the Mormon teachings the promise of a pure kingdom of Christ in America and an alternative to the turmoil of the times. The early Mormons were ecstatic worshippers. They fainted at their gatherings, spoke in tongues, and were said to receive revelations directly from God. To escape persecution, the Mormons moved westward until they reached Great Salt Lake where they created their own community.

The awakening of the American spirit was not restricted to religion; writers woke to the spirit was well. The American Renaissance was romantic from the start, fueled by the transcendentalists. This emphasis on those things that transcended the limits of reason had roots in New England Puritanism. Ralph Waldo Emerson was a spokesman, as was his friend Henry David Thoreau. Nathaniel Hawthorne, Herman Melville, and Walt Whitman wrote their classics of the American Renaissance. The poets Emily Dickinson, Henry Wadsworth Longfellow, John Greenleaf Whittier, James Russell Lowell, and Oliver Wendell Holmes also made their contributions. Not to be left out are Edgar Allan Poe, James Fenimore Cooper, and Washington Irving. No other period in American history had seen such a display. Every facet of American life was re-examined and improved. Education saw the likes of Horace Mann and the lyceum movement. Other reform movements addressed the evils of drinking, slavery, the conditions in prisons, and the plight of the mentally ill.

The role of women in society was also becoming an important issue. Women's suffrage was the focus of the Seneca Falls Convention of 1848. Their *Declaration of Sentiments* announced women were not inferior to men, and that such beliefs were "contrary to nature." Women did not gain full acceptance overnight, but change was on the horizon.

abolition

This term refers to the belief that slavery should be abolished everywhere in the country. White abolitionists spoke out in protest, the American Colonization Society attempted to re-settle African Americans, African American abolitionists helped organize and assist fugitive slaves to freedom, and a few African Americans advocated that slaves should take action themselves by rising up in revolt.

American Colonization Society

This organization promoted the idea of transporting freed slaves to an African colony. The idea had appeal in that African Americans would be removed from U.S. society. In 1822, a settlement was established in Monrovia, Liberia. Colonization proved never to be a practical option in light of the rapidly expanding numbers of African Americans in the United States.

Susan B. Anthony

Anthony was an active crusader for temperance, anti-slavery, and women's rights.

Commonwealth v. Hunt

The Massachusetts Supreme Court ruled in this case that forming a trade union was not illegal. Although the federal courts did not adopt this position until many years later, this case was an important victory for the early labor movement that encouraged the movement's growth.

James Fenimore Cooper

Author of *The Spy* and *The Leather-stocking Tales*, Cooper created Hawkeye, a character who pitted himself against nature and won every time. Cooper's most famous work is *The Last of the Mohicans*.

KAPLAN
Test Prep and Admissions

Emily Dickinson

This poet saw little of her work published in her lifetime. She wrote of death, fear, loneliness, and God.

Dorothea Dix

Dix began a two-year investigation of jails and poorhouses in Massachusetts and published a scathing report. Her work received national attention and by 1860, 20 states had made improvements. She would go on to press for changes in prisons and asylums across the country.

Frederick Douglass

Douglass was a former slave who spoke of the brutality and degradation of slavery from firsthand experience and became the most well-known African American man in America. He published *Narrative of the Life of Frederick Douglass.* He left the country for two years to avoid capture and returned with enough money to buy his freedom.

Ralph Waldo Emerson

Emerson is the man with whom the transcendental movement is most associated. He believed that there had to be intuitive ways of thinking as a means of discovering one's inner self and finding the spirit of God in nature. He attacked materialism in American society by suggesting that artistic expressions were more important than having or seeking wealth.

Charles Finney

Finney preached in Rochester, New York, and it is estimated that he helped to generate 100,000 conversions. Finney preached that conversion was up to the individual and believed that it was the loneliness of that decision that prevented many from converting. He transformed revivals into communal experiences and spectacular public events. In 1835 he began a teaching career at Oberlin College, the first college in America to admit women and African Americans.

William Lloyd Garrison

Garrison was the newspaper publisher of *The Liberator* who advocated the immediate abolition of slavery. He once burned the Constitution because he believed it to be a pro-slavery document. He and other abolitionists established the American Anti-Slavery Society in 1833.

Susan and Angelina Grimke

These South Carolina sisters dedicated themselves to the causes of anti-slavery, feminism, and other reform work. Angelina Grimke wrote *Appeal to the Christian Women of the South* in 1836 and Sarah Grimke wrote *Letter on the Condition of Women and the Equality of the Sexes* in 1837. They later went on speaking tours despite criticisms that they were not properly subordinating themselves to men. Angelina Grimke responded that it was her right to be heard.

Nathaniel Hawthorne

Hawthorne was the author of *The Scarlet Letter* and *The House of the Seven Gables*. He wrote of sin, pride, secret guilt, and the impossibility of eliminating sin from the human soul. His greatest novels examined these themes.

KAPLAN
Test Prep and Admissions

Horace Mann

Originally from Massachusetts, Mann is associated with the reforms in public education, such as the first state-supported "normal school" for the training of teachers and a minimum school year of six months. He also defended the school system as the way to equal opportunity through education.

Herman Melville

Melville was one author whose early work was well received but who later had to support himself with a mundane job. He wrote *Moby Dick* (1851) after serving on a whaler. This story was both a good adventure story and a story of obsession.

Mormons (Church of Jesus Christ of Latter-Day Saints)

Joseph Smith founded this religious group, officially named the Church of Jesus Christ of Latter-Day Saints, in 1830. He and his followers moved westward to Illinois, where Smith was murdered by an anti-religious mob. Brigham Young took over and the group moved westward again to the shore of the Great Salt Lake in Utah.

Lucretia Mott

Mott was one of the first advocates for women's rights. With Elizabeth Cady Stanton she engineered the Seneca Falls Convention, the first women's meeting of its kind. The *Declaration of Sentiments* was presented there. She would go on to work with Susan B. Anthony in holding a series of women's rights meetings.

Robert Owen

As leader of the utopian community known as New Harmony, Owen built a model factory town and set out his ideas in a pamphlet, *A New View of Society*. He was concerned about the social effects of the factory system. His call for colonists at New Harmony was answered by over 900 people, but the community failed when colonists each wanted their own plan put into action.

Edgar Allan Poe

Poe was the originator of the detective story. A tormented man, he drank heavily. He was a literary genius and considered fear to be the most powerful emotion. His works include "The Tell-Tale Heart" and "The Pit and the Pendulum."

romanticism

This was a movement that emphasized the spirit over the dry logic of reason and the desire for material gains. Begun in Europe, Americans took to the emphasis on individualism, the promise of the common people, and the value of original ideas.

Second Great Awakening

This revival of enlightened spirit influenced every facet of American life. The new breed of evangelical preachers, inspired by Reverend Timothy Dwight and Charles Finney, allowed free will to play a role in salvation. See also: Charles Finney.

Seneca Falls Convention (1848)

Elizabeth Cady Stanton and Lucretia Mott organized the convention in New York, the first of its kind. The *Declaration of Sentiments* was adopted at the Convention; it parodied the Declaration of Independence, and made the first step forward for women's rights.

Joseph Smith, Jr.

Smith founded the Mormon Church in upper state New York in 1830. The group moved westward and settled in Illinois. A crisis rose in 1844 when dissenters accused Smith of justifying polygamy. He and his brother were shot during an anti-Mormon riot.

Elizabeth Cady Stanton

She was one of the first women's rights activists. She was associated with both Lucretia Mott and Susan B. Anthony, was author of the *Declaration of Sentiments* adopted by the Convention, and worked tirelessly for her cause. See also: Seneca Falls Convention.

temperance

The temperance movement was an example of the shift from moral to political action. Those concerned with the effects of excessive drinking founded the American Temperance Society in 1826. The society tried to persuade drinkers to take a pledge of total abstinence. The Washingtonians (recovering alcoholics) argued that alcoholism was a disease. By the 1840s, temperance societies had more than a million members.

Henry David Thoreau

Author of *Walden* and "Civil Disobedience," Thoreau was determined to practice plain living. He spent a year in a cabin near Walden Pond reflecting on nature and writing.

transcendentalism

Ralph Waldo Emerson was the spokesman of the movement that drew its inspiration from those things that transcended, or rose above, the limits of reason. The movement had its roots in New England, but was not restricted to that region. It drew upon the teachings of Buddha, the Mohammedan Sufis, and other Indian sects.

Sojourner Truth

An African American female abolitionist leader, Sojourner Truth was a slave until she escaped in 1827. She traveled the country preaching about the sins of slavery and the inequality of women.

Unitarians

This Christian denomination emphasized the oneness and kindness of God, the goodness of mankind, and the ability of reason and conscience to triumph over established creeds. People were not inherently depraved, stressed Unitarians; they were capable of great works, and all were eligible for salvation.

Universalists

A parallel movement to the Unitarians, Universalists stressed the salvation of all men and women, not just a select few. God, they taught, was too merciful to condemn anyone to eternal punishment.

Utopian community

Plans for new, more perfect communities remarkably different from the prevailing society have long been proposed and often attempted. The visions of the 19th century often had economic and social objectives, but those of a religious nature proved to be the most long-lived. Brook Farm and New Harmony were two that flourished longer than most.

Walt Whitman

One of America's most provocative writers, Whitman was relatively unknown until *Leaves of Grass* was published. He served as a nurse during the Civil War and went on to rewrite *Leaves* into several editions.

Brigham Young

Young's odyssey westward, as leader of the Mormons, occurred after the death of Joseph Smith. Settling near the Great Salt Lake in Utah, Young planned the new community carefully, even organizing way stations along the westward trail to assist other Mormons traveling to the Utah Territory. He became the chief political and theocratic authority of the Mormon community. By 1869 there were 80,000 Mormons; today there are 9 million.

SECTIONALISM

The United States was growing by leaps and bounds. However, each section of the country had its own problems particular to that region; and each section of the country was most interested in its own problems. Building the Erie Canal through New York state was of interest to those who owned land near the development, those who wanted to cut their shipping costs, and those who understood the geography well enough to see the unlimited possibilities of having better access to the Great Lakes and the middle of the country.

The southern part of the country was looking for a continuation of the plantation system that produced so much wealth for southern planters. Slaves were needed to maintain the great cotton fields. More hands were needed to harvest and others were needed to process the raw cotton through the cotton gin. Southern society also saw itself as the last bastion of civilization. The disdain with which southerners held most of northern society was not easy to comprehend.

The West was an entirely different story. In the West, a man could start all over and build a new life for himself. There, the younger children of a family could settle and have a chance at making a life and a homestead that was not inherited. Because of its peculiar circumstances, the frontier played an important role in the development of the country. Without it, Frederick Jackson Turner would later argue, the United States would not have been made up of rugged individuals—people who were independent in thought and in deed.

Because of each set of needs and problems, finding consensus in the Congress grew increasingly difficult with each election. The North grew to abhor slavery and the abolitionists were more and more vocal. The South grew to fear the rhetoric—their very way of life was being threatened. The West, being large enough to absorb almost anything, was not so obsessed with the slavery issue. But it was interested in getting its concerns heard and getting its fair share of governmental support. Curious developments were ahead for the whole country.

Erie Canal

Governor De Witt Clinton of New York wanted to connect the Hudson River and Lake Erie. His dream came true in 1825 when the canal was opened all the way from Albany to Buffalo. Branches were immediately added and the price of transporting cargo from the Atlantic coast to the West fell dramatically.

Irish immigration

The Irish came to America to escape destitution in their own country; an epidemic of potato rot in 1845 brought starvation to more than a million. They congregated in the eastern cities because they were too poor to move inland. Some lived out their lives in squalor, others used the opportunity to succeed. There was intense prejudice against the Irish and Catholics, and they, in turn, spoke out against the African Americans. The greatest achievement of the Irish immigration was the revival of the Catholic Church in the United States.

Know Nothing Party

The Order of the Star Spangled Banner was formed in 1849. It became a powerful political party by 1854 and included secret rituals, much like a fraternal order. When asked about the party, followers were to say: "I know nothing." They called for restrictions on immigration and demanded that immigrants and Catholics be excluded from public office. They were extremely successful and might have taken a greater role if slavery had not become the focal issue of the 1850s.

German immigration

The Germans who came to this country in the 1830s joined those who had come in response to William Penn's invitation a hundred years before. Collectively they were more educated than the Irish and their religious convictions were more varied. They generally settled in rural areas in family groups.

Lowell System

This was the factory system developed in Massachusetts that brought all the processes of spinning and weaving using power machinery under one roof. This mechanization of the process—from raw material to finished cloth—created a new industry. The founders of the system also tried to design model communities that would reward "moral" behavior.

manumission

This term refers to formally freeing someone from slavery; following this, one would be a slave no more.

McCormick's Reaper

Cyrus McCormick invented a primitive grain reaper in 1834. He improved the models for ten years, then applied for a patent and began manufacturing six years later. His invention revolutionized the scale of agriculture; now two men could harvest 12 acres in a day, as opposed to one man harvesting a half an acre a day by hand.

nativism

Nativism refers to the anti-immigrant behavior in response to the waves of German and Irish immigrants that were coming into the country. There were fears of voting blocs, but the greatest fear was that of unfamiliar religious practices.

steamboat

Robert Fulton and Robert Livingston launched the first steam-powered boat, the *Clermont*, in 1807. The steamboat was not affected by wind or current, and proved to be a faster and more reliable form of water transportation. By 1836 there were 361 steamboats navigating the rivers of the United States.

Turner's Rebellion of 1831

This was the first violent revolt by African American slaves in the United States. Nat Turner, an African American overseer and religious fanatic, led the rebellion. A small group killed Turner's master's household and then set off to do the same at other households, with other slaves joining as the group progressed. Before the end, 55 whites had been killed. After trials, 17 African Americans were hanged.

Eli Whitney

Whitney was the Yale graduate who engineered a mechanism for removing the seeds from cotton. He realized little profit from his invention, but it revolutionized the South and its production of cotton, fueling a new and profitable use for slavery. Whitney's greatest contribution, however, was in the production of goods by using interchangeable parts.

Working Men's Party

This labor party, first formed in 1828, that was devoted to the interests of labor. The party was relatively ineffective due to the inexperience of its leaders, which left them open to the manipulation of professional politicians.

MULTIPLE-CHOICE QUESTIONS

1. Andrew Jackson appealed to the "common man" because:

   (A) the federal government was overtaxing the poor.

   (B) he had the support of Henry Clay.

   (C) he was a self-made man of humble beginnings who had become a war hero.

   (D) John Quincy Adams was so unpopular.

   (E) he had a large family.

2. A leading advocate of the reform of mental health care was:

   (A) William Garrison.

   (B) Clara Barton.

   (C) Dorothea Dix.

   (D) John Quincy Adams.

   (E) Ralph Waldo Emerson.

3. Emerson and the transcendentalists:

   (A) were important supporters of western expansion.

   (B) popularized individualist and idealist philosophies.

   (C) were best known for their struggles on behalf of equal rights for women.

   (D) frequently clashed with abolitionists.

   (E) argued that intellectuals should separate themselves from political struggles.

4. Calhoun defended the doctrine of nullification because it:

   (A) was basic to the beliefs of the land owners in the South.

   (B) was an extension of the implied powers clause.

   (C) gave states a means of redress against national law.

   (D) was a constitutionally established principle.

   (E) was stated in the Federalist Papers.

5. The political purpose for proposing the Tariff of 1828 was to:

   (A) further the anti-slavery movement.

   (B) get even with the Federalists.

   (C) bolster the political reputation of New England candidates.

   (D) discredit the administration of President John Quincy Adams.

   (E) gain favor from the producers of rice and flax.

6. Which reform was achieved in many states during the Jacksonian era?

   (A) Abolition of prison sentences for those in debt

   (B) Compulsory attendance of schooling through high school

   (C) Mandatory inspections of factories

   (D) Child labor laws

   (E) Women obtaining the vote

7. Which of the following is NOT a correct statement about the presidential election of 1824?

   (A) Andrew Jackson received more popular votes than the other candidates did.

   (B) It was the first election where regional candidates split the vote.

   (C) Andrew Jackson was elected president.

   (D) It was an election where no candidate achieved a majority of electoral votes.

   (E) There were multiple candidates.

8. In the history of American education, the first half of the 19th century was marked by the:

   (A) the creation of a Department of Education in the federal government.

   (B) establishment of tax supported public schooling.

   (C) more coeducation in universities.

   (D) laws that mandated school attendance up to age 16.

   (E) introduction of church-sponsored high schools.

9. In the early 1830s, the majority of workers in New England textile mills were:

   (A) married women with grown children.

   (B) newly arrived immigrants from Ireland.

   (C) veterans of the War of 1812.

   (D) married men with children.

   (E) young, unmarried women from rural areas.

10. In the 1830s and 1840s the Mormons encountered violent opposition because:

   (A) they built temples everywhere they went.

   (B) Brigham Young led them to a new settlement in Utah.

   (C) they were pro-slavery.

   (D) they believed in polygamy and modern-day prophecy.

   (E) they favored unlimited immigration.

11. The Whig Party was most identified with:

   (A) the policies of Martin Van Buren.

   (B) Catholic immigrants from Europe.

   (C) radical reforms during the Jacksonian era.

   (D) the nationalism of Henry Clay and opposition to Jacksonian principles.

   (E) the growing temperance movement.

12. In 1842, the Massachusetts Supreme Court ruled in *Commonwealth v. Hunt* that:

   (A) forming a trade union was not illegal.

   (B) forming a trade union was illegal.

   (C) slavery in Massachusetts was illegal.

   (D) immigration quotas established in the late 1830s were unconstitutional.

   (E) immigration quotas established in the late 1830s were constitutional.

13. One of the hallmarks of Jacksonian democracy was the growth of:

   (A) mass political parties.

   (B) private schools across the country.

   (C) an elite business class.

   (D) trade agreements with other countries.

   (E) nationalism in the North.

14. The *Declaration of Sentiments* at the Seneca Falls Convention in 1848 argued for:

    (A) natural equality between men and women.

    (B) the redress of wrongs committed against the Native Americans.

    (C) the abolition of slavery.

    (D) compulsory public education.

    (E) stronger temperance laws.

15. Jackson opposed nullification because he:

    (A) was a landed slave owner.

    (B) had supported the Tariff Acts of 1828 and 1832.

    (C) was a westerner.

    (D) disliked Calhoun and feared that acceptance of the nullification doctrine would undermine the Union.

    (E) was a former supporter of the Federalist Party.

16. Which of the reforms below is characteristic of the Jacksonian period rather than the period following the American Revolution?

    (A) Abolition of the law of primogeniture

    (B) Decrease in the power of the state assemblies

    (C) Elimination of property requirements for voters

    (D) Confiscation of Loyalists estates

    (E) Creation of tariffs

17. *The Liberator*, a well-known anti-slavery newspaper, was the work of:

    (A) Daniel Webster.

    (B) Carrie Nation.

    (C) Sojourner Truth.

    (D) William Garrison.

    (E) Abraham Lincoln.

18. In rebutting the state-compact theory, Daniel Webster was affirming:

    (A) a nationalistic view of the Constitution.

    (B) a view that Calhoun would agree with.

    (C) the right of states to nullify national laws.

    (D) Congressional authority to pass tariffs to raise revenue.

    (E) the growing sectionalism of his day.

19. The Trail of Tears refers to:

    (A) white settlers who died on the way to the Oregon territory.

    (B) the reaction to the Panic of 1837.

    (C) tragic losses in the fighting over Florida.

    (D) the forced relocation of the Cherokee Native Americans to Oklahoma in the 1830s.

    (E) the exodus of the Mormons to Missouri.

20. The principal result of the widespread use of the cotton gin was that it:

    (A) made millions of dollars for its inventor.

    (B) made cotton easier to pick.

    (C) kept cotton out of the Old Southwest.

    (D) made the cotton industry less dependent on slavery.

    (E) made cotton a major export commodity.

ESSAY QUESTIONS

1. How did the United States evolve as a democracy in the 1815–1840 period?

_____

_____

_____

_____

_____

_____

_____

_____

_____

2. Why was the tariff issue so controversial in the Jacksonian period?

_____

_____

_____

_____

_____

_____

_____

_____

_____

ANSWER KEY

Multiple-Choice Questions

1. C
2. C
3. B
4. C
5. D
6. A
7. C
8. B
9. E
10. D
11. D
12. A
13. A
14. A
15. D
16. C
17. D
18. A
19. D
20. E

Test Prep and Admissions

Answers and Explanations

1. C

Part of Jackson's appeal was that he was a frontiersman who had risen to become a military and political leader. His integrity was as real as his courage. He was the veteran of many duels, as he adhered to the backwoods code of honor. All preceding presidents had been from the 'aristocracy' of Virginia and Massachusetts. Jackson, who was from Tennessee, was the first president not from one of the original 13 states.

2. C

Dorothea Dix was a schoolteacher from Boston who worked tirelessly on behalf of the mentally ill. She called for the inspection of mental wards in Massachusetts and pressured the state legislature to make tougher laws to oversee patient care. Eventually her campaign became national and other states followed her advice on health care reform.

3. B

In New England Emerson and Thoreau were popular philosophers who promoted a radical individualism. They wrote essays on an ideal return to nature and the need to disagree with the government if one's conscience demanded it.

4. C

The Jeffersonian argument in the Kentucky and Virginia Resolutions contained the arguments used by Calhoun in opposing the Tariff of 1828. The Kentucky and Virginia Resolutions held that the Union is a compact that sees the states as sovereign and superior to the federal government. Each state can decide if a federal law is unconstitutional. Nullification was a central principle for those who supported states' rights.

5. D

The Tariff of 1828 passed at the end of the one term Adams served as president. However, he was already so unpopular that the tariff was only one of the causes of his defeat in the election of 1828.

6. A

The abolition of debtor's prisons was in keeping with the other social reform movements of the Jacksonian era. Child labor and women's suffrage did not become an issue until years later.

7. C

In the election of 1824 Jackson received the most popular votes but did not get a majority of the electoral votes needed to be elected. As the Constitution states, the election then goes to the House of Representatives, which then chooses the president. In the House, Jackson was defeated by John Quincy Adams after Henry Clay, another presidential candidate in the election, threw his support to Adams. Adams made Clay Secretary of State and Jackson suggested that Adams had made a deal with Clay to gain his support. In the end it only delayed Jackson's election; he won handily over Adams in 1828.

8. B

America established the local tax support for education early in its history. Schools are organized into local districts and property taxes are often levied to build schools and pay for teachers. This grass roots approach to schooling differs greatly from most other nations, which have national educational systems.

9. E

Most factory workers in the early industrial period were single women who lived in company-run dormitories. Most came from rural areas or small towns in the Northeast and worked until they married.

10. D

Mormons (members of the Church of Jesus Christ of Latter-Day Saints) were viewed with suspicion as their church condoned multiple wives for men and followed a "latter-day" prophet who was their patriarch. They moved from community to community in New York, Illinois, and Missouri encountering sporadic harassment along the way.

After their founder and self-proclaimed prophet, Joseph Smith, was murdered in Illinois they left for the far West to establish present-day Utah.

11. D

The Whigs were an anti-Jacksonian coalition who rallied around the leadership of Henry Clay. Farmers who valued national improvements to help get their crops to market supported the Whig Party as did northerners who had industrial interests and supported a protective tariff. The Whigs elected one president in 1840 but soon faded as a national party.

12. A

This court ruling helped establish the right of workers to create their unions. The state Supreme Court in Massachusetts said that unions were not illegal and this precedent was used in other states to argue for the right to strike and bargain collectively.

13. A

Political parties were transformed in the first half of the 19th century. More people became involved in local and national elections. The Democratic Party was founded out of the Jacksonian movement. It used large rallies to promote its candidates across the country and organized itself in each state.

14. A

In the 1840s women met in upstate New York to create the first female political agenda in American history. Its central goal was to promote equality between the sexes. The women who organized this convention were the pioneers of the suffrage and temperance movements of their day.

15. D

As a slave owner from a slave state it might have been assumed that Jackson would side with Calhoun on the issue of states' rights. But the two men came to dislike one another intensely. Calhoun resigned as vice president and fought with Jackson over the issue of states' rights. As a Democrat and lawyer, Jackson saw the dangers to the Union if states could nullify national laws.

16. C

Removing the property requirements for voting was an important achievement brought about during the Jacksonian Era. The other reforms were carried out in the period immediately after the American Revolution. Tariffs—taxes on imports—were not a new concept or reform.

17. D

One of the earliest and most vocal opponents of slavery was William Lloyd Garrison. He spoke out often about the evils of the slave trade and published *The Liberator*. He was accused by southerners of inciting slave revolts like Nat Turner's in 1830. Though violently opposed to slavery, Garrison was a pacifist and worked to undermine it through his journalism and speeches in the North.

18. A

Webster argued that the American Revolution had been fought by the united colonies against Britain. True sovereignty belonged to the people as a whole and not with the state they live in. Webster believed nullification would threaten to turn the Union "into a rope of sand" and so he opposed the South's support for states' rights.

19. D

Jackson was typical of westerners in that he believed Native Americans were a problem to be removed. After gold was discovered in the near Cherokee lands, there was pressure to remove the remaining Native American tribes further to the West. Although some whites championed the cause of the tribes, the relocation was enforced by the U.S. Army. Many Cherokee died during the move to the West.

20. E

The cotton gin was a machine used to separate the cotton seed from the cotton fibers. It allowed for more cotton to be produced and stimulated the export of raw cotton. It made the production of cotton more efficient while increasing its demand. This also created a demand for more slaves since they were needed to pick the cotton, which was still done by hand.

ANALYSES OF THE FREE-RESPONSE ESSAYS

Question 1:

How did the United States evolve as a democracy in the 1815–1840 period?

Key Points

American democracy after the War of 1812

- The U.S. embarked on a new phase of development and unity after 1815
- The population was growing and settlement was pushing westward
- Land ownership had long been the prerequisite for the right to vote. With so much land available, voting was more accessible to the common people
- More voters meant politicians had to appeal to the people to be elected

Forces that encouraged the advancement of American democracy

- Since the Revolution white male suffrage had been increasing steadily
- Laborers, small merchants, artisans fought for political power through the ballot box against the rising industrial interests
- Vermont adopted universal white male suffrage first in 1791
- Property requirements for voting were largely gone by 1821
- The transition from the Virginia Dynasty of Washington, Jefferson, Madison, and Monroe to Jackson, the hero of the 'common man,' was largely due to the larger electorate
- Organized political parties (i.e., the Democratic Party of Jackson) which worked on the national and local levels

Features of the New Democracy

Opposition to the power of the business elites or capitalist class

Party organizations to promote candidates for office

'Spoils System' which rewarded party members with jobs when power was gained in the Executive or Congressional branches

Large rallies to grab the attention of the voter

Many immigrants came to America to seek cheap land and the promise of the freedom and equality that Jeffersonian democracy had promoted

Scoring Rubric

There are five scoring ranges:

Excellent

The answer must have a strong, clear thesis that talks of the growth of democracy after 1815. The quality of the writing should be excellent, the answer must show logical patterns, and the student should include many of the major points in the above list (though they may go beyond the list). The organization should be clear. The answer may contain minor errors.

Very Good

The answer must have a thesis that discusses the evolution of the American democracy from the presidencies of Monroe to Van Buren. Organization of the answer must show logical patterns, and the student should include many of the specific points from the above list.

Adequate

The answer must try to make some argument and must include at least some of the points listed above. There may be flaws in the thesis argument.

Flawed

The answer will demonstrate serious weaknesses. It may have no thesis argument at all, and it will include few of the points listed above. The answer may show little understanding of what constitutes a democracy or how it evidences itself in the U.S.

Severely Flawed

The answer will demonstrate almost no attempt to answer the question, and will include very few, if any, of the points listed above.

Question 2:

Why was the tariff issue so controversial during the Jacksonian period?

Key Points

- A tariff is an import tax that is use to raise revenue and also protect industry from foreign competition. Pro-tariff sentiment was strongest in the North since that was where industry was concentrated
- There was increasing conflict between the agrarian and commercial interests in the U.S. after 1815
- Unequal regional economic development within the U.S. made for sectional conflict

KAPLAN
Test Prep and Admissions

Events that form the backdrop of the tariff debate in the 1820s

- Hamilton had first outlined the use of a tariff to raise national revenue in 1791
- Peace with Britain after 1815 brought more cheap British goods to compete with American products
- The Tariff of 1816 had started the debate over who benefited from the import tax
- During the Era of Good Feelings(1815–1820) national interests supported the tariff as good for the nation
- By 1824 the South could see that a tariff did not benefit them and they opposed it
- Population growth and immigration to the North and West was resulting in more votes in the Congress at the expense of the South. Most new states were being formed in the Northwest (Michigan, Illinois, Iowa)
- The Tariff of 1828 was a political scheme that backfired on the South. They devised a tariff that would be disadvantageous to all regions but it passed anyway. Thus the name given to it, the 'Tariff of Abominations'
- Calhoun then dug up the Kentucky Resolutions of 1798 which amplified the 10th Amendment and gave all undefined powers in the U.S. Constitution to the states. He interpreted this to include 'nullifying' federal laws and even secession from the Union
- Jackson remained neutral on the tariff issue and resolved to enforce any act of Congress. Calhoun resigned as his vice president and took the fight for states' rights into the Senate
- South Carolina threatened to refuse to abide by the revised tariff of 1832 and Jackson threatened likewise to force the states to obey the laws of Congress
- Clay sponsored a compromise tariff in 1833 which removed many of the extreme features of the earlier tariffs and helped diffuse the sectional crisis

Sectional Line up on the Tariff Issue

Commercial Interests: North	Agrarian Interests: South
Factories and industry were largely in the Northeast	Large and small farms dominated the economic activity of the South
Canals and roads also were developed first in the North	South Carolina took the lead in fighting against the tariffs that would disadvantage the South
Northern manufacturers sought protection from imports	Southern land owners aspired to the gentleman-farmer ideal of Jefferson
After the War of 1812 the tariff was connected to nationalism.	Sectionalism became more pronounced by the mid 1820s as the North eclipsed the South in terms of development and investment

KAPLAN
Test Prep and Admissions

KAPLAN
Test Prep and Admissions

Scoring Rubric

There are five scoring ranges:

Excellent

The answer must have a strong, clear thesis that explains the nature of the tariff controversy during Jackson's presidency. The essay should focus on the sectional nature of the tariff debate. The quality of the writing should be excellent, the answer must show logical patterns, and the student should include many of the major points in the above list (though they may go beyond these points). The organization should be clear. The answer may contain minor errors.

Very Good

The answer must have a thesis that explains the tariff debate in the 1820s. The answer must be logically organized, and the student should include many of the specific points from the above list.

Adequate

The answer must try to make some argument and must include at least some of the points listed above. There may be flaws in the thesis argument.

Flawed

The answer will demonstrate serious weaknesses. It may have no thesis argument at all, and it will include few of the points listed above. The answer may show little understanding of what a tariff is or why it was so hotly debated in Congress during the Jackson administration.

Severely Flawed

The answer will demonstrate almost no attempt to answer the question, and will include very few, if any, of the points listed above.

Chapter Seven: **The Civil War Era**

- Timeline: 1844–1877

- National Expansion

- The Road to Civil War

- The Civil War

- Reconstruction

- Multiple-Choice Questions

- Essay Questions

- Answer Key

- Answers and Explanations

- Analyses of the Free-Response Essays

TIMELINE: 1844–1877

1844	James K. Polk elected president.
1845	U.S. annexes Texas.
1846	U.S. declares war on Mexico.
1846	U.S. and Britain settle "Oregon question," fixing boundary at 49th parallel.
1846	Rep. David Wilmot proposes banning slavery from all territory acquired from Mexico.
1848	Treaty of Guadalupe Hidalgo ends Mexican War and gives most of modern-day Southwest and California to U.S.
1849	Gold Rush in California increases territory's American population.
1850	Compromise of 1850 again solves problem of slavery in territories temporarily, but new Fugitive Slave Law angers many in North.
1851	Treaty of Ft. Laramie attempts to accommodate both western settlers on over-land routes and Plains Native Americans.
1853	Gadsden Purchase adds land necessary for railroad to New Mexico Territory.
1854	Stephen Douglas introduces Kansas-Nebraska Act.

KAPLAN
Test Prep and Admissions

1856	Preston Brooks assaults Charles Sumner on the floor of the Senate.
1856	Conflicts between pro- and anti-slavery settlers in Kansas escalates into violence ("Bleeding Kansas").
1857	Supreme Court issues decision in *Dred Scott* case.
1859	John Brown's raid on Harpers Ferry.
1860	Abraham Lincoln elected president.
1861	Mississippi, Florida, Alabama, Georgia, Texas, and Louisiana form Confederate States of America.
1861	Civil War begins with South's attack on Ft. Sumter; few significant battles for almost a year.
1861	Lincoln suspends habeas corpus.
1862	Congress passes Legal Tender, Morrill Land Grant, and Homestead Acts.
1863	Lincoln issues Emancipation Proclamation.
1863	Union victories at Gettysburg and Vicksburg start to swing progress of war toward Union.
1863	New York City draft riots.
1863	Lincoln issues plan of Reconstruction, allowing Southern states back into Union once 10 percent of loyal voters had sworn allegiance.
1864	Sherman's March devastates much of Georgia.
1864	Lincoln reelected after Union victories in Georgia and Alabama help discredit Democrats' peace platform.
1865	Civil War essentially ends with Robert E. Lee's surrender to Grant at Appomattox.
1865	Congress establishes Freedmen's Bureau.
1865	Lincoln assassinated by John Wilkes Booth.
1865	Presidential Reconstruction under Johnson.
1865	Southern states pass black codes, send ex-Confederates to Congress.
1865	13th Amendment ratified; slavery abolished.
1866	Congress passes Civil Rights Act.
1867	Congressional Reconstruction.
1868	14th Amendment, guaranteeing citizenship and protection of laws to anyone born or naturalized in the United States, ratified by states.
1868	Johnson impeached but not convicted by Congress for violating Tenure of Office Act.
1868	Grant elected president.
1869	Republican Reconstruction governments begin to collapse in South.
1870	15th Amendment ratified; African American suffrage guaranteed.
1870	Ku Klux Klan engages in campaign of terror against African Americans and prominent white Southern Republicans.
1877	Compromise of 1877: last federal troops leave South, Rutherford B. Hayes becomes president.

NATIONAL EXPANSION

The United States experienced a period of phenomenal growth during the first half of the 19th century. The westward expansion of American settlers, the effort to bring civilization and democratic institutions to the wilderness was to be known as *manifest destiny*. The phrase expressed the popular belief that the United States had a divine mission to extend its influence and civilization across the entire continent. This drive to overcome an untamed environment was explained as the destiny of America. Unexplained would be the consequences of that mission for Native Americans and Mexicans, whose territory the American settlers wanted for their "divine" mission. But move west the settlers did, in untold numbers. Through their westward movement, the settlers threatened to destroy a way of life based on the herds of buffalo. The federal government did little to respond to requests to limit settlers, and after gold was discovered, there was a huge wave of expansion to the west coast.

Mexico became an independent country in 1821. Americans traveled to Mexico's northern areas to settle, develop trade, and expand the reach of the United States. California offered an attractive opportunity for expansion. When John Sutter found gold on the land he had persuaded the Mexican government to give him for a settlement of Swiss immigrants, Sutter's Fort (New Helvetia) became the end of the most traveled trail west.

This westward expansion began to put pressure on the boundaries of the United States. In the Oregon territory, the boundary with Great Britain was in dispute. The boundary dispute was characterized by the American slogan "54° 40' or Fight." The matter would be settled after an 1846 agreement was ratified by the Senate establishing the boundary at the 49th parallel and through the main channel south of Vancouver Island.

Brewing at the same time were tensions on the southern border. Americans had been streaming into Texas and by 1830 there were 20,000 American settlers—a number that alarmed the Mexican government. In 1832 and 1833, Americans organized conventions to demand statehood in the United States. In 1836 the Americans declared Texas an independent country. Mexican Dictator Santa Anna came with an army prepared to fight. He attacked the Alamo and 12 days later succeeded in conquering the old mission/fort. However, two months later Santa Anna was captured; he bought his freedom for the price of a treaty recognizing Texan independence with the Rio Grande River as the boundary. The Lone Star Republic wanted annexation to the United States and would achieve this in 1845.

Mexico broke off relations with the United States two days after James K. Polk took office to protest the annexation of Texas. When an ambassador could not negotiate an agreement on a boundary dispute, Polk sent a war message to Congress in May of 1846. Mexico City was captured 17 months later (1847) and Santa Anna fled. The Treaty of Guadalupe Hidalgo was the formal ending of the Mexican War. By signing the treaty, Mexico gave up all claims to Texas above the Rio Grande and ceded California and New Mexico to the United States as well. It may have been referred to as "Mr. Polk's War," but the result established manifest destiny across the continent.

KAPLAN
Test Prep and Admissions

Alamo

The abandoned mission in San Antonio was the site of the attack by Santa Anna against the Texans. All the American defenders, including Davy Crockett, were killed but the attack inspired the rest of Texas to almost fanatical resistance and the rallying cry "Remember the Alamo" was coined.

annexation of California

After the Mexican War was over, California was ceded to the Americans. Although the Mexican and Native American residents did not accept American rule easily, their revolt was soon put down.

annexation of Texas

The Lone Star Republic gained its independence from Mexico in 1836 in exchange for releasing the Mexican dictator, Santa Anna, who had been captured in battle by the Texans. Texas was not immediately admitted as a state. There were major concerns in Congress that a serious sectional difference would endanger Van Buren's candidacy for president much less lead to a war with Mexico. Van Buren would stay away from the issue during his presidency. Texas was not annexed to the United States until 1845, after James Polk became president.

"Fifty–Four Forty or Fight"

The Oregon Territory stretched from the 42nd parallel north to 54° 40′. Since 1818 Great Britain and the U.S. had agreed to "joint occupation." Immigration into the area began after 1837 and by 1843, there were 5,000 settlers—mostly American—in residence. "Fifty-Four Forty or Fight" was the American rallying cry. The British government proposed the 49th parallel as the boundary—the agreement James Buchanan took to the Senate for ratification.

John Charles Fremont

He was known as "The Pathfinder." He gained his fame by mapping the Oregon Trail and for a historic trip in 1843–44 that created interest in Oregon and northern California. He would later run for president.

Manifest Destiny

This was the belief that justified the American expansion across the continent. It held that Americans had a divine destiny to spread their culture from the Atlantic to the Pacific Ocean. In spite of Native American treaties to the contrary, the U.S. government supported the western movement to Mexican and Native American lands.

Mexican War

The conflict between the United States and Mexico for control of Mexican land lasted for 17 months. Fewer than 2,000 Americans were killed in battle, although almost 12,000 died of diseases. It is still one of the deadliest wars; 110 out of every 1,000 soldiers were killed. The U.S. won and a vast piece of land including California and New Mexico was turned over to the United States.

Oregon Trail

Settlers traveled to the Willamette Valley area of Oregon over this 2,000-mile path. The journey usually took six months. The peak year was 1850, when 55,000 settlers traveled west.

James K. Polk

As president during the Mexican War, which was often referred to as "Mr. Polk's War" by New Englanders, Polk took the stance that the war had been forced on the U.S. following acts of aggression from Mexico. He signed the declaration of war on May 13, 1846.

Antonio Lopez de Santa Anna

This Mexican dictator commanded the Mexican troops that over-ran the Alamo. After Santa Anna was captured, he was granted his freedom in exchange for a treaty recognizing Texan independence.

Santa Fe Trail

The route from Missouri to Santa Fe was about a thousand miles long and required the travelers to survive attacks by Native Americans, as well as rough terrain that included deserts and mountains. The passage on the trail showed that heavy wagons could serve as a viable mode of transportation in the American West.

spot resolutions

Resolutions introduced by Abraham Lincoln, when he was a one-term congressman from Illinois. The purpose was to force President Polk to name the spot where American blood had been shed on American soil, implying that American troops may actually have been on Mexican soil when they were attacked north of the Rio Grande River.

Zachary Taylor

Commander of American troops in the Mexican War, his victories at Palo Alto and Resaca de la Palma gave control of Mexico's northern states to the U.S. without a major battle.

Treaty of Guadalupe Hidalgo

Through this treaty, signed on February 2, 1848, Mexico gave up all claims to Texas above the Rio Grande River and ceded California and New Mexico to the United States for $15 million. In return, the U.S. also agreed to pay off any claims of Americans citizens against Mexico up to $3.5 million.

John Tyler

As William Henry Harrison's vice president, Tyler became president upon Harrison's death 31 days after the inauguration. He opposed everything in Henry Clay's "American System"—meaning protective tariffs, internal improvements at federal expense, and a national bank. He was a strict constructionist and a champion of states' rights.

Webster-Ashburton Treaty

The 1842 treaty, which defined the boundary between Canada and Maine, was negotiated by Daniel Webster and Lord Ashburton of Great Britain. The treaty affirmed the current Canadian-U.S. boundary between the Atlantic and Minnesota and accepted joint occupation of Oregon.

THE ROAD TO CIVIL WAR

During the 1840s and 1850s, American settlers were moving west into the Great Plains and the new lands the United States had annexed, including California and Oregon. The westward movement brought the slavery issue forward over and over. The South hoped to extend slavery westward; southerners believed that keeping the balance between the number of slave and free states was the only way to ensure that their interests, including slavery, would be preserved. In the North, however, both free-soilers and abolitionists were opposed to the extension of slavery to western territories. Free-soilers differed from abolitionists in that they didn't oppose slavery in the South; they just wanted to keep it there and use the western lands for the small independent farms that northerners wanted and that predominated in the North.

From the time of the Missouri Compromise (1820) until the Compromise of 1850, the number of slave sates and free states had been carefully kept equal. This meant that the Senate was equally divided between slave-state senators and free-state senators. When Congressman David Wilmot proposed in 1846 that any lands to be acquired from Mexico in the Mexican war be slave-free, he had strong support in the North from both free-soilers and abolitionists. The Wilmot Proviso passed in the House of Representatives. The Senate, however, where the sectional interests of the South were preserved by the balance of free-state and slave-state senators, never passed it. The issue of slavery in the territories could never really be resolved since the majority of Americans supported the free-soil position, but the South, through its control of half the Senate, was able to block the free-soilers.

Senator Lewis Cass proposed another idea to resolve the issue. Cass proposed a way around the growing conflict that became known as "popular sovereignty." He suggested that the citizens of a territory make their own decisions regarding slavery. Such a process, he argued, would put the issue in the hands of those who would be directly affected by it. This position appealed to southerners who maintained their right to take their "property" into the new territories and expand the number of slave states. It also had some appeal in the North, where issues of slavery had been decided through the democratic process in each individual state.

In 1854 Congress passed the Kansas-Nebraska Act, which embodied the principle of popular sovereignty. Both pro- and anti-slavery settlers poured into Kansas, but the result was "bleeding Kansas"—armed struggle between the two opposing camps. This was the prelude to civil war.

Thomas Hart Benton

The Missouri Senator who, even though he owned slaves, tried to find compromises that would bypass the conflict and preserve the Union.

bleeding Kansas

The principle of popular sovereignty was embodied in the Kansas-Nebraska Act. Both pro-slavery and anti-slavery settlers moved to Kansas. The mix of settlers led to a confrontation in Lawrence in 1856. They destroyed the newspaper press, set fire to the governor's home, stole property, and destroyed the Free State Hotel. History reports this battle between the pro-slavery and anti-slavery Americans as a prelude to the Civil War.

KAPLAN
Test Prep and Admissions

John Brown

He was a free-soiler who had a history of instability. He fought the pro-slavery forces in Kansas and then conducted a raid on the federal arsenal at Harpers Ferry, West Virginia. Brown expected African American slaves to revolt and join him but they did not. He was captured, tried, and ultimately hanged. He became a martyr for the anti-slavery cause and was responsible for causing panic in the slaveholding states.

John C. Calhoun

He left his sickbed to speak to the Senate one last time regarding the Compromise of 1850. He said that to avoid war the South needed acceptance of its rights: equality in the territories, return of fugitive slaves, and some equilibrium between the sections of the country.

California gold rush

Gold was discovered at Sutter's Mill in California in 1848. The Gold Rush was the greatest migration to the West, changing California in a matter of months. Towns sprung up overnight and lawlessness abounded. Women were a minority; in 1850 less than 8 percent of California's total population was female.

caning of Charles Sumner

Ardent anti-slavery Senator Sumner of Massachusetts gave a speech, "The Crime Against Kansas," on the floor of the Senate. Preston Brooks of South Carolina brooded for two days, then found Sumner writing at his desk in the Senate and began beating him with a cane. Sumner collapsed and suffered effects of the beating for the rest of his life. Preston Brooks resigned but was re-elected.

Henry Clay

Clay was the 73-year-old primary author of the Compromise of 1850. Clay tried to find compromises to preserve the Union, arguing that secession would only lead to war. Clay did not live to see his words come true; he died in 1852.

Compromise of 1850

Henry Clay's attempt to settle the dispute over slavery. Propositions included admitting California as a free state, having no restrictions on slavery in the remainder of the Southwest, upholding slavery in the District of Columbia but abolishing the slave trade there, and enforcing a more effective fugitive slave act.

Crittenden Compromise

A series of amendments proposed by Senator John Crittenden that would recognize slavery in territories south of 36° 30′ and guarantee slavery where it already existed. This was a last minute effort to ward off secession.

Stephen A. Douglas

The "Little Giant" was an Illinois Senator who included the concept of popular sovereignty to gain passage of the Kansas-Nebraska Bill. He also rescued Clay's Compromise of 1850 and found support for its passage by breaking it into five different measures. California entered as a free state, the Utah Act set up another territory, a new fugitive slave act required northern participation in returning runaway slaves to their owners, and finally, the slave trade, but not slavery, was abolished in the District of Columbia.

Dred Scott Case

Dred Scott, a slave, sued for his freedom after his master's death, claiming his residences in the North entitled him to freedom. Chief Justice Roger B. Taney ruled that Scott lacked legal standing because he was not a citizen. Taney went on to write that one became a federal citizen by birth or naturalization, which eliminated any former slaves.

Free-Soil Party

The political party was a coalition of three major groups: northern Democrats, anti-slavery Whigs, and members of the Liberty Party. Inspired by Wilmot, the party advocated land for white farmers while keeping the African Americans in the South.

Fugitive Slave Act

The legislation required citizens to help capture and return escaped slaves, many of whom were living openly in northern states. Whites who did not comply could be fined $1,000 and face six months imprisonment. Jury trials were not allowed. The abolitionists were incensed and many of them helped slaves escape to Canada.

Gadsen Purchase

The 1853 purchase consisted of 30,000 square miles south of the Gila River. The U.S. paid $10 million to Mexico for the territory, which was a likely route for a Pacific Railroad. This was the last territory added to the contiguous 48 states.

Harpers Ferry raid

John Brown's raid on the federal arsenal quickly turned into a melee. Two of Brown's sons died in the fight. Brown had planned to arm slaves, set up an African American stronghold in the mountains of West Virginia, and provide support for slave revolts throughout the South.

Kansas-Nebraska Act

This legislation sponsored by Senator Stephen Douglas created the new territories of Kansas and Nebraska. Douglas incorporated the idea of popular sovereignty to gain support for his plan.

Lecompton Constitution

The Kansas convention met in Lecompton to draw up a constitution under which Kansas would be admitted as a slave state. The constitution was written in such a way that voters could not amend the proposed document, just approve or reject it. The document was rejected, demonstrating that the majority was against slavery.

Lincoln-Douglas debates

The debates took place in Illinois between August 21 and October 15, 1858, between two candidates for the U.S. Senate, Abraham Lincoln and Stephen A. Douglas. The two men met and traded innuendos as to their political support of slavery. Douglas supported popular sovereignty. Lincoln contended that Douglas did not "care" whether or not slavery was extended to new territories. Lincoln claimed it was a moral decision to care. Douglas won the Senate seat; however, Lincoln would win the presidency in another race with Douglas two years later.

Ostend Manifesto

This began as a diversion involving the Spanish colony of Cuba and the launching of expeditions against the Spanish from American soil. The U.S. offered $130 million for Cuba, one of the last Spanish possessions, but Spain refused. A confidential memo suggested the U.S. might want to take Cuba from Spain by force, but publication of the memo left the U.S. no choice but to disclaim it.

Panic of 1857

Several factors created the crisis. A reduction in demands for American grain (caused by the end of the Crimean War), a surplus of manufactured goods, and the continued confusion over the state banking system combined to throw the economy into a panic. The U.S. did not recover until 1859.

popular sovereignty

The policy, established to prevent violent acts, said that residents of the territories themselves should make the decision about whether slavery was to be allowed in that area. The "squatter sovereignty" did not directly challenge slaveholders' access to new lands.

Pottawatomie Massacre

John Brown and others dragged five men from their homes in Kansas and killed them in front of their families as "revenge" for the deaths of free-state men. The massacre (May 24–25, 1856) set off a guerrilla-style war in Kansas. See also: bleeding Kansas.

Republican Party

Abraham Lincoln was the first presidential candidate of this new political party that emerged from Free-Soil and other single-issue parties in 1860. Lincoln won the election and the Republican Party remains one of the country's two leading parties.

Uncle Tom's Cabin

Harriet Beecher Stowe's 1852 novel of slavery, *Uncle Tom's Cabin*, originally appeared in installments in a ladies' magazine. Northerners rallied around the dark descriptions of Uncle Tom, Little Eva, Simon Legree, and slavery in general. Southerners criticized Stowe as inaccurate. Lincoln, when meeting her, is reputed to have said, "So this is the little lady who started this great big war."

Daniel Webster

Webster, a senator from Massachusetts, is reputed to have been the Senate's greatest orator. Three days after Calhoun's speech in the Senate, Webster spoke on preserving the Union, ending his speech with "Liberty and union, one and inseparable, now and forever." Although he opposed slavery, Webster urged finding a compromise to preserve the Union. His efforts contributed to the Compromise of 1850.

Wilmot Proviso

Three months into the Mexican War, David Wilmot made a speech favoring expansion of the United States but limiting slavery to the areas where it already existed. The speech politicized the issue and kept it in the minds of the Congress. The Proviso was adopted by the House, but not by the Senate.

KAPLAN
Test Prep and Admissions

THE CIVIL WAR

Fort Sumter sits on an island in the middle of Charleston harbor in South Carolina. After South Carolina's secession, the Union forces there were cut off from supplies and reinforcements. President Lincoln informed South Carolina that he was sending two unarmed boats to supply the fort. He presented the Carolinians with the choice of allowing the fort to be supplied or beginning an armed conflict between the North and South. South Carolina's guns fired upon the fort for three days before the garrison surrendered. Thus, on April 12, 1861, Civil War began.

Lincoln realized quickly that fighting this war successfully would depend on several important factors. The first was to keep the border states—those slave states that bordered on the North (Kentucky, Maryland, Missouri)—from seceding as well. Keeping these states aligned with the Union was strategically important, especially in the case of Maryland, whose secession would have required the North to abandon Washington, D.C. Federal troops in Maryland resorted to martial law after pro-secessionists attacked Union troops.

At the beginning of the conflict, both the North and the South possessed advantages. The South only had to fight a defensive war, this meant the North had to try to conquer a huge area that was not home territory. The South also had the more experienced military leaders. Robert E. Lee, offered command of the Union Army in the field, spent the night thinking and then resigned his commission to go home to Virginia and lead the Confederate army. The North's advantage was its huge population that would continue to grow as the war progressed (free African Americans and immigrants). The Northern economy controlled most of the banking, factories and supplies of manufactured goods, and over 70 percent of the railroads. The North could also count on the U.S. Navy remaining intensely loyal and blockading the southern ports. As a result, the South's hope for foreign demand of its cotton in order to provide needed cash and recognition as a separate entity from the North never really materialized.

The Civil War has never been described as a clear-cut war of clear-cut sides. Too often families were split by their positions on the slavery and states' rights questions. Fathers and sons faced each other across battlefields, brothers fired at each other and sank ships under each other. In fact, many southerners remained loyal to the Union. In every Confederate state except South Carolina there was at least one regiment raised in support of the Union.

The further history moves away from those events of 1861–1865, the more the events become clouded. The Northern victory has acquired a sense of inevitability; the Southerners' fight for independence has the aura of a romantic lost cause. The South was doomed from the start, but felt compelled to strike out for the preservation of their way of life is one version of the Civil War story. Another version suggests the inevitability of a Northern victory was not nearly so clear. It places distinct advantages in the hands of the South: a captive labor force, superior officers, home field advantage while fighting, and the prospect of assistance from Great Britain, while suggesting that the northern victory was only accomplished through good leadership and popular commitment.

In the first year of the war, the South proved that this conflict was going to be more than a few months in duration. Confederate victories at Bull Run, Antietam, and Fredericksburg resulted in huge losses and a loss in confidence on the part of Lincoln and his commanders. The Battle of

Gettysburg, in July of 1863, became the turning point of the war. Lee's Confederate Army sustained massive losses, some 28,000 men in the two real days of pitched battle. General Pickett's division was annihilated after attacking the front line of the Federals. Colonel Joshua Chamberlain and the 20th Maine held the end of the Union line at Little Round Top and charged the surprised Alabamians with bayonets when their supplies of ammunition gave out.

While the confrontations continued on the battlefield, Lincoln had his own congressional worries. Early in 1863 he issued the Emancipation Proclamation, a document that freed the slaves. History often forgets to qualify this broad-sweeping document, as the freeing applied only to the areas not under federal control, i.e. the confederate states. Later the freedoms would be extended to all areas of the United States and to all slaves. Additionally, Lincoln was beset with worries about the medical care of the soldiers. Women nurses became a vital component to the survival of troops; 20,000 women served under difficult conditions as nurses. Clara Barton would use these experiences as inspiration to found the American Red Cross.

Finally Ulysses S. Grant emerged as a commander in whom Lincoln could have confidence. The day after Gettysburg, Vicksburg fell to Grant's six-week siege. Lincoln recalled Grant to conduct the remainder of the war. The campaigns continued; William Tecumseh Sherman began his "March through Georgia," a campaign of destruction though the state and into South Carolina. In its path Sherman's army destroyed and burned anything that could be of use to the southern army. Grant's approach was just to outlast Lee by fighting a war that drained the South's resources and destroyed their supplies. The effects of the Navy blockades, combined with Sherman's march and Grant's continued pursuit of Lee spelled the end for the confederacy. Finally, when the fighting had reduced Lee's army into a defensive line around the Confederate capital at Richmond, Lee was forced to surrender to Grant at Appomattox on April 9, 1865.

The Civil War was the first "total war" as it was fought against civilians as well as soldiers. Much of the South had been destroyed, its dead numbered upwards of 620,000. Almost an entire generation was lost. The assassination of Abraham Lincoln, which occurred three days after the surrender, placed incredible pressure on the new president, Andrew Johnson. The war would affect the country—its politics, economy, government, society, and racial relations—for generations to come.

13th Amendment

Because the Constitution contained phrases legitimizing slavery, a constitutional amendment was needed to free slaves in the border states. The amendment was ratified by 1865 and held that neither slavery nor involuntary servitude, except as a punishment, shall exist in the United States.

Antietam

General Lee followed up his victory at Bull Run with a campaign into Maryland. He hoped his victories would convince Great Britain to recognize and support the Confederacy. Lee's battle plan was known to the Union (a copy had fallen into their hands). General McClellan intercepted the Confederates at Antietam Creek in the Maryland town of Sharpsburg. This single battle was the most costly of the war; over 22,000 men were killed or wounded in a single day's fighting.

KAPLAN
Test Prep and Admissions

Appomattox

This was the site of the surrender of General Lee to General Grant on April 9, 1865. Grant treated his enemy with great respect, allowing the surrendering troops to keep their guns and horses.

Bull Run

The First Battle of Bull Run (July 1861) was a rout of federal troops. The Union forces seemed close to victory when General Thomas "Stonewall" Jackson counterattacked and caused the rout. This first win had two effects: it ended the supposition of a short war and served to create the myth that the rebels were invincible.

Confederacy

The 11 southern states which seceded from the United States in 1861 formed the Confederate States of America, commonly called simply the Confederacy. A confederacy is a union in which the individual members retain most of the power, creating a weak central government. Since southerners had long argued in favor of states' rights and proposals such as nullification, it is not surprising that they chose a confederation as their form of government.

Copperheads

During the Civil War, the Democratic Party in the north had several factions within it. The Copperheads were the extreme fringe of the Peace Wing (those who wanted to end the fighting, even at the expense of the Union). They opposed the war against the South and mounted a forceful protest against the Lincoln administration's policies and war conduct.

Jefferson Davis

Davis was the first and only president of the Confederate States of America, elected for a six-year term. He was described as indecisive, but once he made up his mind, nothing could shake him from the decision.

Emancipation Proclamation

Lincoln issued the proclamation in 1863 that emancipated slaves in the states not under federal control; he called it a military necessity. The proclamation would not affect all the states until combined with the 13th Amendment, passed after the Civil War.

Fort Sumter

Site of the first pitched battle of the Civil War, where federal troops withstood two days of bombardment before surrendering the fort and its arsenal to South Carolina troops.

Gettysburg

This three-day battle was arguably the turning point of the Civil War. General Lee's army met General Meade and the Army of the Potomac. Over 50,000 died between July 2–4, 1863. Heroes included Joshua Chamberlain of the 20th Maine with their defense of Little Round Top and the federal troops withstanding a charge that decimated General Pickett's division. After the battle, Lee's Army of Virginia never again ventured into northern territory and the South fought a defensive war for two more years.

Ulysses S. Grant

Grant directed the siege of Vicksburg, a seven-week standoff before the city surrendered. Grant earned Lincoln's notice and was summoned to take command of the Army of the Potomac; Lincoln said that at least Grant would "move" the troops, as opposed to George McClellan's tactics after Antietam. Grant would fight a war of attrition and command the troops until the surrender at Appomattox.

Robert E. Lee

Lee was considered to be the most able of all the officers in the Army. When asked by Lincoln to take command of the troops in defense of the Union, Lee resigned his commission instead and went "home to Virginia." He then became the leading general of the Confederacy. Even after the war, Lee would still be admired and respected by Army personnel from both sides of the conflict.

George B. McClellan

He had twice commanded the Army of the Potomac and was removed for the second and last time after he failed to pursue Lee's troops after Antietam (Lincoln suggested he had a "case of the slows"). He was a popular candidate for president in 1864 against Lincoln. He was nominated by the Democratic Party with a platform calling for peace. He won 45 percent of the popular vote, but only 21 electoral votes.

National Banking Act

This legislation created a uniform system of banking and bank note currency and helped to finance the war.

New York draft riots

The Union allowed men to "purchase" the service of others in the war instead of being drafted themselves. For $300, a man could serve in another's place. The draft riots protested this practice and opposed the draft in general.

Radical Republicans

The radicals in Lincoln's Republican Party wanted confiscation of plantations, emancipation of slaves, and a stronger war effort. Their members included Thaddeus Stevens, Charles Sumner, and Benjamin Wade. After the war had ended, the Radical Republicans pushed for extreme measures designed to punish the South.

Sherman's March

General William Tecumseh Sherman led a force of 100,000 from Chattanooga, Tennessee, on a march that destroyed everything for a 100-mile swath that the South might use in its war effort. He marched through Georgia and captured Atlanta in 1864 and advanced to set fire to Columbia, the capital of South Carolina. The march had its intended effect in that it broke the will of the South to fight. This was the prime example of the war strategy that had changed from a "gentlemen's war" to all out war against civilians as well as military targets.

Vicksburg

In 1863, the Union determined that total control of the Mississippi River was strategically important. General Grant began his siege of Vicksburg with a bombardment. The fighting continued for seven weeks before the Confederates (29,000 soldiers) surrendered on July 4th. Texas, Alabama and Louisiana were now cut off from the rest of the Confederacy.

RECONSTRUCTION

The Civil War was over and it was time to reassemble the country. Three days after the Confederate surrender at Appomattox, President Lincoln was assassinated by John Wilkes booth at Ford's Theatre. Andrew Johnson, a Union man from Tennessee, stepped into the fray.

Johnson, from Tennessee, had stayed with the Union at the beginning of the Civil War. The surprise assumption of the presidency by a southerner did not inspire confidence in the Republicans. The Radical Republicans detected an opportunity to push their programs, knowing that Johnson was not Lincoln and could not command much public support in the North.

The destruction to the country was immense. Sherman's march through Georgia had laid waste to a 100-mile wide swath. Georgia was not the only state that had sustained great damage; rebuilding the country was to be the first priority.

Rebuilding did not just mean physical reconstruction. It meant determining the character of the new South: Would it be forced to make fundamental changes or would it return to its old character, just without slaves? In the South, the end of slavery alone brought little change as ways were found to keep African Americans in their previous economic and political condition even without the institution of slavery. However, the Radical Republicans in the North sought to force southerners to accept African Americans as equals. Reconstruction brought some important changes; however, in 1877, when Reconstruction formally ended and southerners were again in control of their state governments, there remained big differences between North and South and little progress for African Americans toward equality.

13th Amendment

Because the Constitution contained phrases legitimizing slavery, a constitutional amendment was needed to free slaves. The amendment was ratified by 1865 and held that neither slavery nor involuntary servitude of any type, except as a punishment, shall exist in the United States.

14th Amendment

The amendment held that all persons born or naturalized in the United States were to be citizens. The amendment also extended equal protection and due process rights to citizens, protecting them from state governments as well as the federal government.

15th Amendment

This amendment, passed in 1870, guaranteed the right to vote in federal elections to all citizens—regardless of race, color, or previous condition of servitude.

black codes

These were rules that restricted the rights and movements of African Americans. Among many other things, the codes prohibited African Americans from borrowing money to buy land, forced them to sign work contracts, and prohibited African Americans from testifying against whites in court.

carpetbaggers

These were often Northern opportunists who supposedly went south with all their possessions in a carpetbag to grab the political "spoils." More often than not they were drawn south by the hope of economic opportunity or political power.

Civil Rights Act of 1866

This act proclaimed all African Americans to be U.S. citizens (negating the Dred Scott decision) and attempted to provide a legal shield against the implementation of the black codes.

Compromise of 1877

The election of 1876 brought a crisis: Samuel Tilden, the Democratic candidate, won the popular vote but was one vote shy of victory in the Electoral College. A deal was worked out: Republican Hayes, in return for the presidency, would end Reconstruction, ceasing the military occupation of the South, readmitting southern sates to the Union, and allowing southerners to regain control of their own state governments. Hayes also agreed to support the building of a southern transcontinental railroad.

Crédit Mobilier scandal

This was one of the scandals of the Grant administration. Crédit Mobilier, a construction company, had billed the Union Pacific Railroad exorbitant fees, which lined the pockets of insiders who controlled both the construction company and the railroad. The scandal touched many, including the future president James Garfield. When the scandal broke, the rank-and-file shareholders were left holding the worthless shares of railroad stock.

Freedmen's Bureau

The Bureau of Refugees, Freedmen and Abandoned Lands was established to provide for the new African American citizens. Agents of the Bureau were to negotiate contracts, provide medical care, and set up schools. The Bureau had its own courts to deal with labor and land disputes. Failure to understand the depths of racial prejudice interfered with the effectiveness of Bureau agents.

Homestead Act

The 1862 legislation that said a farmer could get a homestead of free federal land (160 acres) if he staked out a claim and lived there for five years, or if he bought the land for $1.25 an acre after six months. Loopholes in the law made it possible for the railroads to secure thousands of acres.

KAPLAN
Test Prep and Admissions

impeachment of Johnson

Johnson deliberately violated the Tenure of Office Act passed by the Radical Republicans in Congress, in order to test its constitutionality. Secretary of War Edwin Stanton had become less than supportive of the president, so Johnson suspended him and named General Grant in his place. Grant was not confirmed by the Senate, and on February 24, 1868 Johnson was impeached by the House of Representatives. The Senate, however, did not convict Johnson; the vote was one less than the two-thirds majority needed. Johnson served out the remainder of his term.

Andrew Johnson

He was a self-taught tailor who learned, with the help of his wife, to become an orator. He served as a mayor, congressman, governor, and senator before serving as military governor of Tennessee. His loyalty to the Union came from his strict interpretation of the Constitution. Lincoln named Johnson his vice president and Johnson became president after Lincoln's assassination. He is best known for surviving an attempt by the Radical Republicans to remove him from office through impeachment.

Johnson's Plan for Reconstruction (Presidential Reconstruction)

After Lincoln's assassination, Johnson adopted a plan for Reconstruction that closely resembled the requirements of Lincoln's. Johnson added an amnesty program. Those excluded (wealthy planters, bankers, and merchants) could apply for a pardon; he granted over 13,000 in 1865 alone. Johnson also called upon each of the states to ratify the 13th Amendment; most of the state conventions met the requirement.

Ku Klux Klan (KKK)

The Klan was founded in 1867 by ex-Confederate general Nathaniel Bedford Forrest. The Klan burned African American–owned buildings, and flogged and murdered African Americans to keep them from exercising their voting rights. The Klan has experienced periodic revivals ever since.

Lincoln's Plan for Reconstruction

Lincoln's plan held that as soon as 10 percent of those who had voted in 1860 had taken an oath of allegiance to the Constitution and the Union, and swore to support emancipation laws, then that rebel state could be readmitted to the Union and form its own government.

Morrill Land Grant Act

This 1862 legislation encouraged states to use the sale of federal land grants to organize and support and maintain agricultural and technical colleges. Many state universities got their start from these appropriations.

Proclamation of Amnesty

After the Civil War amnesty was granted to most southerners for their role in the rebellion against the Union. Johnson added to the list of those excluded from amnesty anyone with taxable property worth more than $20,000. These were the people that Johnson thought had led the South into secession.

Radical Republicans

After the Civil War, the Radical Republicans sought to punish the South for seceding from the Union and instigating the Civil War. They also sought to force the South to make political and social changes, including granting equal rights to African Americans. The Radical Republicans clashed with President Andrew Johnson but were unable to remove him from office through impeachment.

scalawags

They were the native white Republicans in the South who had opposed secession. They were often vilified in the press. Among the scalawags was Confederate general James Longstreet, who had decided after Appomattox that the South must change its ways.

sharecropping

The sharecropper provided the labor and worked the land in return for supplies and a share of the crop. It did not produce self-sufficiency for African Americans.

Tenure of Office Act

This law, passed over President Johnson's veto, required the consent of the Senate for the president to remove any officeholder whose appointment had to be confirmed by the Senate in the first place. The purpose was to protect Secretary of War Edwin Stanton, the one Radical in Johnson's cabinet. There was an ambiguity in the wording, which stated that cabinet officers should serve during the term of the president who appointed them. Lincoln had appointed Stanton; Johnson was, however, serving out Lincoln's term.

Wade-Davis Bill

This bill was passed in 1864. As an alternative to Lincoln's plan, the Wade-Davis Bill required that a majority of white male citizens had to declare their allegiance to the Union before a state's government could be readmitted to the Union, and that only those who had taken an oath affirming their "past" loyalty could vote or serve in the government. The bill never became law as Lincoln exercised a pocket veto.

MULTIPLE-CHOICE QUESTIONS

1. What border states did Lincoln do everything he could to keep in the Union after Fort Sumter?

    (A) Kentucky, Maryland, and Missouri

    (B) North Carolina and Arkansas

    (C) Kentucky and Tennessee

    (D) Pennsylvania and Maryland

    (E) Virginia and Delaware

2. Manifest destiny was a common belief in the 1800s. It was based on the idea that:

    (A) the Union must be preserved.

    (B) the United States was destined to grow from the Atlantic to the Pacific.

    (C) all new territories would abolish slavery.

    (D) slavery would eventually die out of its own accord as farming became more mechanized.

    (E) the West was a land of opportunity.

3. Which of the following groups would most likely have used the slogan: "54° 40' or fight"?

    (A) Lincoln's generals at the end of 1862

    (B) Texans fighting for independence from Mexico

    (C) Easterners taking part in the California Gold Rush

    (D) South Carolina secessionists

    (E) Americans calling for Britain to surrender the Oregon Country

4. Hopes for a Confederate victory in the Civil War began to fade after:

    (A) the Battle of Antietam.

    (B) the Emancipation Proclamation was issued.

    (C) Lee was defeated at Gettysburg, PA.

    (D) the Freedmen's Bureau was created by Lincoln.

    (E) Jefferson Davis resigned.

5. Which statement is LEAST accurate in describing slavery in the 1850s:

    (A) Slaves were generally provided with clothes, shelter, and enough corn meal and pork to keep them in good health.

    (B) Slaves performed a variety of duties and sometimes were able to escape.

    (C) Many overseers treated the slaves kindly in the South.

    (D) Household slaves generally received better treatment than those in the fields.

    (E) Most white farmers did not own slaves in the South.

6. The 13th Amendment contained which of the following provisions?

    (A) Abolition of slavery throughout the United States

    (B) Granting the right to vote to all citizens, including former slaves

    (C) Granting citizenship to freed slaves

    (D) Granting equal protection of the laws to all citizens

    (E) the loss of voting rights for Confederate officers

BRITISH CANADA

UNORGANIZED
U.S.TERRITORY
(slavery prohibited)

(extending to
Pacific Ocean)

SPANISH
TERRITORY

ATLANTIC OCEAN

GULF OF MEXICO

Free states
Free territory
Slave states
Slave territory

7. The map represents the United States immediately after the

   (A) Louisiana Purchase.
   (B) Civil War.
   (C) Proclamation of 1763.
   (D) Northwest Ordinance.
   (E) Missouri Compromise.

8. The raid at Harpers Ferry was of great concern to southerners because:

   (A) they feared African American slaves being armed by northern radicals.
   (B) it took place in the deep South.
   (C) John Brown had once been a slave owner himself.
   (D) it came so close to succeeding.
   (E) the federal government condoned it.

9. The Anaconda strategy to defeat the South was to:

   (A) march into Richmond and arrest the leaders of the Confederacy.
   (B) defend Washington, D.C., and invade the border states.
   (C) march to Texas and cut off its supply of beef to the southern army.
   (D) blockade southern ports and cut the Confederacy in two by controlling the Mississippi.
   (E) infiltrate southern cities and spread Union propaganda.

10. Which group of men represented the interests of the South and were most likely to support a breakup of the Union?

   (A) Charles Sumner, Stephen Douglas and Daniel Webster
   (B) William Crawford and John Brown
   (C) John Quincy Adams and Alexander Stephens
   (D) Jefferson Davis and John Calhoun
   (E) Henry Clay and Thomas Hart Benson

11. In 1860 the slavery position of the Republican party most resembled the views of:

(A) Know Nothing Party.

(B) the Free-Soil Party.

(C) Whig Party.

(D) the Freeport Doctrine.

(E) the Democratic Party.

12. The Mexican War brought about all the following EXCEPT:

(A) popular support for President Polk in the West.

(B) opposition to the war in New England, due to concerns about the expansion of slavery.

(C) U.S. acquisition of the Mexican Cession which included most of the present-day Southwest.

(D) improved Mexican-American relations.

(E) the Treaty of Guadalupe Hidalgo between the U.S. and Mexico.

13. The initial cause of the political debate that resulted in the Compromise of 1850 was:

(A) the publication of *Uncle Tom's Cabin*.

(B) the Texas war for independence.

(C) the death of President William Henry Harrison.

(D) the Dred Scott decision.

(E) California's bid to enter the Union as a free state.

14. The primary objective of the founders of the Know Nothing party was:

(A) to promote the idea of popular sovereignty.

(B) forming workers' unions in the big cities.

(C) restricting the rights of immigrants.

(D) to limit the enforcement of the Fugitive Slave Law.

(E) the abolition of slavery in the territories.

15. Passage of the Kansas-Nebraska Act was a victory for:

(A) proponents of popular sovereignty.

(B) nativist groups.

(C) southerners who wanted a transcontinental railroad with an eastern terminus at New Orleans.

(D) opponents of permanent Native American reservations.

(E) abolitionists.

16. The rapid growth of settlements in the West was stimulated most by:

(A) new and improved transportation from Chicago to San Francisco.

(B) the success of the Mormon settlement in Utah.

(C) the railroad companies promising free land.

(D) successful pacification of the native peoples.

(E) the discovery of precious metal deposits in Utah, Colorado, and California.

17. The Union financed the war by:

   (A) using tariff revenues to help pay for the military.

   (B) printing paper money.

   (C) excise or sales taxes on goods and services.

   (D) selling bonds to citizens and banks.

   (E) All of the above

18. "Bleeding Kansas" refers to:

   (A) wartime casualties in Kansas during the Civil War.

   (B) a mini war between pro- and anti-slavery groups in Kansas in the 1850s.

   (C) the capture of fugitive slaves in the West.

   (D) cruelty towards slaves in Kansas City.

   (E) the raid on Lawrence, Kansas by Quatrills Raiders.

19. The direct economic impact of the Civil War included all of the following EXCEPT:

   (A) large investment losses on Wall Street.

   (B) large fortunes made by military suppliers.

   (C) the growth of manufacturing corporations in the North.

   (D) runaway inflation in the South.

   (E) disruption of cotton exports from the South to Great Britain.

20. Dred Scott was:

   (A) an abolitionist who argued that the North should secede from the Union.

   (B) the founder of the Union League.

   (C) a slave who sued for his freedom after his master took him to the North.

   (D) a Supreme Court justice who declared that the Missouri Compromise was unconstitutional.

   (E) an escaped slave who gave many speeches denouncing slavery.

ESSAY QUESTIONS

1. "The Civil War was fought not over slavery but for the right of a state to leave the Union." Agree or disagree with this statement.

    _____

    _____

    _____

    _____

    _____

    _____

    _____

    _____

    _____

2. What economic challenges faced the Confederate States of America during the American Civil War of 1861–1865?

    _____

    _____

    _____

    _____

    _____

    _____

    _____

    _____

    _____

ANSWER KEY

Multiple-Choice Questions

1. A
2. B
3. E
4. C
5. C
6. A
7. E
8. A
9. D
10. D
11. B
12. D
13. E
14. C
15. A
16. E
17. E
18. B
19. A
20. C

KAPLAN
Test Prep and Admissions

Answers and Explanations

1. A

Lincoln used every political and military tactic possible to keep these three states connected to the Union in 1861. If Maryland had seceded then Washington, D.C., itself would have been cut off from the North. Kentucky, Maryland, and Missouri were slave states that stayed with the Union throughout the Civil War.

2. B

Most Americans believed it was inevitable that the United States should one day stretch "from sea to shining sea." The fast-paced expansion of American settlers brought conflict with Mexico, Britain, and, of course, the Native Americans who already lived in the West. Manifest destiny was questioned by few people and most Americans believed it should be pursued at whatever cost.

3. E

The Oregon territory was at one time claimed by Russia, Britain, and the United States. Newly arriving American settlers strengthened the American claim. The boundary between British-held Canada and the U.S. had to be negotiated and many American settlers hoped for a border at the 54th parallel. In the end, the settlement extended the existing U.S.-Canada border at the 49th latitude.

4. C

Lee tried to end the war in 1863 with his second invasion of the North. After three days the battle of Gettysburg resulted in Lee's defeat and his hasty retreat back to the South. The Confederate army never again threatened the North. The South was forced to fight a defensive campaign that allowed the North to outlast them.

5. C

While some slaves were treated better than others, their role was that of inferiors and most slaves lived lives of hard physical labor and deprivation. The overseer's job was to force the slaves to work; few could be genuinely kind and keep their job. Southerners argued that the Africans were content with their situation and that northern claims of cruel treatment were exaggerated.

6. A

The 13th Amendment made the abolition of slavery official by adding it to the U.S. Constitution. The 14th Amendment defined U.S. citizenship to include the freed slaves and the 15th Amendment gave African Americans the right to vote. However, it still was difficult for African Americans to exercise their right to vote in the South until the Civil Rights Movement of the 1960s.

7. E

The map depicts the agreement reached in 1820 in the Missouri Compromise. Missouri was admitted as a slave state and Maine was admitted as a free state, keeping the balance between the number of slave and free states and thus an equal number of votes for both sides in the U.S. Senate. At the same time a line was drawn westward from the southern boundary of Missouri; slavery was prohibited above that line but allowed below it.

8. A

Southerners had long accused abolitionists from the North of stirring up trouble among the slave population. Earlier slave revolts like Nat Turner's in 1830 were thought to have northern inspiration. John Brown was living proof that some abolitionists would not stop at violence and killing to advance the cause of African American liberation. After the failure of the Harpers Ferry raid, John Brown's trial and execution in Virginia were sensational events covered by many newspapers throughout the nation.

9. D

The Union strategy evolved into a two-fold campaign; one in the West and the other in the East. In the West the successful control of the Mississippi by the Union army brought military fame to Ulysses S. Grant. The U.S. navy bottled up the southern ports to keep the South from selling cotton or getting supplies abroad.

10. D

The most ardent defender of states' rights in the South was John Calhoun, who championed the doctrine of nullification. Jefferson Davis, a senator from Mississippi who in 1861 became the president of the Confederate States of America, was a southern leader favoring secession.

KAPLAN
Test Prep and Admissions

11. B

After the Mexican War, which added vast territory to the U.S., anti-slavery forces supported the Wilmot proviso which would have banned slavery in the West. The anti-slavery forces formed a coalition of former Whigs and Democrats. Later the Republican Party was formed to further resist the expansion of slavery in the western territories.

12. D

The Mexican War soured American relations with Mexico for many years. The loss of so much land was a source of shame to Mexicans and only in the 20th century have the two nations been more friendly.

13. E

As a result of the Gold Rush, California grew in population and sought to be admitted as a free state. The problem was that the admission of California as a free state would have upset the balance between slave and free states, which had been carefully maintained since 1820. If California were to be admitted, the free states, which already had a majority in the House of Representatives, would gain a majority in the Senate as well. In the Compromise of 1850, the South received a strong fugitive slave law (that required runaway slaves living in the North to be returned to their masters) in return for the admission of California as a free state. The Compromise of 1850, worked out by Henry Clay, also ended the slave trade—but not slavery—in the District of Columbia, and opened New Mexico and Utah to settlement with no restrictions on slavery.

14. C

Members of the anti-immigration American Party were instructed to keep party activities secret. When asked about party activities, they claimed to "know nothing," which became the common term for the party. It opposed immigration, especially the growing Catholic immigration from Ireland, believing that this immigration threatened the character of America.

15. A

The Kansas-Nebraska Act, passed in 1854, incorporated the idea of popular sovereignty: whether a state became a free or slave state would be determined democratically by the settlers at the time of the admission of the state into the Union. This allowed both slaveholders and abolitionists

to settle in the territory in the hope that their side would prevail. In practice, this led to armed conflict in Kansas between the two sides.

16. E

Gold and silver 'fever' was caught by tens of thousands of people who made their way west with dreams of quick wealth. The gold strikes in Leadville, Colorado and Sutter's Mill in California helped inspire many people to head west.

17. E

The Union first tried to pay for the war through taxes, but when that was seen as too slow it started printing more money. Bonds were also sold to investors on the promise of repayment after the war.

18. B

The doctrine of popular sovereignty, embodied in the Kansas-Nebraska Act, encouraged both sides—slaveholders (with their slaves) and abolitionists—to settle in Kansas in the hope that their side would prevail when it came time for the settlers to decide whether Kansas would be a free or slave state. In practice this was a recipe for armed conflict. Bloody fighting broke out between the two sides in the 1850s and Bleeding Kansas became a dress rehearsal of the coming Civil War.

19. A

Commonly during war, business investments tend to do well. Losses on Wall Street on the stock and bond exchange were rare during the war and many fortunes were made.

20. C

The Dred Scott case was a test of whether slavery could exist in non-slave states. Dred Scott sued for his freedom because he had moved with his master to the Wisconsin Territory. If he was still legally a slave, then it followed that slavery was not limited to the South. When the Supreme Court ruled that he was not a citizen and could not even bring his case to court, it created fears that slavery had the potential to expand beyond the 'slave states' at the time.

KAPLAN
Test Prep and Admissions

ANALYSES OF THE FREE-RESPONSE ESSAYS

Question 1:

"The Civil War was fought not over slavery but for the right of a state to leave the Union." Agree or disagree with this statement.

Key Points

Agreeing with the statement: Nullification and Secession arguments

- Jefferson was the original advocate of states' rights in U.S. history as he favored a weak central government
- The Kentucky Resolutions of 1799 stated that a state could ignore a federal law
- During the Tariff debates of the late 1820s, the southerners had used the 'nullification' theory as a threat to ignore an Act of Congress
- South Carolina was the hotbed of nullification sentiment and adopted an ordinance of nullification in 1832
- Lincoln stated from the start that 'secession' was illegal under the U.S. Constitution and this was why the war was forced upon him

Disagreeing with the statement: The slavery argument

- Slavery had been a divisive political issue since before Independence in 1781
- Sectionalism had increased during the Jacksonian Era
- The South had evolved into a distinct subculture and economy with slavery as one of its cornerstones
- The abolition movement had gathered strength after 1840 which threatened the Southern way of life
- *Uncle Tom's Cabin* by Stowe portrayed slavery as inhuman
- Congress had dealt with the issue of slavery in the territories and newly created states since 1820
- Compromises of 1820 and 1850
- The Dred Scott decision of 1854 further fueled the slavery controversy
- The Republican party was formed in 1854 which openly opposed the expansion of slavery
- John Brown's raid in the South made southerners even more defensive about anti-slavery sentiment emanating from the North

Main Personalities associated with both sides

States' Rights: Nullification	Proponents of Abolition
Jefferson, Madison	Washington (freed slaves upon his death)
Hayne in the Webster-Hayne debate	John Adams, John Quincy Adams
Calhoun	Garrison, Emerson
Jefferson Davis	Lincoln

Scoring Rubric

There are five scoring ranges:

Excellent

The answer must have a strong, clear thesis that either agrees or disagrees with the statement about why the Civil War was fought. The writer must have a firm grasp of the states' rights debate from the early years of U.S. history. The quality of the writing should be excellent, the answer must show logical patterns, and the student should include many of the major points in the above list (though they may go beyond the list). The organization should be clear. The answer may contain minor errors.

Very Good

The answer must have a thesis that suggests either slavery or the right of a state to secede from the Union was the primary cause of the war. Organization of the answer must show logical patterns, and the student should include many of the specific points from the above list.

Adequate

The answer must try to make some argument and must include at least some of the points listed above. There may be flaws in the thesis argument.

Flawed

The answer will demonstrate serious weaknesses. It may have no thesis argument at all, and it will include few of the points listed above. The answer will show little understanding of the states' rights issue or why the Civil War was fought.

Severely Flawed

The answer will demonstrate almost no attempt to answer the question, and will include very few, if any, of the points listed above.

Question 2:

What economic challenges faced the Confederate States of America during the American Civil War of 1861–1865?

Key Points

Economic realities for the Confederate States of America (C.S.A.)

- A weak central government that had to ask Confederate States for revenues
- A small industrial base which yielded little tax revenue
- Revenues were never able to keep up with war costs
- The South had to fight the war on the cheap; Lee's army often had to live off the land

Fiscal dilemmas faced by the C.S.A.

- Confederate paper money was not backed by gold
- The C.S.A. was forced to print its own money to pay for the war which led to inflation
- After Gettysburg the Confederate dollar was worth about 1.5 cents
- Income from excise taxes and bond sales never paid for more than 15 percent of the war
- The cotton trade with England was largely stopped by the Union naval blockade of southern ports

Foreign relations and financial aid for the C.S.A.

- France made a substantial loan to the Confederacy during the Reign of Napoleon III
- Britain gave some tacit help in building Confederate war ships and recognized the 'belligerency' of the C.S.A.

Scoring Rubric

There are five scoring ranges:

Excellent

The answer must have a strong, clear thesis that gives an assessment of the difficulties the South faced in financing the war. The essay should focus on efforts of the Richmond government to pay for the war. The quality of the writing should be excellent, the answer must show logical patterns, and the student should include many of the major points in the above list (though they may go beyond these points). The organization should be clear. The answer may contain minor errors.

Very Good

The answer must have a thesis that details the financial challenges faced by Jefferson Davis and his government from secession to Appomattox. The answer must be logically organized, and the student should include many of the specific points from the above list.

Adequate

The answer must try to make some argument and must include at least some of the points listed above. There may be flaws in the thesis argument.

Flawed

The answer will demonstrate serious weaknesses. It may have no thesis argument at all, and it will include few of the points listed above. The answer will show little understanding of the realities of managing a wartime economy in the context of the 1860s.

Severely Flawed

The answer will demonstrate almost no attempt to answer the question, and will include very few, if any, of the points listed above.

KAPLAN
Test Prep and Admissions

Chapter Eight: **Industrialization**

- Timeline: 1862–1901

- Industrial Development

- The New South and New West

- Multiple-Choice Questions

- Essay Question

- Answer Key

- Answers and Explanations

- Analysis of the DBQ

TIMELINE: 1862–1901

1862–1890	Indian wars.
1864	Colonel John Chivington's massacre of Cheyennes at Sand Creek in Colorado.
1869	First transcontinental railroad completed.
1870	John D. Rockefeller incorporates Standard Oil.
1874	Gold discovered in the Black Hills in South Dakota.
1876	Battle of Little Bighorn; George Custer becomes a legend after his complete defeat by Sioux confederation.
1876	Alexander Graham Bell patents telephone.
1877	Massive railroad strikes across the country.
1878	"Exodusters" begin migration from South to western plains.
1878	Knights of Labor becomes national organization.
1881	Helen Hunt Jackson publishes *A Century of Dishonor*.
1883	The Supreme Court's ruling in the Civil Rights Cases establishes constitutionality of segregation or discrimination by corporations or individuals.
1886	Haymarket Affair in Chicago.

KAPLAN
Test Prep and Admissions

1886	American Federation of Labor becomes national presence under leadership of Samuel L. Gompers.
1887	Dawes Act allows president to break Native American reservations into individual allotments.
1888	Edison's General Electric company created.
1889	Andrew Carnegie publishes the "Gospel of Wealth."
1890	Mississippi disenfranchisement convention establishes pattern for South.
1890	Sherman Antitrust Act passed.
1890	Ghost Dance massacre at Wounded Knee.
1892	Homestead strike.
1893	Frederick Jackson Turner presents "The Significance of the Frontier in American History" at Chicago's Columbian Exposition.
1894	Pullman strike.
1895	Booker T. Washington speaks at Atlanta Cotton States and International Exposition.
1896	The Supreme Court's ruling in *Plessy v. Ferguson* establishes constitutionality of segregation by state law.
1901	J. P. Morgan buys Carnegie's steel holdings.

INDUSTRIAL DEVELOPMENT

The industrial age came to the United States in a rush; the transformation was evident in several areas. The railroads, working to connect the continent in spite of the Civil War, had achieved success at Promontory Point, Utah, on May 10, 1869. As the symbolic golden spike was hammered into the last railroad tie, plans were already in place to build more lines across the country. By 1893, there would be four such routes connecting the West to the rest of the country, creating one great national market. War veterans, the Irish, and over 6,000 Chinese immigrants provided the primary manpower for the construction of the railroads through the mountain passes.

The railroads combined entrepreneurial spirit with capital, technological advances, a ready labor pool, and government support for the nation's first big business; mileage increased from 35,000 miles in 1865 to 199,000 miles in 1900. The development of the network of rails did more for the development of economic life in America than any other single invention. Railroads made it possible for a national market to grow and this new, expanded market made possible other economic refinements such as mass production. The availability of products encouraged mass consumption; the economy was moving ahead.

All this prosperity was made possible, in part, by new business practices. Andrew Carnegie pioneered vertical integration, whereby a company controls every stage of the process, from mining raw materials to delivering the finished product. Standard Oil and John D. Rockefeller illustrate horizontal integration, whereby companies that previously competed are brought under the control of one corporate head. Rockefeller and his board of trustees controlled 90 percent of the oil refinery business.

All the industrialists were not hardened men. Andrew Carnegie was an exception in that he came to this country at the age of 12, reportedly with thirty-five cents in his pocket. Through hard work he became the owner of United States Steel. He retired in order to devote himself to philanthropic pursuits. In his most famous article, "Wealth," which outlined what came to be known as the "Gospel of Wealth," Carnegie wrote that the wealthy had a "God-given" responsibility to carry out projects that benefited everyone (civic philanthropy).

Most of this wealth was controlled by a few, the "robber barons." The richest 10 percent controlled nine-tenths of the nation's wealth. The industrialists had the ability to dictate to their workers the pay and working conditions. Most American workers were wage earners working ten hours a day, six days a week. Working conditions were poor, but since there was so much competition for even the most menial jobs, management held the advantage. When workers went on strike there were several tactics that could be employed to break the strike. The lockout closed the factory; blacklists could be circulated; yellow-dog contract signatures held workers to the promise not to join a union; private guards had their uses; and court injunctions could be issued against strikes.

The first major strike, in 1877, was against the railroads. When the Baltimore and Ohio cut wages to reduce costs, the strike spread quickly and shut down two-thirds of the system across the country. A half million workers from other industries joined as well. President Rutherford B. Hayes had to use federal troops to put a stop to the violence, but not before 100 had died.

Labor unions, as organizations, had been originally created as craft unions. The National Labor Union was the first attempt to organize all types of workers—skilled and unskilled, agricultural and industrial. Founded in 1866, the union worked for higher wages, an eight-hour day, and a host of social programs such as equal pay for women and African Americans and workers' cooperatives. Its major accomplishment was winning an eight-hour day for federal government workers.

The Knights of Labor was the second national labor union to be established. The union was idealistic and encouraged the membership of all workers, including women and African Americans. The Knights of Labor lost both members and popularity after the Haymarket Riot, which occurred when fighting broke out between striking workers and strikebreakers at a workers meeting in Haymarket, Illinois. Seven policemen were killed in an explosion and two union men were shot by police.

The American Federation of Labor (originally an association of 25 craft unions) was led by Samuel Gompers. From 1886–1924, Gompers led the effort for higher wages and improved working conditions. He told his local unions to walk out until employers agreed to negotiate through collective bargaining. Although the union would become the nation's largest, it would not achieve major successes until the early part of the 20th century.

American Federation of Labor

This labor organization concentrated its efforts on the practical. Originally an association of 25 craft unions, the AF of L did not want to remake society. Samuel Gompers, the leader from 1886–1924, went after such basic goals as higher wages and improved working conditions. He directed his local unions to walk out until employers agreed to negotiate new contracts through collective bargaining.

Alexander Graham Bell

A teacher of the deaf, his original goal in 1876 was to invent a machine that would help the deaf to hear; his wife and mother were both deaf. He ended up inventing the telephone. He called to his assistant the famous words: "Mr. Watson, come here, I want you." His words carried through the amplifier.

Andrew Carnegie

He came to the U.S. from Scotland in the 1850s and started earning money by delivering telegrams. Through a combination of salesmanship and the use of the latest technology, he used vertical integration to make Carnegie Steel the largest producer in the United States. He sold out in 1900 for $500 million to J. P. Morgan to devote himself to philanthropic work. United States Steel became the first billion-dollar company.

Eugene V. Debs

Debs would lead the American Railroad Union during the Pullman Strike. After being jailed and serving a six-month sentence for ignoring a federal court injunction requiring an ending to the strike, he decided that more radical solutions were needed to solve the labor problems. He turned to Socialism and founded the Socialist Party of America.

Thomas Edison

Edison was possibly the greatest inventor of the 19th century; his 1869 patent for a machine to count votes was the first of over 1,000 patents he would receive. His research laboratory was the first place where mechanics and engineers worked as a team. Established in 1876 in Menlo Park, New Jersey, it may be his greatest legacy. Edison's inventions include the phonograph, the incandescent lamp, a dynamo for generating electrical power, a mimeograph, and the motion picture camera.

Samuel Gompers

Gompers was the leader of the American Federation of Labor from 1886–1924. He was instrumental in establishing some of the practices utilized by labor unions today, including the walkout, the strike, and the negotiation of contracts through collective bargaining.

"Gospel of Wealth"

Andrew Carnegie wrote in his article "Wealth" that the wealthy had a God-given responsibility to practice philanthropy. This belief became known as the "Gospel of Wealth." Carnegie distributed over $350 million of his estate to support the building of libraries, universities, and public institutions.

Great Railroad Strike of 1877

This was one of the most violent labor strikes, which began when the railroad companies cut wages to reduce costs during an economic depression. The strike began on the Baltimore and Ohio Railroad and quickly spread across the country. President Hayes had to call out federal troops to end the violence, but not before more than 100 people were killed. After the strike, some employers addressed the grievances by raising wages and improving working conditions; others took a harder line and busted the workers' organizations.

Haymarket Affair

Workers at Chicago's McCormick Harvester plant met on May 4, 1886 in Haymarket Square. As police came to break up the meeting, someone threw a bomb that killed seven police officers. The bomb thrower was never found, but seven anarchists, a large group of whom lived in the Chicago area, were sentenced to death. Many Americans came to believe the union movement was radical and violent, and the Knights of Labor lost popularity and membership.

Homestead Strike

The manager of Carnegie's Homestead Steel plant cut wages by almost 20 percent and probably incited the 1892 strike. Henry Clay Frick used the lockout, private guards, and strikebreakers to defeat the steelworkers' walkout after five months. This failure set the union movement back until the 1930s.

Industrial Workers of the World

The Wobblies, as they came to be called, began among mineworkers in Butte, Montana. Their ultimate goal was called "syndicalism," the destruction of the state and its replacement by one big union.

Knights of Labor

This was the second of the labor unions established first as a secret society. Led by Terence Powderly, it went public in 1881. The union opened its membership to all workers, including African Americans and women. It advocated a number of reforms: worker cooperatives, abolition of child labor, and the abolition of trusts and monopolies. Powderly advocated settling labor problems through arbitration rather than strikes. The Knights would lose their popularity after the Haymarket Riot in Chicago in 1886.

Molly Maguires

Taking their name from an Irish patriot who had fought against the British, these miners were provoked by their brutal treatment and the miserable conditions in the mines. In the 1870s these workers used intimidation, beatings, and killings to right perceived wrongs against the Irish workers in the eastern Pennsylvania coal mines. Some later evidence suggests that mine operators themselves instigated the violence. Pinkerton detectives infiltrated the group; 24 Molly Maguires were tried and 10 were hanged.

J. P. Morgan

Morgan was a wealthy investment banker who bought corporate stocks and bonds wholesale and sold them for a profit. He realized early that railroads were the key to a prosperous economy. He was convinced that the stability brought on by his involvement in an industry helped the economy and the public. His greatest achievement was the consolidation of the steel industry. He created the first billion-dollar corporation, an achievement in itself but helped along by the lack of an income tax at the time.

Pullman Strike

In 1894 George Pullman (Pullman railroad cars) cut wages and fired the leaders of the workers' delegation that came to bargain with him. The workers put down their tools and asked Eugene V. Debs, the leader of the American Railroad Union, to help. Debs directed railroad workers not to handle any trains with Pullman cars, and the boycott tied up rail transportation across the country. Railroad owners appealed to President Grover Cleveland. A federal court issued an injunction against interfering with the delivery of the mail and ordered the workers to give up the strike. For failing to respond, Debs and other union leaders were jailed, thus effectively ending the strike. In its ruling on the case in 1895, the Supreme Court approved the use of court injunctions against strikes.

John D. Rockefeller

Rockefeller began to build his empire in the oil refinery business in 1863. He used technology and efficiency to grow. After gaining control of many of the oil refineries, he used his monopolistic power for activities such as forcing the railroad to issue rebates and cutting kerosene prices to drive the competition out of business. His empire was valued at $900 million at his retirement.

Sears and Roebuck

Richard Sears and Alvah Roebuck began offering a variety of goods by mail in the early 1890s. Their ability to buy in volume meant they could offer goods at prices below those offered in rural general stores. The company also advertised fast service and by 1907 it was one of the largest businesses in the country. The Sears catalog helped create a national market. Families on farms and in small towns could now buy products through the catalog and rural free delivery mail.

Social Darwinism

Charles Darwin's theory of natural selection was applied to the business world. Herbert Spencer, the English philosopher, concluded that the concentration of wealth in the hands of the "fit" was a benefit to the human race. Survival of the fittest would lead to a better and brighter human race.

socialism

This philosophy advocated collective ownership; Marxism was one example. The Socialist Party of America, founded by Eugene V. Debs, was dedicated to working for the welfare of the working class. The platform called for radical reforms, such as public ownership of the railroads, utilities, and even major industries such as oil and steel.

Standard Oil

In 1863, John D. Rockefeller founded a company that became the leader in the oil refinery business. By utilizing the latest technologies and cutthroat business practices, Standard Oil grew into the largest oil company, controlling 90 percent of the business. As a result of his monopolistic power in the oil refinery business, he could cut prices to drive competitors out of business and demand rebates from the railroads.

Transcontinental Railroad

Congress authorized grants and loans for building a transcontinental railroad connecting California and the rest of the Union during the Civil War. The task was completed on May 10, 1869 at Promontory Point, Utah. By 1900, there were four other transcontinental railroads, three completed in 1883 and the fourth in 1893. All were built with federal help with the exception of James Hill's Great Northern Railroad, connecting St. Paul and Seattle.

trusts

The first instance of a large monopolistic trust was Standard Oil Trust, the 1881 company that John D. Rockefeller organized which controlled 90 percent of the oil refinery business. The trust consisted of various companies, all managed by a board of trustees that Rockefeller controlled. This represented the horizontal integration of an industry, whereby all the former competitors were brought under a single corporate name.

vertical integration

A new business strategy by which a company would control every step of the industrial process, from mining the raw materials to delivering the finished product. Carnegie first used this strategy to grow his steel company into an employer of more than 20,000.

THE NEW SOUTH AND NEW WEST

The task of rebuilding the United States after the Civil War was monumental. In every direction the country seemed to be growing. But there were major problems to overcome in both the West and the South. In the West, the Homestead Act encouraged colonization by offering plots of 160 acres to the person or family that would settle there and stay for at least five years. Responding to the opportunity to farm their own land were thousands of immigrants. The influx of settlers placed great pressure on the occupants of the Great Plains, the Native Americans. The buffalo, on which the Native Americans depended, were hunted to near extinction. The tribes realized their cultures were endangered. Then the Dawes Act tried to "civilize" the tribes—or eliminate their tribal organization entirely. Several Native American leaders tried to remove themselves and their tribes from the onslaught. Chief Joseph tried to lead the Nez Percé to Canada, but surrendered to authorities in 1877; Chief Crazy Horse annihilated General Custer at Little Big Horn. Native Americans would make their final stand at Wounded Knee. Fearing an uprising through a new faith dubbed by whites as the Ghost Dance Religion, U.S. Army officials fired upon Native Americans and killed over 200.

In the South, leaders had ideas to create a self-reliant economy built on modern ideas, industrial growth, and the installation of miles of railroad track. There were all sorts of incentives to make the vision a reality. Local governments offered tax exemptions to new industries, and the textile industry moved south encouraged by cheap (low wage) labor rates. By 1900 there were 400 cotton mills employing almost 100,000.

Despite the progress, the South remained primarily an agricultural area. Northern financing had dominated much of the southern economy before the Civil War, and that continued to be the pattern; investors from the North collected most of the profits. The North was not the "bad guy" in this pattern. Decisions over the long-term in the South contributed to the slow recovery. The South was the last area of industrialization because it had a largely uneducated workforce. Having failed to invest in technical and engineering schools, there were few trained in the skills that were needed for industrial development. In addition, political leadership provided little support for education. Without adequate training, the southern workforce was unready to take advantage of economic opportunities.

Commentators abounded. Booker T. Washington and W. E. B. DuBois represented the two viewpoints regarding African American progress, or the lack of it, in the South. Washington taught the virtues of hard work and earning money, believing these virtues would empower African Americans. He advocated compliance, saying in a speech in Atlanta in 1895 that: "...the agitation of the questions of social equality is the extremest folly." DuBois suggested Washington was willing to settle for too little, that African Americans should strive not only for economic freedom but also to develop leaders willing to challenge the laws of segregation.

The segregation in the South would last well into the mid-20th century. Jim Crow laws, passed after Reconstruction ended in 1877, did nothing to advance the case of African Americans; they served only to maintain the status quo. The Supreme Court would support the segregation through its *Plessy v. Ferguson* decision, which would not be overturned for almost 60 years. Other groups would experience the effects of segregation as well. Native Americans barely survived the assault on their culture and their way of life. Millions of immigrants flooded this country and remained on the lowest rungs of the economic ladder. In spite of the obstacles, however, the country continued to grow and prosper and all things seemed possible.

Battle of Little Bighorn

A battle during the Red River War in which the Comanche and Sioux attacked the whites. Before they were defeated, the Sioux ambushed and destroyed General George Armstrong Custer's cavalry unit in retaliation for a massacre of primarily women and children a few weeks previous. The only American survivor of the battle was Custer's horse, who lived out the rest of his days in comfort.

Battle of Wounded Knee

In December 1890, over 200 Native Americans were gunned down by the U.S. Army in the "battle" (massacre) at Wounded Knee in South Dakota. This was the last instance of resistance by Native Americans to white domination and efforts to move them from their ancestral lands. The Native American leader, Sitting Bull, had been killed during an effort to suppress the movement.

buffalo soldiers

Congress passed legislation right after the Civil War authorizing two "colored" cavalry units. Sent to the western frontier, the units built and maintained forts, mapped areas of the Southwest, ran miles of telegraph lines, and protected railroad crews. They were nicknamed "buffalo soldiers" by the Native Americans. Eighteen won congressional Medals of Honor for their service.

A Century of Dishonor (1881)

Helen Hunt Jackson chronicled the injustices done to Native Americans. Although the book created sympathy for the Native Americans, most suggestions for help incorporated assimilation as the solution. Schools were established that stressed formal education, segregating Native American children from their culture and teaching them farming and industrial skills.

crop lien system

One of several methods of tilling land in the South after the Civil War. Country merchants furnished supplies to small farmers in return for liens (mortgages) on their crops. This created a cycle of perennial debt. The merchant charged interest on the debt and required his farmers to grow a cash crop that could be readily sold at harvest time.

Dawes Severalty Act

This 1887 legislation was designed to break up the tribal organizations of Native Americans and to make them "civilized" and "law-abiding." The Dawes Act divided lands into plots of 160 acres or less (the Homestead Act's acreage). U.S. citizenship was granted to those who stayed on the land for 25 years and assimilated into a "civilized life."

disenfranchisement

The process of creating barriers for groups to make them unable in practice, if not in theory, to participate in the political process, particularly voting. Although the 15th Amendment granted all races the right to vote, many states in the South made voter participation a difficult or even fearful experience for African Americans.

W. E. B. DuBois

As Booker T. Washington's critic, DuBois demanded that disenfranchisement and legalized segregation cease and that the laws be enforced. With a Ph.D. in history from Harvard and teaching experience, DuBois said education for African Americans should be more than vocational in nature; it should develop leaders willing to work towards desegregation and ending discrimination.

Homestead Act

The 1862 legislation encouraged the settlement of the western plains by giving away 160 acres of public free land to anyone who built a 12′ × 12′ structure and settled on it for five years. The railroads found a loophole in the law and acquired thousands of acres. Thousands of acres were dotted with 12′ × 12′ structures. About 500,000 immigrant families took advantage of the offer between 1870 and 1900.

Indian wars

The white settlement of the Great Plains was the invasion of the lands of the Native Americans, their homeland and source of their livelihood. The Indian wars saw instances of fighting from 1864 (Colorado militia massacred a Cheyenne camp of men, women, and children) through the 1870s. The Native Americans made several stands: Chief Joseph trying to lead his Nez Percé to Canada and ultimately surrendering in 1877; the Red River War led by Sitting Bull and Crazy Horse; and the massacre at Little Big Horn. The last confrontation was the Battle of Wounded Knee.

Jim Crow

African Americans faced disenfranchisement in the South in spite of the 13th, 14th, and 15th Amendments. Jim Crow laws were instituted to restrain African Americans from participating in the political process. Named for the minstrel character of the 1830s, these laws promoted racial segregation in all aspects of life, beginning first with railroad cars. The laws required segregated washrooms, drinking fountains, park benches, and most other public facilities. Only the use of the streets and stores were unrestricted.

manumission

This term refers to the formal emancipation from slavery.

New South

After the Civil War, some southerners advertised a new vision of the South with a self-sufficient economy built on modern capitalistic values, industrial growth, and improved transportation. Local governments helped to encourage the economy by offering tax exemptions to investors. Cheap labor was another incentive for industry to move south.

Plessy v. Ferguson

The 1896 landmark Supreme Court case that upheld a Louisiana law mandating "separate but equal" facilities for white and African American passengers on the railroad; the Court said that the law did not violate the 14th Amendment's "equal protection" clause. This doctrine was expanded to justify separate facilities throughout the South.

sharecropping

One of the methods of farming land in the South that was developed to promote self-sufficiency. The sharecropper offered his labor in return for supplies and a share of the crop, usually about half. There were many variations that ranged from cash rental to almost slavery. The system was inefficient because the tenant had no incentive to care for the land and the owner had little chance to supervise the work.

Frederick Jackson Turner

Historian author of the influential 1893 essay, "The Significance of the Frontier in American History." Turner developed the thesis that the 300 years of the American frontier had played a fundamental role in the development of the country. The presence of a frontier had produced independence and individualism in Americans. He also suggested that the challenges of the frontier had produced Americans who were practical and inventive. The closing of the frontier was troubling to Turner, he saw it as a "safety valve" for releasing the discontented to a new life.

Booker T. Washington

Washington was a former slave who graduated from Hampton Institute. In 1881, he founded an industrial and agricultural school at Tuskegee, Alabama, that would become the largest and best known school for African Americans in the South. His mission, he said, was to teach African Americans a skill, the virtues of hard work, moderation, and economic self-help. He preached racial harmony and economic cooperation. His position of racial peace would give later civil rights leaders cause to criticize him.

KAPLAN
Test Prep and Admissions

MULTIPLE-CHOICE QUESTIONS

1. The establishment of trusts in the post Civil War period is best explained as the result of:

    (A) the expansion of the railroads and continued settlement of the West.

    (B) the application of mass production techniques in factories.

    (C) the prevalence of intense competition between companies that produced goods and services.

    (D) government policies encouraging monopolistic practices.

    (E) the demands for cheaper shares by investors.

2. In the case of *Plessy v. Ferguson*, the Supreme Court:

    (A) ruled that a federal civil rights act could not extend to individual action.

    (B) declared that "grandfather clauses" were constitutional.

    (C) upheld a Louisiana segregation law.

    (D) decided that segregation on railroad cars was illegal under the 14th Amendment.

    (E) ruled that the 14th Amendment's guarantee of "equal protection of the laws" applied to private businesses.

3. Which industries did labor find most difficult to organize in the late 19th century?

    (A) Those that depended on skilled labor such as steel

    (B) Those that employed large numbers of foreign-born workers

    (C) Those engaged in large scale exports to other countries

    (D) Those that depended on a protective tariff

    (E) Those that provided benefits such as health care to the workers

4. Which did NOT contribute to the expansion of farm production from 1870–1890?

    (A) Establishment of land grant colleges

    (B) Federal loans to agricultural cooperatives

    (C) Transportation subsidies

    (D) Liberal land policy

    (E) Increase in population

5. One reason for the lagging industrialization of the New South from the 1870s to the 1890s was:

    (A) the lack of tax incentives by the state governments.

    (B) the logging boom that took place after the war.

    (C) the continued reliance on cotton as a cash crop.

    (D) a large undereducated and unskilled workforce.

    (E) a surplus of investment capital.

6. The massacre at Wounded Knee in 1890 was the:

    (A) result of gold being discovered in the Utah territory.

    (B) work of Geronimo and his Apache bands in the Southwest.

    (C) beginning of a decade of Indian wars in the West.

    (D) last armed resistance by Native Americans towards the U.S. government.

    (E) final battle fought by the Nez Percé under Chie

KAPLAN
Test Prep and Admissions

7. Who said that African Americans should concentrate their efforts "upon the everyday practical things of life, upon something that is needed to be done, and something which they will be permitted to do in the community in which they reside"?

   (A) Benjamin "Pap" Singleton

   (B) Booker T. Washington

   (C) Eugene V. Debs

   (D) Supreme Court Justice John Marshall Harlan

   (E) W. E. B. DuBois

8. The major strikes in the latter part of the 19th century show that the:

   (A) public did not generally support the unions in their effort to establish themselves.

   (B) use of violence to break the strikes was becoming less necessary.

   (C) strikers were usually successful in winning their demands.

   (D) federal government's intervention usually benefited the employers, not the workers.

   (E) workers only wanted higher wages.

9. Which contributed most to the growth of 'big business' in the United States?

   (A) Growing support for the unions in the late 19th century

   (B) The 14th Amendment

   (C) The growth of government regulation after the Civil War

   (D) The 16th Amendment

   (E) The Sherman Antitrust act

10. In 1896 a business entrepreneur engaged in the manufacture of steel would probably NOT share a bankers view on:

    (A) interest rates.

    (B) raising the protective tariff on textiles.

    (C) the Populist movement in the West.

    (D) trust busting in the Democratic party.

    (E) the gold standard.

11. The American Federation of Labor:

    (A) encouraged minorities and women to join.

    (B) was the first labor union established in the United States.

    (C) called to end the capitalist system.

    (D) was concerned more with concrete economic gains than with social or political reforms.

    (E) excluded craft unions until 1948.

12. Social Darwinism would most likely be supported by:

    (A) Irish immigrants.

    (B) the well educated middle class.

    (C) Chinese railroad workers.

    (D) the wealthy business class.

    (E) African Americans.

13. Which of the following was a consequence of the shift to sharecropping and the crop lien system in the post Civil War South?

    (A) Unemployed farmers in Georgia and Alabama

    (B) A significant rise in cotton production per acre

    (C) A cycle of debt and depression for Southern tenant farmers

    (D) A more diversified economy

    (E) A major redistribution of land ownership

14. Helen Hunt Jackson's *A Century of Dishonor* was significant because it aroused public awareness of the:

    (A) plight of sharecroppers in the deep South.

    (B) range wars between cattlemen and farmers in the West.

    (C) wrongs inflicted on Native Americans by the U.S. government.

    (D) need for reform of government land policies.

    (E) injustice of the treaty of Guadalupe Hidalgo.

15. The popularity of the doctrine of anarchism in the late 19th century stemmed in part from:

    (A) socialistic ideas and tensions between labor and management.

    (B) transplanted fascism from southern Europe.

    (C) government regulation of factories.

    (D) the success of the robber barons.

    (E) the Knights of Labor organization.

16. Which of the following would most likely have been in favor of Jim Crow laws?

    (A) Chinese immigrants

    (B) Poor whites in the South

    (C) Southern Republicans

    (D) Miners during the Gold Rush

    (E) African Americans

KAPLAN
Test Prep and Admissions

ESSAY QUESTION

Document-Based Question (DBQ):

"Americans have always worshipped success in the business world."

Agree or disagree with the above statement in the context of the late 1800s.

Use evidence from the documents **and** your knowledge of the period from 1865 to 1900 to compose your answer.

Document A

Andrew Carnegie's "Gospel of Wealth" (1889):

"This, then, is held to be the duty of the man of wealth: first, to set an example of modest, unostentatious living, shunning display or extravagance; to provide moderately for those dependent upon him; and after doing so to consider all surplus finds which come to him as trust funds, which he is called upon to administer. These must be looked after in a manner, which in his judgement, is best calculated to produce the most beneficial results for the community. A man of wealth thus becomes a mere agent and trustee for his poorer brethren, bringing to their service his superior wisdom, experience, and ability to administer, doing for them better than they could do for themselves. . . ."

Document B

Mr. Dunne in the *The Nation*, 1901:

"Mr. Carnegie's philosophy is perfectly simple, and it is stated clearly and forcibly. He holds first that the present competitive system, which necessarily creates millionaires, or allows men to get rich, is essential to progress, and should not be altered. Secondly, rich men should not leave their fortunes to their children, because their children will be demoralized by having money to spend which they have not earned. Thirdly, rich men should not indulge in luxury. Fourthly, they should dispose of their wealth while living, or the government should confiscate them at their death."

Document C

Rev. Conwell preaching in 1900:

"You have no right to be poor. It is your duty to be rich.

Oh I know well that there are some things higher than money. Ah yes there are some things sweeter and holier than gold! Yet I also know that there is not one of these things but is greatly enhanced by the use of money.

'Oh,' you will say, 'Mr. Conwell, can you, as a Christian teacher, tell the young people to devote their lives to making money?'

Yes I do. Three times I say, I do, I do, I do. You ought to make money. Money is power. Think how much you could do if you had money now? Money is power, and it ought to be in the hands of good men. It should be in the hands of godly men who read the Scriptures. You should be righteous and rich."

Document D

Horatio Alger, *Paul the Peddler*:

"You will want to know how I succeeded. Well, at first only moderately; but I think I had some tact in adapting myself to the different classes of persons with whom I came in contact; at any rate, I was always polite, and that helped me. So my sales increased, and I did a good thing for my employer as well as myself. He would have been glad to employ me for a series of years, but I happened to meet a traveling salesman of a New York wholesale house, who offered to obtain me a position similar to his own. As this would give me a larger field and larger profits, I accepted gladly, and so changed the nature of my employment. I became very successful. My salary was raised from time to time, till it reached five thousand dollars. I lived frugally and saved money, and at length bought an interest in the house by which I had been so long employed. I am now senior partner, and, as you may suppose, very comfortably provided for.

"Do you know why I have told you this?" asked Mr. Preston, noticing the eagerness with which Paul had listened.

"I don't know, sir; but I have been very much interested."

"It is because I like to give encouragement to boys and young men who are now situated as I used to be. I think you are a smart boy."

"Thank you, sir."

"And, though you are poor, you can lift yourself to prosperity, if you are willing to work hard enough and long enough."

"I am not afraid of work," said Paul, promptly.

ANSWER KEY

Multiple-Choice Questions

1. C
2. C
3. B
4. B
5. D
6. D
7. B
8. D
9. B
10. A
11. D
12. D
13. C
14. C
15. A
16. B

KAPLAN
Test Prep and Admissions

Answers and Explanations

1. C

The purpose of the trusts was to eliminate competition and maximize profits. The holders of controlling shares in competing firms would turn over their shares to a group of trustees in exchange for trust certificates. The elimination of competition was to boost profits and share prices.

2. C

Louisiana had passed a law requiring separate railroad cars for African Americans and whites. This was challenged and went to the Supreme Court in 1890. Homer Plessy was a man of mixed race but had been required to sit in the 'colored only' car. In the end the Supreme Court upheld the state law, saying that segregation was a state's policy not regulated by the federal government.

3. B

Differences in language and custom made it difficult to organize immigrants into labor unions. Also, many foreigners were unskilled and there was much more success in organizing skilled workers into defined groups such as machinists or cigar workers.

4. B

The federal government did not assist farmers financially until the mid 20th century. The abundance of land in the West, better education for farmers, an increase in the market due to population growth, and subsidies for the railroads all helped to stimulate farming.

5. D

The Civil War had a devastating impact on the South and it took decades for it to rebuild. One reason was the lack of a large, educated workforce. The education system in much of the South continues to lag behind the rest of the nation to this day, and hinders the economic development of some states.

6. D

The Indian wars took place from the 1860s to the 1890s after the Civil War. With famous successes such as the Battle of Little Big Horn, Native tribes incited fear among settlers who cried for the U.S. Army to protect them. Tribe after tribe were defeated and with the massacre of about 200 Natives at Wounded Knee, South Dakota, the pacification of the Native American was completed.

7. B

Washington believed African Americans must first establish themselves and then work for change when the time was right. He advised his fellow African Americans to work hard and be friendly with all races and acceptance would come in time. He generally avoided political activity and sought better education for his race.

8. D

Unions were often treated by the government as conspiracies that disrupted business and trade. The Sherman Antitrust Act of 1890 was used to deny labor unions the right to organize. Union leaders were often imprisoned at this time in history when the law favored the factory owners.

9. B

Meant to grant equal legal rights to African Americans, the 14th Amendment stated that no one can be denied 'due process' of the law. Corporations used this clause to argue that federal regulation denied them due process of the law. They claimed that the government cannot oversee business unless companies can challenge the government in court. This legal stalling tactic was used by many corporate lawyers to delay federal action in regards to business.

10. A

Low interest rates would encourage business people to buy steel with cheap borrowed money and also encourage factory expansion for the steel makers. Low rates would mean lower profits for the bankers while high interest rates would mean more money for a bank.

KAPLAN
Test Prep and Admissions

11. D

The AF of L, led by Samuel Gompers, fought for concrete economic gains for its membership. It wanted pay increases and better working conditions. This focus contributed to its success as labor fought hard for many concessions from business owners.

12. D

Charles Darwin's theory of natural selection was adapted to the business world in the late 19th century. Just as animals fought and competed in the natural world, corporations fought one another in the business setting. This 'natural' law of the jungle was not to be controlled; it reflected the way things are in the world. This was used by many as a rationalization for brutal business practices. Competition was crushed and only the strongest and most aggressive survived.

13. C

Sharecropping meant that poor farmers rented land to work in return for a possible 'share' of the harvest. Low crop prices made it difficult to pay rents or make a profit. Most sharecroppers barely made a minimal living for themselves and their families. This became a trap for many poor African Americans and whites who were never able to afford their own farms.

14. C

Like *Uncle Tom's Cabin*, the book *A Century of Dishonor* informed and provoked readers to see an injustice in the American experience. Ms. Jackson wrote the book in 1881 and underscored the dishonesty of the U.S. government in its dealings with the Natives since the 18th century.

15. A

Anarchists believed that all government was evil, and shared with socialists of the day some utopian dreams of a perfect world. A favorite tactic of anarchists was dramatic violence often in the forms of random bombings. Assassinations by anarchists also made headlines, the most notorious example being the murder of President McKinley in 1901.

16. B

In the post-war South, it was poor whites who were often the most aggressive defenders of white superiority. They were near the bottom of the economic ladder themselves, and could take some solace in the fact that African Americans were lower than they were. The Jim Crow laws were worded to keep African Americans in their 'place' and to disallow them their civil rights.

ANALYSIS OF THE DBQ

Question:

"Americans have always worshipped success in the business world."

Agree or disagree with the above statement in the context of the late 1800s.

Use evidence from the documents **and** your knowledge of the period from 1865 to 1900 to compose your answer.

Use of the Documents

Each of the documents offers a perspective on wealth in America and its effects on the country and society as a whole.

Document A is a famous book on wealth by one of the richest men of the era, Andrew Carnegie. He sees the effects of what they are doing as positive for society.

Document B is a commentary on Carnegie's philosophy in a well known magazine of the time.

Documents C and D were both authored by ministers in different denominations. In C, Rev. Conwell sees great potential in wealth controlled by Bible-reading Christians. In D, the author is a former minister who became an author of stories about boys who became successful through honest hard work. Carnegie was once such a boy who worked his way up until he controlled the steel industry in the United States.

Key points from Outside Information

Famous industrialists and their actions

- Jay Gould: a good example of the negative effects of unrestrained business activity; became enormously wealthy and contributed little to the building of the railroads

- George Westinghouse: like Edison, an inventor and businessman who developed alternating current, making possible long-distance electrical power

- John D. Rockefeller: succeeded in developing oil refining as an economically successful business, with long-term effects on power and transportation; however, his methods of driving out competitors ultimately brought government response

- Andrew Carnegie: created much personal wealth in the steel and iron industries by, like Rockefeller, driving out competition; provided thousands of jobs, shared his wealth responsibly, yet suppressed labor movement and used violence against union action at his Homestead Steel Works

- J. Pierpont Morgan: used power of his bank to fund industrial development; helped bring in European investment to help American development; became enormously powerful as a member of many companies' boards

Students could make the case that Americans have always been fascinated by the ultra-rich and yet also hold that the wealthy have a responsibility to use their money for the greater good.

KAPLAN

Test Prep and Admissions

Interesting connections

- Carnegie was an immigrant from Scotland and that was a Calvinist stronghold. Calvin believed that God wanted people to live simply and work hard. This is the foundation of the 'Protestant work ethic.' Carnegie was clearly a product of this and made a huge fortune but also did not want to make a display of his money

- Alger's books were morality tales that had a capitalistic thrust. America was the place where the poor could improve their station in life through hard work and diligence.

- Rev. Conwell is an example of many flamboyant preachers in American history who spoke to their times. The rise of rich capitalists in the 19th century made wealth a topic that people wanted to hear about. And if the church condoned success in business there was a kind of green light from God to go out and earn how ever much money you could.

Scoring Rubric

There are five scoring ranges:

Excellent

Argument: The essay must have a strong, clear thesis. The student should take a clear position either in support of or against the proposition stated in the question. The essay should also indicate a grasp of the complexity of the issue, referring to pros and cons of entrepreneurial behavior in this time period.

Critical Thought: The student should explain how each document supports or undermines the thesis. The student should address conflicts and contradictions in the evidence. Any outside information must be relevant to the argument.

Evidence: The student should use documents and outside information (see lists above) throughout the essay. Most of the documents must be used, and students might address the relationship between the sources.

Writing Style: The essay must be well organized and well written; it must make sense throughout.

Very Good

Argument: The thesis must be consistent with the question, but it may not be sufficiently focused.

Critical Thought: The answer must include an analysis of several of the documents and must incorporate outside information.

Evidence: The student should make use of the documents and outside information (see lists above) that support the position being argued. Discussion of relationships between the sources used may be limited.

Writing Style: The essay should be well organized and clearly written; it must be logical, but some points may be unclear.

Adequate

Argument: The thesis is only partially developed. It may address the question, but it does so in a way that doesn't acknowledge the question's complexity. The essay will most likely fail to prioritize the arguments.

Critical Thought: The essay is primarily descriptive or narrative, and doesn't provide an analysis of the question or of the evidence provided. It will not address all the relevant issues, and will ignore the opposing position.

Evidence: The student may paraphrase the documents and may misinterpret a document to better fit the argument. The student will use only a little outside information and may refer to some but not all of the documents. The answer may contain errors.

Writing Style: The writing and organization is unclear, but acceptable.

Flawed

Argument: The thesis will be unclear and will not be supported in the body of the essay. Use of evidence will be unclear, and the argument will be poorly developed.

Critical Thought: The essay will show only a limited understanding of the question, and will offer little or no analysis. What little analysis there is will be inaccurate. The student will show little understanding of the issue of industrialization.

Evidence: The student will not make use of the documents appropriate to their argument, and may use documents that actually support the opposing position. The use of documents will be haphazard, with references only to brief excerpts or paraphrases. There will be little outside information. The argument may contain errors.

Writing Style: The answer will be weakly organized and the writing will be unclear.

Severely Flawed

Argument: The student provides no thesis, or provides one that is not relevant to the question.

Critical Thought: The student demonstrates little or no understanding of the question.

Evidence: The student makes almost no use of the documents provided, and makes little or no use of outside information. The answer contains major errors.

Writing Style: The answer is disorganized and poorly written.

Chapter Nine: **Change and Reform**

- Timeline: 1877–1917

- Urbanization

- Political and Agricultural Reform

- The Progressive Era

- Multiple-Choice Questions

- Essay Question

- Answer Key

- Answers and Explanations

- Analysis of the DBQ

TIMELINE: 1877–1917

1870s	Immigration from southern and eastern Europe starts to increase.
1880s	Farmers' Alliance movement gathers strength, especially in South and Midwest.
1882	Chinese Exclusion Act passed.
1883	Pendleton Civil Service Reform Act passed.
1887	Interstate Commerce Commission established to regulate railroads.
1889	Jane Addams and Ellen Starr open Hull House in Chicago.
1890	National American Woman Suffrage Association founded.
1892	Ellis Island opens.
1892	Populist party founded by Farmers' Alliance supporters; wins a million votes in presidential election.
1893	American economy suffers major depression.
1893	Anti-Saloon League founded.
1896	William Jennings Bryan (Democrat with Populist endorsement) loses to William McKinley in presidential election.

c. 1900	Development of urban mass culture: amusement parks, spectator sports, vaudeville, and outdoor recreation all become popular.
1901	Theodore Roosevelt begins the first of his terms as president upon the death of McKinley.
1902	Roosevelt administration attacks Northern Securities Company as illegal monopoly.
1902	Roosevelt intervenes in anthracite coal strike.
1904	Publication of Ida Tarbell's *McClure's* series attacking Standard Oil.
1906	Upton Sinclair's *The Jungle* published.
1906	Meat Inspection and Pure Food and Drug Act passed.
1908	Supreme Court upholds 10-hour workday for women in *Muller v. Oregon*.
1911	Triangle Shirtwaist Factory fire
1912	Woodrow Wilson elected to first of two terms as president.
1913	16th and 17th Amendments (income tax and direct election of senators, respectively) ratified.
1913	Federal Reserve system established (Glass-Owen Act).
1913	Wilson pushes through tariff reform.
1914	Clayton Antitrust Act passed.
1914	Federal Trade Commission established.
1916	Keating-Owen Child Labor Act passed (later declared unconstitutional).
1917	18th Amendment (prohibition) passed by Congress; ratified in 1919.

URBANIZATION

Industrialization characterized the development of the United States in the latter part of the 19th century. The rapidly improving industrial complex needed labor, raw materials, capital, and the men to manage it. Cheap labor came in the form of thousands of immigrants each year. Chinese coming into the United States through Angel Island in the West, and eastern Europeans coming to Ellis Island in New York City, provided the bulk of the needed manpower.

Many Americans responded negatively to this influx of population. Immigrants were often willing to work for lower wages, threatening American workers who often complained that their culture was at risk. Nativist groups were founded, their mission to protect American culture and values. The settlement house movement, designed to assimilate these new immigrants to American life, provided jobs, education, and classes in being an American.

During the time, many reform movements began that would later form the Progressive movement. Women's suffrage, long a goal of many, became a focus. While Wyoming had granted suffrage to women in 1869, the eastern part of the country was less willing to agree. It was 1920 before the constitutional amendment (19th) would mandate the change.

KAPLAN
Test Prep and Admissions

More reforms were seen in the field of education. Standards changed. Schools and universities began to teach; doctors were required to actually study medicine and be certified. There was support for tax-supported public high schools that taught vocational skills and citizenship education for the changing society. Colleges saw change in that elective courses were introduced and research was emphasized. The United States began to produce scholars who could compete with those educated in Europe.

The reform movement had just begun, as subsequent years would show. Influencing societal change was not yet accepted as a legitimate role of government.

Jane Addams

Addams founded Hull house, a settlement house, in Chicago in 1889 with Ellen Starr. Workers could enroll their children in clubs, kindergarten or nursery school. Immigrants were offered health care, lectures, music and art, an employment bureau, men's clubs, and job training. She organized political support for housing laws, pensions for widowed mothers, workers' compensation laws, and legislation against child labor.

American Protective Association

One of the more prominent nativist associations, it was based in the upper Mississippi River Valley in the 1880s. The organization promoted restrictions on immigration and citizenship requirements, fought against the employment of Catholics, and supported the teaching of the "American" language in schools.

Susan B. Anthony

A veteran leader of the women's rights movement, Anthony was active in demanding the expansion of all rights to women. She argued for 14th Amendment protections for women.

Carrie Chapman Catt

A leader of the Women's Suffrage Movement, Catt followed in the footsteps of Susan B. Anthony and Elizabeth Cady Stanton.

Chinese Exclusion Act of 1882

Immigration restrictions began in the 1890s in response to the large numbers of Chinese entering the country on the West Coast. The Chinese were resented in part because they were willing to accept lower wages. The legislation of 1882 closed the door on new immigrants. The exclusions would not be eliminated until 1943.

John Dewey

Dewey believed that students learned by "doing" rather than by the rote memorization methods widely used at the time. He also supported the flexibility in education to help children prepare for a changing world.

KAPLAN
Test Prep and Admissions

Ellis Island

Opened in 1892, Ellis Island was the reception center for European immigrants. Its busiest year, 1907, saw over a million go through its doors; by the time of its closing in 1954, over 12 million had been processed there.

Morrill Act

In 1862, Congress voted support for vocational training at the college level. The legislation granted 30,000 acres to each state per representative and senator, the income of which was to be dedicated to the teaching of agricultural and mechanical arts. A second act in 1890 provided additional federal funds for education.

nativism

This anti-immigrant attitude by Americans was a reflection of concerns generated by the wave of immigration. The perception that American culture and values were threatened began as mainly anti-Catholic sentiment.

new immigration

Motivated by the promise of jobs and the threat of persecution in Europe, many immigrants came to the United States. After 1870, those from southern Europe (Latin, Slavic, and Jewish peoples) increased sharply and dominated the immigrant stream. They brought with them different cultures, religions, and languages.

Frederick Law Olmstead

Olmstead was one of the first formal designers of public spaces that incorporated natural beauty with functionality. In 1858 he designed Central Park in New York City, seeking to create a space for culture within the urban area. He also designed spaces for the cities of Boston, Philadelphia, Chicago, and San Francisco.

political machines

Political parties were the mechanism for getting elected to public office. Political machines took it one step further, controlling the entire political process from fielding a slate of candidates, to canvassing the district, to encouraging voters to participate, to reaping the rewards in the form of political patronage.

professionalization

The demand for higher learning increased after the Civil War. Colleges multiplied, elective courses were added to curriculums, and there was an increase in the number of women's colleges. The growth of professionalism and its improved standards, licensing requirements for medical school graduates, and accreditation of schools were evidence of rising standards.

settlement house movement

This effort addressed the problems of the slums. Educated workers tried to narrow the gap between newly arrived immigrants and Protestant white Americans, and to improve the lives of slum dwellers. Although the work was demanding, it was expanded to sponsoring legislation that improved conditions for all. Settlement houses provided child care, health clinics, and an employment bureau.

Social Darwinism

Charles Darwin published *On the Origin of Species* in 1859. He argued that all species go through a process of "natural selection." Those most likely to survive are those that possess quickness, shrewdness, and other advantages. Their survival over weaker individuals who die off strengthens the species. Although Darwin was writing of the natural world, many applied his ideas to human civilizations. Social Darwinism held that support for the poor and weak only weakened the human race.

social gospel

This describes the response of religion to the changing social conditions—the applying of Christian principles to social problems. Religious leaders urged their congregations to work to improve society. The Young Men's Christian Association and the Salvation Army are two examples.

Elizabeth Cady Stanton

The co-founder of the National American Woman Suffrage Association (1890), Elizabeth Cady Stanton worked to secure the vote for women with Susan B. Anthony.

Frederick Jackson Turner

Historian and author of the influential 1893 essay, "The Significance of the Frontier in American History." Turner developed the thesis that the 300 years of the American frontier had played a fundamental role in the development of the United States. The presence of a frontier, he argued, had produced independence and individualism in Americans. He also suggested that the challenges of the frontier had produced Americans who were practical and inventive. The closing of the frontier was troubling to Turner; he saw it as a "safety valve" for the discontented to find a new life.

Mark Twain

Twain wrote of life in America. Samuel Langhorne Clemens took his pen name from the call of the Mississippi River boatmen who measured the depth of the river with a lead line (a twain was six feet). He wrote pieces that would become uniquely American: *Life on the Mississippi*, *Huckleberry Finn*, and *Tom Sawyer*. Additionally, he coined the phrase that came to epitomize the latter part of the 19th century, the "Gilded Age."

urbanization

This describes the movement of millions of Americans from farms to cities. Coupled with this movement was the influx of immigrants that helped to swell the population of the urban centers, straining the services and giving rise to city areas that became known as "slums."

vaudeville

These variety shows became the staple of the entertainment world. The term comes from the French word for a play with music. The shows featured musicians, comedians, singers, blackface minstrels, animal acts, jugglers, gymnasts, dancers, mimes, and magicians. Because the shows were usually held in beer halls, they developed a "seedy" reputation; to combat that, show organizers built new theaters, banned alcoholic beverages, and upgraded performers, security, and show material.

KAPLAN
Test Prep and Admissions

Women's Suffrage Movement

The single focus of this reform movement was to expand the Constitution to include the right to vote for women. In 1869 Wyoming granted full suffrage to women, but the eastern half of the country did not readily support the idea. Not until 1920 was a constitutional amendment passed granting women's suffrage.

POLITICAL AND AGRICULTURAL REFORM

During the Gilded Age, big business and politics were hand-in-hand. Politicians thought nothing of accepting retainer fees, stock options, railroad passes, free entertainment and other favors, and their reputations were in no way injured when such were made public. Yet the voters took their responsibilities seriously, voting at the rate of 70 to 80 percent; they believed they were dealing with the critical issues of the day. Immigration, currency, civil service reform, and monopolies were all important issues.

Motivated by concern over local economic issues and cultural conflicts, the politicians and the voters had much at stake. The political effects of local, ethnic, cultural and religious backgrounds cannot be ignored. Historians now look at the Gilded Age as a complex interwoven tapestry of motivations, including economics, ethnic prejudices, cultural heritage, and religious convictions.

The most significant political activity took place at the state and local levels. For example, cities spent their own funds on social services; the federal government was not involved either from a financial or regulatory perspective.

Special interest groups played an important role in this period. The Grangers, formed to give a political voice to the farmers so isolated in the Midwest, gave way to the Alliance, which sought to merge the farmers with other reformers. Only in large groups, the organizers realized, was there sufficient power to affect the political process. Politics, it is said, is not a spectator sport.

Chester A. Arthur

He became president upon the death of Garfield. By distancing himself from the "Stalwart" faction of the Republican Party, he supported a bill reforming the civil service, the Pendleton Civil Service Act (1883), and approved the development of the modern navy. He vetoed the Chinese Exclusion Act (the veto was overridden) and also began to question the high protective tariffs. He was limited to one term.

Bland-Allison Act

This legislation required a limited expansion of silver currency through the government's purchase of $2 million to $4 million worth of silver bullion each month, which was to be coined into silver dollars. Congress would override Hayes's veto to affect passage.

William Jennings Bryan

He would gain recognition almost overnight with his "Cross of Gold" speech at the Democratic Convention in 1896. At 36, he was the youngest candidate yet to run for president. He would be hurt later by a rise in wheat prices and employers spreading fear into the hearts of their workers by saying the workers would be out of a job if Bryan were elected. William McKinley would win the presidency by 271 to 176 in the Electoral College.

Grover Cleveland

He was the only man to serve two unconnected terms as president. In his first term he implemented the new civil service system that had been passed. He vetoed hundreds of private pension bills for those claiming injury in the Civil War. He signed into law the Interstate Commerce Act (1887) as government's first try at regulating business. He also signed the Dawes Act, which was intended to help Native Americans. During his first administration, 81 million acres of government land was recovered from cattle ranchers and the railroads.

election of 1896

At 36 years of age, William Jennings Bryan made his "Cross of Gold" speech and won the Democratic nomination. The Democrats favored the unlimited coinage of silver. The Republicans nominated William McKinley, a friend of labor and a supporter of a high tariff and the gold standard.

Farmer's Alliance

The Farmer's Alliance grew as the Grangers lost favor. The Alliances offered social and recreational opportunities and emphasized political action. Women were welcomed as well.

free silver

This referred to the unlimited coinage of silver. After discoveries of silver in Nevada, the demands for the re-issuance of the coins spoke to the expansion of the money supply. Farmers, debtors, and western miners were the most insistent groups.

James A. Garfield

Garfield was the candidate nominated to replace Hayes, whose election had always been disputed. Garfield was shot by a deranged office seeker. After 11 weeks he died and Chester Arthur became president.

Gilded Age

This was the name, coined by Mark Twain, of the period between 1880 and 1900. Although the industrial complex was booming, the societal ills were merely being covered up, "gilded" over by those with economic power. The gap between the rich and poor grew; 90 percent of the wealth was controlled by less than 10 percent of the population. There was no government regulation to control any aspect of business practices.

KAPLAN
Test Prep and Admissions

Granger Movement

The Patrons of Husbandry was founded in 1867. The Grange (an old word for granary), as it came to be known, was started as a social and educational organization to combat the isolation of farmers. It would later grow to promote farmer-owned cooperatives for buying and selling. It became involved in politics through independent third parties. Its chief political goal was to regulate the rates charged by railroads.

Benjamin Harrison

Benjamin Harrison was the grandson of William Henry Harrison. He would lose the popular vote for president but win the Electoral College vote (233 to 168). He had hopes of civil service reform but would bow to party leaders. His postmaster-general (allegedly selected because of a generous campaign contribution) made thousands of changes. His Pension Commissioner was removed six months later for approving millions of dollars in questionable pension payments.

Rutherford B. Hayes

In the election of 1876, Democrat Samuel Tilden won the popular vote, but neither he nor Republican candidate, Rutherford B. Hayes, had a majority in the Electoral College. Hayes became president through agreements referred to as "backroom deals." His most significant action was to end Reconstruction in the South in 1877 by withdrawing the last of the federal troops. He did support civil service reforms and worked to end the corruption; merit appointments would pave the way for effective government. His wife, a temperance supporter, was nicknamed "Lemonade Lucy" because no alcoholic beverages were served in the White House.

Interstate Commerce Act

Passed in 1887, this act was the first attempt at federal regulation of the railroads. It created the Interstate Commerce Commission (ICC), the first independent regulatory commission. It was empowered to investigate carriers and prosecute the violators. The Commission was to make sure all rates were reasonable and just, that there was no discrimination against people, places, or commodities, and that there were no secret agreements to fix rates. When first tested in the courts, the commission's powers seemed weak. Later legislation gave more teeth to the ICC.

William McKinley

McKinley served as Chairman of the House Ways and Means Committee, raising duties on manufactured goods an average of 50 percent through the McKinley Tariff of 1890. As president he supported the industrial complex that now dominated the country. His first act was to call for a special session of Congress to raise the tariff once again. The economy flourished until the Gold Standard Act was passed in 1900. International concerns, the Spanish-American-Cuban War, finally took attention away from the issues of tariffs and currency. McKinley was assassinated in 1901 by an anarchist.

Munn v. Illinois

In 1877 the Supreme Court ruled in a case involving warehouse regulation. The Court said that a state, using its police powers, had the right to regulate property in the interest of the public good where that property was clothed with a public interest. In other words, a state could make regulations regarding private businesses.

Pendleton Civil Service Act

The legislation, passed in 1883, set up a three-member independent commission to oversee the filling of 14 percent of all government jobs through competitive exams rather than political favor. The president could enlarge the class of affected jobs, something later presidents would use to shield their own appointees.

People's Party

In 1891 delegates from farm, labor, and reform organizations joined forces to form the People's Party. The platform, agreed upon at the Omaha, Nebraska convention, would focus on financial issues, transportation issues, and the dispensation of land. It would support free and unlimited coinage of silver, and a graduated income tax.

populism

This term refers to the position of the People's Party, which adopted positions popular with workers and farmers. The party called for restrictions on railroads, free silver, an eight-hour workday, and restrictions on immigration. The Populists nominated a Union general for president and balanced the ticket with a Confederate general as the vice president. The Populists were perhaps the spoilers in the 1892 election, as Democrat Grover Cleveland defeated Republican Benjamin Harrison. In 1896, the Populists supported William Jennings Bryan for president because of his stand on the silver question.

Sherman Antitrust Act

Named for John Sherman, Chairman of the Senate Judiciary Committee, it tried to incorporate into federal law principles against "restraint of trade." The legislation forbade contracts, combinations, or conspiracies in restraint of trade or in the effort to establish monopolies in interstate or foreign commerce. The legislation was primarily symbolic; from 1890 to 1901 only 18 lawsuits were filed.

spoils system

This was the system by which the winning political party filled government jobs by dispensing them as rewards to the party faithful for their support in the campaign. Prior to civil service reform, an entirely new government could be established with every change in administration. The scandals inherent in the spoils system became apparent with the administration of General Grant.

stalwarts and half-breeds

After Reconstruction, the Republican Party was split into two factions. The stalwarts were led by Senator Roscoe Conkling of New York and the half-breeds were led by Senator James G. Blaine of Maine. The stalwarts supported President Grant, the spoils system and a radical policy with regards to the South. The half-breeds took an opposing view on Grant and the southern policy and even supported a loose form of civil service to replace the spoils system.

THE PROGRESSIVE ERA

The Progressive Era marks the beginning of the 20th century. Formed from the Populists and aided by the muckrakers, the Progressives tried to improve every aspect of American life. They tried to democratize the political process through the use of the direct primary rather than back-room politics to select candidates for office. The initiative and referendum were first adopted in many states. There was a process for the recall of elected officials in over 20 states by 1915. In 1913 the popular election of senators was established by the 17th Amendment; previously they were chosen by state legislatures.

Efficiency was another theme of the Progressives. Frederick W. Taylor developed techniques for efficiency. Scientific management promised to reduce waste, cut costs and help establish per-formance standards for each job. Although many workers saw Taylor's improvements as a way to make them work faster for the same money, some production improvements resulted. Government was also a target of efficiency studies. Identifying overlapping agencies, fixing clear lines of authority, and the ability to assign responsibilities were improvements sought by Progressives.

The Progressives also took on the problem of economic power and its abuses. They were reluc-tant to let businesses police themselves or to adopt the socialistic view of public ownership, instead trying to find a middle ground of private enterprise with government regulation. Social jus-tice was another goal. This motivated all sorts of actions, including campaigns against child labor and liquor. The settlement house movement created social workers. Labor legislation, particularly the employment of children, was documented and banned for children under a minimum age and efforts were made to improve working conditions for women.

Prohibition began to gain a following; merging the opposition to strong drink with social ethics made for a powerful political group. The evils of drink would take on mammoth proportions, and make for strange political allies. When the prohibition amendment was proposed in 1913, it took only six years for it to receive ratification.

Theodore Roosevelt, who became president in 1901 after McKinley's assassination, was young and energetic. The public appreciated his approach to government: he wanted action. In domes-tic affairs he supported the Progressives and is particularly known for setting aside millions of acres of federal lands for parks and conservation. In international affairs, he stated the Roosevelt Corollary (to the Monroe Doctrine), negotiated a peace treaty ending a war between Russia and Japan, and sent the American fleet on a round-the-world tour to demonstrate American naval power.

17th Amendment

Ratified in 1913, the amendment took the senatorial appointment power away from state legisla-tures and provided for the direct election of all future senators by popular vote.

19th Amendment

Ratified in 1920, the amendment expanded the right to vote to women. It was the culmination of a 50-year fight for women's suffrage.

anthracite coal strike (1902)

The UMW (United Mine Workers) went on strike in Pennsylvania and West Virginia demanding a 20 percent wage hike, official union recognition, and a workday that was nine hours long instead of ten. The mine operators, having granted a 10 percent wage hike two years previously, refused to comply, and shut down the mines. Theodore Roosevelt, facing a nationwide coal strike, called the sides to the White House. There was an impasse and Roosevelt threatened to run the mines with the army. The mine owners feared his threat and the loss of public support and so both sides agreed to reopen the mines and submit the issues to an arbitration commission named by Roosevelt. The miners won a partial victory with a 10 percent wage increase and a nine-hour workday but no union recognition was given.

Bull Moose campaign

In 1912, Theodore Roosevelt broke with the Republican Party of his handpicked successor, William Howard Taft, and ran for president again. He took a number of Republicans with him, split the vote and Democrat Woodrow Wilson became the next president.

Carrie Chapman Catt

Catt became head of the National Suffrage Association in 1915 and revived it with funding from Mrs. Frank Leslie, the publisher of *Leslie's Weekly*. The money was used to organize a final campaign for voting rights for women. President Wilson worked closely with organization leaders in support of an amendment. This group would become the League of Women Voters.

Child Labor Act

The 1916 resurgence of progressive ideals persuaded President Wilson to sign the Keating-Owen Child Labor Act that restricted goods manufactured by children under 14 from interstate commerce. True child labor legislation would not become a reality until the New Deal of the 1930s.

Clayton Antitrust Act

This legislation, passed in 1914, made illegal several different types of business practices. Price discrimination (charging different customers different prices), agreements that limited the right of dealings to handle the products of competing manufacturers, interlocking directorates connecting corporations with more than $1 million in capital, and the practice of corporations acquiring stock in other corporations.

Eugene V. Debs

As the leader of the American Socialist Party, Debs campaigned for workers' rights. He ran for president and received over 900,000 votes in 1912. He opposed intervention into World War I and was arrested for suggesting men refuse to serve in the military. He served 20 years in jail for encouraging draft resistance. In 1920, while still in jail, he received a million votes for president.

election of 1912

This was one of the most watched presidential elections in U.S. history. It was the height of power for the Progressives and it was the first election to use primaries. The Republicans nominated William Howard Taft for reelection and the Democratic candidate was Woodrow Wilson.

KAPLAN
Test Prep and Admissions

Other candidates included Theodore Roosevelt (Bull Moose Party) and Eugene V. Debs (Socialist Party). Wilson won but Theodore Roosevelt came in second—the strongest showing by a third party in the 20th century. Progressives abandoned the Republican party, supporting Roosevelt and Wilson and the Republican Party began to become more conservative.

Glass-Owen Federal Reserve Act

This established the Federal Reserve, a new banking system of 12 reserve banks with a central Board of Directors. Federal Reserve notes would replace silver and gold certificates. The new system addressed three problems in the financial world: Bank reserves could be pooled; currency and bank credit became more elastic; and the government became actively involved in the country's banking system.

Hepburn Act

The 1906 legislation gave the ICC the power to set maximum freight rates. While carriers could challenge the rates in court, the burden of proof was now on them rather than the ICC. The ICC's sphere of responsibility had also been widened to include other modes of interstate commerce, such as pipelines, express companies, sleeping car companies, bridges, and ferries.

initiative and referendum

These are reform procedures that allow voters to enact laws directly. The initiative requires a designated number of signatures on voters' petitions to have a measure put on a ballot. A referendum means the right of the people to vote the initiative up or down. Oregon was the first state to adopt all of the reforms.

Robert La Follette

As a governor of Wisconsin and presidential candidate, La Follette believed wholeheartedly in a grassroots democracy, in the power and judgment of the people. He was intense, sincere, and determined. He also worked for reforms such as stronger railroad regulation, the conservation of natural resources, and workman's compensation.

Mann-Elkins Act

The Mann-Elkins Act was passed in 1910. For the first time, the ICC was empowered to initiate rate changes. It also extended its regulatory power to telephone and telegraph companies and set up a commerce court to expedite appeals.

Meat Inspection Act

This 1906 legislation required federal inspection of meats headed for interstate commerce and gave officials in the agriculture Department the power to impose sanitation standards.

muckrakers

These writers thrived on scandal. They wrote exposés on Standard Oil, the meat packing industry, slum conditions, the stock market, life insurance, and politics. Jacob Riis, Lincoln Steffens, Ida Tarbell, and Upton Sinclair are some of the best known muckrakers.

Gifford Pinchot

Pinchot was Roosevelt's appointee to head the National Park Service. As a scientific forester, Pinchot worked to develop programs and public interest in conservation. He would support conservative use of resources.

Progressive Movement

This reform movement took on a multitude of forms. The goals of the Progressives were to achieve greater democracy and social justice, honest government, more effective regulation of business, and a commitment to public service. Theodore Roosevelt was the presidential version of the Progressives.

Theodore Roosevelt

Roosevelt became president upon the death of William McKinley in 1901. The youngest man to serve as president, he was a progressive reformer. He worked to gain support of party leaders in Congress and stayed away from volatile issues until he had garnered support. He took on the trusts, coal mine owners, negotiated the peace treaty for the Russo-Japanese War (Nobel Peace Prize in 1904), and worked to set aside over 55 million acres for public lands for parks and conservation. He left the presidency in 1908 at the age of 50, after the election of his vice president, William Howard Taft, as president. However, four years later in 1912, he would run again on the Bull Moose Party ticket when he felt William Howard Taft no longer represented the country.

Standard Oil breakup

President Roosevelt brought the antitrust suit that resulted in the breakup of the huge oil refining monopoly. A number of competing oil refining companies were created from Standard Oil.

Swift and Company v. U.S. (1905)

The Supreme Court created the "stream-of-commerce" doctrine, reasoning that as livestock and meat products crossed state lines, they were subject to federal regulation. This decision allowed the federal government to regulate the meat industry.

William Howard Taft

He was Roosevelt's handpicked successor for the presidency. Taft was expected to continue to set aside lands for the public and enforce government regulations. Once in office, however, Taft could not restrain the forces that pulled at every fiber of the administration. His true vocation was achieved after his presidency when he was appointed Chief Justice of the Supreme Court.

Ida Tarbell

Tarbell wrote *History of the Standard Oil Company* (1904) and saw its publication in *McClure's* magazine. This detailed account provided an unflattering treatment of the business practices of the conglomerate and led to its breakup.

The Jungle

Upton Sinclair's 1906 novel served as a shocking exposé on the meat packing industry. Roosevelt read it and immediately sent agents to Chicago to verify the charges. The resulting Meat Inspection Act and the Pure Food and Drug Act were both passed in 1906.

KAPLAN
Test Prep and Admissions

Triangle Shirtwaist Company fire

The 1911 fire caused the deaths of 146 workers, mostly women, who died because the exits of the building they were working in were locked or blocked off. The investigation that followed resulted in stricter building codes and factory inspection acts. Accident insurance and workers' compensation laws were also instituted.

Woodrow Wilson

Wilson became president after the Republicans split their votes between Theodore Roosevelt and William Howard Taft in 1912. He supported progressive ideas, advocated tariff reductions, and oversaw the establishment of the Federal Reserve. He would lead the country through the First World War and suffer a nervous breakdown trying to garner support for his League of Nations.

KAPLAN
Test Prep and Admissions

MULTIPLE-CHOICE QUESTIONS

1. City governments between 1870 and 1900 often came under the control of political "machines" because:

    (A) upper class Americans were concerned about the treatment of new immigrants by existing city administrations.

    (B) political "machines" provided urban dwellers in rapidly growing cities with services that previous city governments weren't effectively providing.

    (C) federal officials took control of chaotic municipal governments.

    (D) there was so much political corruption that new methods were needed to reintroduce honesty in government.

    (E) city government had come under the control of big business and the bankers.

2. The Progressive movement of the early 20th century was LEAST successful in:

    (A) getting child labor laws passed to protect children in the workplace.

    (B) introducing election reforms.

    (C) exposing the practices of 'big business.'

    (D) reforming corrupt city governments.

    (E) calling attention to inner city slum conditions.

3. Which internal reform passed during the Wilson administration was most acceptable to "big business"?

    (A) Federal Reserve Act

    (B) Federal Trade Commission Act

    (C) Underwood Tariff

    (D) Clayton Antitrust Act

    (E) Adamson Act

4. Which tended to be the biggest stumbling block for the promotion of women's rights?

    (A) Common law

    (B) The influence of the press which was anti-female

    (C) Frontier conditions

    (D) Corporate policies that discriminated against women in the factories

    (E) Lack of leadership in the suffrage movement

5. Which of the following ideas was included in the platform of the Populist Party during the election of 1892?

    (A) Reviving the Bank of the United States

    (B) A new sales tax

    (C) Nationalizing the railroads

    (D) Sticking to the Gold Standard

    (E) Regulating the stock market

6. In his novel *The Jungle*, Upton Sinclair strongly criticized:

    (A) the American Tobacco Company.

    (B) J. Pierpont Morgan and the banking industry.

    (C) America's wealthy families for fighting against an income tax.

    (D) corruption in the stock market.

    (E) the meatpacking industry.

7. Which act of Congress specifically targeted an ethnic group and restricted their immigration to the United States?

    (A) The Jewish Reclamation Act

    (B) The Vandenberg Sicilian Bill

    (C) The Italian Exemption Act of 1896

    (D) The Chinese Exclusion Act of 1882

    (E) The Irish Regulatory Act of 1852

KAPLAN
Test Prep and Admissions

8. Most Progressives sought all of the following EXCEPT:

   (A) more regulation in the food processing industry.

   (B) the creation of a Socialist system.

   (C) expansion of women's rights.

   (D) reformation of child labor laws.

   (E) democratization of the political process.

9. Why did many labor leaders object to immigrants coming to the United States?

   (A) Immigrants seemed unable to adapt to the new culture.

   (B) Some immigrants were suspected of being former criminals.

   (C) Most immigrants could not speak English.

   (D) Immigrants were willing to work for lower wages.

   (E) Many immigrants were Catholics.

10. Activists for female suffrage in the late 1800s had their greatest successes in:

   (A) electing women to local city positions in the South.

   (B) organizing female workers in northern textile mills.

   (C) winning the vote in western states.

   (D) getting female suffrage included in the Democratic party platform.

   (E) large eastern urban areas.

11. Which of the following is NOT associated with government land policy?

   (A) Railroad land grants

   (B) The Homestead Act of 1862

   (C) The Northwest Ordinance of 1787

   (D) The Interstate Commerce Act

   (E) The Compromise of 1850

12. When William Jennings Bryan said, "You shall not crucify mankind upon a cross of gold!" in 1896 he was advocating a policy of:

   (A) higher government spending.

   (B) deficit spending.

   (C) free silver.

   (D) issuing greenbacks redeemable in gold at banks.

   (E) strict adherence to the Gold Standard.

13. Theodore Roosevelt showed his support for labor when he:

   (A) allowed the White House staff to unionize.

   (B) threatened to use Army troops to run coal mines during the strike of 1902.

   (C) alienated leaders in Congress.

   (D) helped organize the American Federation of Labor.

   (E) supported the National Securities Act.

14. What accounts for the passage of women's suffrage in 1920?

   (A) Women worked in the government and had more influence.

   (B) Women could already vote in the South so it was logical to extend this right to the whole nation.

   (C) Suffragettes became better organized and more radical in pressing for their right to vote.

   (D) The Democratic Party endorsed women's suffrage.

   (E) Women's suffrage was supported by the wives of politicians.

15. Progressives achieved their goal of direct election of U.S. Senators in 1913 with the:

   (A) Supreme Court decision in *Gibbons v. Ogden*.

   (B) ratification of the 17th Amendment.

   (C) endorsement of the Sherman Antitrust Act.

   (D) ratification of the 15th Amendment.

   (E) passage of the Election Reform Act.

16. Which of the following does NOT describe the majority of immigrants who came to the United States between 1880 and 1920?

   (A) They were unskilled and undereducated when they arrived.

   (B) They were generally young.

   (C) They came to urban areas.

   (D) They were Protestant.

   (E) They were from Southern and Eastern Europe.

17. Which of the following politicians were considered to be Progressives in their day?

   (A) William McKinley and William Jennings Bryan

   (B) Theodore Roosevelt and Woodrow Wilson

   (C) Grover Cleveland and Upton Sinclair

   (D) J. P. Morgan and William H. Taft

   (E) Robert La Follette and Henry Cabot Lodge, Sr.

18. The Populist (or People's) Party was overwhelmingly supported by:

   (A) urban bankers.

   (B) farmers.

   (C) religious leaders.

   (D) corporate executives.

   (E) small town businessmen.

19. The creation of the Federal Reserve system in 1913 did which of the following?

   (A) Regulated the stock market

   (B) Allowed farmers more credit

   (C) Insured bank deposits

   (D) Established a floating exchange rate for the dollar

   (E) Made currency and credit more elastic

20. The writers and journalists who criticized certain features of American society, particularly business, during the Progressive Era were called:

   (A) muckrackers.

   (B) abolitionists.

   (C) prohibitionists.

   (D) anarchists.

   (E) Social Darwinists.

KAPLAN
Test Prep and Admissions

21. Civil service reform was accomplished under President Arthur with:

    (A) the passage of the Commerce Act of 1887.

    (B) the arrest of the leaders of the Knights of Labors.

    (C) the passage of the Granger Laws.

    (D) the passage of the Civil Service Act of 1890.

    (E) the passage of the Pendleton Act of 1883.

22. Which was designed to have a deflationary effect on the American economy?

    (A) Printing more paper money

    (B) The Gold Standard Act of 1900

    (C) The Sherman Silver Purchase Act

    (D) More government spending

    (E) Abandonment of specie payments

23. The post Civil War Grange movement in American rural areas was well known for:

    (A) cooperating with railroad companies in settling the West.

    (B) supporting the early suffrage movement.

    (C) promoting anarchy.

    (D) creating a social and educational outlet for farmers in the West.

    (E) helping found the Democratic party.

ESSAY QUESTION

Document-Based Question (DBQ):

Why did American farmers organize themselves politically in the late 19th century?

Use evidence from the documents **and** your knowledge of the period from 1880 to 1900 to compose your answer.

Document A

Consumer Prices and Farm Product Prices, 1880–1900.

Year	Consumer Prices	Farm Product Prices
1880	80	80
1885	82	75
1890	84	70
1895	80	62
1897	82	55
1900	80	70

Document B

F. B. Tracy and W. A. Peffer, "The Farmer's Situation" (1890s).

Nothing has done more to injure the [Western] region than these freight rates. The railroads have retarded its growth as much as they first hastened it. The rates are often four times as large as Eastern rates. . . . The extortionate character of the freight rates has been recognized by all parties, and all have pledged themselves to lower them, but no state west of the Missouri has been able to do so. . . .

These freight rates have been especially burdensome to the farmers, who are far from their selling and buying markets, thus robbing them in both directions. . . .

Closely connected with the land abuse are the money grievances. As his pecuniary condition grew more serious, the farmer could not make payments on his land. Or he found that, with the ruling prices, he could not sell his produce at a profit. In either case he needed money, to make the payment or maintain himself until prices should rise. When he went to the moneylenders, these men, often dishonest usurers, told him that money was very scarce, that the rate of interest was rapidly rising, etc., so that in the end the farmer paid as much interest a month as the moneylender was paying a year for the same money. In this transaction, the farmer obtained his first glimpse of the idea of "the contraction of the currency at the hands of Eastern money sharks."

Document C

F. B. Tracey, "Why the Farmers Revolted," *Forum*, October 1893.

Farmers are passing through the "valley and shadow of death"; farming as a business is profitless; values of farm products have fallen 50 per cent since the great war, and farm values have depreciated 25 to 50 per cent during the last ten years; farmers are overwhelmed with debts secured by mortgages on their homes, unable in many instances to pay even the interest as it falls due, and unable to renew the loans because securities are weakening by reason of the general depression; many farmers are losing their homes under this dreadful blight, and the mortgage mill still grinds. We are in the hands of a merciless power; the people's homes are at stake. . . .

Document D

William Allen White, "A Response to the Farmers' Protests," 1896.

Oh, yes, Kansas is a great state. Here are people fleeing from it by the score every day, capital going out of the state by the hundreds of dollars; and every industry but farming paralyzed, and that crippled, because its products have to go across the ocean before they can find a laboring man at work who can afford to buy them. Let's don't stop this year. Let's drive all the decent, self-respecting men out of the state. Let's keep the old clodhoppers who know it all. Let's encourage the man who is "posted." He can talk, and what we need is not mill hands to eat our meat, nor factory hands to eat our wheat, nor cities to oppress the farmer by consuming his butter and eggs and chickens and produce. What Kansas needs is men who can talk, who have large leisure to argue the currency question while their wives wait at home for the nickel's worth of bluing.

Document E

Populist Party Platform, 1892.

The conditions which surround us best justify our cooperation; we meet in the midst of a nation brought to the verge of moral, political, and material ruin. Corruption dominates the ballot-box, the Legislatures, the Congress, and touches even the ermine of the bench.

The people are demoralized; most of the States have been compelled to isolate the voters at the polling places to prevent universal intimidation and bribery. The newspapers are largely subsidized or muzzled, public opinion silenced, business prostrated, homes covered with mortgages, labor impoverished, and the land concentrating in the hands of capitalists. The urban workmen are denied the right to organize for self-protection, imported pauperized labor beats down their wages, a hireling standing army, unrecognized by our laws, is established to shoot them down, and they are rapidly degenerating into European conditions. The fruits of the toil of millions are badly stolen to build up colossal fortunes for a few, unprecedented in the history of mankind; and the possessors of these, in turn, despise the Republic and endanger liberty. From the same prolific womb of governmental injustice we breed the two great classes—tramps and millionaires. The national power to create money is appropriated to enrich bond-holders; a vast public debt payable in legal-tender currency has been funded into gold-bearing bonds, thereby adding millions to the burdens of the people.

Document F

William Jennings Bryan's Cross of Gold Speech, 1896.

We say to you that you have made the definition of a business man too limited in its application. The man who is employed for wages is as much a business man as his employer; the attorney in a country town is as much a business man as the corporation counsel in a great metropolis; the merchant at the cross-roads store is as much a business man as the merchant of New York; the farmer who goes forth in the morning and toils all day—who begins in the spring and toils all summer—and who by the application of brain and muscle to the natural resources of the country creates wealth, is as much a business man as the man who goes upon the board of trade and bets upon the price of grain; the miners who go down a thousand feet into the earth, or climb two thousand feet upon the cliffs, and bring forth from their hiding places the precious metals to be poured into the channels of trade are as much business men as the few financial magnates who, in a back room, corner the money of the world. We come to speak for this broader class of business men.

Document G

Eva McDonald-Valesh, "The Strength and Weakness of the People's Movement," 1892.

Today there is the agricultural population, on one hand, producing more than enough to feed the world; on the other, the city workmen; producing, in their many occupations, more than enough to clothe and supply all other civilized needs of the race. The two classes are quite distinct, so far as environment is concerned; yet consuming each other's products and supplying both necessities and luxuries to all other classes, there is between them a bond of common interest, stronger than either realizes.

ANSWER KEY

Multiple-Choice Questions

1. B
2. A
3. A
4. A
5. C
6. E
7. D
8. B
9. D
10. C
11. D
12. C
13. B
14. D
15. B
16. D
17. B
18. B
19. E
20. A
21. E
22. B
23. D

KAPLAN
Test Prep and Admissions

Answers and Explanations

1. B

As cities grew, organizations controlled by political parties came into being that delivered city services to immigrants and members of the working class, groups to whom most city services had not generally been available previously. Local political leaders traded favors and used their influence to get things done. The system was corrupt but it also allowed access to people who previously had no access to city government. City officials often illegally profited from their position.

2. A

A National Child Labor Committee was formed in 1904 to promote the abolition of child labor through legislation. A book by John Spargo, *The Bitter Cry of the Children*, revealed deplorable conditions, especially in the textile and coal industries. While some states passed laws to limit child labor it was not until 1938 when the Fair Labor Standards Act really abolished child abuse in the workplace.

3. A

This 1913 Act provided U. S. financial reserves, so that a bank could be helped in times of temporary difficulty. This would happen when too many people tried to take their deposits out of the bank in one day. The 12 Federal Reserve Banks provided for local needs and made it easier to move money from one part of the country to another.

4. A

Common law, established through court decisions over centuries, consists of traditions and values that can be very hard to change. Males had been responsible for establishing this law and were not open to changing it. The women's movement needed specific legislation in order to overturn common law and this was hard to accomplish, especially since it had to happen on a state-by-state basis. Strong and tenacious leaders fought for decades to advance the legal and political struggles of women until they were finally successful in the early 20th century.

5. C

Farmers in the West were fighting constantly with the railroads that moved their products to the cities for sale. Railroad companies usually had no competition at the local level and were able to set prices that in the view of farmers were too high. The Populists, who were supported by the farmers, pushed for the railroads to be nationalized by the government. This was a rather radical position and suggested a move toward socialism in the United States.

6. E

The Jungle was a book that focused on the unsanitary way that food was handled in the United States. Meatpacking in particular was done in the most filthy conditions and the end products were often unhealthy for the consumer. This helped inspire a political movement to have the federal government oversee food production so fresh and healthy food would be assured. Today the Department of Agriculture oversees all meat and food processing.

7. D

In the 1880s there was a severe backlash against the Chinese in many western cities and this resulted in a law that disallowed Chinese from immigrating to the United States. The 1882 Act was a 10-year suspension of Chinese immigration which was renewed into the 1930s. Attempts to limit other groups such as the Japanese were not as successful because those nations protested through diplomatic channels.

8. B

Although they wanted more government oversight over business, Progressives were not Socialists since they did not support government ownership of industry. Progressives sought to pass laws that would benefit the general public and encourage the growth of democratic processes. They were liberals who pushed for change within the system and successfully advanced many reforms between 1902 and 1916.

9. D

Many labor leaders were afraid that the new immigrants arriving in the United States would take lower wages than Americans, thus taking jobs away from Americans and hurting the effort to form labor unions. Thus, many labor leaders became nativists. Eventually many immigrants did join labor organizations and became members of the working class.

10. C

The first state to give women the vote was Wyoming. It was in the West that women were first accepted in the political sense. Throughout American history, the push to extend the right to vote to new groups was usually most successful in the West. Frontier life had a powerful leveling influence that encouraged democracy, and it required a partnership of men and women. The women's movement was able to exert more influence in the West than in the already established political systems of the eastern states.

11. D

The Interstate Commerce Act was a law regulating business and did not have anything to do with land policy. The other choices established policies that opened western land for settlement.

12. C

Farmers were in favor of "cheap" money and they felt that if silver as well as gold were used to back the U.S. dollar, there would be more money and it would be easier to borrow. Bryan's speech was a famous plea for using silver as part of the currency policy of the U. S. Treasury.

13. B

President Roosevelt was enraged when the coal industry leaders would not show any flexibility in ending a strike in 1902. He urged the two parties to compromise but threatened the mine owners with using military troops to work the coal mines if they did not settle the strike. This helped resolve the dispute and resulted in the striking miners winning some of their demands.

14. D

After 1905 new leadership came to the fore in fighting for the right of women to vote. Borrowing more violent tactics from the British suffragettes, American women picketed the White House, chained themselves to gates, and made headlines. After constant campaigning, the Democratic Party endorsed female suffrage in 1916.

15. B

One of the main features of the Progressive movement was to make politicians more responsive to the people. Direct elections were a means to achieve this goal. Formerly the senators were chosen indirectly by the state legislatures. After 1913, candidates had to appeal directly to the people to get elected.

16. D

Many immigrants who came after 1880 were from Russia and Italy. This meant a large influx of Catholic and Jewish people into the U.S. Few of the later immigrants were Protestant except for some Scandinavians and Germans. The U.S. maintained its Protestant majority while Catholics grew in numbers and influence.

17. B

Three presidents were considered Progressives. These were Theodore Roosevelt, William Taft, and Woodrow Wilson. The most famous Progressive governor was Robert La Follette who ran unsuccessfully as a third-party candidate for the presidency in 1924. Others included in the answer choices are not considered Progressives.

18. B

In the 1890s, economic depression hit the nation's farmers very hard. This gave rise in part to the Populist Party, which championed many issues to help farmers. They wanted credit from bankers to help them through the bad years and government assistance in dealing with the railroad companies.

19. E

Wilson pushed for reform of the nation's banking system. The new Federal Reserve System created 12 banking districts to oversee the cost of money. By controlling the interest rate at which it loans money to banks, the "Fed" has a strong influence on how much it costs businesses and consumers to borrow money in the United States. The federal insurance of bank deposits came later during the Great Depression.

20. A

An important role was played in the Progressive movement by writers and reporters. The press examined areas of politics and economics that needed to be reformed and wrote about them. These articles and books became popular reading and had an impact on popular and political thought between 1895 and 1920. This tradition of an investigative press continues to suggest changes that need to be made in local and federal laws.

KAPLAN
Test Prep and Admissions

21. E

Corruption and cronyism were common in government on the local and federal levels after the Civil War. When Garfield was shot, Arthur became president and, to the surprise of many, pushed for civil service reform. The Pendleton Act set standards for employment and set up competitive exams for those wishing to work for the government.

22. B

The Gold Standard Act declared that the U.S. would back its currency with gold held by the government. People could redeem any paper money for gold upon request at a bank. Limiting the amount of money in circulation that could be exchanged for gold was deflationary. This means that the value of money remained high and prices stayed low.

23. D

Local units in rural America formed Granges with a hall for meetings and social events. Lecturers would also come and speak to farmers about their businesses. Men and women worked together and the Grange provided a break from the loneliness and isolation of farm life.

ANALYSIS OF THE DBQ

Question:
Why did American farmers organize themselves politically in the late 19th century?

Use evidence from the documents **and** your knowledge of the period from 1880 to 1900 to compose your answer.

Use of the Documents
Each of the documents offers a perspective on the Populist movement and its effects on the country and society as a whole.

Documents A, B and C provide economic reasons why farmers were under great financial stress after the Civil War—these documents show the effects of falling agricultural prices.

Document B criticizes the railroads for charging too much for shipping goods to market.

Document D offers a sarcastic commentary on the conditions of farmers in Kansas.

Document E is a run down of the Populists parties platform in 1892.

Document F is a short piece of the most famous speech in the 1890s which urged reforms to benefit the common farmers.

Document G offers reasons why farmers and urban workers should join together and fight for common benefits.

Key Points from Outside Information

The dilemma of farmers in 1895
- Production had created surpluses that drove down prices of farm produce
- Many farmers had to borrow to remain in business and were heavily in debt
- The Depression of the 1890s hit farmers very hard
- Farmers were politically isolated from the center of power and not well connected politically
- The struggle took on a regional character as western farmers felt powerless against the banking interests in the East

Students could make the case that farmers had to become political and organize to survive. They had become marginalized during the Industrial Revolution and needed to combine to get support in the government. The thesis should contain two to three reasons for the organization of farmers in the 1890s.

What farmers wanted:

- Cheaper money to pay their debts which could be backed by silver as well as gold
  - This would also benefit mining interests in the West where silver was plentiful
- More power for their organizations such as the Granges and Farmer's Alliance
- Government ownership of the railroads
- A graduated income tax
- Direct election of U.S. senators

Scoring Rubric

There are five scoring ranges:

Excellent

Argument: The essay must have a strong, clear thesis. The student should take a clear position either in support of or against the proposition stated in the question. The essay should also indicate a grasp of the complexity of the issue, referring to pros and cons of entrepreneurial behavior in this time period.

Critical Thought: The student should explain how each document supports or undermines the thesis. The student should address conflicts and contradictions in the evidence. All outside information must be relevant to the argument.

Evidence: The student should use documents **and** outside information (see lists above) throughout the essay. Most of the documents must be used, and students might address the relationship between the sources.

Writing Style: The essay must be well organized and well written; it must make sense throughout.

Very Good

Argument: The thesis must be consistent with the question, but it may not be sufficiently focused.

Critical Thought: The answer must include an analysis of several of the documents and must incorporate outside information.

Evidence: The student should make use of the documents and outside information (see lists above) that support the position being argued. Discussion of relationships between the sources used may be limited.

Writing Style: The essay should be well organized and clearly written; it must be logical, but some points may be unclear.

Adequate

Argument: The thesis is only partially developed. It may address the question, but it does so in a way that doesn't acknowledge the question's complexity.

Critical Thought: The essay is primarily descriptive or narrative, and doesn't provide an analysis of the question or of the evidence provided. It will not address all the relevant issues, and will ignore the opposing position.

Evidence: The student may paraphrase the documents and may misinterpret a document to better fit the argument. The student will use only a little outside information, and may refer to some but not all of the documents. The answer may contain errors.

Writing Style: The writing and organization is unclear, but acceptable.

Flawed

Argument: The thesis will be unclear and will not be supported in the body of the essay. Use of evidence will be unclear, and the argument will be poorly developed.

Critical Thought: The essay will show only a limited understanding of the question, and will offer little or no analysis. What little analysis there is will be inaccurate.

Evidence: The student will not make use of the documents appropriate to their argument, and may use documents that actually support the opposing position. The use of documents will be haphazard, with references only to brief excerpts or paraphrases. There will be little outside information. The argument may contain errors.

Writing Style: The answer will be weakly organized and the writing will be unclear.

Severely Flawed

Argument: The student provides no thesis, or provides one that is not relevant to the question.

Critical Thought: The student demonstrates little or no understanding of the question.

Evidence: The student makes almost no use of the documents provided, and makes little or no use of outside information. The answer contains major errors.

Writing Style: The answer is disorganized and poorly written.

KAPLAN
Test Prep and Admissions

Chapter Ten: **Imperialism and World War I**

- Timeline: 1867–1919
- Imperial Expansion
- World War I
- Multiple-Choice Questions
- Essay Questions
- Answer Key
- Answers and Explanations
- Analyses of the Free-Response Essays

TIMELINE: 1867–1919

1867	Purchase of Alaska for $7.2 million.
1878	Treaty with Samoa marks beginning of U.S. expansion in Pacific.
1890	Alfred Thayer Mahan publishes *The Influence of Sea Power upon History, 1660–1783*.
February 1898	*Maine* explodes and sinks in Havana harbor.
April 1898	Spain and the U.S. declare war on each other over Cuba.
April 1898	Dewey occupies Manila.
Summer 1898	Hawaii annexed to U.S. after two decades of increasing American military and economic presence in islands.
December 1898	Treaty officially ending Spanish-American War adds Puerto Rico, Guam, and the Philippines to American possessions and guarantees Cuban independence; U.S. pays Spain $20 million.
1899	Anti-Imperialist League founded.
1899	U.S. declares Open Door Policy toward China.
1900	Boxer Rebellion suppressed in China with help of American, European, and Japanese forces.

1901	Theodore Roosevelt becomes president after McKinley assassinated by anarchist.
1902	Filipino military resistance to U.S. occupation ends.
1903	With U.S. help, Panama declares independence from Colombia; U.S. purchases Canal Zone.
1905	Roosevelt mediates settlement of Russo-Japanese War.
1907	"Gentlemen's Agreement" between Japan and United States.
1912	Wilson elected president.
1912–1934	U.S. troops in various Caribbean countries (Dominican Republic, Haiti, and Nicaragua).
1914	Declaration of war in Europe after assassination of Archduke Ferdinand in Sarajevo triggers activation of various alliances.
1914	Panama Canal opens.
1914–1916	U.S. involvement in Mexican Revolution; Marines land at Veracruz, Pershing chases Pancho Villa through northern Mexico.
1915	Sinking of *Lusitania* in north Atlantic triggers crisis over neutral rights, shipping, and submarine warfare.
1916	U.S. increases size of military, passes income tax.
1916	Wilson reelected.
1917	Zimmermann telegram and more submarine warfare in North Atlantic pushes U.S. public opinion toward war with Germany.
April 1917	U.S. enters war.
November 1917	Bolshevik Revolution in Russia.
January 1918	Wilson announces Fourteen Points.
March 1918	Russian government makes peace with Germany; focus of war swings west.
March 1918	German offensives on western front.
September 1918	American Meuse-Argonne offensive pushes Germans east.
November 1918	Armistice declared, ending World War I.
1918–1919	Influenza epidemic.
1919	Peace negotiations in Paris finally result in Treaty of Versailles.
1919–1920	Senate debates Treaty of Versailles, but fails to ratify.
1919	Race riots in the North and South.
1919	Beginning of Red Scare.
1919	Wilson suffers disabling stroke.

IMPERIAL EXPANSION

Imperialism was the name of the game at the beginning of the 20th century. The United States had come out of the Spanish-American War with a sprawling empire. The U. S. granted immediate independence to Cuba but retained the right to a naval station at Guantánamo Bay. Puerto Rico and Guam were to remain as American possessions; both were strategically positioned to be important fueling stations and naval bases for the growing U.S. navy. However, the fate of the Philippines was uncertain as Congress debated whether to grant it its independence or maintain control over it as an American colony. For years a Filipino independence movement had battled the Spanish and now it shifted its target to the United States. However, the Philippines did not become an independent nation until 1946.

In 1900, William McKinley conducted a dignified presidential campaign from his front porch in Canton, Ohio while his vice presidential candidate, Theodore Roosevelt, a hero of the Spanish-American War, traveled around the country. The party bosses, in an effort to get Roosevelt out of New York where he vetoed over a thousand bills during his governorship, got him to accept the vice presidential nomination. McKinley and Roosevelt were sworn into office in March 1901. That September, while strolling the grounds of the Buffalo Exposition with his wife, McKinley was shot by an anarchist. After being operated upon to remove one of the two bullets, he rallied for a few days. But 12 days after the shooting, McKinley died and Theodore Roosevelt became president. When Mark Hanna, the Republican Party Chairman, heard the news, he is reported to have said: "Now that damn cowboy is President." Hanna had been particularly pleased when Roosevelt had left New York for Washington where it was supposed that Roosevelt would labor in obscurity.

Roosevelt entered the presidency with the same enthusiasm he exhibited for almost everything he did. He was the first president to ride in a plane, stand before a camera that recorded sound, and go down in a submarine. No job was too small. He wrestled with big business and broke up several trust arrangements. He read Upton Sinclair's exposé on the meat packing industry, *The Jungle*, and instigated the Pure Food and Drug Act and the Meat Inspection Act. He worked with Gifford Pinchot to preserve and reserve over 55 million acres all over the United States for the public. He supported independence for Panama from Colombia (for the price of rights to a waterway through their country). The U.S. took control of the Canal Zone and built a canal connecting the Atlantic and Pacific Oceans, completing the monumental feat in 1914.

All over the world, the United States began to assert its new power and influence. In China, the U.S. was able to force the European powers to open up the ports they controlled, thereby giving access to Americans (the Open Door Policy). Closer to home, the Roosevelt Corollary made it known to the world that the United States was ready to intervene militarily anywhere in the Western Hemisphere to protect its interests. Roosevelt sent the U.S. fleet around the world. Although painted white as a symbolic gesture of peace, there was no mistaking the message of power that the United States wanted to project.

KAPLAN
Test Prep and Admissions

big stick diplomacy

This referred to a description of the diplomacy practiced by the United States in the Western Hemisphere. Roosevelt's big stick was the growing military power of the country that was starting to consider itself to be Latin America's policeman.

Boxer Rebellion

Chinese nationalists known as Boxers (Fists of Righteous Harmony) rebelled against foreigners whose power in China rivaled that of the Chinese government. A multinational force of British, German, Japanese, and American forces mobilized to control the situation. Six weeks later the foreign forces reached Peking and quelled the rebellion. China agreed to pay indemnity of $33 million.

Hawaii annexation

A series of agreements had given United States exclusive rights in Hawaii, including duty-free sugar and the right to build a fortified naval base at Pearl Harbor. In 1887, the Americans forced the Hawaiian king to accept a constitution that created a white-dominated constitutional government. The king's sister, Liliuokalani, tried to regain power; the white population (mostly Americans) seized power and Marines were sent to support them. President Cleveland did not support the coup and proposed restoring the queen to power. On July 4, 1894 the Republic of Hawaii was proclaimed. When McKinley became president, he wanted to annex the islands and sent warships in response to Japanese ships there. Although the Senate did not approve the treaty to annex, a joint resolution of the House and Senate bypassed the problem, and U.S. annexation was achieved in 1898.

Alfred Thayer Mahan

President of the Naval War College and author of *The Influence of Sea Power upon History, 1660–1783*, Mahan argued that national greatness and prosperity came from sea power. A modern country should have a strong navy, a strong merchant marine, foreign commerce, and naval bases. Coaling stations were needed around the world. He also argued for a canal across the Isthmus of Panama. The U.S. government heeded his advice and built up its navy.

Open Door Policy

With the United States in possession of Hawaii and the Philippines, interest in trading with Asia was strong. China, with its vast population and nearly nonexistent industrial capacity, was a logical market for U.S. goods. However, the major European powers had already carved up China into spheres of influence where they held exclusive trading rights. By pushing for all nations to have equal access to Chinese ports and markets, the United States was promoting its own interests. This policy of equal access to China was called the Open Door Policy. The Europeans agreed to U.S. demands and opened Chinese ports to Americans.

Panama Canal

The United States, with ports on both the Atlantic and Pacific sides of the North American continent, supported a canal across Panama. The canal would cross Panama, which was a province of Colombia. However, Colombia did not agree to all the U.S. demands for land to construct a canal through its territory, and President Roosevelt decided to support a military coup to replace the Colombian government with one more favorable to the U.S. position. With the intervention of the U.S. navy, a new government came to power in Colombia and granted independence to Panama. The United States received a zone 10 miles wide in which to construct a canal. The huge construction project lasted 10 years and cost 5,000 lives, but the canal was opened in 1914. The United States returned the Canal Zone to Panama in 1999.

Philippine annexation debate

After the Spanish-American War, the United States found itself in possession of the Philippines. A debate raged in Congress over whether to grant the islands independence or make them an American colony. President McKinley set up a civil government in the islands, sending William Howard Taft there in 1901 to govern the islands. In 1916 the Jones Act confirmed the intention to grant the Philippines independence at an indefinite date. In 1934 the Tydings-McDuffie Act legislated independence after a 10-year tutelary period. Full independence was achieved on July 4, 1946.

purchase of Alaska

In 1867, Secretary of State William Seward learned of Russia's desire to sell Alaska. For $7.23 million, the United States purchased the area. Although criticized at the time as "Seward's Folly" and the Alaskan "icebox," it would prove to be the biggest bargain since the Louisiana Purchase.

Roosevelt Corollary to the Monroe Doctrine

Theodore Roosevelt, in his State of the Union Address in 1904, set forth what would become known as the Roosevelt Corollary. Theodore Roosevelt affirmed what was stated in the Monroe Doctrine, that the United States would oppose any European intervention in the Americas. But he went further. He said the United States, as the dominant power in the region, reserved the right to intervene in Latin American nations to preserve order and make sure U.S. interests aren't violated. The situation that motivated the action was the crisis over debts owed by the Dominican Republic to the United States and European countries. In this case, the United States installed a collector of customs in the Dominican Republic who would set aside 55 percent of the collections for debt repayments.

Spanish-American War

The war was fought in a few months in 1898 after the sinking of the *U.S.S. Maine* in Havana harbor, an event that killed 266 and incensed the nation. In April 1898, President McKinley asked Congress for a declaration of war. The United States subdued the Spanish in the Philippines and defeated them in Cuba. The Spanish asked for terms of peace in August. The United States emerged from the war in control of former Spanish colonies in the Caribbean and Asia. The Spanish-American War is also referred to as the Spanish-American-Cuban War.

KAPLAN
Test Prep and Admissions

Treaty of Paris, 1898

The peace treaty ending the Spanish-American War was signed in Paris on December 10, 1898. Its terms provided for Cuban independence and the U.S. acquisition of Puerto Rico (in the Caribbean) and Guam (in the Pacific). The U.S. also acquired the Philippines for $20 million.

yellow journalism

This type of newspaper reporting was sensationalistic, with bold headlines promising stories of crime, disaster, and scandals. The competing newspapers in New York, *The World* and *The Journal*, printed ever-growing stories of Spanish atrocities in Cuba, helping to instigate the Spanish-American War.

WORLD WAR I

The world was involved in The Great War, as it was known at the time. Although the United States claimed neutrality, the economy was tied closely to that of Europe, so strict neutrality was in name only. Factors such as the discovery and publication of the Zimmermann Telegram and the sinking of American ships inflamed American public opinion against Germany.

The European nations had fought to a standstill. The border of France and Germany became a long string of trenches; the two sides fought back and forth and traded negligible acreage. The entry of the United States into the conflict broke the deadlock and forced German withdrawals from the trenches and their eventual surrender.

Back in the United States, mobilizing a military of less than a half million into a fighting force of four million was a monumental undertaking. Associated with that mobilization was the re-tooling of factories to produce war materials. Auto manufacturers made ambulances, former icebox builders now made shell casings and cannon barrels. Everyone contributed to the effort; women contributed by going to work outside the home and children collected war materials. African Americans used the closing off of immigration and the movement of men into the military as an opportunity to get jobs. Millions moved north to fill the vacancies. However, radicals, anarchists, and foreigners were all treated with suspicion and deportations were carried out with little regard for civil rights.

Fighting the war, or "making the world safe for democracy" as President Wilson put it, was the beginning of change in the United States. When men returned from the front, they told not of a "noble cause," but of the brutal warfare of the trenches. The Great War was the first war in which poisonous gases were used as weapons; nerve gas and mustard gas caused long-term disabilities. When the war was over, men streamed back into the United States. The public's reaction, particularly to the many wounded, was to leave the Europeans to their own devices. Isolationism became the watchword. When President Wilson tried to get Senate approval of the Treaty of Versailles and its League of Nations, he found little support. His trip around the country to try to appeal directly to the people on this issue would prove to be his undoing.

KAPLAN
Test Prep and Admissions

Allied Powers

Those countries allied with Great Britain, France, and Russia against Germany during World War I. Eventually the United States joined the Allied Powers.

Central Powers

Those countries allied with Germany during World War I. The list includes Austria-Hungary and the Ottoman Empire.

Election of 1916

President Wilson knew his first election in 1912 was due, in part, to the split in the Republican Party. In 1916 the Democrats' slogan was: "He kept us out of war." It was an extremely close election, but Wilson prevailed.

Espionage and Sedition Acts

The Espionage Act of 1917 said that anyone who tried to incite a rebellion in the armed forces or obstruct the draft was subject to punishment up to 20 years. The Sedition Act of 1918 went further and prohibited anyone from making disloyal or abusive remarks about the United States government.

Food Administration

The Lever Food and Fuel Control Act of 1917 created a Food Administration that was headed by Herbert Hoover. Hoover raised production while reducing the civilian use of the foodstuffs. He created "Meatless Tuesdays, Wheatless Wednesdays, and Porkless Saturdays," and promoted victory gardens and the use of leftovers.

Great Migration of African Americans

As the United States mobilized for war, immigration from Europe was cut off. At the same time four million men left their jobs and went to war. A large number of factory jobs opened as a result. Over 400,000 African Americans took advantage of the opportunities and moved to the North.

League of Nations

Woodrow Wilson had a vision of a multinational organization that would mediate any disagreements between countries so that a world war would never happen again. He went to Versailles to present his proposals as part of the peace treaty ending the war.

Henry Cabot Lodge

The Chairman of the Senate Foreign Relations Committee became a leading voice for isolationism. His opinion was based on a dislike of Wilson and a fear that the United States often promised more than it could deliver. He joined forces with Theodore Roosevelt to defeat the ratification of the Treaty of Versailles in the Senate.

KAPLAN
Test Prep and Admissions

"irreconcilables" and "reservationists"

The U.S. senators opposed to the Treaty of Versailles were divided into two groups. The irreconcilables would not accept U.S. membership in the League of Nations no matter how it was worded. The reservationists said they could accept the League if certain restrictions were added. Wilson had to choose. He did not want the reservations added, so he chose to appeal directly to the voters to win their support and pressure the Senate to approve the treaty with its League of Nations.

Lusitania

On May 7, 1915, the British ship, *Lusitania*, was torpedoed and sunk by a German submarine. Most passengers drowned, including 128 Americans. The United States, claiming neutrality in the war, sent a warning to Germany that it would be held "strictly accountable" for any other such actions.

A. Mitchell Palmer

As Attorney General, Palmer capitalized on the Red Scare to set up a General Intelligence Division (to be headed by J. Edgar Hoover) within the Department of Justice to investigate radicals. Palmer authorized mass arrests of anarchists, socialists, and other radicals. Palmer had presidential aspirations and saw the witch hunt as a way to gain support. The first Red Scare began to dissolve in 1920 and Palmer saw his support fall off.

Red Scare

Public reaction to the Bolshevik Revolution in Russia was characterized by the fear that labor strikes and race riots might be in store for the United States. Bombs mailed to several prominent citizens incited fear. Many Americans saw "Reds" everywhere and reacted with attacks on minorities.

Schenk v. United States

The 1919 Supreme Court decision upheld the conviction of a man accused of distributing anti-draft leaflets among members of the armed forces. The justices applied the "clear and present danger" test in that such speech in wartime could create evils that Congress had a right to prevent in spite of the First Amendment's guarantee of freedom of speech.

Spanish Flu

In 1918–1919 the pandemic killed more than 22 million around the world, more than twice the number that died in the war. It killed more than 500,000 in the United States alone; 43,000 were servicemen. Some blamed it on the Germans. It ended as quickly as it began; a mild recurrence in 1920 did not have the same devastating effects probably because people had built up some immunity.

Treaty of Versailles

Signed in 1919, the Treaty of Versailles formally ended World War I. In contrast to the United States, the other Allied Powers made it clear that they wanted both revenge and compensation from Germany. Germany was stripped of all its colonies and ordered to pay reparations to Great Britain and France. Many new nations were created and an international peacekeeping organization was established by the treaty. The U.S. Senate did not ratify the treaty, and the United States eventually signed its own peace treaty with Germany.

War Industries Board

The Board was established in 1917 to mobilize the economy. The Board took the needs of the American and Allied governments, prioritized them, and planned production. The Board allocated materials, told manufacturers what to produce, and sometimes fixed prices.

Wilson's Fourteen Points

These were Wilson's famous principles for peace. He presented them to a joint session of Congress in 1918. They included open diplomacy, freedom of the seas, the removal of trade barriers, reduction of military arms, and self-determination for nationalities.

Zimmermann Telegram

The Germans had made a secret offer to Mexico: If Mexico allied itself with Germany, then Germany would work to help Mexico recover its lost territories of Texas, New Mexico, and Arizona. The telegram was intercepted by Great Britain and forwarded to the United States, where it inflamed public opinion against Germany.

KAPLAN
Test Prep and Admissions

MULTIPLE-CHOICE QUESTIONS

1. Some Americans used Social Darwinism as a rationale for imperialism because:

   (A) scientific journals were suggesting that westerners were superior to other peoples.

   (B) Republicans saw a need for more U.S. naval stations around the world.

   (C) Theodore Roosevelt believed in a vigorous foreign policy.

   (D) it suggested that some nations will always be dominant just as some animals are in the natural world.

   (E) Darwin believed in colonization.

2. Which of the following best explains the role of the American battleship *Maine* in American history?

   (A) The *Maine* was the first naval ship to use oil as its source of energy.

   (B) It exploded and sank in Miami harbor as it was leaving for Cuba.

   (C) It disappeared at sea with no trace, but newspaper reporters claimed that Spain had ordered it sunk.

   (D) It exploded in Havana harbor and became a battle cry in the Spanish-American war.

   (E) The *Maine* transported arms to Cuban rebels.

3. What territories were added to the United States after the Spanish American War?

   (A) The Marianas and Haiti

   (B) Western Samoa and the Sandwich Islands

   (C) The Philippines and Guam

   (D) Cuba and Puerto Rico

   (E) Hawaii and Wake Island

4. Which of the following group in the United States Senate would most likely NOT have supported the League of Nations?

   (A) Republicans

   (B) Wilsonians

   (C) Midwestern senators

   (D) Western Progressives

   (E) Internationalists from Eastern States

5. The Versailles Treaty was never ratified by the United States because:

   (A) The House of Representatives was opposed.

   (B) Theodore Roosevelt refused to sign the treaty since it was inconsistent with his "Big Stick" diplomacy.

   (C) The Senate wanted the United States to remain at war with Germany.

   (D) The Senate supported U.S. membership in the League of Nations.

   (E) Republican leaders, including Roosevelt and Lodge, did not support American internationalism and were able to block the treaty.

6. The Open Door policy came into being because:

   (A) China had successfully repelled the Westerners during the siege of Beijing.

   (B) China was expected to allow foreign officials to collect taxes in its port cities.

   (C) Chinese authorities demanded a new foreign policy initiative.

   (D) The U.S. had little desire to expand its trade in Asia.

   (E) America was becoming a regional power in the Pacific and did not want China partitioned.

7. Which of the following is NOT a reason the U.S. sent troops into Mexico shortly before World War I?

   (A) Pancho Villa had raided an American town.

   (B) Socialists in the U.S. were sympathetic with the Zapatistas.

   (C) General Huerta had seized power from Madera.

   (D) Mexico was unstable politically and revolution was possible.

   (E) American investments in Mexico were large and needed protecting.

8. Which of the following statements is NOT true in regards to American railroads during World War I:

   (A) Overall the railroads did a good job moving personnel and goods to where they were needed.

   (B) Wilson called a conference of railroad owners to coordinate wartime movement of goods.

   (C) The Adamson Act dealt with government oversight of the railroads.

   (D) There were initial shipping problems right after the declaration of war.

   (E) The government nationalized the railroads before 1917.

9. Which event delayed the annexation of Hawaii by the United States?

   (A) An impartial investigation into the Hawaiian revolt of 1893

   (B) The prospective annexation of the Philippines

   (C) The isolationist policies of the Republican Party

   (D) The decline of American naval power after the Spanish-American War

   (E) The growth of Japan as a world power

10. President Wilson's Fourteen Points included all of the following elements except:

    (A) admission by Germany and the other Central Powers of complete guilt and responsibility for the war.

    (B) a call for open, not secret, diplomacy.

    (C) creation of an international association of nations.

    (D) a call for removal of all tariffs and trade barriers.

    (E) reduction of armaments.

11. In the late 19th century all the following encouraged jingoism EXCEPT:

    (A) Social Darwinism.

    (B) Spanish atrocities in Cuba.

    (C) foreign goods being sold in American stores.

    (D) yellow journalism.

    (E) the new naval policy supported by Admiral Mahan.

12. In November 1916 President Wilson was re-elected partly because America had stayed out of the war in Europe. However, less than six months later the U.S. declared war on Germany due to:

    (A) Germany's resumption of unrestricted submarine warfare in the Atlantic.

    (B) the collapse of Russia.

    (C) the effectiveness British anti-German propaganda.

    (D) the sinking of the *Lusitania*.

    (E) Germany's failure to stop its attacks on British shipping.

KAPLAN
Test Prep and Admissions

13. During the First World War the Committee on Public Information issued propaganda to convince the American people of all the following EXCEPT:

   (A) German words should not be used in every-day language.

   (B) Italy and Austria were also responsible for starting the war.

   (C) Buying bonds was everyone's patriotic duty.

   (D) The Germans were a barbarous people.

   (E) The country was fighting a war to promote democracy.

14. The United States was able to gain control of the isthmus of Panama to build the canal by:

   (A) using the U.S. Navy to blockade Colombian ports.

   (B) threatening to march in with the U.S. Army and take it.

   (C) signing a treaty with Nicaragua.

   (D) offering to buy half of Colombia.

   (E) supporting a Panamanian rebellion against Colombia.

15. Wilson's primary objective at Versailles was to:

   (A) make Germany take responsibility for starting the war.

   (B) establish an international organization to prevent future wars.

   (C) organize a relief program for war torn Europe.

   (D) get support for the construction of a canal in Panama.

   (E) secure peace in the American hemisphere.

16. Which person would have been most likely to oppose the entry of the U.S. into World War I in 1917?

   (A) An American manufacturer who sold goods to France

   (B) An admirer of Theodore Roosevelt

   (C) An owner of British bonds

   (D) An editor of a Midwest newspaper

   (E) A congressman from New York

17. As ex-president, Theodore Roosevelt criticized President Wilson's foreign policies and believed that:

   (A) the United States should broker the peace in Europe.

   (B) America should rearm and prepare to enter the war.

   (C) war with Mexico was imminent.

   (D) Wilson was too aggressive in using the U.S. military.

   (E) America must stay out of the war in Europe at all costs.

18. Theodore Roosevelt's "Big Stick" diplomacy transformed U.S. foreign policy by:

   (A) intervening in Asia during the Chinese Revolution in 1911.

   (B) following in the footsteps of Thomas Jefferson.

   (C) arguing for a one-ocean Navy.

   (D) supporting U.S. interests in the Caribbean through U.S. military intervention.

   (E) promoting the interests of American business in Europe.

19. Which of the following best explains why Wilson sent American troops to Russia in 1918 after the Bolshevik Revolution?

    (A) The United States wanted to support Russia on the Eastern Front against Germany.

    (B) The United States wanted to make sure that Russia did not decide to switch sides and fight for the Central Powers against the Allied Powers.

    (C) Wilson wanted to encourage anti-Bolshevik forces in the Russian civil war.

    (D) Wilson wanted to protect Americans caught in Russia in the midst of the Bolshevik Revolution.

    (E) Wilson decided to prevent the arrival of the Bolshevik revolutionaries in Moscow.

20. When President Wilson first suggested a "peace without victory" after World War I he was suggesting that:

    (A) neutral shipping rights should be included in the peace treaty.

    (B) the Allies should work to redraw the map of Europe after the war.

    (C) no nation be blamed or punished for starting the war.

    (D) every nation would lose something in the peace settlement.

    (E) France should be awarded reparations after the armistice.

21. William Seward's chief motivation in buying Alaska from Russia was:

    (A) Japan's imperialistic designs on North America.

    (B) the fulfillment of America's 'manifest destiny' in North America.

    (C) rumors that Britain was also interested in the territory.

    (D) the rich oil fields near Fairbanks.

    (E) fear that Russian bases in Alaska would be used to attack the United States.

ESSAY QUESTIONS

1. Assess the validity of the following statement: "Woodrow Wilson's idealism was his greatest weakness."

_____

_____

_____

_____

_____

_____

_____

_____

_____

2. What interests in the United States argued for the acquisition of the Philippines after the Spanish-American War and why?

_____

_____

_____

_____

_____

_____

_____

ANSWER KEY

Multiple-Choice Questions

1. D
2. D
3. C
4. A
5. E
6. E
7. B
8. E
9. A
10. A
11. C
12. A
13. B
14. E
15. B
16. D
17. B
18. D
19. C
20. C
21. B

Answers and Explanations

1. D

On a macrocosmic level, Social Darwinists said that nations do resemble the animal world because some are strong while others are weak. It is the destiny of stronger peoples to dominate weaker peoples just as happens in nature with predator and prey. Many Westerners believed that the white peoples had demonstrated their superiority over non-white peoples and therefore the building of empires in Africa and Asia was part of the natural order. Later Nazism would take this argument to a more extreme level and systematize the subjugation and murder of peoples they believed to be sub-human.

2. D

"Remember the *Maine*" was a battle cry used by jingoists who wanted war with Spain in 1898. The mysterious explosion of the American warship in Havana, which still has not been explained, made some people suspicious that Spanish agents had been guilty of the sabotage.

3. C

In the Peace of Paris in 1898, the United States gained the Philippines, Guam and Puerto Rico. Puerto Rico and Guam still belong to the U.S. today; Guam is currently the site of a large U.S. military base. The Philippines remained an American colony until 1946.

4. A

Leading Republicans were isolationists and did not feel that the president consulted with them when he helped frame the Peace at Versailles in 1919. Republican senators such as Lodge of Massachusetts were not in favor of the U.S. joining an international body. When the League of Nations was debated in the Senate most Republicans opposed U.S. membership.

5. E

President Wilson would not compromise on the League of Nations and promised to go to the people to persuade them about the issue. Republicans felt America should take care of itself and should not be bound by international agreements. They were hearkening back to George Washington's admonition that the U.S. be detached from European affairs.

6. E

After the Spanish-American War, the United States controlled new possessions in the Pacific and Asia and wanted to expand trade with China. The United States was concerned at seeing European nations scrambling for exclusive concessions from China and feared the partitioning of China into European spheres of influence that could exclude the U.S. The Open Door Policy proclaimed that China should remain intact and that all nations should have equal access to trade there.

7. B

Mexico was politically unstable after the 1913 military takeover by Huerta. Different rebel groups vied for power and created unrest that spilled across the border into America. This was the beginning of the Mexican Revolution. However, American troops being sent to Mexico had nothing to do with the views of American socialists, who had little political influence in the U.S. at the time.

8. E

While the Populists had wanted the government to nationalize the railroads back in the 1890s, there was no chance of that happening. The railroads had always been under the firm control of powerful business interests in America. When the war started, the government did coordinate the use of the rails for the war effort but never took them over.

9. A

American business interests in Hawaii wanted the United States to take control of Hawaii. A revolt in 1893 overthrew the Hawaiian queen and American businessmen argued that, to maintain stability, the United States should declare the islands a protectorate. However, an investigation revealed that the revolt had been staged by American business interests seeking a U.S. takeover. It was not until 1898 that the annexation went through.

KAPLAN
Test Prep and Admissions

10. A

The Fourteen Points embodied Wilson's view of what should result at the end of the World War I. They sought to address the causes of the war, such as secret treaties and agreements that European nations were infamous for. The Fourteen Points did not state that Germany was responsible for the start of the war. This point and whether or not Germany should pay reparations was debated later at the Peace Conference in 1919.

11. C

Jingoism is extreme nationalism marked by a belligerent foreign policy. Jingoes often support war as a means of making the nation greater and more powerful. Some Americans in the late 19th century believed that war with Spain would be a means to gaining more territory and power. In fact, this did happen and, after the war with Spain in 1898, the U.S. gained new possessions in the Caribbean and the Pacific. However, jingoism was mostly a political agenda and had little to do with goods being imported into the U.S.

12. A

As President, Wilson wanted to push his Progressive reforms. Most Americans viewed the war in Europe with interest but detachment. While many Americans were shocked by the sinking of ships by the Germans they did not see it as an act of war. With the Sussex pledge, Germany promised to stop sinking neutral ships, including those of the United States. It changed this policy after the 1916 election, gambling that by cutting off American supplies to Britain and France, it could win the war in Europe even if this caused the United States to enter the war on the Allied side.

13. B

World War I was the first American war where the government created an office to issue propaganda directed towards the American public. There were many vehicles for the "selling" of the war, from newspaper stories to posters printed by the government. The propaganda effort told of war aims to promote democracy and painted the Germans as cruel villains who wanted to dominate the world. It did not focus on Austria who was fighting with Germany nor Italy which had joined the Allied cause.

14. E

Roosevelt was determined to build the canal so that America could move more freely between its two oceans. He first negotiated with Colombia which controlled the isthmus of Panama. But when this did not work, the U.S. supported a revolt by Panamanians who favored the American-built canal. This was the "Big Stick" diplomacy that Roosevelt became known for.

15. B

Wilson was a firm believer in democratic values. He helped propose the idea that an international body that debated and voted on world problems could be the solution to the unending cycle of war that had always plagued humankind. This League of Nations was the main goal he hoped would be his greatest achievement. Though the U.S. did not join this League, America used Wilson's ideas to help found the United Nations a generation later.

16. D

The Midwest was the most isolationist and pro-German part of the country in 1917. Many immigrants of German descent had moved there and were not in favor of being involved in the European conflict. Many towns in Wisconsin, Minnesota and Missouri were founded by German settlers and many of them left Europe to escape the draft and war.

17. B

Theodore Roosevelt had always been a jingo, believing that war was manly and virtuous if it legitimately advanced the national interest. The cerebral Wilson could not have been more unlike him. When war clouds threatened in 1915, Roosevelt argued that the nation should prepare for war. Wilson continued to hope for peace and was re-elected as a staunch supporter of neutrality. Most Americans agreed with the president. Once war came, Roosevelt supported the Wilson administration in its war effort.

18. D

Latin America and the Caribbean were the scenes of most of Theodore Roosevelt's aggressive foreign policies, and the term "Big Stick" diplomacy applies to U.S. relations with that region. He backed the breakup of Colombia to create the Panama Canal and sent U.S. troops to the Dominican Republic to protect American business interests.

KAPLAN
Test Prep and Admissions

19. C

The U.S. was alarmed about the new radical regime in Russia and sent troops to encourage a possible counter-revolution. The expedition was also sent to prevent supplies sent to Russia to fight Germany from falling into Bolshevik hands. By doing this, the Americans earned the distrust of the Communist regime for many years.

20. C

Wilson had a vision of ending the war in such a way that no nation would be the loser or be punished. In an atmosphere of mutual trust and good will, the war would stop and the post war order could be discussed among equals without the need for revenge. This was too much to hope for and the peace settlement negotiated at Versailles blamed Germany and punished it economically, thus helping lead the world towards World War II. While Wilson did not agree with this, he placed great faith in the League of Nations and hoped it would make amends in the years to come.

21. B

The secretary of state under Lincoln and Johnson shared a common view that it was only a matter of time before the U.S. controlled Canada and other territories in North America. When Russia suffered defeat in the Crimean War it needed to unload its North American claims. As had happened in 1803, another nation's problem became an opportunity for America to increase its territory. Alaska added another 25% to the U.S. land holdings.

KAPLAN
Test Prep and Admissions

ANALYSES OF THE FREE-RESPONSE ESSAYS

Question 1:

Assess the validity of the following statement: "Woodrow Wilson's idealism was his greatest weakness."

Key Points

- To be 'idealistic' means that one must have a vision of what would be best for one's self or the world. Wilson had such a vision in attempting to adapt American democratic principals to help solve world problems

- Forced by the Great War to engage in international issues, Wilson brought his American viewpoint with him in trying to solve the post-war problems in 1919

- Wilson is the only 'academic' to become a president in U.S. history. He was a political science professor and president of Princeton University before becoming governor of New Jersey

- Wilson's promotion of the League of Nations was the final expression of his belief in a 'global democracy' that needed a place and forum to debate and vote on international issues

Arguments for and against the statement

Idealism was Wilson's greatest weakness	Idealism was not Wilson's greatest weakness
Wilson had a deep conviction that democratic principles could save the world from future wars	Wilson failed to promote his ideas because of his inherent inflexibility
Wilson believed that America had a chance to share its egalitarian beliefs with the world after the devastating war of 1914–1918	Could not relate well to his European peers and gain support for his ideas
As an idealist, Wilson could not understand the cynical views of Clemenceau in negotiating the Treaty at Versailles	Wilson blundered as a politician, not an idealist, by not selling his post-war vision to the Republicans in the Senate
Wilson put all his prestige behind the promotion of the League of Nations believing in the support from the voters. In this he underestimated the disillusionment in post-war America.	Personal traits such as stubbornness and arrogance may have been more to blame for Wilson's failure to have his policies ratified in Congress

KAPLAN
Test Prep and Admissions

Scoring Rubric

There are five scoring ranges:

Excellent

The answer must have a strong, clear thesis that explores the meaning of 'idealism' and how it applies or does not apply to Woodrow Wilson. The quality of the writing should be excellent, the answer must show logical patterns, and the student should include many of the major points in the above list (though they may go beyond the list). The organization should be clear. The answer may contain minor errors.

Very Good

The answer must have a thesis that states clearly whether Wilson was an idealist or not. The discussion must also determine if this was a factor in Wilson's post-war political problems. Organization of the answer must show logical patterns, and the student should include many of the specific points from the above list.

Adequate

The answer must try to make some argument and must include at least some of the points listed above. There may be flaws in the thesis argument.

Flawed

The answer will demonstrate serious weaknesses. It may have no thesis argument at all, and it will include few of the points listed above. The answer may show little understanding of who Wilson was and what an idealist is.

Severely Flawed

The answer will demonstrate almost no attempt to answer the question, and will include very few, if any, of the points listed above.

Question 2:

What interests in the United States argued for the acquisition of the Philippines after the Spanish-American War and why?

Key Points

- Europeans had been engaged in a fierce competition for Asian and African territories for many years prior to 1890
- The United States had once fought for its freedom as a colonial possession. For the U.S. to become a colonial power is an historical irony
- As American power grew, there were those Americans who advocated its use to expand its territories
- Darwinism was becoming a popular theory that was used to explain why strong nations were destined to dominate the weaker peoples of the world
- American imperialism was a very polarizing debate as many prominent Americans took opposing sides on the issue

The battle for the colonization of the Philippines 1898

- Anti-imperialists such as Andrew Carnegie felt that the acquisition of the Philippines would undermine democracy

- Traditional isolationism was appealed to in declining to become an imperial power. 'Foreign entanglements' seemed certain if America transplanted itself overseas

- The difficulty of defending a far flung empire was also seen as a disadvantage

- William Jennings Bryan came out for the Treaty of Paris and acquisition as he believed that democracy would be encouraged under American guidance

- Pro-imperialists saw unbounded commercial opportunities in Asia

- Taft, the first American governor of the Philippines, took a paternalistic attitude towards his 'little brown brothers.'

Scoring Rubric

There are five scoring ranges:

Excellent

The answer must have a strong, clear thesis that gives an assessment of American imperialism and who favored an American empire at the dawn of the 20th century. The essay should focus on the arguments for the colonization of the Philippines. The quality of the writing should be excellent, the answer must show logical patterns, and the student should include many of the major points in the above list (though they may go beyond these points). The organization should be clear. The answer may contain minor errors.

Very Good

The answer must have a thesis that details the reasons why some Americans were outspoken in promoting the acquisition of foreign territories. The answer must be logically organized, and the student should include many of the specific points from the above list.

Adequate

The answer must try to make some argument and must include at least some of the points listed above. There may be flaws in the thesis argument.

Flawed

The answer will demonstrate serious weaknesses. It may have no thesis argument at all, and it will include few of the points listed above. The answer may show little understanding of 19th century imperialism or why some Americans were attracted to the idea.

Severely Flawed

The answer will demonstrate almost no attempt to answer the question, and will include very few, if any, of the points listed above.

Chapter Eleven: **The Twenties and Thirties**

TIMELINE: 1920–1939

1920	Warren G. Harding elected president.
1920	Prohibition (18th Amendment) takes effect.
1920	Women's suffrage (19th Amendment) ratified.
1920–1924	Ku Klux Klan flourishes nationally with "100% Americanism" campaign.
1920s	Organized labor hurt by the growth of "open shop" plans and company unions.
1920s	Harlem Renaissance artists and activists draw attention to new urban African American culture.
1923–24	Teapot Dome scandal further tarnishes Harding's administration.
1924	Calvin Coolidge elected president.
1924	Restrictive immigration quotas imposed.
1925	Scopes's "monkey trial" in Tennessee.
1925	F. Scott Fitzgerald publishes *The Great Gatsby*.
1927	*The Jazz Singer* (first feature-length movie with sound) released.
1927	Charles Lindbergh flies solo across the Atlantic.

1928	Herbert Hoover elected president.
October 1929	Stock market crash.
1930	Hawley-Smoot bill increases tariffs to record highs.
1931	Drought begins in Great Plains region.
1932	Reconstruction Finance Corporation established.
1932	"Bonus Army" marches on Washington, D.C.
1932	Franklin D. Roosevelt elected president.
March–June 1932	"Hundred Days": Congress passes laws authorizing banking relief; Civilian Conservation Corps; abandonment of gold standard; agricultural relief; Tennessee Valley Authority; National Recovery Administration; Home Owners' Loan Corporation.
1934	"Indian New Deal" passed.
1935	Drought and dust storms in southern Plains begin to peak; dispossessed farm families move west.
1935	NRA declared unconstitutional.
July–August 1935	Second New Deal; Congress passes Wagner Act, Social Security Act, and authorizes Works Progress Administration.
1936	Roosevelt reelected easily by New Deal coalition of workers, African Americans, and farmers.
1937	Roosevelt's court-packing plan fails.
1937	CIO organizes auto and steel industries.
1937	"Roosevelt recession."
1939	John Steinbeck publishes *The Grapes of Wrath*.

CULTURE OF THE 1920s

The bonds of war had been thrown off and the consumer became the king—that sums up much of the 1920s. Materialism was the word, having new things and buying to keep pace with the neighbors seemed to be the thing to do. Women had gone through a radical transformation from homemaker to modern woman. No longer were they content to endure a life bounded by a home and children. This perspective clashed with the traditional values of the rural areas where the new modern woman was someone to be feared. Women danced, smoked, drove cars, went out without chaperones; it was wild. Jazz came into the American landscape; the new, modern music form was the first to be uniquely American. Automobiles gave people the ability to move. By 1929 there were 26.5 million autos registered. The auto transformed culture; it affected every facet of life. Americans used automobiles to shop, go to work, travel; autos became the replacement for the couch in the front parlor, they were used for dating. Ancillary industries were spawned. The steel, glass, rubber, gasoline and all the highway construction depended upon the auto as well.

KAPLAN
Test Prep and Admissions

There was also a "dark side" to the twenties. On the one hand were the bright lights and music, on the other hand was the nativism and isolationism of a post-war country. The isolationists wanted to turn their backs on the rest of the world and look only inward. The nativists wanted to turn their backs and close the borders to all who might want to enter the country. Some historians describe it as a time when the middle class abandoned progressive reforms and either supported or condoned the reactionary forces of nativism, racism and fundamentalism.

One of the most extreme groups of nativists was the Ku Klux Klan. These Klanners were not the same as their ancestors of the 1860s and 1870s; these were more extreme. They directed their wrath against African Americans and Catholics, Jews, foreigners, and suspected Communists. Their tactics included terrorizing and punishing their victims with whips, tar and feathers, and even lynching. The Klan might have continued to flourish in the Midwest but reports of graft and corruption began to be published and the leader, the Grand Dragon, was convicted of murder.

Fundamentalist religion saw a rebirth of interest in the 1920s. Modernists accepted a less literal interpretation of the Bible and thought that they could accept Darwin's theory of evolution without completely abandoning their religious faith. The fundamentalists differed and said that every word of the Bible was to be taken literally. The key to the fundamentalists was creationism, the idea that God had created the universe in seven days as told in the Book of Genesis. The radio became the new medium as the evangelists spoke to the masses.

Creationism was challenged in the schools when John T. Scopes volunteered to test the Tennessee law banning the teaching of evolution. In 1925 he taught a biology class and was quickly arrested. The American Civil Liberties Union volunteered to conduct his defense. The trial was riveting. Clarence Darrow spoke for the defense, William Jennings Bryan represented the state. The culmination of the trial saw Darrow call Jennings to the stand as an expert on the Bible and expose Jennings with clever questions. Jennings died five days later of a stroke. Scopes was found guilty, but the case was overturned on a technicality. It did, however, call attention to some of the inconsistencies of fundamentalism. Although there are laws on the books today banning the teaching of evolution, they are rarely enforced. The division between church and the schools seems to have survived, although every year there are still cases heard by the Supreme Court that involve schools and religion.

The 1920s were a high point of American literature. Novelists F. Scott Fitzgerald, Ernest Hemingway, and Sinclair Lewis and poets Ezra Pound and T. S. Eliot became known as the "lost generation" as they wrote about their disillusionment with America. Criticizing religion as hypocritical and condemning the sacrifices of a war they believed represented only the monied interests were the themes. Fitzgerald took to a life of drinking and Eliot and Hemingway expressed their disillusionment by moving to Europe.

The Harlem Renaissance took place in a section of New York City that was home to 200,000 African Americans by 1930. Their artistic achievements were legendary: the Jazz Age of Duke Ellington and Louis Armstrong began here. Bessie Smith sang the blues; Paul Robeson was a singer and actor who also came out of Harlem. At the Cotton Club, whites were entertained by African Americans who came in and out through the back door.

18th Amendment

Ratified in 1919, the manufacture, sale or transportation of intoxicating liquors in or out of the United States was prohibited. Prohibition had begun.

Birth of a Nation

D. W. Griffith directed the film in 1915, proving that the new celluloid invention could be a serious form of art. It showed a view of Reconstruction complete with stereotypical villains, sinister characters, pure white southerners, and faithful "darkies." It grossed $18 million and opened the door to a new industry. The next advancement would come in 1927 with "talkies." By the mid-1930s, every town had a movie theater.

consumer culture

After the war was over, factories re-tooled and began making consumer goods instead of war materials. The influence of a growing materialism and prosperity changed American society. Affluence, advertising, and a mass culture mentality redefined social values.

F. Scott Fitzgerald

One of the "lost generation," he wrote of surface gaiety and impending doom. He became famous at 24 with *This Side of Paradise* (1920). His most acclaimed work was *The Great Gatsby* (1925).

flappers

When fashionable women allowed their galoshes (boots) to flap about their ankles, they created "flappers." This new feminism was seen by some as a sign of a deteriorating society.

Marcus Garvey

Garvey was the founder of the United Negro Improvement Association and a spokesman for "Negro nationalism." He supported the position that African Americans should leave America and form their own nation in Africa. He would be found guilty of mail fraud (used in fund-raising) and sent to the Atlanta penitentiary. President Coolidge commuted his sentence and deported him to Jamaica in 1927.

Harlem Renaissance

During the 1920s, there was an unprecedented outburst of creative activity among African Americans in all fields of art. Centered in the predominantly African American section of New York City known as Harlem, it came to be called the Harlem Renaissance. It was fueled in part by the migration of African Americans to northern cities and the greater cultural and intellectual freedom they found there. Names associated with the Harlem Renaissance include intellectuals Alain LeRoy Locke, Marcus Garvey, and W. E. B. DuBois as well as authors Langston Hughes and Countee Cullen. The Harlem Renaissance influenced not only African American culture, but the culture and thought of American society as a whole.

Ernest Hemingway

He wrote of the search for the meaning of life. *The Sun Also Rises* (1926) focused on a group of Americans in Europe looking from the bars of Paris to the bullrings of Spain for the meaning of life. *A Farewell to Arms* (1929) told of a lost love between an ambulance driver in World War I and a nurse and was based on his own experiences.

KAPLAN
Test Prep and Admissions

Ku Klux Klan

This secret organization was the most extreme expression of nativism in the 1920s. The KKK directed their violence against African Americans, Catholics, Jews, foreigners, and suspected Communists. They terrorized their victims by burning crosses and punished their victims with whips, tar and feathers, and even hanging. In 1925 the leader of Indiana's Klan was convicted of murder, and membership began to decline. The Klan continues to exist today.

modernism

The range of influences that caused Protestants to re-examine their faith also reflected the tension between traditional values of rural areas and the modernizing forces in the cities. Modernists took a more historical view of the Bible and believed they could accept the theory of evolution without compromising their religious faith.

National Association for the Advancement of Colored People (NAACP)

The organization started with the call for a revival of the abolitionist spirit in response to a race riot in Springfield, Illinois in 1908. Their main strategy was to focus on legal actions designed to enforce the 14th and 15th Amendments. Their second task was to get lynchings declared illegal.

nativism

After the war, immigration was revived. Over a million foreigners came into the country between 1919 and 1921. Workers again feared for their jobs. Isolationists wanted only minimal contact with Europe and many believed the immigrant ranks were filled with undesirable radicals. The belief that anyone who was not white, of English ancestry, and Protestant was not to be trusted. Ethnic discrimination, racial discrimination, and religious discrimination all were used to justify behaviors that would not be tolerated today.

"new women"

After 1920 women saw themselves differently. They were no longer willing to settle for a life in the home. They were working outside the home and defied the societal restrictions of former years. Women revolted against sexual restrictions and took up dancing the new steps (foxtrot, Charleston), wearing the new fashions, smoking, and driving cars. Contraceptives became more accepted and divorce laws began to be liberalized.

Sacco and Vanzetti

The two anarchists were arrested after an armored car robbery in which a guard was killed. Their trial was sensationalistic, reflecting the fear many had of anarchists and the other "agitators," including the Reds (Communists). The two were executed after six years of appeals; many suggested that they were sentenced to die simply because they were poor and Italian.

Scopes Trial

John T. Scopes was a biology teacher in Tennessee who challenged the law banning the teaching of evolution. In the 1925 trial, Clarence Darrow defended Scopes and William Jennings Bryan, a three-time presidential candidate, defended the Biblical account. Darrow questioned Bryan as an expert on the Bible, which made him appear to be mocking fundamentalist positions. Bryan died a week later. Scopes was found guilty, but the verdict was overturned on a technicality.

KAPLAN
Test Prep and Admissions

POLITICS AND ECONOMICS IN THE 1920s

During the 1920s, the country moved towards that watershed moment in 1929 when the bottom fell out of the economy and the country entered "The Depression." President Harding's lack of oversight laid his government friends open to the temptations of corruption (Albert Fall) and negligence (Veterans Bureau medical and hospital supplies being sold for an individual's profit). When Harding died, Coolidge wisely stayed away from the investigations and let the chips fall.

Coolidge was a different kind of president and politician. He supported business but thought that the government and business should not be intertwined. He saw the prosperity in the mid-1920s as confirmation of his policies. Everything seemed to be booming. There were the new inventions of the movies and radio that tied the country together as never before. Transportation saw vast improvements through the airplane and the automobile. Henry Ford made ownership of an automobile an economic reality for his workers and all other workers when he raised the wages to $5 a day and lowered the cost of the Model T (the "tin lizzie") to $290 in 1924. "You can get any color car you want, so long as it's black," Ford was reported to have said. Ransom Olds would challenge that philosophy when he brought out the Oldsmobile in green and blue and established General Motors.

The prosperity of the manufacturing world did not extend to agriculture. The purchasing power of the farmer fell in almost direct correlation to the products available. Organized labor fared no better in the 1920s than did the farmers. The Red Scare and strikes left people with the impression that unions were filled with subversives and anarchists. The open shop concept allowed the discrimination against unions to manifest itself.

Herbert Hoover came into office as probably the most experienced man in the government. He had pushed the economy to new heights during World War I and re-organized the Commerce Department into a dynamic agency. However, he was unable to forecast the coming financial difficulties or deal with the economic crisis. He believed in voluntarism rather than government social action. He also thought the nation's business structure was sound and just needed a dose of confidence. He did move up the schedule for public works projects to provide jobs, and the Federal Reserve reverted to an easier credit policy, but his efforts were not enough.

Hoover could do little as the country slid further into a depression. The dark times fell over the country, and it would take a new president and an entirely new way of looking at the role of government to bring the United States out of the depression. However, full employment—always a goal of the New Deal—would not happen until the onset of World War II.

Bonus Army

World War I veterans had been promised bonuses for their military service to be paid in 1945. As times grew more difficult, veterans marched on Washington, D.C., demanding their bonus money. The Bonus Expeditionary Force camped on the Mall and was finally driven off when Hoover called out the military, under the command of General Douglas MacArthur (assisted by junior officers Dwight D. Eisenhower and George S. Patton, Jr.), to knock down their camp and burn it. Hoover was roundly criticized for the action, but said government would not be held hostage by the veterans' demands.

KAPLAN
Test Prep and Admissions

Calvin Coolidge

As Harding's vice president, he took over after Harding's death and wisely remained aloof from the fallout of the scandals of the Harding administration. He believed that government and business should not interfere with each other: "The man who builds a factory builds a temple." He was a conservative, pure and simple.

The Crash

The name given to the single largest fall that the stock market ever had experienced. More than 16 million shares were unloaded on October 29, 1929, signaling that all was not right with the economy and the country. Although connected to the worldwide depression, the United States did not recover quickly, and it would take revolutionary new practices on the part of government to reinvigorate the economy.

Emergency Relief and Construction Act

Herbert Hoover did not believe in federal assistance at the beginning of the Depression, he said volunteerism would be the answer. By 1932, he was persuaded that governmental assistance was needed. The Emergency Relief and Construction Act was signed on July 21, 1932. The money was not given to individuals directly, but was dispensed through relief loans to the states ($300 million), loans for state and local public works (up to $1.5 billion), and federal public works ($322 million)

Henry Ford

Ford revolutionized the industry with mass production and the assembly line. He further affected the auto industry when he paid his workers $5 a day, so that they could also afford to buy the cars they made.

Warren G. Harding

As the Republican candidate for president in 1920, Harding told audiences that he stood for a "Return to Normalcy." At the end of World War I and the Progressive Era, people were not in the mood for more experimentation and activism either abroad or at home. As president, Harding is best known for allowing his friends to work unchecked and appointing conservative Supreme Court Justices including William Howard Taft. Harding died while on a speaking trip to the Alaska Territory after suffering an attack of food poisoning.

Herbert Hoover

Hoover made his reputation as the man who mobilized the American economy in World War I. As Commerce Secretary under Harding and Coolidge, he made the department one of the most important in the government. He created the Bureau of Aviation in 1926 and the Federal Radio Commission in 1927. As president, however, he is best known for his inability to envision and organize a strong governmental response to the stock market crash and the Great Depression.

Hoovervilles

This was the name given to the squalid settlements that sprang up along railroad tracks during the Depression. Constructed of tarpaper and galvanized iron old packing crates and junk cars, these settlements of families who had lost their jobs and homes came to represent the poor and oppressed.

KAPLAN

Test Prep and Admissions

Charles Lindbergh

In 1927, he was the first to fly nonstop across the Atlantic Ocean and live to tell about it; for the rest of his life, he would be heralded for the 33-hour, 30-minute flight. He won the $25,000 prize that had been promised to the first successful transatlantic flight. Unfortunately, his son was kidnapped and later found dead; the trial of the kidnapper was sensationalism at its best. Later in life he would grow to be an admirer of the Nazis.

McNary-Haugen Bill

This agriculturally related bill was the first attempt to get for agriculture the benefits of the protective tariff. The plan was to dump American farm surpluses on the world market in order to raise prices at home; to raise the domestic farm prices to a point where they would have the same purchasing power they had (relatively speaking) had from 1909 to 1914 (viewed as the golden age of agriculture). Coolidge vetoed the first attempt and the second, calling the efforts unsound. The debates did bring the farm problem into the national limelight and define it as a problem of surpluses.

open shop

In theory, an open shop meant that the employer had the right to hire anyone whether or not they belonged to a union. In practice it often meant discrimination against unionists and the refusal to recognize unions even when most of the workers belonged to one.

Reconstruction Finance Corporation

In 1932, Congress forced Hoover to use governmental resources to help out the financial institutions in the country. With $500 million to start, and the authority to borrow up to $2 billion more, the RFC was to make emergency loans to banks, life insurance companies, building and loan societies, farm mortgage associations and railroads. It was criticized as favoring businesses, but remained a key agency during the Depression.

Scottsboro case

In 1931, nine African American farm boys were accused of raping two white girls on a freight train in Alabama. From that case came two important Supreme Court decisions, one detailing "due process" and the second stating that the "systematic exclusion" of African Americans from juries denied the defendants equal protection of the law.

Al Smith

Smith was the Democratic candidate for president against Herbert Hoover. Governor of New York, Smith represented many of the things people mistrusted; he was the son of Irish immigrants, he was Catholic, and anti-Prohibition. He lost handily to Hoover.

Teapot Dome scandal

President Harding's Interior Department Secretary, Albert Fall, allowed private interests to drill in a naval oil reserve without completing the competitive bidding process. Fall's standard of living suddenly improved and called attention to his actions. Bribery charges resulted. Conservationists were outraged and a senatorial investigation ensued. Teapot Dome, Wyoming was actually one of two drilling sites for which Fall had signed contracts; the other was in Elk Hills, California.

DEPRESSION AND THE NEW DEAL

The election of Franklin Roosevelt and the implementation of the New Deal changed the face of America. With 25 percent unemployment, the country was mired in a depression that seemed to have no end. Herbert Hoover, president as the country slid, acted too slowly. The sheer number of Americans in need overwhelmed his programs and measures of assistance. Hoover was hampered by his philosophical view of the role of government in relation to the lives of Americans. He came from the viewpoint that the division between the two should be clear; that government should not be involved in the day-to-day lives of the citizens.

Roosevelt held the opposite view. He understood that the need was too great to let philosophy keep the federal government from assisting. The scope of the New Deal defied all descriptions. Roosevelt's first move was to close all the banks to stop the run on the currency. FDR spoke on the radio to the country (the first president to use the media in this way). He told the citizens through the fireside chats, as the addresses came to be called, why the banks had been closed and what would happen next. He spoke as a father, allaying fears and asking for help and support. It worked. The Emergency Banking Act served to solidify the people behind the first of many New Deal Programs.

Government stepped into every facet of American life. In the first phase of the New Deal, Congress passed into law everything FDR asked. Congress repealed Prohibition (the 21st Amendment would make this final later) and established financial recovery programs. The Civilian Conservation Corps (CCC) took young men off the streets and put them to work in the woods. The Tennessee Valley Authority (TVA) harnessed the Tennessee River and brought electricity to rural America. The Civil Works Administration created more construction jobs. The United States went off the gold standard; which meant that the value of a dollar was set at $35 per ounce of gold, although Americans could no longer redeem dollars for the actual gold.

The second phase of the New Deal, sometimes called the Second New Deal, continued the relief programs. The Works Progress Administration continued the efforts to get people off relief rolls; workers built new bridges, roads, airports and public buildings. The reforms of the New Deal included the Wagner Act (and the resulting National Labor Relations Board), which guaranteed a worker's right to join a union and a union's right to bargain collectively. A revenue act of 1935 increased the tax on incomes, especially the incomes of the rich. Probably the most influential piece of legislation was the Social Security law. It created a federal insurance program based on payments made during a person's working life. Today, the Social Security Administration still monitors payments to millions of Americans.

Although the New Deal was projected to achieve full employment for Americans, this would not be achieved until the country's entrance into World War II. One of the last pieces of legislation of the New Deal was the Fair Labor Standards Act. This act provided a minimum wage (originally set at $.40 an hour), a maximum workweek of 40 hours, time and a half for overtime, and labor restrictions for children under the age of 16.

Certainly Roosevelt had his detractors. The Republicans, philosophically opposed to the New Deal, continually attacked the use of the billions of tax dollars for relief aid. They were outvoted. Democrats stood behind FDR and passed more sweeping new legislation in the first 100 days than most people thought possible. The New Deal, although targeted at all Americans, helped farmers and labor unions and did not do as much for some other groups, particularly women, African Americans, and Latinos.

Most of the New Deal programs were phased out as World War II began and the Depression ended. Some of the programs, such as social security and the TVA, continue to exist. What also continues to exist is the degree of involvement that government has in the everyday lives of Americans. Government dispenses funds for a myriad of programs, writes rules and regulations, and sets standards for all corners of American life.

Agricultural Adjustment Act (AAA)

This legislation encouraged farmers to reduce production by offering to pay government subsidies for every acre they did not plant. It was designed to raise the prices of agricultural produce so farmers could make a decent living, slowing the wave of farm foreclosures. The act was declared unconstitutional in 1935.

Civilian Conservation Corps (CCC)

This program employed young men in projects on federal lands and paid their families $25 of the $30 monthly wage directly.

Father Coughlin

This Catholic priest is known for his weekly radio program. As the founder of the National Union for Social Justice, Coughlin called for inflating currency and nationalizing all banks. He attacked the New Deal and made anti-Semitic as well as Fascist remarks until his superiors ordered him to stop.

Court-packing plan

FDR saw the Supreme Court as an obstacle to his New Deal programs, several of which it had declared unconstitutional. He proposed the judicial reorganization plan, which would have authorized the president to appoint another Supreme Court justice for every justice over the age of 70.5 years. The bill would have authorized six more justices.

Emergency Banking Relief Act

This legislation authorized the government to check the books of banks closed by the Banking Holiday and reopen those that were on sound financial footing.

Fair Labor Standards Act

In 1938 this legislation was enacted to provide regulations on businesses in interstate commerce. It mandated a minimum wage (fixed at $0.40 an hour), a maximum workweek of 40 hours with time and a half for overtime, and child labor restrictions for workers under 16.

Federal Emergency Relief Act (FERA)

This act gave grants of federal money to states and local governments that were operating soup kitchens and other forms of relief for the unemployed.

Federal Housing Administration (FHA)

This administration provided support to home purchasers that addressed needs in every geographic area for every group, or so it was intended. The FHA, however, refused to guarantee mortgages on houses purchased by African Americans in white neighborhoods.

Federal Securities Act

This legislation passed during the first 100 days of FDR's first administration required full disclosure in the issue of any new securities.

Grapes of Wrath

The John Steinbeck novel told the story of displaced farmers who took to the road and headed for the farms of California. Their story mirrored many other stories of personal tragedy and suffering brought on by the Depression.

Home Owners' Loan Corporation (HOLC)

This New Deal program provided refinancing of homes to prevent foreclosures.

Indian Reorganization Act

John Collier, a Native American rights spokesman, won FDR's support for a major policy change in 1934. The Dawes Act was repealed and lands were returned to the control of the tribes. The government would also support the preservation of the tribal cultures. In spite of the reforms, critics of the New Deal accused FDR of being paternalistic and withholding control from the Native Americans.

National Recovery Administration (NRA)

The NRA was an attempt by the government to guarantee reasonable profits for business and fair wages and hours for labor. With antitrust laws temporarily suspended, the NRA could help each industry set codes for wages, hours worked, levels of production, and prices of finished products. The law also gave workers the right to organize and bargain collectively.

National Industrial Recovery Act (NIRA)

This was the industrial equivalent to the AAA. Contained within its scope were two major parts: one section created the Public Works Administration (PWA) with resources of $3 billion for public buildings, highways, and flood control. Workers built the permanent improvements such as the Triborough Bridge in New York and Chicago's subway system. The other piece of the NIRA was the National Recovery Administration (NRA). Its purpose was to set wages and prices to stabilize business and to generate more purchasing power. The legislation would later be declared unconstitutional.

New Deal

FDR gave this name to the programs he would quickly introduce upon his inauguration. In his acceptance speech at the Democratic National convention, he had said: "I pledge you, I pledge myself, to a new deal for the American people."

Eleanor Roosevelt

As the wife of the president, she was the most active first lady to date. She served as FDR's eyes and ears and visited many places in his stead. Although their personal relationship had some problems, they had great respect for each other. Eleanor was the social conscience of the president and always reminded him to support minorities and others who were less fortunate.

Franklin Delano Roosevelt (FDR)

Born to wealth and privilege, Roosevelt could have retired after he was paralyzed by polio while summering at his cottage on Campobello Island in New Brunswick, Canada. Instead, he choose to remain in politics. His greatest strengths were his personality, his ability to speak to the country, and his ability to work with and inspire people. He is the only president to be elected to four terms. He died 83 days into his fourth term and was succeeded by his vice president, Harry Truman.

Second Agricultural Adjustment Act

This legislation followed up on the first agricultural act, which had been declared unconstitutional by the Supreme Court. The Soil Conservation and Domestic Allotment Act was pushed through Congress in six weeks to provide benefit payments for land taken out of production and set aside for conservation. This second act was not declared unconstitutional.

Second New Deal

After FDR's reelection in 1936, the Second New Deal was instituted. FDR was pragmatic in that he kept the programs that worked and eliminated those that did not. The New Deal left American changed forever as government moved more directly into the lives of all. In spite of that movement, the capitalistic nature of the economy remained intact.

Share Our Wealth

Huey Long, as governor of Louisiana and later a U.S. senator, proposed to liquidate large personal fortunes, guarantee every family a $5,000 allowance and every worker a $2,500 wage, grant pensions, lower the number of hours worked, pay veteran's bonuses, and assure a college education for every student. His plan, named Share Our Wealth, called attention to the problems of the distributions of wealth, a topic most politicians refused to address. He had enormous popular appeal especially in the South, but was assassinated in the Louisiana state capitol in 1935.

Social Security Act

The 1935 legislation created a federal insurance program for workers. Based on automatic collections from both employers and employees, the trust fund created would make regular monthly payments to retirees over 65. Others benefiting from this new law were the unemployed, the disabled, and dependent children. The program exists to this day.

Tennessee Valley Authority (TVA)

The TVA was established as part of FDR's New Deal and was designed to help get the economy going again. It was to build dams, operate electric power plants, and control the flooding and erosion for the Tennessee River Valley. It brought electricity to an area of the country that was as yet without power. The TVA exists to this day.

Wagner Act

The National Labor Relations Act of 1935 replaced the labor provisions of the National Industrial Recovery Act that had been declared unconstitutional. The Wagner Act guaranteed a worker's right to join a union and a union's right to bargain collectively. A new agency, the National Labor Relations Board, was created to enforce the law and make sure worker's rights were protected.

Works Progress Administration

Led by Harry Hopkins, the WPA spent millions from 1935 to 1940 to provide jobs. Most WPA projects were building bridges, roads, airports and public buildings. Unemployed artists, writers, photographers and actors were paid to continue to practice their crafts. Photographers were sent around the country to document the depression and the effects of the government programs.

KAPLAN
Test Prep and Admissions

MULTIPLE-CHOICE QUESTIONS

1. When World War I veterans marched in the Bonus Expeditionary Force in 1932 they were trying to:

    (A) support the Civil Rights Movement for African Americans.

    (B) convince the government to rearm the military.

    (C) get Congress to release a promised payment to the soldiers who had fought in the war.

    (D) petition the president to legalize the Socialist Party in America.

    (E) protest the collapse of farm prices during the Depression.

2. Which of the following best characterizes the federal immigration policy of the 1920s?

    (A) In the face of strong opposition to immigration from labor unions, restrictions brought immigration to a standstill.

    (B) The "Gentlemen's Agreement" was canceled, increasing immigration from Japan.

    (C) It was aimed at increasing the proportion of immigrants from northern and western Europe.

    (D) It was aimed at increasing the number of immigrants from southern and eastern Europe.

    (E) It was aimed at decreasing the number of immigrants from Mexico.

3. The use of the assembly line to manufacture automobiles by Henry Ford had resulted in which of the following by 1930?

    (A) Working class people could borrow half the amount needed to buy a car

    (B) A marked decrease in railroad travel

    (C) Cheaper imported cars began to flood the market

    (D) Average American families could purchase a car for less than $1,000

    (E) Ford went broke trying to make an inexpensive car for America

4. The U.S. government under Franklin Roosevelt made a marked change in its policies toward Native Americans with the passage of:

    (A) the Bureau of Indian Affairs.

    (B) the Arapaho Lease Act.

    (C) the Native Judicial Act.

    (D) the New Dawes Act.

    (E) the Indian Reorganization Act.

5. The 1925 Scopes "monkey trial" pitted religious conservatives against:

    (A) the laws of the state of Tennessee.

    (B) William Jennings Bryan's support of academic freedom.

    (C) liberals who believed that Darwinism should be taught in the school curriculum.

    (D) Clarence Darrow, who believed the Bible to be infallible.

    (E) The Supreme Court, which ruled that the teaching of evolution was unconstitutional in American schools.

6. In the 1920s the farmers demanded a change in the government's farm program in order to obtain:

   (A) direct farm subsidies from the federal government.

   (B) more credit so they could get out of debt.

   (C) a federal program that would reduce surpluses rather than acreage.

   (D) a higher tariff on agricultural goods being imported into the U.S.

   (E) better prices for their crops.

7. The neutrality legislation of 1935–1937 was based on the contention that one of the chief causes of World War I had been:

   (A) a public that was eager to join the war in Europe.

   (B) American economic ties with the belligerents.

   (C) a press that had created hostility toward Germany.

   (D) no consensus about what American foreign policy should be.

   (E) lack of public support for the idea of collective security.

8. To alleviate unemployment, the Works Progress Administration (WPA) attempted to provide all of the following except:

   (A) jobs building bridges, dams, and public buildings.

   (B) part-time employment and technical training for jobless youth.

   (C) jobs for artists to create murals and other works of art for federal buildings.

   (D) jobs for writers to collect materials on folklore and regional culture.

   (E) jobs for veterans to help train new draftees in the Army.

9. Congressional legislation in the 1930s reflected an abandonment of America's historic position on:

   (A) entangling alliances.

   (B) freedom of the seas.

   (C) the Monroe Doctrine.

   (D) the Good Neighbor policy.

   (E) the Open Door policy in Asia.

10. The appointments of Henry Stimson and Frank Knox to Franklin Roosevelt's cabinet were unusual because both were:

    (A) bankers from New York.

    (B) Republicans.

    (C) isolationists.

    (D) former members of the Coolidge administration.

    (E) corporation lawyers.

11. The most important event in aviation history in the 1920s was:

    (A) Charles Lindbergh's flight from New York to Paris.

    (B) the barnstorming of Eddie Rickenbacker.

    (C) the round-the-world flight of U.S. Navy pilots.

    (D) Richard Paines' flight from Japan to the west coast of the U.S.

    (E) the invention of the monoplane.

12. All of the following were root causes of the Great Depression EXCEPT:

    (A) falling crop prices for farmers.

    (B) overly generous wage increases in U.S. factories.

    (C) a growing imbalance between rising productivity and purchasing power.

    (D) tax reductions that led to oversaving.

    (E) unsound banking practices.

13. Which of the following statements about the Social Security Act is true?

    (A) It provided old-age pensions and unemployment insurance.

    (B) It was a temporary relief measure to help people hurt by the Depression.

    (C) It provided childcare to working mothers.

    (D) If offered universal medical insurance.

    (E) It was based on a regressive tax that took a smaller percentage of higher incomes.

14. Which reason best explains the growth of the Ku Klux Klan in the 1920s?

    (A) Motion pictures romanticized the Klan and its history.

    (B) Large scale immigration from Europe swelled the membership of the Klan.

    (C) There was a conservative reaction against shifting moral standards.

    (D) More Americans went to church and listened to sermons praising the "new piety."

    (E) Many Americans were anti-foreign after the Treaty of Versailles was reported in the press.

15. All of the following statements agree with the New Deal liberalism of the Democratic Party in the 1930s EXCEPT:

    (A) The minimum wage should be set high enough to keep people off the welfare rolls.

    (B) Modifying the gold standard was one way to counteract deflation.

    (C) Minimum wage laws promote unemployment and welfare.

    (D) Economic health lies in the purchasing power of the lower and middle classes.

    (E) High taxes in prosperous times tend to control inflation by limiting spending power.

16. An important result of the Hawley-Smoot Tariff Act was:

    (A) new increases in wages for American factory workers.

    (B) tariff reprisals from a number of foreign countries.

    (C) general improvements in business in the U.S.

    (D) more imports being shipped into the U.S.

    (E) an increase in farm incomes.

17. Franklin Roosevelt's disagreement with the Supreme Court differed from that of previous presidents because:

    (A) he feared the growth of power of the judicial branch.

    (B) he was the first president to back labor when they went on strike.

    (C) he proposed a national minimum wage for workers.

    (D) he proposed to limit the number of justices who sit on the Court.

    (E) he was angered when the Court declared major parts of his legislative program unconstitutional.

18. All of the following were a part of the African American experience in the 1920s and 1930s EXCEPT:

    (A) a flowering of African American culture in Harlem.

    (B) a large migration from the rural South to northern urban areas.

    (C) gains made in voting rights in the South.

    (D) a "new Negro nationalism" that exalted African American culture.

    (E) an increase in the number of lynchings in the South.

19. The isolationist policies of the United States in the 1930s were broken down in the face of:

    (A) German imperialism in North Africa.

    (B) British trade agreements in Latin and South America.

    (C) a possible two-ocean war against an Asian and European enemy.

    (D) a united Asia under the leadership of the People's Republic of China.

    (E) the growing imperialism of Soviet Russia after 1932.

20. The conservative Democratic opposition to the New Deal in the late 1930s:

    (A) was strongest in the South.

    (B) supported plans to replace Roosevelt with Henry Wallace as the Democratic presidential candidate in 1936.

    (C) supported plans to replace Roosevelt with Huey Long as the Democratic presidential candidate in 1936.

    (D) succeeded in removing three of Roosevelt's cabinet members.

    (E) was strongly opposed to Roosevelt's agricultural policies.

KAPLAN

Test Prep and Admissions

ESSAY QUESTION

Document-Based Question (DBQ):

How did Franklin Delano Roosevelt appeal to the 'common man' and depart from the policies of his Republican predecessors?

Use evidence from the documents **and** your knowledge of the period from 1932 to 1940 to compose your answer.

Document A

Franklin D. Roosevelt, "First Inaugural Address," March 4, 1933:

"Plenty is at our doorstep, but a generous use of it languishes in the very sight of the supply. Primarily this is because the rulers of the exchange of mankind's goods have failed, through their own stubbornness and their own incompetence, have admitted their failure, and abdicated. Practices of the unscrupulous money changers stand indicted in the court of public opinion, rejected by the hearts and minds of men.

True they have tried, but their efforts have been cast in the pattern of an outworn tradition. Faced by failure of credit they have proposed only the lending of more money. Stripped of the lure of profit by which to induce our people to follow their false leadership, they have resorted to exhortations, pleading tearfully for restored confidence. They know only the rules of a generation of self-seekers. They have no vision, and when there is no vision the people perish."

Document B

Franklin D. Roosevelt, "Second Inaugural Address," January 20, 1937:

"Instinctively we recognized a deeper need—the need to find through government the instrument of our united purpose to solve for the individual the ever-rising problems of a complex civilization. Repeated attempts at their solution without the aid of government had left us baffled and bewildered. For, without that aid, we had been unable to create those moral controls over the services of science which are necessary to make science a useful servant instead of a ruthless master of mankind. To do this we knew that we must find practical controls over blind economic forces and blindly selfish men."

Document C

Herbert Hoover, "Inaugural Address," March 4, 1929:

"The election has again confirmed the determination of the American people that regulation of private enterprise and not Government ownership or operation is the course rightly to be pursued in our relation to business. In recent years we have established a differentiation in the whole method of business regulation between the industries which produce and distribute commodities on the one hand and public utilities on the other. In the former, our laws insist upon effective competition; in the latter, because we substantially confer a monopoly by limiting competition, we must regulate their services and rates. . .

Business has by cooperation made great progress in the advancement of service, in stability, in regularity of employment and in the correction of its own abuses."

Document D

Calvin Coolidge, "Authority and Religious Liberty," Address delivered to the Holy Name Society, Washington, D.C., Sept. 21, 1924:

"Coincident with the right of individual liberty under the provisions of our Government is the right of individual property. . . . When once the right of the individual to liberty and equality is admitted, there is no escape from the conclusion that he alone is entitled to the rewards of his own industry. . . .

Socialism and communism cannot be reconciled with the principles which our institutions represent. They are entirely foreign, entirely un-American. We stand wholly committed to the policy that what the individual produces belongs entirely to him to be used by him for the benefit of himself, to provide for his own family and to enable him to serve his fellow men."

Document E

Warren G. Harding, "Inaugural Address," March 4, 1921:

"We can reduce the abnormal expenditures, and we will. We can strike at war taxation, and we must [do so]. . . . Our most dangerous tendency is to expect too much of government, and at the same time do for it too little. We contemplate the immediate task of putting our public household in order. We need a rigid and yet sane economy, combined with fiscal justice, and it must be attended by individual prudence and thrift...

The forward course of the business cycle is unmistakable. . . . The call is for productive America to go on. I know that Congress and the Administration will favor every wise Government policy to aid the resumption and encourage continued progress.

I speak for administrative efficiency, for lightened tax burdens, for sound commercial practices, for adequate credit facilities, for sympathetic concern for all agricultural problems, for the omission of unnecessary interference of Government with business, for an end to Government's experiment in business. . . ."

Document F

President Herbert Hoover, letter to Senator Simeon Fess of Ohio, Feb. 21, 1933:

"They have begun to realize what the abandonment of a successful program of this administration which was bringing rapid recovery last summer and fall now means and they are alarmed at possible new deal policies indicated by the current events. . . .

What is needed, if the country is not to drift into great grief, is the immediate and emphatic restoration of confidence in the future. The resources of the country are incalculable, the available credit is ample but lenders will not lend, and men will not borrow unless they have confidence. Instead they are withdrawing their resources and their energies. The courage and enterprise of the people still exist and only await release from fears and apprehension."

Document G

"Leases upon Naval Oil Reserves," Senate, 70th Congress 1st Session, Report 1326, pt. 2, pg. 3, May 28, 1928:

"The investigation has uncovered the slimiest of slimy trails beaten by privilege. The investigation has shown, let us hope, privilege at its worst. The trail is one of dishonesty, greed, violation of law, secrecy, concealment, evasion, falsehood, and cunning. It is a trail of betrayals by trusted and presumably honorable men—betrayals of a government, of certain business interests and the people who trusted and honored them; it is a trial showing a flagrant degree of the exercise of political power and influence, and the power and influence of great wealth upon individuals and political parties; it is the trail of despoilers and schemers, far more dangerous to the well-being of our Nation and our democracy than all those who have been deported from our shores in all time as undesirable citizens."

Document H

Calvin Coolidge, "Government and Business," Address before the Chamber of Commerce of the State of New York, New York City, November 19, 1925:

"It is the important and righteous position that business holds in relation to life which gives warrant to the great interest which the National Government constantly exercises for the promotion of its success. This is not exercised as has been the autocratic practice abroad of directly supporting and financing different business projects, except in case of great emergency; but we have rather held to a democratic policy of cherishing the general structure of business while holding its avenues open to the widest competition, in order that its opportunities and its benefits might be given the broadest possible participation. While it is true that the Government ought not to be and is not committed to certain methods of acquisition which, while partaking of the nature of unfair practices, try to masquerade under the guise of business, the Government is and ought to be thoroughly committed to every endeavor of production and distribution which is entitled to be designated as true business. Those who are so engaged, instead of regarding the Government as their opponent and enemy, ought to regard it as their vigilant supporter and friend."

ANSWER KEY

Multiple-Choice Questions

1. C
2. A
3. D
4. E
5. C
6. E
7. B
8. E
9. B
10. B
11. A
12. B
13. A
14. C
15. C
16. B
17. E
18. C
19. C
20. A

Answers and Explanations

1. C

Veterans who had fought in the Great War had been promised a retirement bonus. When the Great Depression struck, many of these men were jobless and desperate. They organized a march on Washington to petition Congress to give them their bonuses earlier. This was refused and the U.S. Army cleared the demonstrators out of the capital.

2. A

Fears of job competition and a new nativism made the 1920s a decade when immigration into the United States was virtually stopped. Quotas and restrictions passed into law made it very difficult to immigrate to the U.S. from overseas. Part of this was the result of a growing concern about radical revolutions being imported into the country. Labor unions also feared that immigrants would take jobs away from "real" Americans.

3. D

Ford's goals were to make money through mass production and to make cars affordable to the average American. Increases in the efficiency of his factories actually brought car prices down after World War I. Buying on credit became popular and the general prosperity of the 1920s caused automobile sales to boom.

4. E

The Bureau of Indian Affairs under Roosevelt reversed the government policy towards Native American tribes that had been defined by the Dawes Act. The Indian Reorganization Act dealt with the tribes more individually and without the attempt to forcibly "Americanize" or assimilate Native Americans.

5. C

The Scopes trial was sponsored by the American Civil Liberties Union, which wanted to make a test of state laws limiting academic freedom in the classroom. Scopes agreed to be the defendant and the trial received much publicity as two great legal minds, Clarence Darrow and William Jennings Bryan, opposed one another. Liberals believed that religion should have no role in dictating school curriculum and that this was a constitutional issue that needed to be decided. Scopes was convicted and fined a small amount for teaching evolution in his class.

6. E

During the war farmers had prospered when crop prices were high. They purchased more land and machinery with these profits. After the war, farm prices fell because farmers were overproducing. Farmers wanted price controls for their produce but until the surplus issue was resolved this remained impossible.

7. B

These laws barred the sale or transportation of arms to warring nations and refused loans to nations at war outside the Western Hemisphere. Americans were ordered to stay out of war zones and not to travel on ships belonging to nations at war. This hearkened back to the loss of American life on British ships prior to the U.S. entering World War I.

8. E

Roosevelt's general philosophy was that the 'dole' or welfare was "a narcotic that destroyed the human spirit." His programs were to employ Americans to do things that would benefit the nation. These included building public facilities and improving federal lands including national parks and forests. He did not use the military as a jobs program but did offer veterans other types of opportunities within the WPA program.

KAPLAN
Test Prep and Admissions

9. B

Historically, the U.S. had always fought for the right of U.S. citizens to travel on any ships even in time of war. In the 1930s the American government did not champion this right and urged its citizens to travel on U.S. vessels only—or better yet, not to travel overseas at all.

10. B

Previous presidents tended to appoint only members of their own party to the cabinet. Roosevelt took a bold step to appoint members of the opposing party and sought to have bipartisan support for his programs in the 1930s.

11. A

Aviation was greatly stimulated by the First World War and afterwards planes were used to carry goods and the mail from city to city. Speed and distance records were set and larger planes were designed. Still, long distance flights between nations were not a part of the American experience until an unknown mail pilot named Charles Lindbergh made the first flight across the Atlantic from New York to Paris. He became the most sensational hero of the decade and helped promote the growth of aviation.

12. B

Throughout the boom of the 1920s the buying power of the average American was shrinking. There were no significant wage increases for American workers and farmers were especially hard hit when crop prices collapsed.

13. A

The Social Security Act offered a compulsory insurance program overseen by the federal government. Money would be taken out of payrolls and saved for each American until retirement. This provided a small 'safety net' for the aged and gave them a supplemental income after age 65. This is one of the longest lasting of the New Deal programs and millions of Americans receive these payments today.

14. C

The 1920s was a time of cultural change in the U.S. and there was a conservative reaction to this. Nativism and racism have always been a part of the American psyche but it is brought to the fore when history is in flux. The Klan expanded beyond the South and appealed to many Americans who were attracted to the secret society that promised to defend what they believed to be American values.

15. C

The New Deal was successful in establishing a minimum wage and establishing the belief that workers needed laws to protect them against being paid too little. Today there is widespread acceptance of the minimum wage concept as one way the government protects the working class from being exploited by employers. However, the argument against a minimum wage law—that it reduces the number of jobs, thus increasing unemployment—is still heard during debates over increases in the minimum wage.

16. B

The Hawley-Smoot Tariff Act of 1930 pushed protectionism to its highest level in U.S. history. This brought prompt retaliation from other nations: Twenty-five nations put up similar barriers to American goods and U.S. foreign trade fell 50 percent in 18 months. This came at a time when the economy was already plummeting at the start of the Great Depression.

17. E

The Court had struck down two key Roosevelt programs including the National Recovery Act and the Agricultural Adjustment Act. This was a great blow to the president's plans for the recovery of the nation during the Great Depression and he strongly criticized the Supreme Court for being out of touch with the needs of the people. He even tried to change the Constitution and increase the membership of the court so he could appoint new justices himself.

18. C

The 1920s were an interesting and contradictory period in terms of African American culture. New musical forms such as jazz were produced by African American artists and in Harlem there was a literary and artistic renaissance detailing the African American experience. Racial segregation was still the custom though, and there were few political gains made by African Americans in the U.S.—especially in the South, where lynchings were on the rise.

19. C

While most Americans remained isolationist in attitude right up to Pearl Harbor, there was a rising fear that war would come. This led to a rare peacetime build up of the military and also the first peacetime draft ever. With Germany and Japan arming, the U.S. was faced with fighting two nations on opposite sides of the world. This called for a larger Navy at least, which led to the enlarging of the Pearl Harbor base in Hawaii.

20. A

Southern Democrats were more conservative than their northern counterparts and came to oppose some of the social programs that FDR wanted. These Democrats were losing their regional voting block in the party and were angered when African Americans were allowed to participate in the national convention in 1936. The Southern Democrats started to join with Republicans in Congress to vote against Roosevelt's program by 1937.

KAPLAN
Test Prep and Admissions

ANALYSIS OF THE DBQ

Question:

How did Franklin Delano Roosevelt appeal to the 'common man' and depart from the policies of his Republican predecessors?

Use evidence from the documents **and** your knowledge of the period from 1932 to 1940 to compose your answer.

Use of the Documents

Each of the documents offers a perspective on the New Deal and its effects on the country and society as a whole.

Documents A and B: These are inaugural speeches by Roosevelt—both attack the 'selfish' business interests in American society and suggest that government needs to help those in need.

Documents C, D, E, F, and H: These are all speeches by Republican presidents in the decade before the Depression.

Document C: Hoover, who would be blamed for the Depression, suggests that business has been able to regulate itself.

Documents D and H: Coolidge says only that everyone should enjoy the fruits of their labor and that socialism is anti-American. He puts forth the idea that government is a friend of business.

Document E: A bland commentary from one of America's worst presidents about a 'sane economy.' Harding's inaugural address shows him to be in favor of lower taxes, and for an end to "unnecessary" government interference with business. Harding also argues that the "forward course of the business cycle" must go on, and that it deserves government support to encourage the productivity and progress brought by business.

Document G: A Senate report of the scandal that rocked the Harding administration where cabinet officials were found guilty of corruption when arranging oil leases in Wyoming.

Key Points from Outside Information

Republican views on American business

- Calvin Coolidge once said, "The business of America is business"
- Unions were suspected of having Socialist ideas that were antithetical to American progress. Unions fell out of public favor especially when strikes were organized
- The Supreme Court largely appointed by Republican administrations overturned a minimum wage law for women and nullified some child labor restrictions
- All Republican presidents in the 1920s followed conservative economic policies
- They pushed for lower income tax rates
- Businesses offered workers more benefits to dissuade them from organizing. This was called 'welfare capitalism' which was supported by the Republican Party

Roosevelt's (FDR) approach to the economy in the 1930s

- The Depression was so severe by 1932 that Roosevelt was able to attack the business interests and blame them and the Republicans for much of the nation's economic problems
- The scandals of the 1920s suggested that the government would have to oversee some parts of private industry to protect ordinary people
- Unlike the 'hands off' Republicans of the 20s, FDR promised Americans that he would revive the economy through government action
- Roosevelt promised to experiment with solutions and keep the ones that worked

Students could make the case that Roosevelt saw government as a 'helper' of the common citizen. The Democratic Party drew support from workers, farmers, and small businesses that had been battered by the Depression.

The government's response after 1932

- An active economic policy: laid groundwork for large federal programs that created employment and provided services for the needy
- Created price supports for farmers and legal protection for labor unions
- The government responded to Republican critics by saying they had led the nation to economic ruin and now it had to be saved
- The New Deal was a large combination of programs that dealt with such economic problems as farm surpluses, unemployment, deflation, and bank failures

Scoring Rubric

There are five scoring ranges:

Excellent

Argument: The essay must have a strong, clear thesis. The student should take a clear position either in support of or against the proposition stated in the question. The essay should also indicate a grasp of the complexity of the issue, referring to pros and cons of entrepreneurial behavior in this time period.

Critical Thought: The student should explain how each document supports or undermines the thesis. The student should address conflicts and contradictions in the evidence. Any outside information must be relevant to the argument.

Evidence: The student should use documents **and** outside information (see lists above) throughout the essay. Most of the documents must be used, and students might address the relationship between the sources.

Writing Style: The essay must be well organized and well written; it must make sense throughout.

KAPLAN
Test Prep and Admissions

Very Good

Argument: The thesis should be consistent with the question, but it may not be sufficiently focused.

Critical Thought: The answer must include an analysis of several of the documents and must incorporate outside information.

Evidence: The student should make use of the documents and outside information (see lists above) that support the position being argued. Discussion of relationships between the sources used may be limited.

Writing Style: The essay should be well organized and clearly written; it must be logical, but some points may be unclear.

Adequate

Argument: The thesis is only partially developed. It may address the question, but it does so in a way that doesn't acknowledge the question's complexity. The essay will most likely fail to prioritize the arguments.

Critical Thought: The essay is primarily descriptive or narrative, and doesn't provide an analysis of the question or of the evidence provided. It will not address all the relevant issues, and will ignore the opposing position.

Evidence: The student may paraphrase the documents and may misinterpret a document to better fit the argument. The student will use only a little outside information and may refer to some but not all of the documents. The answer may contain errors.

Writing Style: The writing and organization is unclear, but acceptable.

Flawed

Argument: The thesis will be unclear and will not be supported in the body of the essay. Use of evidence will be unclear, and the argument will be poorly developed.

Critical Thought: The essay will show only a limited understanding of the question, and will offer little or no analysis. What little analysis there is will be inaccurate. The student will show little understanding of the issue of industrialization.

Evidence: The student will not make use of the documents appropriate to their argument, and may use documents that actually support the opposing position. The use of documents will be haphazard, with references only to brief excerpts or paraphrases. There will be little outside information. The argument may contain errors.

Writing Style: The answer will be weakly organized and the writing will be unclear.

Severely Flawed

Argument: The student provides no thesis, or provides one that is not relevant to the question.

Critical Thought: The student demonstrates little or no understanding of the question.

Evidence: The student makes almost no use of the documents provided, and makes little or no use of outside information. The answer contains major errors.

Writing Style: The answer is disorganized and poorly written.

KAPLAN
Test Prep and Admissions

Chapter Twelve: **World War II and Containment**

- Timeline: 1922–1953

- Path to War

- World War II

- Containment and the Cold War

- Multiple-Choice Questions

- Essay Questions

- Answer Key

- Answers and Explanations

- Analyses of the Free-Response Essays

TIMELINE: 1922–1953

1922	Major powers sign treaties pledging to halt some naval arms buildups, to respect the status quo in the Pacific, to maintain a commitment to Open Door policy in China.
1928	Scores of countries sign Kellogg-Briand pact renouncing war as an instrument of policy.
1928–1936	Coolidge, Harding, and Roosevelt implement "Good Neighbor" policy towards most Latin American nations.
1931	Japan invades Manchuria.
1934	Hitler becomes the leader of Germany.
1934–1937	Nye Committee investigates profiteering in World War I.
1935	Roosevelt signs Neutrality Act of 1935 forbidding sale of arms or munitions to nations at war.
1935	Italy (led by Mussolini) invades Ethiopia.
1936	Germany occupies the Rhineland.
1936–1939	Spanish Civil War; though Mussolini and Hitler aid Franco's forces, democracies do little to help republicans.

1937	Japanese troops advance farther in China.
1937	Roosevelt gives "quarantine" speech, apparently signaling move away from isolationism; his speech has few concrete results.
1938	Hitler forces the *Anschluss* uniting Austria with Germany.
1938–1939	Hitler invades Sudetenland, and then occupies all of Czechoslovakia.
September 1939	Hitler invades Poland shortly after signing nonaggression pact with Russia.
June 1940	France falls to German troops.
November 1940	Roosevelt defeats Wendell Willkie for third term.
March 1941	Lend-Lease program passes Congress.
June 1941	Germany attacks Russia.
July 1941	Japan takes control of Indochina.
August 1941	Churchill and Roosevelt meet and draft Atlantic Charter.
September 1941	U.S. imposes oil embargo on Japan.
Fall 1941	Undeclared naval war in north Atlantic.
November 1941	Negotiations between Japan and U.S. over Indochina, China, and oil fail.
December 1941	Surprise Japanese attack on Pearl Harbor; U.S. declares war.
1941–1942	Philip Randolph's plans to organize a march on Washington pressures FDR to issue executive order forbidding racial discrimination in defense contracts; African American press leads "Double V" campaign.
1942	Defense jobs begin to draw hundreds of thousands to West.
1942	Russians hold off German armies in lengthy siege of Stalingrad.
February 1942	Roosevelt issues Executive Order 9066, interning Japanese Americans on the West Coast.
May-June 1942	Battles of Coral Sea and Midway Island end string of Japanese victories in Pacific.
1942	Price freezes and rationing go into effect as mobilization intensifies.
1942	Conservative gains in midterm elections lead to end of many New Deal programs.
1942–1943	Allied victories in North Africa and North Atlantic.
1943	Allied troops land in Sicily.
June 6, 1944	D-Day—Allied troops land in Normandy in largest naval invasion in history.
November 1944	Roosevelt reelected to record fourth term.
1944	Congress passes GI Bill.
February 1945	Churchill, Stalin, and FDR set terms of postwar world at Yalta conference.
April 1945	Roosevelt dies in Warm Springs, Georgia.
Spring 1945	Berlin falls to Soviets; Soviet Union extends sphere of influence across Eastern Europe.
August 1945	Atomic bombs dropped on Hiroshima and Nagasaki; Japan surrenders.

1946	Strikes in major industries, including coal, steel, and railroads.
1946	United Nations established.
1946	George Kennan sends "Long Telegram" warning of Soviet expansionism; expands on these ideas in later *Foreign Affairs* article spelling out idea of containment.
1947	Taft-Hartley Act passed.
1947	Truman outlines "Truman Doctrine" while calling for aid to Greece and Turkey.
1947	Jackie Robinson joins Brooklyn Dodgers, becoming the first African American to break the color barrier in professional baseball.
1947	National Security Council and Central Intelligence Agency established.
1947	Truman orders background checks and loyalty oaths for federal employees.
1948	Marshall Plan to aid Western Europe passed.
1948	State of Israel established.
1948	Truman desegregates armed services.
1948–1949	Soviet blockade of Berlin and Allied airlift.
1948	Truman reelected, defeating Thomas Dewey and Strom Thurmond.
1949	NATO established.
1949	U.S.S.R. tests atomic bomb.
1949	Mao Zedong victorious over Chiang Kai-Shek's Nationalists in China.
February 1950	Senator Joseph McCarthy begins rise to notoriety with speech in Wheeling, West Virginia.
June 1950	North Korea invades South Korea across 38th parallel.
1950	Alger Hiss convicted of perjury.
1950–1953	Korean War; conflict ends with 38th parallel boundary still in place.

PATH TO WAR

The seeds of World War II were planted at the end of World War I. Germany was kept out of the negotiations that led to the Treaty of Versailles. The European countries held out for retribution from Germany for so long that President Wilson gave up in exasperation and acquiesced if his League of Nations remained intact (although Wilson was never able to get the United States to join). Germany was assessed huge reparations, far beyond anything the country could pay, considering that Germany was in no better position than any other nation at the end of the war.

Adolf Hitler, the charismatic German army corporal, arrived on the scene and began to speak about the injustices Germany suffered from. He gained a following among the unemployed and his following grew. The Nazi Party began to win votes. Ultimately Hitler would be elected Chancellor, and then made Chancellor for life. The Nazis were firmly in power.

KAPLAN
Test Prep and Admissions

In Italy, Benito Mussolini and the Fascist Party attracted war veterans and those who were afraid of the Communists. Dressed in black shirts, the Fascists marched into Rome with Mussolini as their leader. Fascism is the idea that a strong nationalistic government is needed to organize the country and prevent the chaos that results if political groups are all allowed to pursue their own interests.

In Japan the nationalists and militarists increased their power. They persuaded the emperor that the way to ensure a steady supply of raw materials was to invade China and Southeast Asia.

Mindful of the recent world war events, France and Great Britain employed a policy known as appeasement. Trying to avoid war at all costs, Hitler was allowed to take portions of several countries in return for peaceful co-existence. First Mussolini invaded Ethiopia and nothing was done. German troops marched into the Rhineland in 1936 and again no one stopped them. In 1937 Japan invaded China and an apology for sinking an American gunboat was quickly accepted. In 1938, the Munich Pact, signed by Britain, France, Italy, and Germany, gave the Sudetenland (part of Czechoslovakia) to Germany in exchange for a promise of no further acts of aggression; however, in March 1938, Germany took the rest of Czechoslovakia as well. In September 1939, when the German blitzkrieg struck in Poland, the war was on.

The United States was involved with World War II from the beginning, even if the actual date of combat was not until the attack on Pearl Harbor on December 7, 1941. Roosevelt knew that Great Britain could not survive without American assistance, and directed aid to them from the beginning.

Not wanting to get caught unawares (as the United States had done at the beginning of the first World War) the Selective Service Act was passed providing for the registration of all Americans between the ages of 21–35. The legislation also provided for the training of 1.2 million troops. The last component of the readiness program was the destroyers-for-bases deal. Roosevelt knew that U.S. destroyers could not be sold without creating a problem with the isolationists. Instead, he engineered a deal where Britain received 50 older but serviceable destroyers in exchange for Britain giving the United States the right to build military bases on British islands in the Caribbean Sea area.

Franklin Roosevelt saw Germany's conquest of most of Europe as a direct threat to the United States. After his election to a third and unprecedented term, Roosevelt said, in a fireside chat, that the United States must be the "arsenal of democracy." In January of 1941, Roosevelt spoke to Congress and suggested lending money and material aid to Great Britain. He said the United States must stand and be counted with the nations that were committed to the four freedoms: "the freedom of speech, freedom of religion, freedom from want, and freedom from fear."

Recognizing the risks, Roosevelt met secretly with Britain's Prime Minister Winston Churchill on a destroyer off the coast of Newfoundland. There the two men drew up the Atlantic Charter, which confirmed what their peace objectives would be when the war ended. They agreed that any principles of a sound peace treaty would include self-determination for all people, no territorial expansion, and free trade.

Allied Powers

Britain, France, the Soviet Union, and the United States and their allies were referred to as the Allied Powers in World War II. See also: Axis Powers.

appeasement

Trying to avoid war at all costs, the nations of Europe adopted the policy of appeasement, allowing Hitler to get away with a succession of relatively small acts of aggression and expansion. The United States went along with the policy.

Atlantic Charter

In August of 1941, Winston Churchill and Franklin Roosevelt met off the coast of Newfoundland where they drew up the Atlantic Charter. It was a joint statement of war aims. It called for self-determination of all peoples, freedom of the seas, and a new system of general security. Fifteen nations, including the Soviet Union, endorsed the charter by September of the same year.

Axis Powers

Germany, Italy, and Japan constituted the Axis Powers in World War II. Aiding them were Hungary, Romania, and Bulgaria. See also: Allied Powers.

fascism

A political system that exalts nation—and often race—above the individual and suppresses the rights and freedoms of individuals and groups of individuals in the name of national glory. It involves a strong autocratic national government, usually headed by a charismatic dictatorial leader. Fascism grew out of the political chaos that resulted in Europe with the Great Depression.

Good Neighbor Policy

Roosevelt promised such a policy towards the other nations of the western hemisphere in his first inaugural address. His motives made sense; intervening in Latin America in support of dollar diplomacy made no sense as the United States in the midst of the Great Depression did not have the resources to invest in other countries. In addition, the militaristic behavior from Italy and Germany suggested a better course would be to ask for Latin American assistance in defending the area. The Pan-American conferences heard Roosevelt pledge the United States would never again intervene in the internal affairs of a Latin American country, in contrast to Theodore Roosevelt's Corollary to the Monroe Doctrine.

isolationism

After World War I was over, the prevailing opinion of Americans was that the U.S. should not get involved with problems in other nations. Peace conferences and treaties were acceptable forms of involvement. The consensus was that even utilizing economic sanctions against aggressive nations would only lead to military involvement.

Kellogg-Briand Pact

This 1928 agreement was the culmination of some clever diplomatic moves on the part of the French and the Americans. The French wanted the Americans to sign an agreement never to go to war against each other. Secretary of State Frank Kellogg countered with a plan to have all the nations sign. Eventually 62 nations signed; however, the treaty had an escape clause of self-defense.

KAPLAN
Test Prep and Admissions

Keynesian economics

John Maynard Keynes published *The General Theory of Employment, Interest, and Money* in 1936. The Keynesian ideas of using government spending to boost the economy were used to justify New Deal spending and anticipated additional spending. Keynes thought massive spending by government was the way to end the recession.

Lend-Lease Act

This bill authorized the president to sell, transfer, exchange, lend, lease or otherwise dispose of arms and other equipment and supplies to "any country whose defense the President deems vital to the defense of the United States." President Roosevelt knew that Great Britain could not sustain another war and the United States would be the key to its survival.

Nazi Party

The Nazi Party in Germany, similar to the Fascists in Italy, believed that an autocratic government was necessary to organize the nation and save it from the chaos of democracy. With Hitler as its leader, it sought to glorify the German nation and the Aryan race, pursuing an aggressive militaristic foreign policy and a domestic policy that involved extermination of the Jews, who the Nazis perceived to be non-German and non-Aryan. The Nazi Party grew out of resentments over provisions in the Treaty of Versailles and the economic and political chaos caused by the Great Depression in Europe. Hitler seized power through popular appeal and the bullying tactics of his "brown shirts," his supporters.

Neutrality Acts

There were three: one in 1935, 1936, and 1937. Each piece of legislation applied to nations that were proclaimed to be at war. In 1935 the president was authorized to prohibit all arms shipments and forbid U.S. citizens to travel on ships of the warring nations. The 1936 version restricted the extension of loans and credit to warring nations. The 1937 action also disallowed the shipment of arms to the opposing sides in the civil war in Spain. FDR signed each with great reservation.

Nye Committee

Senator Gerald Nye of North Dakota led a committee investigation into the U.S. entry into World War I. The committee concluded that the main impetus for participation in the war was the pressure of the greedy bankers and arms manufacturers. This opinion would influence legislation for years.

Pearl Harbor

On December 7, 1941 Japanese planes staged a surprise attack and bombed the U.S. Navy base at Pearl Harbor, Hawaii. Of the eight battleships there, three were sunk, one grounded, one capsized, and the others were badly damaged. President Roosevelt spoke to Congress the next day and asked for a declaration of war. It was approved with one dissenting vote (Jeanette Rankin of Montana). On December 11, Germany and Italy declared war on the United States. It was now a global conflict.

Washington Armaments Conference

President Harding invited eight major foreign powers to the conference in 1921. Charles Evans Hughes was the hero of the moment when he said: "the way to disarm is to disarm them." The resulting Five-Power Treaty included tonnage limits and a 10-year moratorium on the building of battleships. Other agreements reached at the conference included a mutual respect for possessions in the Pacific and support for the open-door principle for trade and investment purposes. The negative side of the agreements was that the participants were in no way obligated to comply and there was no way to force compliance.

WORLD WAR II

The Second World War was unlike any other confrontation. The United States, again located an ocean away, found itself a spectator on the actions of the Germans. After the German invasion of Poland, all-out war resulted in Europe. During the first year, Germany seemed invincible. France fell quickly. Great Britain, protected by that 23-mile wide waterway, endured 11 months of German bombing. Britain appealed early to the United States. President Roosevelt recognized that the United States was probably the key to a victory in Europe. He also knew that Congress would not condone another war, or even active involvement in a European conflict; the isolationists still held sway. Instead, FDR devised the Lend-Lease Program so that he could justify the millions of dollars of materials that were soon on their way to Great Britain.

On the opposite front, Japan invaded Manchuria, China, and southeast Asia. On December 7, 1941 the Japanese bombed Pearl Harbor and the United States declared war upon them the next day. When Germany and Italy declared war in support of the Japanese, America had a two-front war. The first year of the war, the Japanese also seemed invincible. There was real doubt that the United States could defeat the enemy.

At home, the country threw itself into the entire war effort. Everyone participated. Women worked building ships, welding metal plates together and finishing a Liberty ship at the Bath Iron Works in Bath, Maine, every 11 weeks. Children collected metals of all kinds. Rationing affected everyone; gasoline coupons were hoarded and sugar and coffee were in limited supply. Margarine was invented to replace butter. Tires were patched again and again.

The war effort seemed to bind the country together. Millions of African Americans left the South and headed North, pulled by the attraction of jobs in the factories. Membership in the NAACP increased and the Congress of Racial Equality (CORE) was formed. Mexican Americans worked in defense plants; a 1942 agreement allowed *braceros*, Mexican farm workers, to enter the United States without going through the formal immigration process. Native Americans also contributed; over 25,000 served in the military. The Navajos contributed by creating a code that was used to pass military messages that proved unbreakable to the Japanese. The Code Talkers are only now receiving the recognition they deserve.

The Japanese Americans were not so lucky. After the attack on Pearl Harbor, over 100,000 Japanese Americans were taken from their homes and interred in camps scattered throughout the West. This only applied to the Japanese Americans living on the West Coast. In spite of the internments, over 20,000 Japanese Americans served in the military during the war. Years later the federal government agreed to pay for the injustices done and the property seized. In 1988, a financial payment of $20,000 was made to all those still alive.

The election of 1944 seemed almost anti-climactic. Many felt that to change leaders during the war was not a good idea, and so President Roosevelt was elected for a fourth term. The Democrats chose a new vice president—Harry Truman, the Senator from Missouri who had conducted the Senate investigations into war spending.

By 1945 the tide had turned. American forces were working their way across the Pacific towards Japan. D-Day put thousands of troops on the European continent and they began to push toward Paris, forcing the Germans backwards each day. Then the unthinkable happened: Franklin Roosevelt died in the night of April 12, 1945 in Warm Springs, Georgia. In his place was the untested Harry Truman. Truman had met with the President twice since the election, knew nothing of the atomic bomb, and had never been in the war room. He would say later that he felt as if the sun and the moon and the stars had all fallen in on top of him, yet Truman would rise to the occasion and put in place the policies that governed foreign policy in America for the rest of the century.

On May 6, 1945, Germany surrendered. Hitler committed suicide in a bunker and a fire destroyed his remains. In August 1945 the Americans warned the Japanese that the United States had produced a new weapon of mass destruction and offered them the opportunity to surrender. The offer was met with silence. The first atomic bomb was dropped. Silence. The second bomb was dropped. The Japanese surrendered. The world was at peace.

But a war of a different kind was about to begin: the Cold War.

Bracero Program

To combat the labor shortage in 1942, Mexico agreed to provide farm workers in exchange for a promise on the part of the United States not to draft them. As a result, approximately 200,000 farm workers entered the U.S. on one-year contracts and were paid wages at the going rate.

Winston Churchill

Churchill was the Prime Minister of Great Britain during most of World War II. He was a great friend of FDR. His tenaciousness served as an inspiration to the millions in London who were subjected to nighttime bombings for 11 months and did not surrender.

D-Day

The invasion of Normandy and Europe (Operation Overlord) by the forces of Great Britain and the United States was led by General Dwight D. Eisenhower. It took place on June 6, 1944. It was the largest amphibious assault ever staged. The march towards Paris and Berlin had begun.

Fair Employment Practices Committee (FEPC)

The Commission was established to investigate civil rights abuses. It also worked to withhold federal funding from any state with mandated school segregation and public facilities.

Hiroshima

The United States warned Japan that it had weapons of mass destruction. The Japanese were warned to surrender or suffer the consequences. The first atomic bomb was dropped on Hiroshima on August 6, 1945. 100,000 people died within seconds and thousands more within the next five days. The second bomb was dropped three days later on Nagasaki. The Japanese then surrendered.

Holocaust

The systematic effort by the Nazis to eliminate the Jews of the world. The death camps had ovens that operated day and night to burn the bodies. This genocide eliminated between six and eight million Jews beginning in 1936.

Japanese internment

After the Japanese attack on Pearl Harbor, fears that the Japanese were about to invade the western part of the United States seemed to have some foundation. President Roosevelt was persuaded to issue an executive order calling for the collection and internment of thousands of Japanese Americans. There were 10 camps, one as far away from the west coast as Arkansas. The Japanese were given hours to collect their things and whites argued over the property left behind. Many pieces of property were never returned. Many years after the war was over, the Japanese Americans received compensation from the federal government in the amount of $20,000 for each family member affected by the internment.

Douglas MacArthur

MacArthur commanded the American army forces in the South Pacific and is known for his legendary "I will return" with the troops in the Philippines. He would orchestrate the surrender of the Japanese on the deck of the U.S.S. Missouri and would serve as the commander in Japan for the first few years after the war was over.

Manhattan Project

This top-secret project to build the world's first nuclear weapon began in 1942. Directed by J. Robert Oppenheimer, it spent $2 billion and employed over 100,000 people to build a weapon whose power came from atoms. It was successfully tested in New Mexico on July 16, 1945.

Office of Price Administration (OPA)

The wartime OPA had maintained some price controls while gradually ending the rationing of most goods. After the war, Truman asked for a one-year extension of the powers. There was a campaign to end the controls. Congress passed a bill to extend the life of the OPA, but also set in place many restrictions. Truman vetoed the bill. The OPA expired after the 1946 elections.

Joseph Stalin

He was the Russian leader during World War II who joined the Allied Powers in the fight against Germany. After the war, Stalin led a country that did not demobilize, that took over other countries in what would become known as the Eastern Bloc, and sent thousands of Russians to the Siberian work camps.

Harry Truman

Roosevelt's vice president knew nothing about the Manhattan Project and had met with FDR only twice since the election. He became president upon FDR's death on April 12, 1945 and said he felt like the sun and the moon and the stars had all fallen in on top of him. He was so solicitous of Eleanor Roosevelt that he postponed moving into the White House for over a month to give Eleanor time to collect her things and move out. He would go on to win a second term as president.

War Powers Act

The 1941 legislation gave the president a directive to reassign government agencies to conduct the war effort. The Second War Powers Act gave the president power to allot materials and facilities as needed for defense, with penalties for those who failed to comply.

War Production Board (WPB)

Created in 1942, the WPB was responsible for converting the consumer economy to a wartime economy, for retooling the factories, and for directing manufacturers. Mosquito netting was made in former shirt-making plants, auto manufacturers built ambulances and tanks, and the refrigerator manufacturers would now produce munitions.

Yalta Conference

In February 1945, Roosevelt, Churchill and Stalin planned what would occur after the Allied victory. Germany would be divided into four occupation zones; the Soviets would declare war against Japan, getting control of the southern half of Sakhalin Island in return; and a new world peace organization would be formed.

CONTAINMENT AND THE COLD WAR

The aftermath of the Second World War led not to peace, but to further military and political confrontation that became known as the Cold War. The Soviets refused to commit to a de-mobilization plan; in fact, they seized control of many European countries along the western border of the Soviet Union and in the Balkans. This aggressive, militaristic posture served to frighten nations around the world. The United States, physically less damaged by the war than any other country, became the symbol of democracy and freedom around the world. The United States stood up to the Soviets when they threatened to take over Greece, when the roads to Berlin were closed (The Berlin Airlift), and when the North Koreans crossed the 38th parallel.

This kind of action became known as the Truman Doctrine. Simply put, the United States would respond anywhere in the world when faced or threatened with the advance of Communism. Truman and George Kennan developed the policy based on the premise that the United States had to act as the leader of the free world. Only the United States, they felt, had the strength and ability to stand up to the Soviets.

The Cold War was like a dark cloud that shadowed life. In the United States, people saw Communists everywhere. Joseph McCarthy made a name for himself professing to hunt down the Communists. Many innocent people saw their lives and careers ruined by the suspicion of Communistic beliefs. Many in the Hollywood movie industry were blacklisted; they could not find work, write, or direct often because of long-ago actions. It would take a diminutive woman sena-tor from Maine, Margaret Chase Smith, to face off the hysteria and challenge McCarthy on the Senate floor. She would be subjected to several efforts by McCarthy to have her removed, but ultimately she prevailed and McCarthy would disappear from the political scene without ever pro-ducing the lists he claimed to have of Communists in the U.S. government.

At home, the country was learning to readjust to life. Veterans came home and wanted to get on with their lives. They wanted a home and a family; the baby boom was a result. Civil rights issues were prevalent. Truman desegregated the federal employees and then the armed services. The army took several years to accept the executive order, but finally all branches of the service were desegregated.

Atomic Energy Commission

Created in 1946, the Commission was created to address the disagreements over who would con-trol the use of atomic energy—the military or civilians. The Civilian Commission would work with the president who was given sole power to use atomic weapons during a time of war.

baby boom

With the returning troops at the end of the war, the number of babies born in the following years was much higher than in previous years. The baby boom generation is usually calculated as those born between 1946 and 1949.

Berlin Airlift

Following the closing of the roads to Berlin by the Soviets, Truman knew a direct confrontation was ill-advised. He chose instead to fly over the Soviets, sending 450 tons of food and materials to West Berlin each day and night for 11 months.

containment

This was the 1947 policy with regards to the Soviet Union that Truman adopted on the advice of Secretary of State George Marshall, his undersecretary Dean Acheson, and George F. Kennan, an expert on Soviet affairs. This policy, which was to keep the Soviet Union from further expansion, would be the foundation of foreign policy for years to come.

Dixiecrats

A split in the Democratic Party produced Strom Thurmond as a candidate for president in the 1948 election. Thurmond's conservative southern Democrats were called "Dixiecrats." Truman won the election, beating Thurmond and Republican Thomas E. Dewey, in spite of the division within his party.

Fair Deal

Each president after Roosevelt named his legislative package. FDR had the New Deal, and Truman had the Fair Deal—an ambitious reform program which included national health care, aid to education, civil rights legislation, and a new farm program. Most of his bills were defeated in Congress.

GI Bill

Trying to soften the effects of demobilization, the Serviceman's Readjustment Act of 1944 brought funding to the veterans. Over $13 billion was spent for veterans on education, training, medical treatment, and loans for building houses.

Alger Hiss

Hiss had served in several government departments and had been the secretary-general of the United Nations charter conference. Whittaker Chambers (a former Soviet agent) testified before the House Un-American Activities Committee that he had received certain documents from Hiss 10 years earlier. Hiss denied this and sued for libel. His 1950 perjury trials (one mistrial, then a conviction) were nonconclusive.

House Un-American Activities Committee

Formed in 1938, the Committee (HUAC) kept calling attention to perceived Communist "subversives" in the government. Truman signed an executive order setting up procedures for a federal employee loyalty program. Every person entering civil employment would be subject to a background check.

Korean War

The forces of Communist North Korea crossed the 38th parallel into South Korea. UN forces were called upon to act. The United States responded immediately; in all, 14 nations sent some kind of assistance. Truman was sure that Stalin was behind the aggression and this belief motivated other decisions—to station more U.S. troops in Europe under NATO and to assist the French in Indochina (the seeds of the Vietnam War). There would never be a final peace conference; the truce line near the 38th parallel became the new border.

Douglas MacArthur

MacArthur led the American troops in Korea. His prediction of a total victory by Christmas turned out to be premature. He wanted an "unlimited war" and urged the use of atomic weapons. When he criticized Truman in a letter read on the floor of the House, it left Truman to respond to the act of insubordination, and MacArthur was removed from his command.

Marshall Plan

This extensive program offered economic aid after World War II to European countries devastated by World War II. The European Recovery Program was funded with $12 billion over a four-year period. The Soviet Union and its allies were also offered aid, but they refused fearing a dependence on the United States. The Marshall Plan worked exactly as Truman and Marshall had hoped. Western Europe became a firm ally of the United States and achieved growth by the 1950s.

McCarthyism

In 1950 an obscure Wisconsin senator—Joseph McCarthy—made a speech and charged that the State Department was "infested" with Communists. He claimed to have a list of names. Although he never produced a list of names or uncovered any Communists, he held the government in fear. He continued unchecked until the end of the Korean War, when his charges were refuted. He then left government and disappeared from public view.

KAPLAN
Test Prep and Admissions

National Labor Relations Board (NLRB)

The Taft-Hartley Act of 1947 set up the NLRB and conditions for the operation of labor unions. The NLRB would serve as an agency to which employers could appeal for rulings on the legitimacy of unions as collective bargaining units.

National Security Council (NSC)

The 1947 National Security Act created the NSC, whose role is to coordinate the defense and foreign policies of the United States. It includes the president, vice-president, secretary of defense, and the secretary of state. The Council's special advisers include the chairman of the Joint Chiefs of Staff, the director of the Central Intelligence Agency, and the president's national security adviser.

NATO

The North Atlantic Treaty Organization was founded in 1949 with General Dwight D. Eisenhower as its first head. This organization committed the United States to the defense of Western Europe; this was a military alliance for defending its members from attack—a deterrent against a Soviet invasion. The Soviets responded by forming the Warsaw Pact, an alliance of the Communist states of Eastern Europe.

Julius and Ethel Rosenberg

The Rosenbergs were convicted of passing atomic secrets to the Soviets and executed in 1953. Klaus Fuchs, a British scientist who had worked on the Manhattan project, admitted to giving secrets to the Russians. An FBI investigation uncovered another spy ring, and implicated the Rosenbergs. President Eisenhower denied their appeal for clemency saying that by giving atomic secrets to the Soviets that they had put millions at risk.

Taft-Hartley Act

The 1947 legislation allowed individual states to ban closed shops (where nonunion workers could not be hired) but in other states allowed a union shop (new hires could be required to join the union). It also described "unfair" union practices, such as boycotts and refusals to bargain in good faith. See also: National Labor Relations Board.

Truman Doctrine

This doctrine embodied the containment policy that was implemented because of Soviet-supported uprisings in Greece. Truman asked Congress for $400 million to aid Greece and got bipartisan support. Although the Doctrine at first directed the funds as aid for Greece and Turkey, it would become the standard when dealing with the Soviets everywhere in the world.

Harry Truman

Truman was unpretentious as the president; he had to lead the country following the only man ever elected president more than two times (FDR). He supported civil rights and desegregated the federal government and the armed forces. He got the minimum wage raised from $0.40 to $0.75 an hour and expanded the requirements for people who would be eligible under Social Security. He has always been given credit for keeping the New Deal reforms of FDR alive and making civil rights part of the national agenda.

KAPLAN
Test Prep and Admissions

United Nations

The first meeting of this multinational peacekeeping organization was held in San Francisco in 1945. First conceived during the meetings of leaders of the Allies during World War II, the United Nations, as it was to be called, was designed in eight weeks. The Senate readily approved U.S. participation on October 24, 1945. The headquarters are located in New York City.

Henry A. Wallace

Wallace had been FDR's liberal vice president for three terms until the election of 1944, when FDR dropped him and replaced him with Harry S Truman. Truman was a moderate, a position FDR felt was more in keeping with the changing times. Truman would become president upon FDR's death on April 12, 1945.

KAPLAN
Test Prep and Admissions

MULTIPLE-CHOICE QUESTIONS

1. On the West Coast during World War II Japanese Americans were:

    (A) saved by the Supreme Court from wartime persecution.

    (B) forced to buy war bonds.

    (C) relocated to camps in remote areas and dispossessed of their homes and businesses.

    (D) redefined nonvoting citizens of the U.S.

    (E) forced to take loyalty oaths to the U.S. Constitution.

2. America's entry into World War II produced which of the following impacts on domestic life?

    (A) The loss of jobs in the textile industry

    (B) A growing isolationism in the East

    (C) Racial desegregation in the South and Midwest

    (D) The hiring of many women to do factory work

    (E) A decline in farm income

3. The announced purpose of the Marshall Plan was:

    (A) to advance the development of American military technology.

    (B) to aid in the economic recovery of war-torn Europe.

    (C) to help promote the work of the United Nations in the Middle East.

    (D) to stabilize world currencies.

    (E) mainly to help Truman win re-election.

4. The main purpose of the Taft-Hartley Act was to:

    (A) expand employment opportunities for women.

    (B) investigate Communist influence in the State Department.

    (C) desegregate the armed forces.

    (D) curb the power of labor unions.

    (E) control wartime inflation.

5. The U.S. government departed from the past in regards to conscription in the 1940s by:

    (A) instituting the first peacetime draft in U.S. history.

    (B) allowing pacifists to stay home and work in factories.

    (C) having the U.S. military oversee the draft.

    (D) drafting young men after Japan attacked Hawaii.

    (E) allowing exemptions for all men with special manufacturing skills.

6. Before the Japanese attack on Hawaii on December 7, 1941 the U.S. government knew that:

    (A) there were already saboteurs planning to attack U.S. military bases in California.

    (B) war was imminent.

    (C) Japan was hoping for Nazi Germany to help in the negotiations between it and the U.S.

    (D) the American military was already larger than Japan's was.

    (E) the Philippines were safe from Japanese attack.

7. To preserve the supply of strategic materials for the military in World War II the U.S. government instituted:

   (A) mandatory rationing of gasoline, rubber, and other products such as silk.

   (B) a barter system for citizens to trade their own food.

   (C) higher gasoline prices.

   (D) joint ownership of most of the oil industry.

   (E) a quota system for mining companies.

8. The removal of General MacArthur from command during the Korean War was an example of:

   (A) freedom of speech.

   (B) federalism after World War II.

   (C) civilian control of the military.

   (D) military intrigue between the Army and the Navy.

   (E) constitutional separation of powers.

9. Which of the following is an accurate statement of Truman's victory in the presidential election of 1948?

   (A) African Americans in large numbers supported the "Dixiecrat" Strom Thurmond.

   (B) There was strong support for Truman in the Deep South.

   (C) Congressional support for Truman's civil rights initiatives helped Truman win.

   (D) A strong leftist challenge was mounted by Henry Wallace, a third-party candidate.

   (E) Political polls and pundits were virtually unanimous in predicting, even on election night, that Truman would lose.

10. What happened at the meeting at Yalta between Churchill, Roosevelt, and Stalin?

    (A) They planned a joint invasion of France and a Soviet offensive in the east.

    (B) They discussed the revival of the League of Nations.

    (C) Great Britain, the United States, and the Soviet Union decided to divide up Poland.

    (D) They discussed Jewish emigration to Palestine.

    (E) They planned the post-war military occupation of Germany and agreed that the USSR would join the war against Japan.

11. Franklin Roosevelt preferred to pay for World War II with taxes rather than borrowing the money because:

    (A) it had been done by Wilson before him.

    (B) he believed the wealthy should bear the cost of the war.

    (C) he did not want future generations to be burdened with the war debt.

    (D) business leaders and politicians urged him to do it.

    (E) he wanted to balance the budget.

12. The Peace Treaty with Japan after 1945 provided for which of the following?

    (A) The emperor being tried as a war criminal

    (B) Russian occupation of Hokkaido and Honshu

    (C) Japanese membership in the United Nations

    (D) The breakup of the entire Japanese empire in Asia and the Pacific

    (E) Reparations of over $10 billion

13. Which of the following was an event of the Second Red Scare in the 1950s?

    (A) A small group of suspected Communists was discovered working on the U.S. Senate staff.

    (B) Suspected Fascists from Germany were rounded up and charged with sedition.

    (C) Senator McCarthy claimed many Communists were already entrenched in high levels of the U.S. government, especially the State Department.

    (D) President Truman announced the Potsdam Declaration.

    (E) The trial and conviction of Sacco and Vanzetti led to fears of Communist spies.

14. In a famous analysis of American foreign policy in 1947, George Kennan called for:

    (A) canceling the Soviet war debt to encourage U.S.-Soviet détente.

    (B) cooperation with Great Britain to guard against the rearming of Germany.

    (C) the containment of Communist expansion around the globe.

    (D) the use the atomic bomb on Soviet targets.

    (E) the division of the world into capitalistic spheres of influence.

15. Southern Democrats called "Dixiecrats" opposed President Truman's:

    (A) program to fight inflation.

    (B) desire to increase the size of the standing army.

    (C) civil rights programs.

    (D) plans to reorganize the postal service.

    (E) proposal for a nuclear weapon buildup.

16. Native Americans contributed to the war effort during World War II by:

    (A) joining the military in large numbers and using native languages in military code work.

    (B) working in factories built on reservations.

    (C) buying a large number of war bonds.

    (D) patrolling the borders of the U.S.

    (E) letting reservations be used for military bases.

17. The North Atlantic Treaty Organization (NATO) was created in 1949 to:

    (A) help the democracies of Western Europe recover from wartime devastation.

    (B) encourage the collective security of Western Europe against Communism.

    (C) aid in the rebuilding of Japan's post-war economy.

    (D) prevent Soviet control of the North Atlantic.

    (E) stop Soviet control of Greece and Egypt.

18. Franklin Roosevelt used different political tactics than Woodrow Wilson when he:

    (A) established a special "war cabinet" in 1942.

    (B) publicized U.S. war aims before the surrender of Germany.

    (C) desegregated the military.

    (D) included members of both parties in the delegation to the San Francisco Conference in 1945.

    (E) listed only 10 post-war aims instead of 14.

19. The Nuremberg trials at the end of World War II were important because they:

    (A) were instrumental in cementing U.S.-Soviet relations.

    (B) established Hitler's responsibility for starting World War II.

    (C) helped establish the legal framework of the United Nations.

    (D) set the legal precedent that leaders are responsible for the deeds of their nations.

    (E) showed that Allied cooperation was going to last even after the surrender of Germany.

20. By the mid-1950s many American officials had come to believe that the Soviet Union was moving towards world domination because:

    I. many Soviet spies had been discovered working secretly in the U.S. State Department.

    II. Mao Zedong's Communist revolutionaries had won the Chinese civil war.

    III. Communists had succeeded in taking over the governments of Greece and Turkey.

    IV. radioactivity in the atmosphere showed that the Soviets had developed a nuclear bomb.

    V. North Korea had invaded South Korea.

    (A) I and II only

    (B) II only

    (C) II, IV, and V only

    (D) III and V only

    (E) IV and V only

ESSAY QUESTIONS

1. What was the justification for the forced evacuation of Japanese persons living in the West during World War II?

_____

_____

_____

_____

_____

_____

_____

_____

_____

2. What was the social impact of World War II on the American home front?

_____

_____

_____

_____

_____

_____

_____

_____

_____

ANSWER KEY

Multiple-Choice Questions

1. C
2. D
3. B
4. D
5. A
6. B
7. A
8. C
9. E
10. E
11. C
12. D
13. C
14. C
15. C
16. A
17. B
18. D
19. D
20. C

KAPLAN

Test Prep and Admissions

Answers and Explanations

1. C

Executive Order 9066 in 1942 led to one of the worst violations of constitutional rights in U.S. history. Japanese Americans, most of them U.S. citizens, were sent to remote camps in the American West to be interned for most of the war. This product of war hysteria and racial profiling was not apologized for until 1983 when the U.S. government agreed to pay the survivors a compensation of $20,000.

2. D

While there were many changes in American life during the war, one of the most important was the employment of many thousands of women in industry. With military production on the rise and many men leaving for the war, the use of females was a logical solution to the worker shortage. New skills and responsibilities were gained by many women as they helped build the military machinery needed.

3. B

Alarmed by the threat of a Communist-dominated Europe, President Truman suggested that America, as the wealthiest of the Allies, help the continent to recover from the war. The plan was announced by Truman's Secretary of State, George Marshall, at a Harvard University commencement speech in 1947. More than 12 billion dollars of American aid were used to rebuild European infrastructure and industry.

4. D

The New Deal championed the rights of the worker and produced strong pro-labor legislation such as the Wagner Act. The Republicans got some payback when they passed the Taft-Hartley Act over President Truman's veto in 1947. This act restricted some types of strikes and allowed states to pass legislation prohibiting closed shops, in which workers are required to join the union.

5. A

Military drafts had been used only after wars had started and manpower was needed to mobilize. In 1940, Roosevelt pushed through the first peacetime draft because he had become convinced that war was probable in the near future. The peacetime draft was authorized for one year only but it was renewed in 1941 before Pearl Harbor. Thus, by the time the U.S. entered the war, the buildup of military manpower had already begun.

6. B

Much historical debate has taken place about what the U.S. government did or did not know prior to December 7, 1941. From military documents and communications, it is obvious that the U.S. expected the Japanese to strike somewhere and that war was soon to start. Most estimates at the time were that war would begin in the spring of 1942. The December attack on Hawaii had not been predicted because such a long range military operation had never been carried out previously.

7. A

Certain materials were desperately needed by wartime manufacturers after Pearl Harbor. For example, rubber was needed for many items from tires to engine hoses. Silk was needed for parachutes and fuel was needed for trucks and airplanes. Foods such as sugar and meat were also needed to feed the military. Americans at home were very limited in what they could consume and the government rationed many different items deemed important to the war effort.

8. C

The United Nations command structure was complex during the Korean War but MacArthur, as an American general, was under the command of the U.S. president. Convinced that MacArthur was not following his policies, Truman relieved the general of his command. This action by the president was very unpopular at the time, due to the public's esteem for MacArthur as a hero of World War II. Truman's action demonstrated the president's constitutional power as commander in chief of the American military.

KAPLAN
Test Prep and Admissions

9. E

Never have political experts and the media been more wrong than when most said that Truman was doomed to defeat in 1948. In a spirited come-from-behind campaign, Truman took his program to the people and stole the election from the Republicans. Without much support from his own party, Truman proved that in democracy the people often gravitate toward energetic leadership.

10. E

Yalta took place only months before President Roosevelt died. By this time the defeat of the Axis powers was certain and plans had to be made for Allied post-war cooperation. The issues of how to treat the defeated Germans and how to finish the war in Asia were discussed.

11. C

Although Roosevelt wanted to pay for the war by raising taxes, Congress only approved some of his economic plans. In the end, about 45 percent of World War II was paid for from tax revenues. The rest had to be raised by government bond drives where the people loaned money to the war effort with the promise of repayment after the fighting was over.

12. D

When Japan surrendered on the battleship *Missouri* in Tokyo Bay, it renounced its claim to its empire beyond Japan. This meant that even Korea and Taiwan, which had long been controlled by Japan, would be freed of Japanese control. The islands in the Pacific that had been under Japan's control since the signing of the Treaty of Versailles were transferred to the Trustee Council of the newly formed United Nations.

13. C

The First Red Scare, which occurred during the 1920s, led to the deportations of suspected Socialists and Anarchists. Immigrants Nicola Sacco and Bartolomeo Vanzetti were anarchists arrested in 1920 and sentenced to death in Massachusetts. The newly formed Federal Bureau of Investigation was to watch out for foreigners with radical ideologies. After World War II, as the Cold War started and world Communism became the great enemy of the United States, another wave of American fear of Communism produced the Second Red Scare. Senator McCarthy of

Wisconsin preyed on this fear to make headlines when he claimed to have found Communists in the Truman administration.

14. C

Kennan was a well-known foreign policy expert who believed that America's new challenge was its post-war rivalry with the Soviet Union. He wrote that the U.S. needed to use it resources to stop the expansion of Communism around the world. The policy of containment was adopted by the United States. This meant trying to block any more nations from becoming Communist and joining the Soviet bloc. This policy became the rationale for the later wars in Korea and Vietnam.

15. C

The South felt threatened on two fronts in the late 1940s. Its political power was waning within the Democratic Party because population was shifting to the West and Midwest. Also it feared the liberal policies of President Truman, who was pushing for more rights for African Americans. This was anathema to the racially segregated society in the South and Dixiecrats fought all attempts to expand civil rights for African Americans and end racial segregation.

16. A

Many Native Americans served in the military during the war and were decorated for their service. Members of the Navajo tribe were used as translators because their language was so difficult to learn that it came to be used as a secure means of communication on the battlefield.

17. B

By 1949 the Cold War was well under way and Europe was seen as the most decisive battleground between Western capitalism and Soviet Communism. The United States pushed for a military alliance of the nations of Western Europe and North America to oppose the Communist threat. The result was a collective security agreement in which all the signatory nations agreed an attack on one of them would be considered an attack on all. This treaty was successful in halting Soviet expansion westward into Europe.

KAPLAN
Test Prep and Admissions

18. D

After the failure of Wilson to gain Republican support for the League of Nations in 1919, Roosevelt made every effort to include them in the planning of the post-World War II United Nations. The charter of the United Nations was to be signed in San Francisco and congressional leaders from both parties were there. Even though FDR died before the charter was signed, his inclusion of Republicans was continued by his successor, Truman.

19. D

The trials of German political and military leaders after World War II created a new legal tradition or precedent that those who start war will be held responsible by the international community afterwards. The Allies set up the tribunals in both Europe and Asia to hold Japanese and German leadership responsible for the worst war in human history. Some Germans and Japanese were executed and others served prison terms.

20. C

Numerous events made the U.S. suspicious of the Soviet Union after World War II. The Soviets supported Mao Zedong and the Communist Revolution in China in 1949. But more ominous was the evidence—also in 1949—that the Soviets possessed a nuclear capability. When the Korean conflict broke out, many believed that there was a global Communist offensive that the U.S. had to defend against. However, in spite of Senator McCarthy's claims to the contrary, the State Department was never discovered to be overrun with Soviet spies. American aid to Greece at the beginning of the Cold War was successful in preventing a Communist takeover there and Greece and Turkey never came under Communist control.

ANALYSES OF THE FREE-RESPONSE ESSAYS

Question 1:

What was the justification for the forced evacuation of Japanese persons living in the West during World War II?

Key Points

- The Japanese attack on Hawaii which propelled the U.S. into World War II was a huge shock and surprise to the American people. Part of the reaction was a deep desire for revenge, war hysteria, and racial prejudice against the Japanese

- There was a genuine fear and paranoia that the Japanese military might land on the coast of California in December and January after Pearl Harbor

- Executive Order 9066 was issued in February 1942 which ordered the removal of Japanese Americans from the towns and cities of the western region
  - All non-citizen German, Italian and Japanese were classified as enemy aliens and had to register with the authorities

- The Japanese people living in the United States were a tiny minority who were easily identified because of their race

- Compliance with authority was a cultural trait for the Japanese. They obeyed the Order to evacuate their homes without protest

- The U.S. government hastily built camps in remote regions of the American West for the Japanese Americans to be moved to

- Some resident Germans and Italians were also moved to camps

Reasons for discrimination against the Japanese living in America

- Some Americans were jealous of the success some Japanese had had as farmers in such states as California and Washington

- Japanese Americans tended to do well in school and were hard working

- The attack on Pearl Harbor gave rise to the stereotype that Japanese were 'sneaky' and 'treacherous', and that they acted politely but were actually not to be trusted

- Japanese had been isolated as an immigrant group and were different from the more typical Americans of European descent

- The Japanese in America were not politically organized

- Chinese and Japanese had often been discriminated against in western states since the 1800s

Scoring Rubric

There are five scoring ranges:

Excellent

The answer must have a strong, clear thesis that states the rationale for Executive Order 9066 in 1942. The quality of the writing should be excellent, the answer must show logical patterns, and the student should include many of the major points in the above list (though they may go beyond the list). The organization should be clear. The answer may contain minor errors.

Very Good

The answer must have a thesis that explains why the president ordered the evacuation of Japanese Americans to remote camps soon after Pearl Harbor. Organization of the answer must show logical patterns, and the student should include many of the specific points from the above list.

Adequate

The answer must try to make some argument and must include at least some of the points listed above. There may be flaws in the thesis argument.

Flawed

The answer will demonstrate serious weaknesses. It may have no thesis argument at all, and it will include few of the points listed above. The answer may show little understanding of the World War II period and why the Japanese Americans were singled out for evacuation from 1942 to 1945

Severely Flawed

The answer will demonstrate almost no attempt to answer the question, and will include very few, if any, of the points listed above.

Question 2:

What was the social impact of World War II on the American home front?

Key Points

- The attack on Pearl Harbor created tremendous national unity after 1941
- World War II was fought as a 'total war' and the government mobilized the entire population, young and old, to help with the war effort
- Nearly 15 million Americans, men and women, served in the military until 1945
  - Women played a greater role than ever before in the Armed Services
  - Millions were transported to different parts of the nation and around the world
- More than 6 million women took jobs outside the home, many of them in industry
- Jobs in California, Washington and Texas attracted thousands of workers
  - Many of these workers were African Americans from the South

Examples of societal changes

- Professional sports opened up for some women, i.e. women's baseball
- Native Americans became less marginalized on the reservations because many served in the military
- Unemployment was almost eliminated
- The military trained millions and gave them new skills
- Wartime separations were hard on marriages and the divorce rate increased
- Children were encouraged to participate in rationing, recycling, and helping to pay for the war
  - War stamps and metal drives
- The government sponsored housing projects and child care for workers
- Increased mixing of the races caused riots in some locales (Los Angeles)
- Discrimination and segregation was beginning to be challenged
  - NAACP membership skyrocketed

Scoring Rubric

There are five scoring ranges:

Excellent

The answer must have a strong, clear thesis that gives an assessment of the social changes brought about during the Second World War. The essay should focus on social history. The writing should be excellent, the answer must show logical patterns, and the student should include many of the major points in the above list (though they may go beyond these points). The organization should be clear. The answer may contain minor errors.

Very Good

The answer must have a thesis that details the societal changes in the United States between 1941 and 1945. The answer must be logically organized, and the student should include many of the specific points from the above list.

Adequate

The answer must try to make some argument and must include at least some of the points listed above. There may be flaws in the thesis argument.

Flawed

The answer will demonstrate serious weaknesses. It may have no thesis argument at all, and it will include few of the points listed above. The answer may show little understanding of what happened in the U.S. during the Second World War.

Severely Flawed

The answer will demonstrate almost no attempt to answer the question, and will include very few, if any, of the points listed above.

KAPLAN
Test Prep and Admissions

Chapter Thirteen: **Post-War Politics and Society**

- Timeline: 1944–1969

- Society in the 1950s

- Eisenhower Years

- Turbulent Times—The 1960s

- Multiple-Choice Questions

- Essay Question

- Answer Key

- Answers and Explanations

- Analysis of the DBQ

TIMELINE: 1944–1969

1944	GI Bill passed.
1945	"Baby boom" begins.
1945	Ho Chi Minh declares Vietnam independent.
1946–54	French-Vietnamese war.
1947	First Levittown built on Long Island.
1948	Harry Truman reelected.
1951	J. D. Salinger publishes *Catcher in the Rye*.
1952	Dwight D. Eisenhower defeats Adlai Stevenson in presidential election.
1953	Armistice divides Korea at 38th parallel.
1953	Eisenhower appoints Earl Warren as Chief Justice of the Supreme Court.
1953–54	U.S., through CIA, supports overthrow of governments in Iran and Guatemala.
1954	Army-McCarthy hearings.
1954	*Brown v. Board of Education*.
1954	Geneva accords split Vietnam into North and South.

1955–1956	Montgomery bus boycott.
1956	Elvis Presley has first number one hit.
1956	Ngo Dinh Diem refuses to participate in elections to reunify Vietnam.
1956	Interstate Highway Act passed.
1956	Suez conflict in Middle East.
1957	U.S.S.R. launches Sputnik satellite.
1957	Eisenhower sends in troops to ensure peaceful desegregation of Arkansas high school.
1959	Fidel Castro comes to power in Cuba.
1960	U-2 spy plane crisis.
1960	Sit-in movement begins in Greensboro, North Carolina; SNCC and SDS formed.
1960	John F. Kennedy narrowly defeats Richard Nixon in presidential election.
1961	Bay of Pigs invasion.
October 1962	Cuban missile crisis.
1963	Betty Friedan publishes *Feminine Mystique*.
1963	Martin Luther King, Jr. publishes "Letter from Birmingham Jail."
1963	*Gideon v. Wainwright*.
1963	Ngo Dinh Diem assassinated in South Vietnam.
1963	John F. Kennedy assassinated.
1964	Civil Rights Act passed.
1964	LBJ calls for Great Society initiatives.
1964	Gulf of Tonkin resolution passed.
1965	Civil rights march from Selma to Montgomery.
1965	Bombings of North Vietnam begin.
1965	Riots in Watts.
1965	Voting Rights Act passed.
1965	*Miranda v. Arizona*.
1965	Immigration reform bill passed.
1965	Malcolm X murdered.
1965	Military draft expands.
1965–1970	César Chavez leads strike against California grape growers.
1966	Black Panthers founded.
1966	National Organization for Women founded.
January 1968	Tet offensive.
March 1968	LBJ announces he won't run for reelection.
April 1968	Martin Luther King, Jr. assassinated.
June 1968	Robert F. Kennedy assassinated.
August 1968	Democratic National Convention in Chicago.

1968	Richard Nixon wins presidency over Hubert Humphrey and George Wallace.
1969	Woodstock and Altamont concerts.
1969	American Indian Movement members occupy Alcatraz Island.
1969	Stonewall protests in New York City.

SOCIETY IN THE 1950s

The Second World War affected the United States as if there had been a four-year time warp. Everything had been focused on the war effort. As the veterans returned home, they sought comfort in life as they remembered it. Home and hearth were visions and the housing industry exploded overnight as the demand for housing skyrocketed. William Levitt produced the first suburban housing development, mass-producing 17,000 homes on Long Island, New York. Low mortgage rates made the homes affordable. The highway systems needed major extensions and upgrading as people moved out into suburbia.

The baby boom put a strain on the educational systems. Not only were children going to school, but millions of returning soldiers took advantage of the opportunity to attend college on the GI Bill. And everywhere there was the demand for consumer goods. For four years the economy had been focused on the conflict and the output had met those requirements. Now consumers wanted new things for their homes, their families, and their lives. The technological advances of the war could now be applied to consumer goods.

President Harry Truman called on Congress to pass several progressive measures. He wanted a national health insurance program, an increase in the minimum wage, and a bill committing the government to maintaining full employment. However, most of Truman's reform proposals were not passed. He did use his office to confront racial discrimination; he added to the civil rights division of the Justice Department and in 1948 he desegregated all the departments of the federal government and the three branches of the armed forces. Congress also passed the Taft-Hartley Act which permitted states to pass "right to work" laws outlawing closed shops, and gave the president the power to require an 80-day "cooling off" period before a strike that involved national security could be called.

Harry Truman won re-election in 1948 in spite of a divided Democratic Party. The Southern Democrats who left the party formed the States' Rights Party (better known as the Dixiecrats) and nominated J. Strom Thurmond of South Carolina. (This is the same Strom Thurmond who served in the Senate until 2002.) In addition, a faction of liberal Democrats formed the new Progressive Party and nominated Henry Wallace. New York Governor Thomas Dewey was the Republican candidate. Truman traveled the country in a 12-ton railroad car called the Ferdinand Magellan, gave his "give-'em-hell" speeches, and attacked the "do-nothing Congress." Truman won, in spite of the predictions.

The Cold War—the rivalry between the two superpowers, the U.S. and the Soviet Union—originated as World War II was winding down and continued until 1991. Winston Churchill would coin the phrase that came to characterize the division of Europe into two opposing camps in 1946 when he said: "An iron curtain has descended across the continent."

Truman's policies had much to do with his perception of the Soviet threat. The Berlin Airlift circumvented an armed confrontation and paved the way for the creation, in 1949, of two Germanys: the Federal Republic of Germany (West Germany) and the German Democratic Republic (East Germany). Not until 1992 was Germany reunited as one country. The National Security Act was passed. With this legislation the War Department was replaced with the Defense Department that would coordinate the operations of the Army, Navy and Air Force; The National Security Council was created, as was the Central Intelligence Agency. Truman also broke a long-standing practice of the United States remaining uninvolved with European alliances. Truman suggested, crafted and pushed through Congress the creation of the North Atlantic Treaty Organization (NATO). Its first commander was General Dwight Eisenhower. Here was a military alliance that would monitor the peace in countries around the north Atlantic and serve to rein in the Soviet expansion in Europe.

In the Pacific, Japan was totally under the control of the United States at the end of the war. Under the leadership of General Douglas MacArthur, Japan passed a new constitution. The constitution provided for the emperor to remain as a ceremonial head of state, outlawed war, and provided limited military capability. The United States would become responsible for the defense of Japan. The Philippines became independent in 1946 and in 1949 the Nationalist Chinese, under the leadership of General Chiang Kai-Shek, fled China to the Island of Formosa (Taiwan).

In Korea, however, the Communists were massed for an attack. Korea had been divided after the defeat of Japan. Soviet forces occupied the north half and American forces maintained the south, but by 1949 all these forces had been withdrawn. On June 25, 1950 the North Koreans crossed the 38th parallel and invaded South Korea. Knowing the American people would not support another war, Truman involved the United Nations and referred to American involvement as a "police action." MacArthur took command of the troops. When it became evident that the North Koreans, backed by China, would be difficult to defeat, MacArthur called for an expansion of the war effort and the use of nuclear weapons. Truman, as commander-in-chief, warned MacArthur to stop making public statements that conflicted with American policy. When MacArthur refused, Truman relieved him of his command. The Korean Conflict would sputter to a stalemate, and during the Eisenhower administration, a truce was negotiated. Even today, American troops are stationed along the armistice line in Korea.

The 1950s saw the election of Dwight Eisenhower to two terms as president. As peace and prosperity spanned the nation and the per capita income increased, Americans didn't want to change their leader. Eisenhower was elected to a second term, in spite of his heart attack and surgery. The foreign policies of the United States did take on a new look. Secretary of State John Foster Dulles thought the Truman policies to be too passive. He suggested, instead, pushing the Soviet Union to the brink of war. Called "brinksmanship," Dulles alarmed many with his ideas and Eisenhower stopped him from carrying out the policy. Dulles did place a great emphasis on nuclear weapons. In 1953, the Americans developed the hydrogen bomb; a year later the Soviets had done the same.

When talking with those who were children in the 1950s, one of the recurring stories is that of fear of nuclear war. Children remember practicing for nuclear war by hiding under their desks at school, closing their eyes, and placing their hands over their ears. There was an emphasis on building bomb shelters, and advertisements showed concrete-lined chambers under ground, stocked with provisions for a year. Civil Defense and air raid drills were conducted with screeching sirens. For a child, the 1950s could be a scary time.

beat generation

A term for the students of the 1950s who were the rebellious writers. Led by Jack Kerouac (*On the Road*, 1957) and poet Allen Ginsberg ("Howl," 1956) they supported spontaneous behavior, the use of drugs, and rebellion against social standards.

GI Bill

The legislation made the re-adjustment to civilian life easier for veterans (the GI stood for "government issue") by providing funds for education, vocational training, and a new government agency, the Bureau of Veterans' Affairs. The government spent over $14.5 billion to ease the transition and help more than eight million veterans rejoin American society.

Great Migration of African Americans

During the war, jobs were plentiful, especially once the United States was fully engaged. Many African Americans saw their opportunity to move to the cities of the northern states and get jobs in the manufacturing plants, replacing the men who had gone into the armed services.

Levittown

The first housing project was located on 1,200 acres on Long Island where William Levitt built 10,600 houses. The economies of scale were evident from the speed with which the houses were erected; the houses were all nearly identical and offering the same floor plans and accessories. The houses were affordable for veterans and their families ($7,990 in price, no down payment, and monthly mortgage payments of $56). The concept was duplicated all over the country.

Arthur Miller

Miller was the author of the 1949 play *Death of a Salesman*, a powerful commentary on the sense of alienation in a mass culture that threatens to overpower the individual.

Dr. Spock

His manual on baby care, *The Common Sense Book of Baby and Child Care*, is still in print today. He believed that parents should encourage their children to develop skills and attributes that would help their chances later in life.

suburbanization

With the advent of mass-produced housing projects, life in many places became regimented. Millions moved to the areas surrounding the cities for the employment and educational opportunities. The GI Bill assisted families in making the transitions. Mass transportation facilities, in the form of roads and commuter trains, made living in the suburbs attractive. The downtown areas were losing their populations while the suburbs were gaining.

EISENHOWER YEARS

The world was a frightening place for almost everyone. Communists were flexing their muscles and extending their spheres of influence in many corners of the globe. The United States had said that it would respond to any requests to defend any nation threatened by Communism. There were requests from the French who needed help in Indochina in their war against the

Communists led by Ho Chi Minh, who wanted all the foreigners out of Vietnam. An uprising in Hungary in 1956 succeeded in overthrowing the Communist government but was soon put down with a vengeance by Soviet troops. Just 93 miles off the doorstep of Florida, Communist dictator Fidel Castro came to power in Cuba.

At home there were racial problems. Segregation was still prominent. The 1898 Supreme Court decision in *Plessy v. Ferguson* had found "separate but equal" to be acceptable. The 1954 *Brown v. the Board of Education* was argued before the Supreme Court by Thurgood Marshall, who later became a justice of the Supreme Court himself. The Court's decision reverberated across the nation. The Supreme Court declared that "separate but equal is inherently unequal," overturning *Plessy v. Ferguson.*

While civil rights leaders cheered the decision and announced that they were no longer willing to accept segregation, Governor Orval Faubus in Arkansas thought differently. He and the state's National Guard stood on the front steps of Little Rock Central High School to prevent nine African American students from entering. President Eisenhower sent federal troops to uphold the federal court decision. The federal troops stood guard and protected the African American students as they walked to school.

Martin Luther King, Jr., Malcolm X, and Stokely Carmichael all spoke out against discrimination and segregation. As president of the Southern Christian Leadership Conference, King organized ministers and churches to stage sit-ins and other forms of nonviolent protest. However, southern politicians and police forces reacted strongly and sometimes violently. The violence came into people's living rooms via television. The calm and pleasant existence of the 1950s was being replaced by the turbulence of the 1960s. There was more to come.

Army-McCarthy hearings

Senator Joseph McCarthy's political influence finally came to an end when he accused the army of being "soft" on Communism. From April 22 to June 17, 1954 the Army-McCarthy hearings gave McCarthy the opportunity to be seen at his worst. He insulted witnesses, maligned officials, and bumbled his way into the history books. On December 2, 1954 the Senate voted to "condemn" McCarthy for contempt of the Senate. He died three years later of complications of alcoholism.

brinksmanship

This was the policy of acting "tough" when confronting Communism, of going to the brink of nuclear war to make a point or gain ground.

Brown v. Board of Education of Topeka, Kansas

The challenge to segregation laws was actually five cases, cited by the name of the first case. Chief Justice Earl Warren handed down the decision on May 17, 1954. The unanimous Court held that in education the doctrine of "separate but equal" (from *Plessy v. Ferguson*, 1898) was inherently unequal. The next year the Court ordered compliance, desegregation, with "all deliberate speed."

KAPLAN
Test Prep and Admissions

Fidel Castro

Castro took over as dictator in Cuba in 1959 and is still in power today; he is the longest ruling dictator anywhere in the world. Eisenhower was adamant that Castro should be removed, and even hatched plans to bring about such an event (the Bay of Pigs invasion).

John Foster Dulles

Eisenhower's Secretary of State had been present at the Versailles Conference in 1919. Dulles differed from the Democrats in suggesting that a policy of containment was akin to accepting the status quo. Instead, he argued that the United States should work towards the "liberation" of Eastern Europe. The policy did not materialize beyond words. For all his talk, Dulles did not depart from Truman's policy.

Dwight Eisenhower

Eisenhower was the popular two-term Republican president who succeeded Harry Truman. During his administrations the CIA worked to oust Soviets in several locations around the world while life in the United States continued to focus on the home and family. The St. Lawrence Seaway and the interstate highway system were constructed. Eisenhower was an effective leader who often hid behind a veil of folksy unpretention so that his actual role in policy decisions was not so apparent.

Ho Chi Minh

The leader of the Communists in French Indochina, Ho Chi Minh had received American aid against the Japanese. After World War II, he turned to the Soviet Union and Red China for assistance in his struggle against the French for independence for Vietnam. In 1954 the new French government wanted a quick settlement to the Vietnam problem; they proposed to divide Vietnam at the 17th parallel—the Communist Viet Minh led by Ho Chi Minh would take the north and a pro-French puppet regime would rule in the south.

Hungarian Revolution

After a student-led revolution in 1956, the Soviets allowed a moderate Communist to become head of the government in Hungary. Three days later came the announcement that Hungary was going to withdraw from the Warsaw Pact. The Soviets would not tolerate that action, and so the tanks rolled back into Hungary and brutally suppressed the revolution.

Indochina

Indochina was a French colony in southeast Asia; it included the present-day nations of Vietnam, Laos, and Cambodia. After World War II, the United States got involved by providing supplies and military equipment to the French who were trying to maintain control of Indochina against the Communist Viet Minh, which sought independence for Vietnam. By 1954, the United States was providing almost 80 percent of the French supplies.

Nikita Khrushchev

Khrushchev had prevailed in the internal political struggles in the Soviet Union after the death of Stalin. He supported "de-Stalinization," the relaxing of policies. He confronted the United States from Berlin to Cuba.

KAPLAN
Test Prep and Admissions

Sputnik

On October 4, 1957, the Soviets launched earth's first manmade satellite, *Sputnik*. It weighed 194 pounds. The space race was on, as Americans struggled to catch up and overtake the Soviets in space. As a result, mathematics and science became heavily emphasized in U.S. schools.

Adlai Stevenson

Stevenson ran against Dwight Eisenhower on the Democratic ticket twice, and lost both times. He tried to interest voters in supporting the concept of an all-volunteer army and banning the testing of H-bombs. Neither proposal went very far because he was perceived to be at a disadvantage in military decision-making; it was his word against that of a successful general.

Suez War

Egypt's Soviet-backed leader, Gamal Nasser, seized the Suez Canal, which was administered and operated by Britain. With their supply line of oil threatened, Britain, France and Israel invaded and retook the canal. They took this action without consulting the United States. Eisenhower sponsored a UN resolution condemning the action and, under world pressure, the invaders withdrew. Neither Great Britain nor France would ever again be a major world player.

TURBULENT TIMES—THE 1960s

For the presidential election of 1960, the Democrats nominated John F. Kennedy, a senator from Massachusetts. His vice presidential running mate, Lyndon B. Johnson, was a seasoned campaigner from Texas. Johnson had been asked to be on the ticket to balance Kennedy's youth and Catholicism. The Republicans nominated Richard Nixon, Eisenhower's vice president. The campaign was the first to revolve around the television media. The two candidates participated in a series of televised debates before the American people. If there was a defining moment of the campaign, it was the debates. Richard Nixon came across as an aged politician representing the former administration; John Kennedy was younger and did not have five o'clock shadow on his face. John Kennedy was elected president, but the election was one of the closest ever, with the popular vote difference at less than 100,000 votes.

These times were all about equality and rights. In the South, African Americans marched and protested for civil rights. Many northerners found it difficult to understand why segregation existed. To them, repealing the literacy requirement for voter registration seemed like such a simple process. There was little understanding as to why, historically, these exclusions had been in place.

As African Americans protested, other groups began to demand equal rights as well—Native Americans, then college students, then Latinos. It seemed like every group had reason to protest and wanted things for their people. Farm workers, not covered by any of the U.S. labor legislation, protested the lack of fundamental freedoms afforded them. Women also sought equality and became involved through the National Organization for Women (NOW).

KAPLAN
Test Prep and Admissions

There was a distinct line between the groups protesting and the groups that saw themselves as the bedrock of American society. The middle class values came under direct criticism by the students, and many older members of the middle class answered back that it was that middle class upbringing that made it possible for the students to go to college in the first place. Many a family was placed under great strain by their philosophical differences.

Kennedy inherited the Cold War objections to Fidel Castro, 93 miles off the coast of Florida. The CIA had devised a plan to land Cuban nationals in the Bay of Pigs, expecting the Cubans to rise up and overthrow Castro. The Americans trained in the marshes of Florida and set off for Cuba. When they arrived, the Americans were met by an overpowering Cuban army. Castro used the incident to create a public relations nightmare for the Americans. A few months later, American spy satellites took pictures of missile silos being built in Cuba by the Soviets. Kennedy demanded the Soviets dismantle the silos. The Soviets denied the construction. Kennedy demanded the dismantling and supported his demands with a naval blockade of the island. In October 1962 the United States and the Soviets stood nose to nose. The Russians capitulated and the world breathed a sigh of relief.

Johnson stepped up American involvement in Vietnam by bombing Hanoi and sending hundreds of thousands of troops to fight there. Student protest to the war became more violent and more frequent. Soldiers who served were criticized for their actions. Draft cards and flags were burned. Every night the television news had pictures of demonstrations that had gone from the peaceful march to the frenzied confrontation.

In Dallas, Texas, shots rang out and John Kennedy was assassinated. Lyndon Johnson became the president on November 23, 1963. He managed to secure passage for the Civil Rights Bills of 1964 and 1965 by invoking the memory of the dead president. In 1964, LBJ was re-elected by a wide margin and began to create his "Great Society." Johnson persuaded Congress to pass Medicare and Medicaid; the Democratic president and Congress also passed the elementary and Secondary Education Act, new immigration laws, and more funding for public housing and crime prevention. Lyndon Johnson wanted to be remembered as the president who came to the aid of the poor and forgotten segments of the population in his Great Society programs, but most often he is remembered for getting the country more involved in the Vietnam War and dividing the country over that war.

1964 Civil Rights Act

This legislation made segregation illegal in all public facilities including hotels and restaurants. It also gave the federal government more power to enforce school desegregation and set up the Equal Opportunity Employment Commission. The Commission was charged with ending racial discrimination in employment.

1965 Immigration Act

This legislation removed the quotas based on national origins that had been in place since the 1920s. The new law treated all nationalities equally. Family relationships and education became the leading criteria for applicants.

KAPLAN
Test Prep and Admissions

1965 Voting Rights Act

This legislation was passed to ensure that all citizens had the right to vote, and authorized the Attorney General to send federal agents to register voters. The legislation also disallowed the literacy test as a requirement for voter registration.

1968 Democratic Convention

Held in Chicago, the Democrats nominated Hubert Humphrey. Chicago mayor Richard Daley had told police not to allow demonstrators near the convention hall especially so soon after the assassination of Martin Luther King, Jr. However, massive antiwar protests occurred and were brutally suppressed by the police—all shown on television.

American Indian Movement

The organization spoke for change in the lives of Native Americans. It borrowed tactics from African American activism to call attention to their plight; they had "red power" instead of "black power." AIM occupied Alcatraz Island in 1969, held a sit-in at the Department of the Interior's Bureau of Indian Affairs in 1972, and protested at Wounded Knee in 1973.

Bay of Pigs

The location of the 1961 unsuccessful attempt to overthrow Fidel Castro of Cuba under a plan hatched during the Eisenhower administration. Cuban nationals told CIA operatives that with some assistance, they could land in Cuba and people would rise up and overthrow Castro. Instead, the Cuban army was waiting. The United States was chastised around the world for its subversive behavior.

Black Panthers

A separatist philosophy was at the center of this militant civil rights group headed by Stokely Carmichael. The group eventually broke up over the issue of the use of violence against whites to right racial wrongs.

Black Power

This was the rallying cry for civil rights groups that advocated great changes immediately. They preached anti-white messages and complete separation from the whites. Although quite vocal, the movement, on its own, never really gained widespread support. The movement did help African Americans to develop pride in their heritage and it forced Martin Luther King, Jr. to rethink their strategies concerning poor, inner-city African Americans.

Stokely Carmichael

He was a graduate of Howard University who became head of the SNCC (Student Nonviolent Coordinating Committee) and advocated an African American separatist philosophy. He would later join the Black Panthers and serve as their spokesman as well.

Congress of Racial Equality (CORE)

In 1961 CORE sent "freedom riders" to ride buses in the South and test the law that banned segregation on public transportation. Some buses were attacked and burned, but the riders persisted and got national attention.

KAPLAN
Test Prep and Admissions

counterculture

This term was used to describe the youth revolt of the 1960s. Direct descendents of the "beat generation" of the 1950s, students and other young people rebelled against the society that had brought them the Vietnam War and racism. The counterculture sought an alternative to the established ways of American society and experimented with communes and other alternative lifestyles. The counterculture of the 1960s is known especially for its support of drug usage and the music it produced. Over 500,000 attended the concert at Woodstock in 1969.

Department of Housing and Urban Development

In 1966 the HUD was created to monitor funds for rent supplements to low-income families. The Department, the first headed by an African American person, continues to administer funds for construction and urban renewal.

Betty Friedan

Friedan wrote *The Feminine Mystique* in 1963. It raised women's consciousness and publicized some common misconceptions about women. She was instrumental in founding the National Organization for Women.

Great Society

This was Johnson's name for his legislative program that he presented to Congress and that would attempt to carry the New Deal further and bring prosperity to all segments of American society.

Gulf of Tonkin Resolution

After U.S. Navy ships reported attacks in the Gulf of Tonkin, LBJ went to Congress and asked for unilateral permission to take the offensive in the war and bomb North Vietnam. Until that point, the United States had fought what it called a "defensive war."

Lyndon Johnson

A consummate politician, LBJ was an early New Dealer. As vice president, he brought to the presidential ticket experience and his southern roots, to offset Kennedy's youth and Catholicism. After Kennedy's assassination, Johnson strove to improve conditions for people with his Great Society. He wanted to be remembered as the president who had changed society, but is more often remembered for his role in the Vietnam War. He accelerated the involvement in the Vietnam conflict, and the division this caused in American society forced him not to run for another term.

John F. Kennedy

Kennedy served as president from 1960–1963, when he was assassinated in Dallas, Texas. He brought to the presidency youth and enthusiasm. Although his intentions were good, his lack of a supportive majority in Congress held up most pieces of legislation. His brother Robert, the Attorney General, sent legions of attorneys into the South to hear civil rights cases. Much of the legislation he proposed would be passed after his death. One lasting legacy of his presidency is the Peace Corps.

Martin Luther King, Jr.

King had a Ph.D. in philosophy from Boston College and led the Dexter Avenue Baptist Church in Atlanta. His first foray into civil rights came when he helped to organize the bus boycott in Montgomery. He preached nonviolent civil disobedience, and the teachings of Thoreau and Gandhi, as well as the Bible. In 1957 he helped to organize the Southern Christian Leadership Conference. He went on to epitomize the civil rights movement. In 1964 he was awarded the Nobel Peace Prize.

Little Rock school integration

After the passage of the Civil Rights Act of 1957, Arkansas governor Orval Faubus denied nine African American students from entering a Little Rock high school. Eisenhower sent 1,000 paratroopers to protect the students. The following year Faubus closed the schools rather than allow integration and it was months before the schools reopened.

Malcolm X

He was the spokesman for the black power movement and Black Muslims. He argued that African American men everywhere were "extremists" in that their rights were being violated. Just prior to his death he had begun to soften his message and speak to the advantages of social change. He was assassinated in 1965.

Medicare/Medicaid

Two of the important programs from Johnson's Great Society continue to this day. Medicare is a health insurance program for those 65 and over. Medicaid is a health care plan for the poor and disabled.

National Organization for Women (NOW)

Founded in 1966 by Betty Friedan and other women's activists, NOW advocated ending discrimination in the workplace, a defense of abortion rights, and government support for childcare.

Richard Nixon

For eight years Nixon served as Eisenhower's vice president. He ran against Kennedy in 1960 and lost what, until recently, had been the closest election. He would be elected in 1968 and re-elected in 1972. He has the dubious distinction of being the only president ever to resign.

Silent Spring

The wake-up call by Rachel Carson, published in 1962. Her book detailed the damage being done to the environment by cities and industrial development. Congress acted, passing several pieces of legislation to protect and clean up the environment. The Environmental Protection Agency (EPA) was founded to monitor future activities.

sit-in movement

This was a nonviolent form of protest in which the protestors just sat in place and made it difficult for people to conduct whatever business was meant to take place there. Sit-ins were held in restaurants, in terminals for public transportation, and in offices. Music often was played to inspire the participants.

KAPLAN
Test Prep and Admissions

Southern Christian Leadership Conference

Martin Luther King, Jr. turned this organization into the premier civil rights group. It spearheaded sit-ins, parades, boycotts of public transportation, and other nonviolent forms of protest.

Stonewall riots

Police raided the Stonewall Inn in Greenwich Village in New York in 1969. The gay bar's patrons fought back and the altercation lasted through the weekend. The Gay Liberation Front (GLF) was formed. Most date the modern struggle for gay and lesbian rights to this event.

Students for a Democratic Society

This was one of the more radical student groups of the 1960s. The SDS called attention to issues through protest. Issues addressed included mandatory ROTC program, dress codes, dormitory regulations and faculty tenure decisions. The escalating war in Vietnam changed the group's focus to that of war demonstrators.

Tet Offensive

It was the Vietnamese New Years' invasion of South Vietnam by the North Vietnamese forces that occurred on January 31, 1968. Casualties were heavy, although the Americans proclaimed it a victory. The impact was greater that the actual fighting; Americans now began to think the war was unwinnable.

The Other America

In 1962 Michael Harrington wrote this book to help focus attention on the 40 million Americans still loving in poverty. It motivated President Johnson to declare a "war on poverty." The Congress, controlled by the Democrats, gave him unconditional support. Programs such as Head Start and the Job Corps got their start here along with literacy programs and Community Action Programs.

United Farm Workers (UFW)

The founder of the UFW was César Chavez. He rose from a sharecropper and migrant farm hand to lead farm workers in a struggle to unionize. The workers would strike instead of harvesting until wages were addressed. His final accomplishment was to get growers to bargain collectively.

Earl Warren

Warren was the Chief Justice of the Supreme Court during some of the most turbulent times of segregation. He wrote the decision in *Brown v. Board of Education*, the desegregation case; ruled that a school prayer adopted in New York violated the "freedom of religion" clause; and instituted the Miranda warnings. He resigned to head the Warren Commission which conducted the investigation into the assassination of President John F. Kennedy.

KAPLAN
Test Prep and Admissions

MULTIPLE-CHOICE QUESTIONS

1. In his presidential campaign in 1952, General Dwight Eisenhower promised:

   (A) to end American aid for the French war in Indochina.

   (B) to end the last New Deal programs in the federal government.

   (C) to work towards full civil rights for African Americans.

   (D) to curtail the activities of Senator Joseph McCarthy.

   (E) to bring peace to Korea.

2. The Stonewall riots in 1969 marked the beginning of the:

   (A) the federal government's involvement in the banking industry.

   (B) movement by farmers who wanted better price supports for their crops.

   (C) textile workers' strike during the Nixon years.

   (D) Vietnam protest years.

   (E) gay rights movement in the U.S.

3. The advent of rock 'n' roll in the post-World War II era was:

   (A) the result of white recording stars from the Midwest.

   (B) a reflection of the Eisenhower years.

   (C) was short lived and later replaced by doo wop music.

   (D) widely opposed by concerned parents who thought the music was evil.

   (E) a continuation of the earlier Big Band era.

4. The greatest speech to appeal to American morality and justice after World War II was:

   (A) Martin Luther King's "I Have a Dream" speech in 1963.

   (B) Governor George Wallace's speech at the entrance to the University of Mississippi.

   (C) Eisenhower's announcement of the end of the Korean War.

   (D) Kennedy's speech at the Berlin Wall.

   (E) Kennedy's speech announcing the Peace Corps program.

5. The result of the armistice at the end of the Korean War was that:

   (A) the U.N. had fought its last war.

   (B) no significant territory was won or lost by either side.

   (C) the CIA ended its espionage in North Korea.

   (D) the U.S.S.R. had lost its first war.

   (E) the United States had decisively won the war against the Communist North Koreans.

6. In his farewell address to the American people, President Eisenhower warned against which of the following?

   (A) Racial integration

   (B) Rising world population

   (C) The military-industrial complex

   (D) The international Communist conspiracy

   (E) Environmental pollution

7. After the Cuban Missile Crisis the U.S. agreed to:

   (A) never invade Cuba in the future.

   (B) swear off the use of a naval blockade around Cuba.

   (C) recognize the Castro government in Cuba.

   (D) send Robert F. Kennedy to Moscow to negotiate the removal of the missiles.

   (E) call off air strikes to eliminate the missile threat.

8. What did the launch of Sputnik in 1957 mean to the U.S.?

   (A) The Germans had given their missile technology to the Russians

   (B) NASA was being formed by the U.S. Army

   (C) The Soviet Union had ICBM capability and were ahead in missile technology

   (D) The Russians were going to attack the NATO forces in West Germany

   (E) The U.S. was already ahead in the "space race" with the Soviet Union

9. President Johnson received the authority to send troops to Vietnam when he secured the passage of the:

   (A) 1964 federal budget.

   (B) Cambodian Relief Act of 1967.

   (C) Military Assistance Act of 1963.

   (D) Gulf of Tonkin Resolution in 1964.

   (E) SEATO Act of 1965.

10. Martin Luther King, Jr. borrowed his philosophy of civil disobedience from:

    (A) other African Americans who had protested their lack of civil rights after the Civil War.

    (B) the work of Mahatma Gandhi and the pacifist principles of Christianity.

    (C) the radical writings of Malcolm X.

    (D) young people who had rejected the values of the white middle class in the 50s.

    (E) Kahil Kabran's *The Prophet*.

11. When news of the Montgomery Bus boycott came out, it showed Americans that:

    (A) African Americans were migrating away from the Deep South.

    (B) a new spirit of resistance to racism was growing among African Americans.

    (C) the transportation system needed to be nationalized.

    (D) segregation was indeed supported by the federal government.

    (E) integration was finally achieved in the U.S.

12. *Miranda v. Arizona*:

    (A) overturned the conviction of student Freedom Riders in the Southwest.

    (B) declared school prayer unconstitutional.

    (C) ordered the release of a conscientious objector who refused to fight in Vietnam.

    (D) confirmed the obligation of police to inform arrested suspects of their rights before questioning.

    (E) ruled unconstitutional all suburban residential segregation.

13. The Civil Rights Act of 1964 required:

    (A) that arrested suspects be read their rights by the police.

    (B) free access for all races at public establishments offering food or entertainment.

    (C) the right to campaign for office free of coercion and interference.

    (D) the renewal of some Jim Crow laws in the South.

    (E) a federal judge to deal with all voting rights cases.

14. "Ask not what your country can do for you, ask what you can do for your country."

    This quotation is from:

    (A) John F. Kennedy's inaugural address.

    (B) King's "I Have a Dream" speech.

    (C) Richard Nixon's second inaugural address in 1973.

    (D) A John Birch Society pamphlet.

    (E) Robert Kennedy's 1964 Senate campaign.

15. Native Americans became more radical in their protests against the U.S. government in the 1960s with the forming of the:

    (A) Wounded Knee Alliance.

    (B) Seneca Eight.

    (C) Chickasaw Union.

    (D) Bureau of Indian Affairs.

    (E) American Indian Movement.

16. Which of the following best describes President Johnson's policy toward Vietnam?

    (A) He increased the number of American "advisers" in Vietnam.

    (B) He ordered a secret bombing campaign of North Vietnam.

    (C) He wanted to achieve "peace with honor" in Vietnam.

    (D) He pursued a policy of "Vietnamization" to reduce American involvement in Vietnam.

    (E) He was the main architect of escalating the conflict until over 500,000 troops were involved.

17. The 'counterculture' of the 1960s was characterized primarily by:

    (A) young moderate Republicans who led campus sit-ins.

    (B) working class people who had been marginalized in American culture.

    (C) affluent young people dissatisfied with American materialism and politics.

    (D) violent protests against local governments in regards to welfare issues.

    (E) a love for jazz music and philosophical debate.

18. Which of the following correctly characterizes writers of the beat generation?

    (A) They praised the new rock 'n' roll music.

    (B) Most of them left America to live in Paris.

    (C) They isolated themselves from society and lived in communes.

    (D) They criticized the conventional world of the middle class.

    (E) They had little long-term impact on American culture.

19. Johnson's Great Society attempted which of the following?

    (A) Health insurance for the elderly

    (B) Federal aid to elementary schools

    (C) Development assistance for Appalachia

    (D) Money for housing for the poor

    (E) All of the above

20. What previous Supreme Court decision was negated with the ruling in *Brown v. Board of Education of Topeka, Kansas*?

    (A) *Marbury v. Madison*

    (B) *Plessy v. Ferguson*

    (C) *Miranda v. Arizona*

    (D) *Gideon v. Wainwright*

    (E) *Nichols v. the College Board*

ESSAY QUESTION

Document-Based Question (DBQ):

How is the U.S. government's view of Vietnam after 1954 an example of the post-war policy of containment?

Use evidence from the documents **and** your knowledge of the period from 1954 to 1966 to compose your answer.

Document A

U.S. State Dept: "Aggression from the North," February 27, 1965:

"South Vietnam is fighting for its life against a brutal campaign of terror and armed attack inspired, directed, supplied, and controlled by the Communist regime in Hanoi. This flagrant aggression has been going on for years, but recently the pace has quickened and the threat has now become acute. . . .

The United States seeks no territory, no military bases, no favored position. But we have learned the meaning of aggression elsewhere in the post-war world, and we have met it.

If peace can be restored in South Vietnam, the United States will be ready at once to reduce its military involvement. But it will not abandon friends who want to remain free. It will do what must be done to help them. . . ."

Document B

Joint Resolution of U.S. Congress: Public Law 88-408, August 7, 1964, (The Tonkin Gulf Resolution):

"Whereas the United States is assisting the peoples of southeast Asia to protect their freedom and has no territorial, military or political ambitions in that area, but desires only that these peoples should be left in peace to work out their own destinies in their own way: Now, therefore, be it:

Resolved by the Senate and House of Representatives of the United States of America in Congress assembled, that the Congress approves and supports the determination of the President, as Commander in Chief, to take all necessary measures to repel any armed attack against the forces of the United States and to prevent further aggression."

Document C

President Eisenhower, "The Importance to the United States of the Security and Progress of Viet-Nam," address given at Gettysburg College, April 4, 1959:

"Viet-Nam must have a reasonable degree of safety now—both for her people and for her property. Because of these facts, military as well as economic help is currently needed in Viet-Nam.

. . . . Unassisted, Viet-Nam cannot at this time produce and support the military formations essential to it or, equally important, the morale—the hope, the confidence, the pride—necessary to meet the dual threat of aggression from without and subversion within its borders. . . .

We reach the inescapable conclusion that our own national interests demand some help from us in sustaining in Viet-Nam the morale, the economic progress, and the military strength necessary to its continued existence in freedom."

Document D

White House Statement, "U.S. Policy on Viet-Nam," October 2, 1963:

"The security of South Viet-Nam is a major interest of the United States as other free nations. We will adhere to our policy of working with the people and Government of South Viet-Nam to deny this country to Communism and to suppress the externally stimulated and supported insurgency of the Viet Cong as promptly as possible. Effective performance in this undertaking is the central objective of our policy in South Viet-Nam.

It remains the policy of the United States, in South Viet-Nam as in other parts of the world, to support the efforts of the people of that country to defeat aggression and to build a peaceful and free society."

KAPLAN
Test Prep and Admissions

Document E

Telephone Conversation Between President Johnson and Senator Richard Russell, Washington, May 27, 1964, 10:55 p.m.:

"Johnson: What do you think about this Vietnam thing? I'd like to hear you talk a little bit.

Russell: Well, frankly, Mr. President, if you were to tell me that I was authorized to settle as I saw fit, I would respectfully decline to undertake it. It's the damn worse mess that I ever saw, and I don't like to brag and I never have been right many times in my life, but I knew that we were gone to get into this sort of mess when we went in there. And I don't see how we're ever going to get out of it without fighting a major war with the Chinese and all of them down there in those rice paddies and jungles. . . .

Russell: . . . . I don't think the American people are quite ready for us to send our troops in there to do the fighting. . . ."

Document F

President Lyndon B. Johnson, "Peace Without Conquest" (1965):

"Why are we in South Vietnam? We are there because we have a promise to keep. Since 1954 every American President has offered support of South Vietnam. We have helped to build, and we have helped to defend. Thus, over many years, we have made a national pledge to help South Vietnam defend its independence. And I intend to keep our promise. . . .

We are also there because there are great stakes in the balance. Let no one think for a moment that retreat from Vietnam would bring an end to conflict. The battle would be renewed in one country and then another. The central lesson of our time is that the appetite of aggression is never satisfied. To withdraw from one battlefield means only to prepare for the next. . . .

There are those who wonder why we have a responsibility there. We have it for the same reason we have a responsibility for the defense of freedom in Europe. World War II was fought in both Europe and Asia, and when it ended we found ourselves with continued responsibility for the defense of freedom. . . ."

KAPLAN
Test Prep and Admissions

Document G

Report by Secretary of State Dean Rusk and Secretary of Defense Robert McNamara (1961):

"1. United States' National Interests in South Viet-Nam. . . . The loss of South Viet-Nam to Communism would involve the transfer of a nation of 20 million people from the free world to the Communism bloc. The loss of South Viet-Nam would make pointless any further discussion about the importance of Southeast Asia to the free world; . . .

3. The United States Objective in South Viet-Nam. *The United States should commit itself to the objective of preventing the fall of South VietNam to Communist [sic].* The basic means for accomplishing this objective must be to put the Government of South Viet-Nam into a position to win its own war against the Guerrillas. . . .

We should be prepared to introduce United States combat forces if that should become necessary for success. Dependent upon the circumstances, it may also be necessary for United States forces to strike at the source of the aggression in North Viet-Nam."

Document H

Letter from President Eisenhower to Ngo Dinh Diem, President of the Council of Ministers of Vietnam, October 23, 1954:

"We have been exploring ways and means to permit our aid to Viet-Nam to be more effective and to make a greater contribution to the welfare and stability of the Government of Viet-Nam. . . .

The purpose of this offer is to assist the Government of Viet-Nam in developing and maintaining a strong, viable state, capable of resisting attempted subversion or aggression through military means. . . . It hopes that such aid, combined with your own continuing efforts, will contribute effectively toward an independent Viet-Nam endowed with a strong government. Such a government would, I hope, be so responsive to the nationalist aspirations of its people, so enlightened in purpose and effective in performance, that it will be respected both at home and abroad and discourage any who might wish to impose a foreign ideology on your free people."

KAPLAN
Test Prep and Admissions

ANSWER KEY

Multiple-Choice Questions

1. E
2. E
3. D
4. A
5. B
6. C
7. A
8. C
9. D
10. B
11. B
12. D
13. B
14. A
15. E
16. E
17. C
18. D
19. E
20. B

Answers and Explanations

1. E

The Korean war began in 1950 and dragged on into 1952, which was an election year. Eisenhower, a famous general from World War II, promised to use his prestige as a military figure and go to Korea to help end the war. Eisenhower went to Korea after his election as president and a cease fire was signed in 1953.

2. E

The Stonewall Inn was a gay bar in New York City which became the scene of several days of rioting after police raided it in 1969. The violence was atypical of gays and the event encouraged gays and lesbians across the country to stand up and demand their rights. At the time, gays and lesbians were a hidden and often persecuted subculture. The Stonewall riots led to the beginning of a more open and more vocal gay rights movement in the U.S.

3. D

In the early days of rock 'n' roll, many saw it as the "devil's music." The wild gyrations that teen dances demonstrated alarmed many parents. Some radio stations banned the music but its popularity was immense among young people. Part of the reason for older people being opposed to the music was its roots in the African American culture. This was one reason it was also called "race music."

4. A

The March on Washington in 1963 was the first time the Civil Rights Movement had left the Deep South and made its case in the national capital. King spoke from a symbolic position in front of the Lincoln Memorial of a better America where the children of whites and blacks could grow up together without hatred.

5. B

The Korean War, like the War of 1812, did not result in victory for either side. For Korea it meant as many as a million dead, but the border between the two Koreas remained almost the same as it had been before the war. Basically, it was a return to the pre-war status quo.

6. C

Eisenhower had been a professional soldier before becoming the president. After World War II he watched the military build-up in response to the threat of Communism. For the first time huge government contracts were going out to arms manufacturers during peace time so that the U.S. could maintain a large military capability. The combination of military and business became a powerful partnership that he called the "military-industrial complex." He warned the nation to watch this new combination and be wary of its influence.

7. A

Castro and the Soviets agreed to pull the missiles out of Cuba provided the U.S. would promise no more attempts to invade the island. This was in the aftermath of the CIA-sponsored invasion which was badly defeated in 1961. Since then the U.S. has refused to recognize the Castro regime and to allow nearly all types of trade between the two nations.

8. C

Since 1949, the Soviets and Americans had been pouring a lot of research into nuclear bombs, which both the Soviet Union and the United States possessed. At the same time, the rocket technology which had been pioneered by the Germans in World War II was advancing. It was the Soviets who first launched a manmade object (Sputnik) into Earth's orbit in 1957. In doing so they proved they had a vehicle with the thrust to send a warhead from one part of the world to another. This was a shocking revelation to the U.S. military and there was a rush to pour more money into U.S. rocket development. As a result, the U.S. reorganized its space program and formed NASA.

KAPLAN
Test Prep and Admissions

9. D

The beginning of the buildup to a larger land war in Vietnam began when the U.S. Navy reported an attack by North Vietnamese torpedo boats at night in the Gulf of Tonkin. The president used this report—although the incident is still unverified today—to ask Congress for the authority to hit back at the North Vietnamese Communists. This resolution passed with little opposition and Johnson began a bombing campaign against the North. Ground troops were added to guard the U.S. airfields and the war grew larger and larger.

10. B

Martin Luther King, Jr. had studied theology and history and learned of Gandhi's success using nonviolence against the British, forcing them to grant independence to India 1947. King adapted these tactics to force confrontations with police and white supremacists in the South in the 1950s and 60s. This drew national attention to the injustices suffered by African Americans, and put pressure on the federal government to address the issue and change the system.

11. B

Rosa Parks refused to give up her seat on a public bus and became a famous symbol of African American resistance to racism. African American pastors organized a boycott of the city buses and finally the companies relented. More examples of segregation and discrimination were challenged after that as African Americans and whites staged nonviolent protests in public places.

12. D

This Supreme Court ruling charged that all police had to inform arrested persons of their rights immediately upon being taken into custody. This was an interpretation of the Bill of Rights, which guarantees due process and the right not to incriminate oneself.

13. B

After many sit-ins and extensive TV coverage that showed African Americans being dragged out of restaurants and other public establishments, the Civil Rights Act of 1964 made it illegal to bar access to public facilities for racial reasons. President Johnson, who was instrumental in getting the law passed, was following in the footsteps of President Truman, who had desegregated the military and federal government in the late 1940s.

14. A

President Kennedy struck an idealistic tone in this first speech as chief executive. He talked about the burden that needed to be borne by all Americans in the perilous struggle for freedom around the world. He called on young people to find ways to serve their country and helped start federal volunteer programs, such as the Peace Corps, that many young people joined after college.

15. E

As other minorities became more militant in their demands for equal rights, Native Americans also formed their own strategies and organizations to press for their rights. The American Indian Movement (AIM) staged high profile events such as the occupation of Alcatraz in 1969. AIM demanded the island be given to them and pushed for other compensation from the federal government.

16. E

President Johnson will be remembered for turning Vietnam into a large scale land war that cost the United States $1 billion a month at its peak. Between 1964 and 1968 a million men were cycled through the war and East Asia became a huge staging area for American soldiers. Johnson inherited the policy of containment as a Democrat and believed he had to hold the line against Communism everywhere in the world. Presidents Eisenhower and Kennedy sent advisers to Vietnam; Nixon is associated with the Vietnamization of the war.

17. C

Following the beat generation of the 50s, the counterculture of the 60s became much larger and in the end impacted music and fashion for an entire generation. Critical of the mainstream values of upper and middle class America, many people dropped out and adopted their own dress and lifestyle quite apart from the norm. The war in Vietnam became a major source of disenchantment and the drug culture also fed the fantasy of living a more simple and carefree existence.

18. D

The 'beats' were poets and writers who commented on society through their work. New York's Greenwich Village became a center for coffeehouses where poetry could be read and discussed. Their bohemian lifestyle ran counter to the common desire to seek success and wealth.

19. E

As a young protégé of Franklin Roosevelt, Johnson hoped to continue the work of the New Deal. The public works and contributions of federal monies were all part of the Great Society just as they had been 30 years before. The federal government expanded into the areas of housing and education under the Johnson administration.

20. B

In the 1890s the Supreme Court had ruled that 'separate but equal' was constitutional. The *Brown* case in Kansas forced the Court to reexamine this and they found that 'black only' schools were inferior to those for white children. They ordered the desegregation of all U.S. schools in 1954. The federal government was forced to make sure this happened and used the U.S. military to enforce the ruling.

KAPLAN
Test Prep and Admissions

ANALYSIS OF THE DBQ

Question:

How is the U.S. government's view of Vietnam after 1954 an example of the post-war policy of containment?

Use evidence from the documents **and** your knowledge of the period from 1954 to 1966 to compose your answer.

Use of the Documents

Each of the documents offers a perspective on the political views that shaped the American policy towards Vietnam after 1954.

All the documents are from either the executive or legislative branch of the U.S. government. Dates can be used to associate the documents with the different administrations in power. Eisenhower was president from 1952 to 1960, Kennedy from 1960 to 1963, and Johnson from 1964 to 1968.

Documents A, D and F are explanations to the public from the Johnson administration as to why Vietnam must be defended.

Documents A and **B** emphasize that the U.S. has no desire for territory in aiding Vietnam. The word 'aggression' appears in most of the documents (**A, C, D, G, H**) and is clearly a theme in justifying why America must protect the new nation of South Vietnam.

Document G talks about the possible 'loss' of South Vietnam to the Communists and how 20 million 'free' people will be transferred to the 'Communist Bloc.' Indeed the word 'freedom' or 'free' appears in all but one of the documents. Better students will be able to pick this out and relate it to the policy of containment.

Key Points from Outside Information

- The Victory of the Chinese Communists in the Chinese Civil War in 1949 was seen as a major victory for Marxist Communism. The Republicans blamed the Democrats who were in the White House (Truman) for 'losing' China
- The next move by Communists in Korea in 1950 was met with UN/U.S. military action
- Vietnam was partitioned in 1954 after the French could no longer hold on to its former colony, Indochina
  - The North was allowed to be Communist but the South was defined as a non-Communist state
- 'Containment' held that Communism should be geographically contained so that the 'free' world (which the U.S. was the leader of) would be safe from Marxist totalitarianism. As such it is geopolitical in nature
- The policy of containment which was formulated in the late 40s by George Kennan to stop the spread of Communism was adapted to Southeast Asia by all U.S. presidents from Truman to Ford

KAPLAN
Test Prep and Admissions

Background of the major players in the formulation of America's Vietnam policy

- **President Eisenhower**: World War II general and moderate Republican, gave aid to South Vietnam after the Geneva Conference partitioned Indochina
- **John Foster Dulles**: Sec. of State under Eisenhower took a hard line against Communism in the 1950s
- **President Kennedy**: young Democrat had campaigned in 1960 as being tough on Communism
- **Dean Rusk**: Sec. of State under Kennedy supported military aid to South Vietnam after 1960
- **Robert McNamara**: former Ford executive became Sec. of Defense under Kennedy and Johnson. Took a hard line and supported military intervention in Vietnam from 1961 on
- **President Johnson**: inherited the Vietnam policy from Kennedy and sent more and more U.S. troops to support South Vietnam after 1964
- **Senator Russell of Arkansas**: was opposed to the use of American troops in Vietnam and later became more and more outspoken against the war

Students could make the case that all presidents from Eisenhower to Johnson used the policy of containment to guide them in sending aid and later troops to defend South Vietnam from Communist intrusion from the North. The U.S. effectively drew a line at the 17th parallel and meant to disallow the unification of Vietnam under Communism.

DBQ Scoring Rubric

There are five scoring ranges:

Excellent

Argument: The essay must have a strong, clear thesis. The student should take a clear position either in support of or against the proposition stated in the question. The essay should also indicate a grasp of the complexity of the issue, referring to pros and cons of entrepreneurial behavior in this time period.

Critical Thought: The student should explain how each document supports or undermines the thesis. The student should address conflicts and contradictions in the evidence. Any outside information must be relevant to the argument.

Evidence: The student should use documents and outside information (see lists above) throughout the essay. Most of the documents must be used, and students might address the relationship between the sources.

Writing Style: The essay must be well organized and well written; it must make sense throughout.

KAPLAN
Test Prep and Admissions

Very Good

Argument: The thesis must be consistent with the question, but it may not be sufficiently focused.

Critical Thought: The answer must include an analysis of several of the documents and must incorporate outside information.

Evidence: The student should make use of the documents and outside information (see lists above) that support the position being argued. Discussion of relationships between the sources used may be limited.

Writing Style: The essay should be well organized and clearly written; it must be logical, but some points may be unclear.

Adequate

Argument: The thesis is only partially developed. It may address the question, but it does so in a way that doesn't acknowledge the question's complexity. The essay will most likely fail to prioritize the arguments.

Critical Thought: The essay is primarily descriptive or narrative, and doesn't provide an analysis of the question or of the evidence provided. It will not address all the relevant issues, and will ignore the opposing position.

Evidence: The student may paraphrase the documents and may misinterpret a document to better fit the argument. The student will use only a little outside information and may refer to some but not all of the documents. The answer may contain errors.

Writing Style: The writing and organization is unclear, but acceptable.

Flawed

Argument: The thesis will be unclear and will not be supported in the body of the essay. Use of evidence will be unclear, and the argument will be poorly developed.

Critical Thought: The essay will show only a limited understanding of the question, and will offer little or no analysis. What little analysis there is will be inaccurate. The student will show little understanding of the issue of industrialization.

Evidence: The student will not make use of the documents appropriate to their argument, and may use documents that actually support the opposing position. The use of documents will be haphazard, with references only to brief excerpts or paraphrases. There will be little outside information. The argument may contain errors.

Writing Style: The answer will be weakly organized and the writing will be unclear.

Severely Flawed

Argument: The student provides no thesis, or provides one that is not relevant to the question.

Critical Thought: The student demonstrates little or no understanding of the question.

Evidence: The student makes almost no use of the documents provided, and makes little or no use of outside information. The answer contains major errors.

Writing Style: The answer is disorganized and poorly written.

Chapter Fourteen: **The Modern Age**

- Timeline: 1969–2003
- From the 1970s to the 1990s
- Multiple-Choice Questions
- Essay Questions
- Answer Key
- Answers and Explanations
- Analyses of the Free-Response Essays

TIMELINE: 1969–2003

1969	United States begins bombing Cambodia.
1969	My Lai massacre reported.
1970	Shootings at Kent State and Jackson State University.
1971	*The Pentagon Papers* published.
1971	*Swann v. Charlotte-Mecklenburg* decision permits school busing as a means to desegregation.
1972	Nixon travels to China.
1972	Burglars break into the Democratic National Committee headquarters in the Watergate building in Washington, D.C.
1972	Nixon reelected.
1973	American combat troops leave Vietnam.
1973	OPEC embargo hurts ailing economy.
1974	Nixon resigns before he is impeached; Gerald Ford becomes president.
1975	North Vietnamese troops occupy Saigon and win the war.
1976	Jimmy Carter elected president.
1978	Camp David Accords between Israel and Egypt signed.
1978	*Bakke v. Board of Regents of California* restricts use of racial quotas in higher education.

1979	Americans taken hostage in revolution in Iran.
1980	Ronald Reagan elected for first of two terms as president.
1981	U.S. government begins aiding rebels in El Salvador and Nicaragua.
1983	U.S. successfully invades Grenada.
1986	Iran-Contra scandal unfolds.
1987	Stock market dives on "Black Monday" (October 19, 1987).
1987	Reagan and Mikhail Gorbachev sign treaty eliminating intermediate-range nuclear forces.
1988	George H. W. Bush elected president.
1989	Communist regimes collapse across Eastern Europe.
1991	Soviet Union collapses.
1991	Gulf War against Iraq.
1991	Clarence Thomas narrowly confirmed to Supreme Court.
1992	Bill Clinton elected for first of two terms as president.
1994	Clinton's health plan fails in Congress.
1994	Republicans win both Senate and House in midterm elections.
1995	Oklahoma City bombing.
1995	U.S. brokers uneasy peace in Bosnia.
1996	Congress passes major welfare reform bill.
1998	Clinton impeached, but not convicted, over Monica Lewinsky scandal.
2000	Republican George W. Bush elected president by the Electoral College, although the Democratic candidate, Albert Gore, received more votes than Bush in the popular vote.
2001	Terrorists hijacked four airplanes and used three of them to attack the World Trade Center towers and the Pentagon. The fourth plane crashed in a field in Pennsylvania before hitting its intended target in Washington, D.C.
2003	U.S.-/Britain-led invasion of Iraq.

FROM THE 1970s TO THE 1990s

The last chapter of any history book always reaches into the present. A former CIA director and ambassador to the UN, George H. W. Bush was president from 1988–1992. As Ronald Reagan's vice president, he had been involved in negotiations regarding the ending of the Cold War. It fell to Bush to help define the U.S. role after the Cold War.

The Bush presidency was defined by extraordinary events in the world. In China, the world watched as students demonstrated in Tiananmen Square. During the night, the Chinese government rolled tanks into the Square, killing many of the demonstrators. Although this ended the protest, it garnered for China intense criticism from many democratic countries. Only in 2001 did President George W. Bush (son of the former president) grant normal trading status to China, a status that had been denied because of the human rights violations.

In Eastern Europe the changes were even more astounding. Communist governments were falling. Mikhail Gorbachev, the new Soviet leader who had negotiated the glasnost (openness to end political repression) and perestroika (restructuring the Soviet economy with free- market strategies) with Reagan, announced that he would no longer back the various Communist governments of Eastern Europe with military forces. Immediately, Polish labor leader Lech Walesa organized the fall of Communism in Poland, and other countries soon did the same. In Hungary, Czechoslovakia, Bulgaria, and Romania the Communist party lost their control of government. The Communists in East Germany were forced out and the Berlin Wall, that most frightening symbol of the Cold War, was destroyed in 1989. In 1990 the two Germanys, which had been divided since the end of World War II in 1945, became one again.

The Soviet Union itself imploded and broke up into many smaller republics. In 1990, Estonia, Latvia, and Lithuania (which were part of the Soviet Union) declared themselves free and independent. Gorbachev, who had survived a coup by Communists who tried to stop the breakup, was left with no country after the remaining republics dissolved the Soviet Union in December 1991. Boris Yeltsin, president of the Russian Republic, gained support from nine other former republics to form a confederation, or commonwealth of Independent States. He then disbanded the Communist party and tried to establish a democracy and free-market economy.

Even as the changes were occurring, President Bush did not celebrate a victory. His vast experience suggested that there were likely to be problems. The heavy-handed Soviet domination of the Eastern countries had been lifted; there was the possibility of civil wars. Yugoslavia was the first to disintegrate. Serbia and Croatia fought each other and Bosnia and Herzegovina fell into a destructive civil war. Then, in Serbia, Albanians and Serbs clashed. The actions of Slobodan Milosevic and his systematic elimination of Albanians ultimately brought his arrest and trial in the World Court at The Hague for crimes against humanity.

Unrest was everywhere, or so it seemed. In the Persian Gulf, Saddam Hussein invaded Kuwait. Bush went to Congress and received approval for a military campaign, Desert Storm. In 1991 military units from the United States and 28 other countries conducted air strikes and a ground war that forced Iraq to surrender. There were criticisms in the United States of the action; some said it was "another Vietnam." However, in Iraq, the United States quickly achieved victory and Americans greeted military personnel upon their arrival in the United States with bands and flags and expressions of appreciation.

Although Bush's foreign policy and Desert Storm saw his popularity ratings climb to almost 90 percent, there were other issues. Bush's control over the economy was compromised when he had to reverse a campaign slogan—"no new taxes"—and raise them. The new tax law raised income tax rates, excise taxes, and the taxes on luxury items like boats and cars. Another milestone was reached with the passage of the Americans with Disabilities Act (1992), which made discrimination because of a physical or mental handicap illegal.

The election of 1992 saw a change. William Jefferson Clinton was elected with a substantial majority, defeating both Bush and third-party candidate H. Ross Perot, a Texas billionaire. Clinton's first years were controversial. He faced a scandal in the White House travel office, questions about his involvement with a real estate deal called Whitewater, and controversy over his Cabinet nominations. The administration had its bright moments with the Family and Medical Leave Act,

KAPLAN
Test Prep and Admissions

motor-voter registrations, the Brady Bill (requiring a waiting period for purchasing a handgun), the Anti-Crime Bill (providing funding for more police protection and crime prevention), and the North American Free Trade Agreement (NAFTA) which created a free-trade zone for Canada, the United States, and Mexico.

Perhaps Clinton's greatest accomplishment, however, was Congress' passage of a deficit-reduction budget that included $255 billion in spending cuts and $241 billion in tax increases. With the Republicans gaining control of the House of Representatives in 1994, government came to a standstill twice as the president and the Congress hammered out fiscal reforms. The president agreed to cuts in Medicare and other welfare programs; the Republicans agreed to smaller cuts in other social programs. All helped to significantly reduce the size of the deficit. There were projections of surpluses for the next 10 years.

In foreign policy, the Clinton presidency addressed problems in Haiti, a nuclear threat from North Korea, Bosnian civil war, financial support to keep Russia from collapse, Nelson Mandela's election as president of South Africa, the re-establishment of diplomatic relations in Vietnam, and the continued problems in the Middle East. Clinton also brokered the first uneasy peace in Northern Ireland.

In 1996, Clinton was reelected by a wide margin but faced a scandal involving a White House intern, Monica Lewinsky. The Republicans engineered an impeachment trial (the first since Andrew Johnson). Clinton was not convicted of charges of perjury and obstructing justice. Clinton's vice president, Albert Gore, faced off against Republican George W. Bush, the son of the former president, in the presidential election of 2002. Ralph Nader ran as a third party candidate. Although Gore won the popular vote, the outcome in the Electoral College hinged on a few contested ballots in Florida. The country waited almost five weeks while the votes in Florida were counted and recounted, with the U.S. Supreme Court finally handing down a decision that made Bush president.

On September 11, 2001, planes hijacked by terrorists hit the World Trade Center Towers in New York City. Both towers fell to the ground shortly after the collisions. At the same time, another plane was flown directly into the Pentagon, and a fourth plane crashed in Pennsylvania on its way to another building in Washington, D.C. In the subsequent "war on terrorism," the United States used its military to hunt for Osama bin Laden, leader of the terrorist group Al Qaeda, which had used Afghanistan as a base of operations and was presumed responsible for the attacks. The Taliban government in Kabul was removed and the hunt for bin Ladin and the leadership of Al Qaeda continued.

President Bush also called for a military operation to remove the Hussein regime in Baghdad; the regime was accused of harboring terrorists and weapons of mass destruction. Unable to get United Nations support in the Security Council, the United States and Great Britain attacked Iraq in March 2003. Baghdad was taken within three weeks, leaders of the former Baath party were arrested, and the Hussein regime deposed.

In domestic affairs, Bush was successful in getting a tax cut through Congress. However, the budget surplus vanished and a growing deficit resulted from the tax cut and an economic downturn, as well as from increased government spending to combat terrorism, build up the military, and improve education.

The next chapter in U.S. history is now being written by the Americans themselves. How it develops depends in part on Americans' understanding of themselves (their history) and the world around them.

AIDS

Acquired Immune Deficiency Syndrome (AIDS) is one of the greatest killers of the 20th century. Originally found in Africa, it has spread to all corners of the world. Although no cure has yet been found, new drugs are being developed to slow the disease's progress and give those afflicted a longer and better quality of life.

Bakke v. Board of Regents of California

This Supreme Court decision was the first to take on the question of reverse discrimination. A medical school applicant argued he had been denied entrance into medical school because the school had to fill quotas with women and other minorities. The Court ruled in Bakke's favor, outlawing the use of racial quotas in college and university admissions.

George H. W. Bush

President from 1989–1993, Bush oversaw the Gulf War. He was a pragmatist, and chose to work with rather than confront the Democratic Congress. He supervised the savings and loan bailouts, tried to fight the "war on drugs," saw the Berlin Wall fall, and dealt with Panama.

Camp David Accords

President Carter helped to engineer the first peace treaty signed between the Egyptians and the Israelis. In 1977 President Anwar el-Sadat and Prime Minister Menachem Begin met and agreed to end the hostilities. Land in the Sinai was returned to Egypt in return for Egypt's recognition of Israel and promises of peaceful coexistence.

Jimmy Carter

As the president with no foreign affairs experience, his greatest achievement as chief executive was to manage the Camp David Accords. Probably his greatest failure was his inability to shift the economy and control inflation. He was also unable to gain the release of the American hostages being held in Iran. He won the Nobel Peace Prize in 2002.

Bill Clinton

Clinton was the first Democratic president since Carter. Elected over the incumbent Bush, Clinton came to the White House with no international experience, but he had the skills of a consummate politician. Under the leadership of his wife, Hillary Rodham Clinton, his administration attempted to develop a national health insurance system but ran into a wall and had to abandon the effort. Clinton reduced the deficit to a nonexistent level for the first time since Franklin D. Roosevelt took office. There were budget surpluses forecast well into the future. His second administration saw his impeachment trial for lying under oath about a relationship with an intern, Monica Lewinsky.

KAPLAN
Test Prep and Admissions

détente

This described the more orderly and less competitive relationship between the two superpowers, the United States and the Soviet Union. The two countries traded diplomatic visits and made efforts to work together.

downsizing

This describes the business practice of cutting costs by eliminating jobs.

Earth Day and the Environmental Movement

In March 1970 the first Earth Day was celebrated. This marked the beginning of an organized political movement to protect the environment in the United States. It encouraged ecological activism on all levels of American government and was followed by the passages of such laws as The Clean Air Act, the Toxic Substances Act, and others.

Environmental Protection Agency (EPA)

The federal government made the environment a priority and established, by executive order, a consolidation of the various agencies to control air and water pollution and monitor the disposal of toxic wastes.

Gerald Ford

Richard Nixon's vice president, Ford, became president upon the resignation of Nixon. One of his first acts as president was to pardon Nixon, thus sparing him a criminal trial. Ford lost the 1976 election to Jimmy Carter.

Gulf War

Saddam Hussein, the dictator of Iraq, attacked Kuwait and threatened Saudi Arabia. The United States responded to these actions with American forces, from 200,000 to 400,000 massed on the Arabian peninsula in just a few weeks. Bush called for a cease fire six weeks later. The ground assault began on February 24, 1991 and four days later, Iraqi troops surrendered.

Iran-Contra Affair

During the Reagan administration, arms had been secretly sold to Iran. The sales made Reagan's words about never dealing with terrorists seem hollow. Upon investigation, the profits generated by the sales were being directed to the Contra rebels in Nicaragua after Congress had voted against any such aid.

Iranian hostage crisis

Iranian religious fundamentalists seized the American Embassy in Tehran in 1979 and held more than 54 Americans there. The spiritual and political leader of Iran, Ruhollah Khomeini, approved of the action. President Carter appealed to the UN, froze Iranian assets in the United States, and appealed for a trade embargo of Iran. A rescue attempt by American commandos failed. After 444 days in captivity, and 20 minutes after Ronald Reagan took the oath of office, the hostages were released.

KAPLAN
Test Prep and Admissions

Kent State

Site of the 1970 war protests that resulted in the deaths of four students. Poorly trained National Guardsmen fired on demonstrators after a riot at the campus ROTC building. Although the official investigation did not exonerate the Guardsmen, many thought the students "got what they were asking for."

Henry Kissinger

A professor of international relations at Harvard, Kissinger became Nixon's Special Assistant for National Security Affairs. He negotiated the peace treaty that ended the conflict in Vietnam.

Richard Nixon

Nixon's presidency was characterized by highs and lows. Although he did engineer the withdrawal from Vietnam, the lack of speed in accomplishing the goal demoralized the military and cost an additional 20,000 American lives. He extended the bombing in the war to Laos and Cambodia. He tried to end several social programs, but found the lack of a Republican majority in Congress a liability. History will, however, remember him as the president who resigned in disgrace as a result of his handling of the Watergate crisis.

North American Free Trade Agreement (NAFTA)

This agreement, signed between Mexico, the United States, and Canada, created a free trade zone throughout the three countries. Although it was thought that the tariff reductions would open up foreign markets to American industries, opponents feared that manufacturing jobs would go to where the labor was cheaper. NAFTA is still in effect.

Oklahoma City bombing

On April 19, 1995 a giant truck bomb destroyed the Murrah Federal Building in Oklahoma City. The damage was complete—the front half of the building was blown off, 168 people died, and 600 others were injured. Timothy McVeigh and Terry Nichols were tried and found guilty. Timothy McVeigh was executed in 2001.

Pentagon Papers

These were Department of Defense papers classified as "top secret" that were published by the *New York Times*. Although the government immediately went to court to stop the publication, the Supreme Court would later rule that the publication of the papers was covered under the First Amendment's freedom of the press. The papers showed that the military had been under-reporting casualty numbers for American troops in Vietnam.

Ronald Reagan

President for eight years, this Republican was a "people person." His was not a peaceful tenure; there were problems all over the world and also here in the Western Hemisphere. Reagan found that his promise of tax cuts was not possible to fulfill. He appointed cabinet members not necessarily suited to their positions, such as James Watt at the Department of the Interior. By his second term, there were improvements. His greatest legacy may be his bringing inflation under control and his optimism of all things possible.

Reaganomics

This was the supply-side economic strategy of the Reagan supporters. The contention was that government, instead of trying to control spending (Keynesian theory), should remove restraints on business and let the economy function freely. Price controls on oil were the first to go. Tax concessions, such as a lowered maximum rate and capital gains tax cut, seemed to benefit only a few.

savings and loan crisis

In 1982 Congress, following Reagan's policy of removing restraints on business, allowed savings and loan institutions to invest up to 40 percent of their assets in higher risk nonresidential real estate. Office buildings went up everywhere. After Black Monday, when the stock market fell almost 23 percent in one day, paper value disappeared to the tune of $560 billion. Because the Federal Deposit Insurance Corporation insured the savings and loans, the federal government had to repay consumers, to the tune of $300 billion over 30 years.

stagflation

The term was coined to describe the situation in which the American economy was experiencing a recession and inflation at the same time. This defied the traditional laws of economics.

Strategic Arms Limitation Treaty

Nixon and Leonid Brezhnev (Soviet Union) signed a treaty limiting all future intercontinental ballistic missiles and their construction. The Soviets would retain a greater number of missiles with more destructive power and the United States would retain the lead in the total number of warheads. Each side agreed to work towards a permanent freeze on all nuclear weapons.

Tech Boom

Beginning in the early 1990s, the stock market was stimulated by a boom in technology companies. Led by the explosive growth of hardware companies such as Intel and software companies such as Microsoft, Wall Street enjoyed a tremendous increase in share prices up until 2000.

Vietnamization

This was Nixon's policy of equipping and training South Vietnamese troops. The assumption was that the South Vietnamese would take over the ground war for the Americans. As a result, President Nixon lowered the number of Americans troops in Vietnam. By 1973 there were only 50,000.

Watergate

This was the name of the building in Washington, D.C. where the Democratic National Headquarters was located. The Democratic National Headquarters was burglarized during the 1972 elections by a team organized by the Republican Party. In catching the burglars, who had ties to Nixon's Chief of Staff, the "house of cards" came tumbling down. Although Nixon won the 1972 election by a substantial margin, the investigation of the burglary—and more important, the attempted coverup organized by the White House—continued until Nixon was forced to face impeachment or resign, which he did in 1974.

MULTIPLE-CHOICE QUESTIONS

1. Which of the following showed the strength of the women's movement in the 1970s?

    I.   Ratification of the Equal Rights Amendment

    II. Founding of the National Organization for Women

    III. Nomination of a woman for vice president by one of the major political parties

    IV. Supreme Court decision in *Roe v. Wade*

    V.   Title IX of the Educational Amendments Act of 1972

    (A) I and IV only

    (B) II and IV only

    (C) II, III, IV, and V only

    (D) II, IV, and V only

    (E) V only

2. After the Soviet invasion of Afghanistan in 1979 President Carter declared a:

    (A) national day of prayer.

    (B) military alert for all U.S. troops.

    (C) total trade embargo against the USSR.

    (D) U.S. boycott of the Moscow Olympics in 1980.

    (E) plan for a superpower summit in Washington, D.C.

3. Which of the following does NOT describe challenges faced by President Carter in the late 70s?

    (A) High inflation that threatened the economy

    (B) Lower energy costs that threatened to result in deflation

    (C) Making peace in the Middle East between Egypt and Israel

    (D) A hostage crisis in Iran

    (E) Negotiations for the return of the Panama Canal

4. The Reagan administration was accused of secretly funding Nicaraguan rebels who wanted to overthrow the Sandinista government in the:

    (A) Iran-Contra affair.

    (B) Watergate scandal.

    (C) Contragate scandal.

    (D) early years of their second term.

    (E) Whitewater affair.

5. Which of the following was NOT an example of democratic advances abroad in the 1980s?

    (A) The crackdown against the Tiananmen Square demonstrations in 1989

    (B) The fall of the Berlin Wall

    (C) The Solidarity movement in Poland

    (D) Gorbachev's perestroika policies

    (E) The election loss of Pinochet in Chile

6. President Nixon was accused of what crime as he was threatened with impeachment in 1974?

    (A) Covering up for his associates

    (B) Obstruction of justice

    (C) Perjury before a grand jury

    (D) Grand larceny

    (E) Defying a congressional mandate

7. Arms negotiations between the United States and the Soviet Union achieved a milestone in 1972 with the:

    (A) signing of an anti-ballistic missile treaty and an agreement to limit ICBMs (SALT I).

    (B) negotiation of the START treaty.

    (C) acceptance of a United Nations sponsored proposal to cut back the number of nuclear weapons of both superpowers.

    (D) signing of the Test Ban Treaty.

    (E) signing of the Nuclear Proliferation Agreement.

8. Which of the following describes the effect of Reagan's economic policies on the national debt?

    (A) Because of tax cuts and increased spending on defense, the national debt nearly tripled.

    (B) Despite massive cuts in federal spending on social programs, the debt remained the same.

    (C) Because the United States abandoned the gold standard, the national debt increased tenfold.

    (D) Because of massive cuts in federal spending on social programs, the debt decreased.

    (E) Because of the combination of cuts in federal social programs and a booming economy that increased tax revenues, the debt was cut in half.

9. One of the most significant outcomes of the Yom Kippur War in 1973 was:

    (A) a marked increase in anti-Semitism in America afterwards.

    (B) the closer relationship between Syria and Egypt that followed.

    (C) the massive military support Egypt received from the Soviet Union.

    (D) the Arab oil embargo that created fuel shortages and widespread inflation.

    (E) the military defeat of Israel by Jordan.

10. Jimmy Carter won the election of 1976 by:

    (A) saying he would increase spending on defense.

    (B) convincing Americans of his honesty and reviving the New Deal coalition of southern whites and urban workers.

    (C) promising never to raise taxes.

    (D) proclaiming that America would stay out of all wars.

    (E) accusing the Republicans of corruption and deceit.

11. *Bakke v. the Board of Regents of California* was a legal test case of:

    (A) increased federal spending on social programs in Los Angeles.

    (B) poverty programs that had been put in place during President Johnson's Great Society.

    (C) hiring practices of migrant farm workers in California.

    (D) affirmative action, which gave preference to women and minorities in college admissions.

    (E) inequities of Social Security payments to the elderly.

KAPLAN
Test Prep and Admissions

12. Nixon and Kissinger drew closer to Peoples Republic of China in the 1970s partly because:

    (A) Mao Ze Dong was calling for an end to the Vietnam War.

    (B) they were taking advantage of Sino-Soviet tensions.

    (C) Prime Minister Takamoto of Japan had acted as a go-between.

    (D) they wanted to conclude a nuclear non-proliferation pact with Mao.

    (E) tensions in Korea were threatening the region.

13. Which of the following are true statements about the Gulf War in 1991?

    I. A United Nations coalition sent troops from many nations to fight against Iraq

    II. The war lasted about six weeks

    III. A coup in Iraq overthrew Saddam Hussein during the fighting

    IV. Baghdad was occupied by the United Nations for a year afterwards

    V. The war was precipitated by the Iraqi invasion of Kuwait

    (A) I, II, and V only

    (B) I, II, IV, and V only

    (C) I, II, and III only

    (D) II, III, and V only

    (E) III, IV, and V only

14. Which of the following was the major policy crisis the Clinton administration faced in southeastern Europe?

    (A) A Communist revolution in Grenada

    (B) Military confrontations between Turkey and Greece

    (C) Collapse of democratic governments in the Czech Republic and Romania

    (D) Ethnic conflict and genocide in Yugoslavia

    (E) Soviet efforts to regain control of Eastern European countries

15. All of the following are true of the collapse of the Soviet Union EXCEPT:

    (A) new nations were formed out of the former USSR.

    (B) a change of leadership took place in Moscow with the creation of the Russian Federation.

    (C) a young democracy and free market economy was established in Russia.

    (D) former Communists were arrested and executed in Moscow.

    (E) former Soviet satellites such as Romania also saw leadership changes.

16. A new nativism in the 1970s resulted in grass roots referendums such as:

    (A) the Federal Budget Forum.

    (B) the National Tax Coalition.

    (C) Illinois' Referendum 16.

    (D) the 23rd Amendment to the Constitution.

    (E) California's Proposition 187.

17. Which of the following best describes the Reaganomics of the 1980s?

    (A) Stricter price controls were the best way to help economic growth

    (B) Less government regulation and lower taxes would stimulate the economy

    (C) Raising domestic federal spending would have a positive effect on business in the U.S.

    (D) Slashing the military budget would free up funds for social programs

    (E) A Keynesian approach to government spending would create incentives to work

KAPLAN
Test Prep and Admissions

18. In the 1980s and 90s a general distrust of government and fear that American freedoms were being threatened led to:

    (A) the formation of private militias and domestic terrorism.

    (B) the founding of the Bureau of Firearms and Tobacco.

    (C) declining military enlistments.

    (D) more authority for the Department of Justice.

    (E) greater tensions in urban areas.

19. A free trade zone throughout Mexico, Canada, and the United States was created with the signing of the:

    (A) North American Free Trade Agreement (NAFTA)

    (B) Mericour Trade Agreement

    (C) Trans-Canada Trade Treaty

    (D) North American Tariff Agreement (NATA)

    (E) Bush-Cretan Treaty

20. *The History of the U.S. Decision-Making Policy in Vietnam*, commonly known as *The Pentagon Papers*, included which of the following revelations?

    (A) That high officials in the Department of Defense were advising an immediate withdrawal from Vietnam

    (B) That President Eisenhower had been misinformed by his military advisors about Chinese involvement in Korea

    (C) That President Nixon's plan to bomb Cambodia and Laos were calculated to force China to intervene

    (D) That President Johnson had misled Congress over the events in the Gulf of Tonkin

    (E) That the U.S. Army had developed plans to use chemical weapons to bring a quick end to the war

ESSAY QUESTIONS

1. What defined the economic features of the Reagan Revolution in the 1980s?

_____

_____

_____

_____

_____

_____

_____

_____

_____

_____

_____

2. What impact did the Vietnam War experience have on the foreign policy decisions of the 1980s and 90s?

_____

_____

_____

_____

_____

_____

_____

_____

_____

_____

KAPLAN
Test Prep and Admissions

ANSWER KEY

Multiple-Choice Questions

1. D
2. D
3. B
4. A
5. A
6. B
7. A
8. A
9. D
10. B
11. D
12. B
13. A
14. D
15. D
16. E
17. B
18. A
19. A
20. D

KAPLAN
Test Prep and Admissions

Answers and Explanations

1. D

The women's movement had slowly gathered momentum in the 1960s but had been overshadowed by the anti-war movement and other political issues. By 1970 there was a new activism fueled by many women who fought to have the right to terminate a pregnancy and also to gain equality with males in the workplace. The first was achieved by the Supreme Court decision *Roe v. Wade*, but the latter was harder to accomplish. After considerable debate in many state legislatures, the Equal Rights Amendment was never ratified. It wasn't until 1984 that Geraldine Ferraro became the first female vice presidential nominee of a major political party (Democratic).

2. D

Carter was caught by surprise and angered when the Soviets invaded Afghanistan near the end of his first term. He used two forms of diplomatic retaliation. First he declared a boycott on grain sales to the Russians and then later decided that the U.S. team would not compete in the first Olympics to be held in the Soviet Union. This led the USSR to retaliate and not send its team to the 1984 Los Angeles Summer games. The end result was a worsening of Cold War tensions and a quagmire war for the Russians, which accomplished nothing.

3. B

Carter struggled with a number of political and economic problems. He inherited the inflationary economy from Ford and Nixon and prices continued to rise during his term. Petroleum prices remained especially high and this further fueled inflation. Carter declared a "war" on energy costs and appeared on TV in a sweater to urge Americans to turn down their heat and save fuel.

4. A

Reagan gave considerable freedom to his CIA Director and the National Security Council (NSC) in working to undermine Communism around the world. The Sandinista victory in Nicaragua was a special area of concern as it seemed to suggest Communist advance near the United States. A secret means of funding anti-Sandinista rebels called "contras" was devised via arms sales to Iran. This was against Congressional wishes and a series of hearings were held to uncover the work of a mid-level NSC aid named Lt. Col. Oliver North. He was involved in the secret aid to the contras and was later forced to resign his commission from the U.S. Marines.

5. A

When the Chinese cracked down on young pro-democracy demonstrators in Beijing it was a setback for political reform and liberalism in China. The Chinese Communist Party took a great deal of criticism from the international community but made no changes in its policy to block any further moves towards democracy.

6. B

When the Oval Office tapes revealed that Nixon had been using his authority to impede the FBI and the Congressional investigation into the Watergate breakin, he became open to the charge of "obstruction of justice." Impeachment proceedings were being planned in the House of Representatives when Nixon resigned the presidency in the summer of 1974.

7. A

The SALT I (Strategic Arms Limitation Talks), which began in 1969 came to a conclusion when Nixon traveled to the USSR and met with Premier Brezhnev in 1972. Nixon and Brezhnev announced that the two superpowers had finalized an agreement which would limit the number of ICBMs and the construction of ABMs in both nations. Though it was an agreement of limited impact, since it did nothing to reduce the large nuclear arsenals of the two superpowers, it was hailed as a symbolic first step to control nuclear arms. START (Strategic Arms Reduction Talks) resulted in an agreement to reduce the nuclear stockpiles of the two superpowers in 1991, just before the collapse of the Soviet Union.

8. A

While Reagan believed in less government and lower taxes he also wanted to strengthen the U.S. military, which had downsized since Vietnam. When taxes were cut but military spending soared, the national debt went up dramatically. Reagan's popularity remained high throughout his presidency although the problem of the growing national debt continued into the 1990s.

9. D

When Israel was surprised by the Egyptian attack on Yom Kippur, it requested urgent military aid from the U.S. When Nixon gave it and the war turned in Israel's favor the Arab world was enraged. Leading oil producers such as Saudi Arabia punished the West economically by raising the price of crude oil. This meant a great rise in gasoline costs for the average American and a marked inflationary trend.

10. B

The election of 1976 was quite close but Carter won as a southern Democrat who appealed to working Americans, both African American and white. Similar to the support Franklin Roosevelt had received in the 1930s, Carter won the Deep South as well as the urban North to carry the election.

11. D

This case tested the national trend since the 1960s that had favored minorities and women who were applying to universities and graduate schools. Race and gender quotas in use did not favor white males. Mr. Bakke was a white male military veteran who wanted to go to medical school in California but was rejected. He sued the state and his lawyers argued that he was better qualified to enter than some of the females and nonwhites who had been admitted. The Supreme Court agreed with Bakke, who was allowed to attend medical school. As a result, schools began to reexamine their admission policies and remove specific racial quotas.

12. B

Kissinger and Nixon were practitioners of *realpolitik* and believed that the split between Communist Russia and China could be used to America's advantage. Nixon wanted Soviet concessions on arms control and a settlement in Vietnam. Kissinger traveled secretly to Beijing to arrange a meeting and the first U.S. president went to China in 1972. This would hopefully concern the USSR enough to consider better relations with the U.S.

13. A

The Gulf War was the second United Nations war in the post-1945 era. President Bush reacted aggressively to the invasion of Kuwait just as Truman had in 1950 when South Korea was attacked. A coalition of nations was formed and UN resolutions passed condemning Iraq's aggression. After economic sanctions failed the war began and Kuwait was liberated after six weeks of fighting. Like Korea, the war ended with a return to the status quo before the war with Hussein still the dictator in Iraq.

14. D

With the disintegration of Yugoslavia, ethnic tensions mounted and the country was split into several nations, some of which immediately started fighting. In Bosnia, fighting broke out between different ethnic groups to control the land that they shared. Bosnian Muslims were singled out and massacred by Serbian militias. Clinton responded by sending some troops to help the UN forces already trying to keep the peace. The United States also worked with the UN to seek those who had been guilty of mass murder and bring them to trial.

15. D

The implosion of the Soviet Union was one of the most dramatic events of recent history. It ended the Cold War and led to the birth of new nations that had been part of the Soviet empire for generations. Russia reorganized itself and wrote a new democratic constitution. New leadership was elected and a coup attempt from the military right was foiled.

16. E

California had become the most populated state by the 1970s. Many of the newcomers were recent immigrants and some were illegal workers from Mexico. Proposition 187 was a grass roots movement to limit the access of illegal aliens to public schooling and social services. This was supposed to save the taxpayers money and stem the tide of immigrants to what was one of the fastest growing states in the United States.

17. B

Reagan hearkened back to the 1920s when Republicans favored little government spending and lower taxes. Some believe the prosperity of the 1920s had been based on that economic approach. Reagan was anti-regulation and against "big government" in general. He initiated a hiring freeze in the federal government in his first months in office and promised to slash income taxes. This would force the shrinking of the federal government as there would be no money to pay for the many wasteful programs he wanted to get rid of. The result, however, was rapid growth in the national debt.

18. A

There was a new cynicism in the United States after Watergate and Vietnam. The Reagan years illustrated the idea that one could be proud to be an American but also distrustful of the government. This led some to fall back on the long-cherished tradition that a person and his guns were the last bastion against tyranny. Militias were composed of disenchanted white men who wanted to be 'military' without being in it. They were organized in various states from Michigan to Montana to Texas and reflected the conservative 'gun culture' of rural America.

19. A

With Europe achieving such economic success from the creation of a European free trade zone, the U.S. worked on advancing free trade in North America. Though many opposed this as threatening to American jobs, NAFTA was negotiated between Mexico, Canada and the United States during the first Bush administration. Then Clinton pushed it through Congress in 1993.

20. D

Daniel Ellsberg's release of the top-secret *Pentagon Papers* to *The New York Times* revealed to the public that the "attack" on the U.S. Navy by North Vietnam had been greatly exaggerated. President Johnson used that "attack" to gain Congressional approval for a resolution that gave the president authority to strike back at North Vietnam, which escalated the fighting into a full-fledged war. That the president would use an unverifiable report to wage war was seen as shocking to many. It led to a further distrust of the White House in the early 1970s.

KAPLAN
Test Prep and Admissions

ANALYSES OF THE FREE-RESPONSE ESSAYS

Question 1:

What defined the economic features of the Reagan Revolution in the 1980s?

Key Points

Reaganomics

- Reagan endorsed 'supply side' economics. This is a belief that tax cuts will free up investment monies that will stimulate the economy

- Tax cuts benefit the Americans with higher incomes so it is largely a benefit to the entrepreneurial class

- Cutting corporate taxes would spur businesses to expand production, produce more goods, and hire more workers. The end result in theory would be prosperity for the working class as well. This is also called 'trickle down economics'

- Reaganomics was believed to be a painless way to stop inflation which had ravaged the American economy in the 1970s

- Reagan also believed 'big government' was the cause of many American problems and vowed to downsize the federal bureaucracy. One of his first acts as president was to declare a federal hiring freeze

- The federal deficit was also something the president said he would eliminate as he promised to balance the budget

Domestic economy in the 1980s

- 1981–82 were difficult years as the recession inherited by Reagan deepened
- Farm foreclosures and bankruptcies were increasing
- Unemployment peaked in 1982, but new jobs were being created in 1983
- Military spending increased dramatically and the federal deficit soared
- The economy was recovering by 1984 as inflation was going down and employment was on the rise
- The improving economy and perceived success of 'Reaganomics' set the stage for Reagan's landslide reelection victory in 1984

Scoring Rubric

There are five scoring ranges:

Excellent

The answer must have a strong, clear thesis that details the main features of Reaganomics from 1980–1990. The quality of the writing should be excellent, the answer must show logical patterns, and the student should include many of the major points in the above list (though they may go beyond the list). The organization should be clear. The answer may contain minor errors.

Very Good

The answer must have a thesis that explains the economic approach that Reagan followed as president. Organization of the answer must show logical patterns, and the student should include many of the specific points from the above list.

Adequate

The answer must try to make some argument and must include at least some of the points listed above. There may be flaws in the thesis argument.

Flawed

The answer will demonstrate serious weaknesses. It may have no thesis argument at all, and it will include few of the points listed above. The answer may show little understanding of Reaganomics specifically or of economics in general.

Severely Flawed

The answer will demonstrate almost no attempt to answer the question, and will include very few, if any, of the points listed above.

Question 2:

What impact did the Vietnam War experience have on the foreign policy decisions of the 1980s and 90s?

Key Points

- The failure of American foreign policy in Vietnam and the Watergate scandal that followed had a demoralizing impact on the United States. It cast doubt about American military power and its leadership
- The period of 'détente' or improving relations with Soviet Russia and the Peoples Republic of China in the 1970s lessened the anti-Communist rhetoric of the superpowers
- The invasion of Afghanistan in 1979 brought an end to 'détente' and set the stage for the election of Reagan, a conservative anti-Communist
- A mythology arose that U.S. POWs had been abandoned in Vietnam

Military hotspots for the U.S. after 1980

- Soviet troops in Afghanistan led the U.S. to covertly help Afghanis against the Soviets
- Iran had humiliated the U.S. by holding diplomats hostage and was hostile to America
- Nicaragua was another nation that swung to the left after 1979 when the repressive dictator was ousted by a socialist regime. The U.S. began to support guerilla fighters to destabilize the new government
- El Salvador also was a battle ground between right wing military and leftist groups
- The island of Grenada was the scene of overwhelming U.S. action when Cubans seemed to be supporting a left wing Marxist regime. This local operation was a signal that America was watching events in Central American and would oppose Communism in whatever form
- U.S. Marines were stationed in Lebanon as peacemakers. 241 Marines were killed by a suicide bomber in Beirut in 1984
- The Iraqi invasion of Kuwait in 1990 caused the first war for the United States since the Vietnam period. The U.S. pushed through a U.N. resolution and sent 500,000 troops to fight in the Gulf War which was brief and highly technological. Generals Powell and Schwartzkopf had been junior officers in Vietnam and planned the Gulf War as a brief and victorious campaign.

The big picture

- Many American career military officers who had fought in Vietnam were formed by the experience
- The lesson that many soldiers took away from Vietnam was that there had to be a clear political and military goal if America was to go to war
- Military action must be carefully thought out and well planned. A timetable must be in place and fighting cannot be open-ended as it was in Vietnam

Scoring Rubric

There are five scoring ranges:

Excellent

The answer must have a strong, clear thesis that gives an assessment of the impact of the Vietnam War on American foreign policy after 1980. The essay should focus on efforts to avoid military conflicts. The quality of the writing should be excellent, the answer must show logical patterns, and the student should include many of the major points in the above list (though they may go beyond these points). The organization should be clear. The answer may contain minor errors.

KAPLAN
Test Prep and Admissions

Very Good

The answer must have a thesis that discusses the nature of the 'Vietnam War syndrome.' The answer must be logically organized, and the student should include many of the specific points from the above list.

Adequate

The answer must try to make some argument and must include at least some of the points listed above. There may be flaws in the thesis argument.

Flawed

The answer will demonstrate serious weaknesses. It may have no thesis argument at all, and it will include few of the points listed above. The answer may show little understanding of what the Vietnam war was and what impact it had on America.

Severely Flawed

The answer will demonstrate almost no attempt to answer the question, and will include very few, if any, of the points listed above.

Full-Length Practice Tests

In this section are two full-length practice tests. Tear out or photocopy the answer grids and use them to complete the tests. You'll get the most benefit if you take these exams under test-like conditions.

Before taking a practice test, find a quiet room where you can work uninterrupted. Be sure to bring a watch so you can time yourself. Once you start a test, don't stop until you have finished. You'll have 45 minutes for Section I, and 100 minutes for Section II. Work on only one section at a time, and take a short break in between sections.

The format of the practice tests in this book varies slightly from that of the actual AP exam since you will not be using separate booklets or answering questions about exam preparation.

An answer key and detailed explanations for every question follow each of the tests.

Good luck!

AP U.S. History
Practice Test One Answer Sheet

1. Ⓐ Ⓑ Ⓒ Ⓓ Ⓔ	21. Ⓐ Ⓑ Ⓒ Ⓓ Ⓔ	41. Ⓐ Ⓑ Ⓒ Ⓓ Ⓔ	61. Ⓐ Ⓑ Ⓒ Ⓓ Ⓔ
2. Ⓐ Ⓑ Ⓒ Ⓓ Ⓔ	22. Ⓐ Ⓑ Ⓒ Ⓓ Ⓔ	42. Ⓐ Ⓑ Ⓒ Ⓓ Ⓔ	62. Ⓐ Ⓑ Ⓒ Ⓓ Ⓔ
3. Ⓐ Ⓑ Ⓒ Ⓓ Ⓔ	23. Ⓐ Ⓑ Ⓒ Ⓓ Ⓔ	43. Ⓐ Ⓑ Ⓒ Ⓓ Ⓔ	63. Ⓐ Ⓑ Ⓒ Ⓓ Ⓔ
4. Ⓐ Ⓑ Ⓒ Ⓓ Ⓔ	24. Ⓐ Ⓑ Ⓒ Ⓓ Ⓔ	44. Ⓐ Ⓑ Ⓒ Ⓓ Ⓔ	64. Ⓐ Ⓑ Ⓒ Ⓓ Ⓔ
5. Ⓐ Ⓑ Ⓒ Ⓓ Ⓔ	25. Ⓐ Ⓑ Ⓒ Ⓓ Ⓔ	45. Ⓐ Ⓑ Ⓒ Ⓓ Ⓔ	65. Ⓐ Ⓑ Ⓒ Ⓓ Ⓔ
6. Ⓐ Ⓑ Ⓒ Ⓓ Ⓔ	26. Ⓐ Ⓑ Ⓒ Ⓓ Ⓔ	46. Ⓐ Ⓑ Ⓒ Ⓓ Ⓔ	66. Ⓐ Ⓑ Ⓒ Ⓓ Ⓔ
7. Ⓐ Ⓑ Ⓒ Ⓓ Ⓔ	27. Ⓐ Ⓑ Ⓒ Ⓓ Ⓔ	47. Ⓐ Ⓑ Ⓒ Ⓓ Ⓔ	67. Ⓐ Ⓑ Ⓒ Ⓓ Ⓔ
8. Ⓐ Ⓑ Ⓒ Ⓓ Ⓔ	28. Ⓐ Ⓑ Ⓒ Ⓓ Ⓔ	48. Ⓐ Ⓑ Ⓒ Ⓓ Ⓔ	68. Ⓐ Ⓑ Ⓒ Ⓓ Ⓔ
9. Ⓐ Ⓑ Ⓒ Ⓓ Ⓔ	29. Ⓐ Ⓑ Ⓒ Ⓓ Ⓔ	49. Ⓐ Ⓑ Ⓒ Ⓓ Ⓔ	69. Ⓐ Ⓑ Ⓒ Ⓓ Ⓔ
10. Ⓐ Ⓑ Ⓒ Ⓓ Ⓔ	30. Ⓐ Ⓑ Ⓒ Ⓓ Ⓔ	50. Ⓐ Ⓑ Ⓒ Ⓓ Ⓔ	70. Ⓐ Ⓑ Ⓒ Ⓓ Ⓔ
11. Ⓐ Ⓑ Ⓒ Ⓓ Ⓔ	31. Ⓐ Ⓑ Ⓒ Ⓓ Ⓔ	51. Ⓐ Ⓑ Ⓒ Ⓓ Ⓔ	71. Ⓐ Ⓑ Ⓒ Ⓓ Ⓔ
12. Ⓐ Ⓑ Ⓒ Ⓓ Ⓔ	32. Ⓐ Ⓑ Ⓒ Ⓓ Ⓔ	52. Ⓐ Ⓑ Ⓒ Ⓓ Ⓔ	72. Ⓐ Ⓑ Ⓒ Ⓓ Ⓔ
13. Ⓐ Ⓑ Ⓒ Ⓓ Ⓔ	33. Ⓐ Ⓑ Ⓒ Ⓓ Ⓔ	53. Ⓐ Ⓑ Ⓒ Ⓓ Ⓔ	73. Ⓐ Ⓑ Ⓒ Ⓓ Ⓔ
14. Ⓐ Ⓑ Ⓒ Ⓓ Ⓔ	34. Ⓐ Ⓑ Ⓒ Ⓓ Ⓔ	54. Ⓐ Ⓑ Ⓒ Ⓓ Ⓔ	74. Ⓐ Ⓑ Ⓒ Ⓓ Ⓔ
15. Ⓐ Ⓑ Ⓒ Ⓓ Ⓔ	35. Ⓐ Ⓑ Ⓒ Ⓓ Ⓔ	55. Ⓐ Ⓑ Ⓒ Ⓓ Ⓔ	75. Ⓐ Ⓑ Ⓒ Ⓓ Ⓔ
16. Ⓐ Ⓑ Ⓒ Ⓓ Ⓔ	36. Ⓐ Ⓑ Ⓒ Ⓓ Ⓔ	56. Ⓐ Ⓑ Ⓒ Ⓓ Ⓔ	76. Ⓐ Ⓑ Ⓒ Ⓓ Ⓔ
17. Ⓐ Ⓑ Ⓒ Ⓓ Ⓔ	37. Ⓐ Ⓑ Ⓒ Ⓓ Ⓔ	57. Ⓐ Ⓑ Ⓒ Ⓓ Ⓔ	77. Ⓐ Ⓑ Ⓒ Ⓓ Ⓔ
18. Ⓐ Ⓑ Ⓒ Ⓓ Ⓔ	38. Ⓐ Ⓑ Ⓒ Ⓓ Ⓔ	58. Ⓐ Ⓑ Ⓒ Ⓓ Ⓔ	78. Ⓐ Ⓑ Ⓒ Ⓓ Ⓔ
19. Ⓐ Ⓑ Ⓒ Ⓓ Ⓔ	39. Ⓐ Ⓑ Ⓒ Ⓓ Ⓔ	59. Ⓐ Ⓑ Ⓒ Ⓓ Ⓔ	79. Ⓐ Ⓑ Ⓒ Ⓓ Ⓔ
20. Ⓐ Ⓑ Ⓒ Ⓓ Ⓔ	40. Ⓐ Ⓑ Ⓒ Ⓓ Ⓔ	60. Ⓐ Ⓑ Ⓒ Ⓓ Ⓔ	80. Ⓐ Ⓑ Ⓒ Ⓓ Ⓔ

Practice Test One

Section I: Multiple-Choice Questions

Time: 55 Minutes

80 Questions, 120 points

Directions: Each of the questions or incomplete statements below is followed by five suggested answers or completions. Select the one that is best in each case and then fill in the corresponding oval on the answer sheet.

1. President Franklin Roosevelt's decision to in 1933 to recognize the Soviet Union was probably LEAST influenced by:

    (A) the danger of a Soviet-German alliance.

    (B) a changing attitude among Americans towards Communism.

    (C) Japanese imperial designs in the Pacific.

    (D) the rise of militarism in Germany and Italy.

    (E) a need to increase American exports.

2. Which of the following is evidence that middle-class women had taken on new roles in public life by the middle of the 19th century?

    (A) Many of the reform movements of the time were led by women.

    (B) The wealthy land-owning class began to include women who inherited property from their fathers.

    (C) Many of the leading ministers in the Second Great Awakening were women.

    (D) Women slave owners were among the most outspoken opponents of abolition.

    (E) The women's vote was becoming increasingly important in federal elections.

3. The first Bank of the United States was supported by those who advocated:

    (A) a laissez faire policy by the government towards the banking industry.

    (B) nationalization of the nation's banks.

    (C) a government-controlled banking system.

    (D) a decentralized banking system.

    (E) private control of the banking industry.

4. Which of the following statements most accurately characterizes Woodrow Wilson's stated reason for leading the United States into World War I?

    (A) He wanted to gain colonial lands in the "scramble for Africa."

    (B) He wanted to stand up for freedom of the seas in the face of German submarine warfare.

    (C) He wanted to bolster the American economy by selling arms to the Allies.

    (D) He wanted to stand up for the rights of persecuted minorities in Nazi Germany.

    (E) He wanted to create the League of Nations.

GO ON TO THE NEXT PAGE

5. The ratification of the United States Constitution was most strongly opposed by the:

    (A) small farmers in New England.
    (B) business class and financial interests.
    (C) large plantation owners in the South.
    (D) clergy and areas with well established congregations.
    (E) people in the frontier farming districts.

6. Debates over "internal improvements" during the Jacksonian Era were primarily about:

    (A) whether canal or railroad travel would be most efficient.
    (B) how and to what extent the federal government should subsidize new roads and canals.
    (C) how many immigrants should be allowed into the United States to do unskilled labor.
    (D) the best route for a transcontinental railroad.
    (E) whether cotton or wheat production should be favored in tariff policy.

7. Which of the following statements BEST explains the term *salutary neglect* during the colonial era?

    (A) England did not enforce the trade and navigation acts of Parliament.
    (B) British Americans were reluctant to enter the war with the French and let England do the fighting.
    (C) France neglected her colonial settlements and let them do as they wished.
    (D) England neglected to oppose the French and their native allies until Pitt took over.
    (E) Colonials were casual about paying taxes as required by the crown.

8. All of the following statements are true of the southern gentry during the colonial period EXCEPT:

    (A) The southern gentry tried to emulate the rural culture of the English upper class.
    (B) The southern gentry was often heavily in debt.
    (C) The southern gentry was mostly concentrated in Virginia and South Carolina.
    (D) The southern gentry made money off the sale of staple crops in international markets.
    (E) The southern gentry primarily subscribed to orthodox Calvinist religious beliefs.

9. Secretary of State George Marshall was credited with stemming the spread of Communism in Europe through his proposal to:

    (A) support South Korea against potential threats from North Korea.
    (B) prevent the victory of Communist revolutionaries in Greece and Turkey.
    (C) help all European countries recover from the devastation of World War II.
    (D) establish U.S. military bases in West Germany.
    (E) provide aid to Japan to permit rebuilding from the wartime destruction.

10. Known as the Bill of Rights, the first 10 amendments to the constitution protect all of the following rights EXCEPT:

    (A) the right to vote regardless of gender.
    (B) the right to establish and practice a religion.
    (C) the right to peaceably assemble.
    (D) freedom of speech.
    (E) freedom of the press.

GO ON TO THE NEXT PAGE

KAPLAN
Test Prep and Admissions

11. In which pair is the second an example of the first:

    (A) Closed shop —— lockout

    (B) Tenant farming —— sharecropping

    (C) Laissez faire —— Lend Lease

    (D) Gold standard —— inflation

    (E) Tariff —— excise tax

12. Which of the following arguments was used by southerners who supported the expansion of slavery into the territories acquired in the war with Mexico?

    (A) Spanish colonists' use of forced labor in these territories provided a legal precedent for slavery there.

    (B) If slavery were permitted in the territories, white northerners would be able to dominate American culture and politics.

    (C) Slavery in the territories would help to resolve the sectional conflict that was brewing between North and South.

    (D) Spain would refuse to recognize the United States if slavery were not allowed in its former territories.

    (E) Republican senators would block all pending legislation until slavery was allowed in the newly acquired territories.

13. After World War II, most of the six million women who had entered the workforce during the war:

    (A) lobbied the federal government for pay equity with their male counterparts.

    (B) were offered education grants by the government.

    (C) were encouraged to give up their jobs to the returning GIs.

    (D) continued to provide the main source of income for their families.

    (E) were able to maintain their jobs in the face of rising unemployment.

14. A president and a secretary of state who had sharp differences of opinion with regards to U.S. foreign policy were:

    (A) Ronald Reagan and Alexander Haig

    (B) Woodrow Wilson and William Jennings Bryan

    (C) James Monroe and John Quincy Adams

    (D) Andrew Jackson and Martin Van Buren

    (E) Thomas Jefferson and James Madison

15. The Monroe Doctrine included which of the following provisions?

    (A) The United States reserved the right to intervene in European affairs where American interests were involved.

    (B) All attempts to extend European political systems to the Americas would be considered threats to the peace and safety of the United States.

    (C) The United States should interfere in the remaining European colonies in the Americas.

    (D) The United States would try to prevent any new European immigration to the Americas.

    (E) The United States agreed not to acquire any more Spanish territory in the Americas.

16. "The history of mankind is a history of repeated injuries and usurpations on the part of man toward woman, having in direct object the establishment of an absolute tyranny over her. To prove this let facts be submitted to a candid world."

    This quotation is from which document?

    (A) The Ostend Manifesto (1854)

    (B) The convention of the National Organization of Women in 1973

    (C) The Democratic Party platform (1972)

    (D) The Wilmot Proviso (1846)

    (E) The Seneca Falls Declaration (1848)

GO ON TO THE NEXT PAGE

17. All of the following probably played a significant part in Truman's decision to drop atomic bombs on Hiroshima and Nagasaki EXCEPT:

(A) advice from military and diplomatic experts that Japan would not surrender unless unequivocally defeated.

(B) the success of other incendiary bombing campaigns in the war.

(C) the conviction that without the atomic bomb, the United States would have to invade Japan to end the war.

(D) the belief that a demonstration of nuclear weapons would not be as effective as their use against people and infrastructure.

(E) the fear that Japan was on the verge of developing an atomic bomb and using it against the United States.

18. Where will a president be tried after he has been impeached?

(A) The Senate

(B) The House of Representatives

(C) The Supreme Court

(D) The White House

(E) The State Legislatures

19. During the Great Migration after World War II:

(A) millions of urban African Americans migrated to the fertile regions of the Midwest.

(B) millions of African Americans fled from the Dust Bowl of the Midwest to settle in California.

(C) millions of urban, northern African Americans migrated to Liberia.

(D) millions of rural, Southern African Americans migrated to cities in the North and West.

(E) millions of African Americans moved from the inner cities to the burgeoning suburbs of the South.

20. Throughout the 19th century, pressure for a loose interpretation of the Constitution and more government control came most consistently from:

(A) labor union leaders.

(B) farmers in the West.

(C) railroad owners.

(D) fishermen from New England.

(E) cotton farmers from the South.

21. Which of the following is a correct statement regarding the national government's land policy in the Old Northwest in the early 19th century?

(A) It encouraged wealthy developers to purchase the land in large plots, but only if they paid in cash.

(B) It reduced the price per acre of land in the West.

(C) It began to permit individuals to purchase small plots (as little as five acres) but at substantially higher prices per acre.

(D) It was based on the "homestead" principle whereby an individual could gain ownership of 160 acres free of charge.

(E) It distributed lands seized from Native Americans to veterans of the War of 1812.

22. The constitutionality of federal regulation of 'big business' and labor can be traced to what Supreme Court decision?

(A) *Fletcher v. Peck*

(B) *Roe v. Wade*

(C) *Gideon v. Wainwright*

(D) *Gibbons v. Ogden*

(E) *Marbury v. Madison*

GO ON TO THE NEXT PAGE ⟩

23. President Lincoln's main objective in waging war on the Confederacy was:

    (A) preserving the Union.
    (B) abolishing slavery in the Southern states.
    (C) abolishing slavery in the Western territories.
    (D) eroding the economic base of the South.
    (E) ensuring that the flow of immigrants to the Northern states would continue.

24. The landmark case *Brown v. Board of Education of Topeka, Kansas* established the principle that:

    (A) bussing students to force integration of schools was unconstitutional.
    (B) the doctrine of "separate but equal" had no place in education.
    (C) teaching evolution in schools could not be prevented by law.
    (D) schools could be segregated as long as they provided "separate but equal" facilities.
    (E) American military personnel could obtain low-interest loans for college.

25. "Ordinarily, war tends to submerge sectional differences."

    The best example of a contradiction of this statement would be congressional criticism during:

    (A) World War I
    (B) The Indian Wars in the West
    (C) The Korean War
    (D) The Gulf War
    (E) The Mexican War

26. One difference between the 18th and 19th Amendments lies in the fact that:

    (A) the 19th Amendment was opposed in the West.
    (B) the 18th Amendment was mostly supported by people from northern Europe.
    (C) the 19th Amendment was supported by the people after ratification.
    (D) the 18th Amendment was more popular.
    (E) the 19th Amendment was supported by the farmers in the Northeast.

27. All of the following statements about free African Americans in the South before the Civil War are correct EXCEPT:

    (A) by the early 19th century, they were not permitted to serve on juries or to testify against whites.
    (B) approximately two percent of free African Americans in the South were slave owners.
    (C) free African Americans in the South were prohibited from owning property.
    (D) by 1860 almost half of African Americans in Maryland were free.
    (E) some free African Americans in the South had been able to purchase their freedom.

28. When the Electoral College fails to elect a president what will happen next, according to the U.S. Constitution?

    (A) The votes will be recounted within one week
    (B) The election will be held again in two weeks
    (C) The election goes to the Senate
    (D) The election goes to the House of Representatives
    (E) The Supreme Court will choose the next President

GO ON TO THE NEXT PAGE ⟹

29. The United States went to war with Spain in 1898 because of all of the following EXCEPT:

(A) Spain refused to discuss terms for peace and cut diplomatic ties with the United States.

(B) Newspapers helped increase public support for war with Spain.

(C) Americans tended to compare the Cuban insurrection to their own American Revolution.

(D) There were reports of Spanish mistreatment of Cuban civilians.

(E) The American battleship *Maine* blew up in Havana Harbor under suspicious circumstances.

30. Which problem that confronted the American farmer from 1870–1890 was practically nonexistent by 1935?

(A) Supreme Court opposition to farm legislation

(B) Inadequate farm credit available

(C) Existence of large farm surpluses

(D) Discriminatory practices of the railroad companies

(E) Low income from falling crop prices

31. In the wake of the Cuban missile crisis, all of the following steps were taken to ease Soviet-American tensions EXCEPT:

(A) the signing of a treaty that banned nuclear testing in the atmosphere.

(B) the installation of a "hot line" linking Moscow and Washington.

(C) the decision to halt construction on the Berlin Wall.

(D) the removal of obsolete NATO missiles from Turkey, Italy, and Britain.

(E) the decision by the United States to sell wheat to the Soviet Union.

32. Which of the following best represents the objectives of Henry Clay's "American System"?

(A) Decreased federal spending and less regulation

(B) Funds to the states to improve public schools

(C) More training for state militias and a higher tariff

(D) More credit for land speculators and grants for the railroads

(E) A protective tariff to encourage the growth of American industry and improvements in the national infrastructure

33. John Steinbeck's classic *The Grapes of Wrath* describes the lives of:

(A) the artists of the Harlem Renaissance.

(B) Dust Bowl migrants to California.

(C) former slaves.

(D) child laborers during the Industrial Revolution.

(E) suffragettes in the early 20th century.

34. Which of the following is not a freedom contained in the 1st Amendment to the Constitution:

(A) Freedom of religion

(B) Freedom of the press

(C) Freedom of petition

(D) Freedom of enterprise

(E) Freedom of assembly

GO ON TO THE NEXT PAGE

35. The main intent of the Open Door Policy toward China was:

    (A) to increase the number of Chinese immigrants to America.

    (B) to support the work of American Christian missionaries in China.

    (C) to begin a cultural exchange program with China.

    (D) to further American commercial interests in China.

    (E) to increase America's naval presence in the Eastern Pacific.

36. A major purpose of the Reconstruction Act of 1867 was to:

    (A) further the temperance movement.

    (B) enable the Republican Party to retain control of Congress.

    (C) "bind up the nation's wounds" by providing economic assistance to repair Civil War destruction.

    (D) punish the former generals of the CSA.

    (E) stimulate the industrial development of the South.

37. Which of the following statements correctly describes what happened following the American Revolution?

    (A) Qualifications for voting were raised.

    (B) Legislative representation of rural and inland areas was decreased in order to increase the influence of the coastal cities.

    (C) Although revolutionary ideology had called for an increasingly educated population, opportunities for higher education decreased.

    (D) The people who became most interested in politics after the war were those who had not fought during the Revolution.

    (E) Land and property that had been confiscated from the Tory loyalists was returned to them after the war was over.

38. Jacksonian democracy represented a trend away from the Jeffersonian ideal in its:

    (A) active foreign policy.

    (B) sympathy towards agrarian problems.

    (C) tendency to strengthen the federal government.

    (D) appeal to the common man.

    (E) attitude toward the Bank of the United States.

39. Which of the following statements best describes the War Powers Act of 1973?

    (A) It gave the president so many new powers that the office came to be known as the "imperial presidency."

    (B) It reaffirmed the authority of the president over the leaders of the Armed Forces.

    (C) It granted President Nixon the authority to expand American bombing into Cambodia and Laos.

    (D) It limited the power of the president to send American troops into combat.

    (E) It reorganized the command structure within the Pentagon.

40. The basic case of the 'agrarian crusade' during the late 19th century was most similar to:

    (A) the Whiskey Rebellion.

    (B) Earth Day 1970.

    (C) the Hartford Convention.

    (D) Shay's Rebellion.

    (E) Nat Turner's revolt.

GO ON TO THE NEXT PAGE

41. All of the following statements about the depression of the 1890s are true EXCEPT:

    (A) the depression was widespread because of the interdependence of many sectors in the American economy.

    (B) during the depression, an army of unemployed railroad construction workers marched on Washington to protest conditions.

    (C) most farmers were able to escape the effects of this depression.

    (D) despite large numbers of unemployed and dissatisfied workers, Republicans made gains in the midterm elections of 1894.

    (E) railroad failures set off a panic on Wall Street, which hindered the economy's recovery.

42. One of the ways that the Federal Reserve System exercises control over the economy of the United States is:

    (A) determining the amount banks must have on hand to depositers.

    (B) managing government spending on social programs.

    (C) regulating interest rates banks can charge to high risk borrowers.

    (D) regulation of interest rates for loans by Federal Reserve Banks to banks.

    (E) adjustment of the price of gold per ounce.

43. Which of the following is considered to be the most important foreign policy achievement of the Carter administration?

    (A) Restoration of diplomatic relations with Cuba

    (B) Negotiations of free-trade agreements with Communist countries

    (C) Rescue of the American hostages in Iran

    (D) Negotiation of a peace agreement between Israel and Egypt at Camp David

    (E) Restoration of diplomatic relations with Taiwan

44. During World War II the U.S. government used all the following policies to combat inflation EXCEPT:

    (A) pressuring some industries to cancel planned price increases.

    (B) increasing interest rates.

    (C) nationalizing certain industries that overcharged the public.

    (D) tax increases.

    (E) setting price controls on staple goods.

45. When Jewish leaders proclaimed the existence of an independent state of Israel in 1948, the United States:

    (A) broke diplomatic relations with all Arab countries.

    (B) withheld its recognition until democratic elections could be held and a constitution drafted.

    (C) recognized the new state immediately.

    (D) offered military and financial aid to Arab states.

    (E) applied the Truman Doctrine in Israel as it had in Greece and Turkey.

46. The Chinese Exclusion Act of 1882 was passed to halt emigrants from China because:

    (A) many other immigrant groups were jealous of Chinese success in America

    (B) they made up 30 percent of the population of California at the time

    (C) white laborers feared that jobs were being taken by Chinese workers

    (D) the Chinese birth rate was so high in America

    (E) it was feared that Chinese were bringing disease into the United States

GO ON TO THE NEXT PAGE

47. Andrew Johnson's Reconstruction plan differed from Radical Reconstruction in which of the following ways?

    (A) It required all Southern states to grant African Americans the right to vote before they would be allowed to rejoin the Union.

    (B) It denied freed slaves the right to vote on the grounds that they were not citizens.

    (C) It required freed slaves to attend school for a certain number of years before they would be allowed to vote.

    (D) It called for a Constitutional amendment to guarantee African Americans the vote.

    (E) It left the issue of African American suffrage to the individual states.

48. In its relations with the Arab world since 1945, the United States' most fateful decision was to:

    (A) remain neutral during the Yom Kippur War.

    (B) support Israel in the Suez Crisis of 1956.

    (C) offer economic aid to build the Aswan Dam in Egypt.

    (D) establish the Central Treaty Organization.

    (E) support the United Nations Resolution to partition Palestine and recognize the State of Israel.

49. The détente between Richard Nixon and Leonid Brezhnev led most directly to which of the following events?

    (A) The United States' decision to use the United Nations to solve international problems

    (B) The United States' official recognition of Communist China

    (C) The integration of the economic systems of the United States and Western Europe

    (D) The signing of agreements at the Strategic Arms Limitation Talks (SALT)

    (E) The decision by the United States to increase its nuclear arsenal as a means of deterring Soviet aggression

50. The legal basis for President Truman's use of the American military to defend South Korea in 1950 was:

    (A) the United Nations charter.

    (B) a joint resolution of the U.S. Congress.

    (C) the powers given him as commander-in-chief in the U.S. Constitution.

    (D) precedents in international law.

    (E) a United Nations resolution.

51. When Northern Whigs, independent Democrats, and other factions joined together in 1854 to form the Republican Party, they were united primarily by their:

    (A) fear of disunion and civil war.

    (B) opposition to the extension of slavery to new territories in the West.

    (C) opposition to the annexation of Texas.

    (D) desire to expand further into Mexico.

    (E) desire to keep the Kansas-Nebraska Act from passing in Congress.

52. J. D. Salinger's *Catcher in the Rye* addressed which of the following issues of the 1940s and 1950s?

    (A) Alienated youth in a conformist world

    (B) Employment discrimination against women

    (C) Growing unemployment caused by increased imports from an economically recovering Europe

    (D) Environmental problems brought about by postwar industrialization

    (E) African Americans' limited access to the middle class

GO ON TO THE NEXT PAGE

KAPLAN
Test Prep and Admissions

53. Progressive reformers supported all of the following causes EXCEPT:

   (A) direct democracy.

   (B) free silver.

   (C) government regulation of big businesses.

   (D) child-labor reform.

   (E) prohibition.

54. In the U.S. Constitution the power to admit new states to the Union is given to:

   (A) Congress.

   (B) the Justice department.

   (C) the executive branch.

   (D) the president's cabinet.

   (E) the Supreme Court.

55. All of the following were major issues in Jacksonian politics EXCEPT:

   (A) the status of the national bank.

   (B) South Carolina's refusal to obey federal laws.

   (C) removal of the Cherokees.

   (D) statehood for California.

   (E) tariff policy.

56. In which of the following cases did the Supreme Court uphold segregation in public transportation?

   (A) *Miranda v. Arizona*

   (B) the *Dred Scott* case

   (C) *Gideon v. Wainwright*

   (D) *Plessy v. Ferguson*

   (E) *Roe v. Wade*

57. How did Franklin Roosevelt's method of dealing with the Depression differ from Herbert Hoover's?

   (A) Roosevelt thought that it would be a mistake to give federal funds directly to the unemployed because it would keep them from trying to find jobs.

   (B) Roosevelt believed that the economy was fundamentally sound and that it would recover on its own.

   (C) Roosevelt believed the federal government should actively fund, promote, and oversee economic-recovery efforts.

   (D) Roosevelt used the draft to reduce unemployment.

   (E) Roosevelt promoted the deregulation of businesses.

58. If the policies of the Greenback Party had been enacted it would have had the same effect on the money supply as when the Federal Reserve:

   (A) raises the discount lending rate.

   (B) manipulates the price of gold.

   (C) tightens the money supply.

   (D) lowers the discount lending rate.

   (E) insures bank deposits.

59. Two-thirds of the people of Japanese ancestry who were placed in War Relocation Camps during World War II:

   (A) enlisted in the armed forces and served in combat.

   (B) were under the age of 19.

   (C) were later convicted of espionage.

   (D) were American citizens.

   (E) protested by refusing to comply with curfews.

GO ON TO THE NEXT PAGE

60. Which New Deal measure illustrates support for the Keynesian theory?

   (A) Passing the Agriculture Adjustment Act
   (B) Reforming the Bureau of Indian Affairs
   (C) Starting the Works Progress Administration
   (D) Passing the Social Security Act
   (E) Establishing the Securities and Exchange Commission

61. Senator Henry Cabot Lodge focused on which of the following in his campaign against Senate ratification of the Versailles Treaty that ended World War I?

   (A) Lodge wanted the provision concerning the "racial equality" of all people to be removed from the Treaty.
   (B) Lodge was concerned that the Treaty would lead to the interference by the League of Nations in the domestic affairs of member nations.
   (C) Lodge argued that the Monroe Doctrine, with its Roosevelt Corollary, should be exempted from the provisions of the Treaty.
   (D) Lodge wanted a requirement of Senate authorization for any use of American military forces to help ensure the collective security that the Treaty called for.
   (E) Lodge was willing to consider the Treaty and the League only if the entire Western Hemisphere was removed from its jurisdiction.

Talk softly but carry a big stick (1904)

62. The cartoon above dramatizes what aspect of Theodore Roosevelt's presidency?

   (A) The Republican party was using the 'big stick' to defeat the Democrats in 1904.
   (B) The U.S. needed to become a dominant world power.
   (C) America had used the 'big stick' during the Boxer Rebellion.
   (D) The U.S. was destined to be a regional power and should have an aggressive foreign policy.
   (E) Roosevelt believed that the U.S. should concentrate on domestic issues.

GO ON TO THE NEXT PAGE

63. All of the following correctly describe elements of the policy of containment introduced in 1947 EXCEPT:

(A) it included investigations into the loyalty of American government employees who were suspected of supporting the Soviet Union.

(B) it was a response to the Soviet belief that for the Soviet Union to survive, America's position in the world had to be threatened.

(C) it was based on the belief that American policy toward the U.S.S.R. should be based on a long-term and patient opposition to Soviet activities throughout the world.

(D) it was based on the belief that successful prevention of Soviet expansion would cause, in the long run, an internal decline in the Soviet system and fertilize the "seeds of their own decay."

(E) it was based on the belief that providing aid and assistance to all countries bordering on the U.S.S.R. would help to prevent Soviet expansion.

64. The Platt Amendment, the Ostend Manifesto, and the Roosevelt Corollary were similar in that all three:

(A) departed from previous U.S. foreign policies in the Caribbean.

(B) had to do with U.S. interests in South America.

(C) were extensions of the Monroe Doctrine.

(D) expressed the expanding interests of the United States.

(E) Established colonial policies for the American empire.

65. Which of the following statements is true of immigrants who came to the United States in the late 19th century?

(A) Most came from Asia and the Pacific Islands.

(B) Many could neither read nor write in English.

(C) Most settled in rural and agricultural areas of the country.

(D) A large majority of these immigrants were women.

(E) Most settled in suburbs on the outskirts of America's major cities.

66. The War of 1812 and World War I are similar in that:

(A) in both wars there was widespread dissatisfaction with the post-war settlement.

(B) a world congress was established after a treaty was concluded.

(C) a major American victory was won after the peace was concluded.

(D) the United States entered both wars to defend the trading rights of neutral nations.

(E) national conscription was adopted during both wars.

GO ON TO THE NEXT PAGE

67. Why did supporters of the teaching of evolution in schools claim victory at the Scopes Trial, even though Mr. Scopes was found guilty?

    (A) The Supreme Court, hearing the evidence again, overturned Scopes' conviction.

    (B) In the long run, Tennessee passed a law that permitted the teaching of evolution in public schools.

    (C) Clarence Darrow used the trial proceedings to mount a countrywide campaign against fundamentalism and tradition-bound culture.

    (D) Due to William Jennings Bryan's eloquent support of "academic freedom," this concept gained wide acceptance throughout the country.

    (E) They believed the testimony in the trial had shown the fundamentalist views of biology and history to be illogical and even funny.

68. In foreign affairs, President Lincoln's most important achievement was to:

    (A) emancipate the slaves.

    (B) convince Great Britain not to recognize the Confederate States of America.

    (C) gain Russian support for the North.

    (D) negotiate loans from France to help pay for the Civil War.

    (E) establish diplomatic relations with the Confederacy.

69. Which of the following statements about the Supreme Court's decision in the case of *Marbury v. Madison* is true?

    (A) The Court denied Maryland the right to tax a federal agency.

    (B) The Court declared the Alien and Sedition Acts to be constitutional.

    (C) The Court upheld President Jefferson's right to claim executive privilege.

    (D) The Supreme Court declared an act of Congress to be unconstitutional for the first time.

    (E) The Supreme Court declared a state law to be unconstitutional for the first time.

70. An *ex post facto* law is one that:

    (A) was passed after a president has vetoed it.

    (B) has expired and cannot be used to prosecute a criminal.

    (C) allows a person to be tried for the same criminal act only once.

    (D) punishes a crime that was illegal when it happened.

    (E) makes punishable an act that was not illegal when it was committed.

GO ON TO THE NEXT PAGE

KAPLAN
Test Prep and Admissions

71. One of the main disadvantages faced by the South during the Civil War was:

    (A) the lack of an industrial base.

    (B) a lack of military leadership.

    (C) a lack of conviction that they were on the right side.

    (D) a large number of soldiers who were recent immigrants and could not understand each other.

    (E) the fact that the war was fought on territory unfamiliar to southerners.

72. The House of Burgesses was established in which British colony?

    (A) Pennsylvania

    (B) Rhode Island

    (C) Virginia

    (D) Florida

    (E) New Hampshire

73. The economic theory that described England's goals for its American colonies is most accurately termed:

    (A) imperialism.

    (B) socialism.

    (C) laissez faire capitalism.

    (D) paternalism.

    (E) mercantilism.

74. Which industries did labor find most difficult to organize in the late 19th century?

    (A) Those that had a monopoly and paid higher wages

    (B) Those that were protected by high tariffs

    (C) Those providing fringe benefits to management

    (D) Those engaged in interstate commerce

    (E) Those employing a large number of foreign-born workers

75. The main problem that the United States faced as it entered the War of 1812 was:

    (A) Americans in the West were not willing to take part in the war.

    (B) there was no longer enough British territory nearby that could be attacked.

    (C) France, allied with Britain, continued to attack American shipping.

    (D) America's army was strong but her navy was weak.

    (E) the United States was not prepared militarily to fight a war with Britain.

76. Why did the United States lag behind many European nations in adopting labor and social legislation in the early 20th century?

    (A) Unions were weaker in America.

    (B) Private philanthropy was active in solving social concerns.

    (C) No major political party was pressing for these reforms.

    (D) Legal rulings limited the powers of the federal government and sometimes favored the employer.

    (E) the success of welfare capitalism made it unnecessary.

77. Epidemic diseases of European origin to which Native Americans had no resistance:

    (A) made it more difficult for Europeans to colonize the New World.

    (B) were not significant by the early 17th century.

    (C) had little impact on early Native American-European relations.

    (D) made it much easier for Europeans to colonize the New World.

    (E) hit Africans brought to British colonies harder than they hit Native American peoples.

GO ON TO THE NEXT PAGE ⇨

78. What marked the beginning of the environmental movement in recent American history?

   (A) The Exxon oil spill off Alaska in 1984

   (B) The protests after the Three Mile Island accident in 1979

   (C) The creation of the Environmental Protection Agency by President Nixon

   (D) The celebration of Earth Day in 1970

   (E) The publishing of Buckminster Fuller's books on the cosmos

79. In the Presidential campaign of 1896, William Jennings Bryan emphasized which of the following as his main campaign issue?

   (A) Support for strict immigration restriction

   (B) The end of the gold standard and the free coinage of silver

   (C) Strong opposition to immigration restriction

   (D) The need to increase tariffs

   (E) Removal of government regulation of the banking industry

80. Which of the following principles have been supported by both the League of Nations and the United Nations?

   (A) Global military alliances

   (B) The creation of an international space agency

   (C) The right of self determination

   (D) A Security Council with veto power over lesser nations

   (E) The rights of belligerent nations to defend their shipping lanes

IF YOU FINISH BEFORE TIME IS CALLED, YOU MAY CHECK YOUR WORK ON THIS SECTION ONLY. DO NOT TURN TO ANY OTHER SECTION IN THE TEST. | STOP

Test Prep and Admissions

Section II: Free Response Questions

Time: 130 Minutes

Directions: This section contains five free-response questions. Answer the document-based question in Part A, one of the essay questions in Part B, and one of the essay questions in Part C. The first 15 minutes of the 130 minutes allocated for Section II is a reading period. During this period you should read the document-based question and plan what you will write, including making any notes. However, you cannot begin to write your essay until the 15-minute reading period has ended.

Part A: Document-Based Question

Suggested writing time: 45 minutes

The following question requires you to write a coherent essay incorporating your interpretation of the documents and your knowledge of the period specified in the question. To earn a high score you are required to cite key pieces of evidence from the documents and draw on your knowledge of the period.

1. It is often claimed that the major American wars of the last 150 years have resulted in the most important social and political gains of minorities and women. Evaluate this statement with regard to the experience of minorities and women during World War II.

   Use evidence from the documents **and** your knowledge of the period from 1941 to 1945 to compose your answer.

Document A

"Above and Beyond the Call of Duty." 1943.
National Archives and Records Administration.

Document B

Brigadier General B. O. Davis to General Peterson, 9 November 1943 (Brigadier Davis had just completed an inspection of military bases in Massachusetts, New York, New Jersey and Michigan):

"I was deeply impressed with the high morale and attitudes of the colored officers and soldiers stationed in the states visited in the past two months. They were so different from those of the colored officers and soldiers located in the Southern states. While there has been an improvement in general conditions, there is still great dissatisfaction and discouragement on the part of the colored people and the soldiers. They feel that, regardless of how much they strive to meet War Department requirements, there is no change in the attitude of the War Department. The colored officers and soldiers feel that they are denied the protection and rewards that ordinarily result from good behavior and proper performance of duty. . . .

Continued on the next page.

Document B (continued)

The Press news items and reports of investigations show that there has been little change in the attitudes of civilian communities in Southern states. The colored man in uniform receives nothing but hostility from community officials. . . . The colored man in uniform is expected by the War Department to develop a high morale in a community that offers him nothing but humiliation and mistreatment. Military training does not develop a spirit of cheerful acceptance of Jim-Crow laws and customs. The War Department has failed to secure to the colored soldier protection against violence on the part of civilian police and to secure justice in the courts in communities near-by to Southern stations. In the areas recently inspected, the colored soldier feels that he can secure justice in the civil courts. He has not been set upon by the civilian police. He has not been denied the privilege of occupying empty seats in public buses, street cars, etc. taxicabs to serve him. This is not so in Southern communities. . . ."

Document C

President Roosevelt, "Executive Order 9066," February 25, 1942:

"Whereas the successful prosecution of the war requires every possible protection against espionage and against sabotage to national-defense material, national-defense premises, and national defense utilities. . . .

. . . . I hereby authorize and direct the Secretary of War, and the Military Commanders whom he may from time to time designate, whenever he or any designated commander deems such action necessary or desirable, to prescribe military areas in such places and of such extent as he or the appropriate Military Commander may determine, from which any or all persons may be excluded, and with respect to which, the right of any person to enter, remain in, or leave shall be subject to whatever restrictions the Secretary of War or the appropriate Military Commander may impose in his discretion. . . ."

Document D

Korematsu v. United States, 1944. Mr. Justice Murphy, dissenting:

"This exclusion of 'all persons of Japanese ancestry, both alien and non-alien,' from the Pacific Coast area on a plea of military necessity in the absence of martial law ought not to be approved. Such exclusion goes over 'the very brink of constitutional power' and falls into the ugly abyss of racism.

. . . . Individuals must not be left impoverished of their constitutional rights on a plea of military necessity that has neither substance nor support. . . .

. . . . Being an obvious racial discrimination, the order deprives all those within its scope of the equal protection of the laws as guaranteed by the Fifth Amendment. It further deprives these individuals of their constitutional rights to live and work where they will, to establish a home where they choose and to move about freely. In excommunicating them without benefit of hearings, this order also deprives them of all their constitutional rights to procedural due process. Yet no reasonable relation to an 'immediate, imminent, and impending' public danger is evident to support this racial restriction which is one of the most sweeping and complete deprivations of constitutional rights in the history of this nation in the absence of martial law. . . ."

Document E

Congressman Rankin, Mississippi, February 18, 1942:

"I know the Hawaiian Islands. I know the Pacific coast where these Japanese reside. Even though they may be the third or fourth generation of Japanese, we cannot trust them. I know that those areas are teeming with Japanese spies and fifth columnists. Once a Jap always a Jap. You cannot change him. You cannot make a silk purse out of a sow's ear. . . .

Do not forget that once a Japanese always a Japanese. I say it is of vital importance that we get rid of every Japanese whether in Hawaii or on the mainland. They violate every sacred promise, every canon of honor and decency. This was evidenced in their diplomacy and in their bombing of Hawaii. These Japs who had been there for generations were making signs, if you please, guiding the Japanese planes to the objects of their inequity in order that they might destroy our naval vessels, murder our soldiers and sailors, and blow to pieces the helpless women and children of Hawaii. Damn them! Let us get rid of them now!"

Document F

Franklin D. Roosevelt, "Fireside Chat on the Home Front," October 12, 1942:

"In order to keep stepping up our production, we have had to add millions of workers to the total labor force of the Nation. And as new factories come into operation, we must find additional millions of workers. This presents a formidable problem in the mobilization of manpower. It is not that we do not have enough people in this country to do the job. The problem is to have the right numbers of people in the right place at the right time. . . .

In some communities, employers dislike to employ women. In others they are reluctant to hire Negroes. In still others, older men are not wanted. We can no longer afford to indulge such prejudices or practices."

Document G

"Women are welders [sic] discuss the production of motor mounts and welded parts in a welding booth at the Inglewood, Calif., plant of North American Aviation, Inc." 1942. National Archives and Records Administration.

Document H

President Roosevelt, Executive Order 8802, June 25, 1941:

"WHEREAS it is the policy of the United States to encourage full participation in the national defense program by all citizens of the United States, regardless of race, creed, color, or national origin, in the firm belief that the democratic way of life within the Nation can be defended successfully only with the help and support of all groups within its borders; and

WHEREAS there is evidence that available and needed workers have been barred from employment in industries engaged in defense production solely because of considerations of race, creed, color, or national origin, to the detriment of workers' morale and of national unity;

NOW, THEREFORE, by virtue of the authority vested in me by the Constitution and the statutes, and as a prerequisite to the successful conduct of our national defense production effort, I do hereby reaffirm the policy of the United States that there shall be no discrimination in the employment of workers in defense industries or government because of race, creed, color, or national origin, and I do hereby declare that it is the duty of employers and of labor organizations, in furtherance of said policy and of this order, to provide for the full and equitable participation of all workers in defense industries, without discrimination because of race, creed, color, or national origin; . . . ."

Part B

Suggested time: 35 minutes

Directions: Choose ONE question from this part. You are advised to spend five minutes planning and 30 minutes writing your answer.

2. Compare the relationships of TWO of the following colonial powers with the Native Americans up to 1770.

    - French
    - British
    - Spanish

3. Discuss the impact of TWO of the following wars on the domestic politics in the United States.

    - War of 1812
    - Mexican War
    - Spanish-American War

Part C

Suggested time: 35 minutes

Directions: Choose ONE question from this part. You are advised to spend five minutes planning and 30 minutes writing your answer.

4. Discuss the impact of the second "Red Scare" on American politics in the 1950s.

5. Discuss TWO cultural and societal changes that America experienced during the late 1960s and early 1970s.

Practice Test One: **Answer Key**

1.	A	21.	B	41.	C	61.	B
2.	A	22.	D	42.	D	62.	D
3.	A	23.	A	43.	D	63.	A
4.	B	24.	B	44.	C	64.	D
5.	E	25.	E	45.	C	65.	B
6.	B	26.	C	46.	C	66.	D
7.	A	27.	C	47.	B	67.	E
8.	E	28.	D	48.	E	68.	B
9.	C	29.	A	49.	D	69.	D
10.	A	30.	D	50.	C	70.	E
11.	B	31.	C	51.	B	71.	A
12.	A	32.	E	52.	A	72.	C
13.	C	33.	B	53.	B	73.	E
14.	B	34.	D	54.	A	74.	E
15.	B	35.	D	55.	D	75.	E
16.	E	36.	B	56.	D	76.	D
17.	E	37.	E	57.	C	77.	D
18.	A	38.	C	58.	D	78.	D
19.	D	39.	D	59.	D	79.	B
20.	B	40.	D	60.	C	80.	C

Answers and Explanations

1. A

In 1933 there was no likelihood of a Soviet-German alliance. Hitler had been virulently anti-Communist and viewed the Soviet Union as the great danger in Europe. Stalin also saw the emergence of fascism as a great threat to his regime.

2. A

Middle-class women were important players in the following reform movements: women's rights, temperance, prison reform, abolition, and education. Women such as Dorothea Dix, Catharine Beecher, and Elizabeth Cady Stanton were important reform leaders.

3. A

The Bank of the United States, or BUS, was a central bank established by Congress in 1791. It was privately owned and managed, 80 percent of its stock being reserved for private parties and the remaining 20 percent being owned by the government.

4. B

Wilson tried to keep the United States out of World War I until the last possible moment. But when Germany violated the principle of freedom of the seas by waging unrestricted submarine warfare, Wilson decided to act. Wilson felt he was defending the freedom of all people by entering the war. Wilson's idealism became a foundation for much of American foreign policy for the rest of the century, including World War II, the Korean War, and Vietnam.

5. E

Pockets of Antifederalist sentiment were most prevalent in western areas of New York state and in Pennsylvania, Virginia, the Carolinas, Tennessee and most of Kentucky. These farmers were not in favor of a central government and held deep-seated antiauthoritarian beliefs.

6. B

During Jackson's presidency, the major debate over internal improvements concerned whether it was constitutional to permit the federal government to pay for new roads and canals. Jackson was in favor of further development, but not at federal expense.

7. A

The British trade and navigation acts would have restricted colonial trade, but they were not enforced. This practice of nonenforcement, called salutary neglect, was beneficial to the colonies and indirectly to England as well. This worked fine until the mother country needed the revenue from the acts in question. Salutary neglect came to an end after 1763 when Britain needed to raise revenues to pay war debts from the French and Indian War.

8. E

The upper class South was primarily Anglican, not Calvinist. All other statements accurately portray the upper class of the southern colonies.

9. C

In June 1947, Marshall proposed that the United States finance a massive recovery program for Europe. The Marshall Plan was intended to restore European economies, allowing these nations time to recover from the war and reestablish themselves politically. Under this plan the U.S. would give money, food, and machinery. This served both humanitarian and political ends as western Europe became less susceptible to Communist activity.

10. A

The Bill of Rights does not guarantee the right to vote regardless of gender. The right to vote was not won for women until the passage of the 19th Amendment in 1920.

11. B

Sharecropping is a type of tenant farming. In this case, the tenant who works the land pays the landowner a portion of the crops (cotton perhaps) rather than cash.

KAPLAN
Test Prep and Admissions

12. A

Pro-slavery Southerners advanced many arguments in support of the expansion of slavery into the territories acquired in the war with Mexico, including the idea that Spanish colonists' use of forced labor set a precedent for slavery. They also argued that slavery was a positive, civilizing force, that slavery was crucial to the cotton industry, that the cotton industry was crucial to the American economy, and that it was unconstitutional to ban slavery in the territories.

13. C

Although the entry of women into the workforce during World War II was strongly encouraged, these same women were encouraged to leave their new jobs once war veterans returned home. The idea was that available jobs should go first to men, as men were assumed to be the main breadwinners in each family.

14. B

Wilson won reelection in 1916 with the slogan, "He kept us out of the war." He had urged neutrality and supported laws intended to help keep the country out of the conflict. But when Americans were killed by German submarine attacks, Wilson protested and demanded America's rights as a neutral nation.

Bryan resigned as Woodrow Wilson's Secretary of State because he believed that Wilson was too reckless and that, as a result, war was possible. He favored further steps, including laws that would prohibit Americans from traveling in war areas so that German submarines could not threaten American lives.

15. B

The Monroe Doctrine related entirely to the expansion of European interests in the Americas and did not apply to American involvement in Europe. It wasn't relevant to immigration, which was not yet considered to be a problem by any political factions, nor did the Monroe Doctrine apply to existing European colonies, including those belonging to Spain.

16. E

The Seneca Falls Convention was the nation's first women's rights convention. Organized by Elizabeth Cady Stanton and Lucretia Mott, it issued a ringing declaration of women's rights which interpreted the Declaration of Independence to mean that all "people" are created equal.

17. E

Truman believed that American lives were his main responsibility, not Japanese lives. The decision to use the bomb was a military and strategic one; Truman wanted to bring the war to an end as quickly as possible and with as few American casualties as possible. He did not suspect that Japan was close to being able to produce its own atomic weaponry.

18. A

The Constitution stipulates that for a president to be removed he must first be impeached in the House of Representatives. Then the trial will take place in the Senate chamber with the chief justice presiding. This has happened only twice in U.S. history and both times the presidents (Andrew Johnson and William Clinton) were acquitted by the Senate. Article 1, Section 3 of the Constitution states, "The Senate shall have sole Power to try all impeachments…And no Person shall be convicted without the concurrence of a two-thirds majority."

19. D

After World War II, economic opportunities in the North and West inspired millions of African Americans to migrate to these areas. The economy boomed during this period.

20. B

Western farmers favored cheap land, squatters rights, and internal improvements. They wanted the government to build roads and canals so their produce could get to market. By the end of the 1800s most farmers favored governmental control of the prices that railroads (which often had local monopolies) could charge.

21. B

After the "Panic of 1819," Congress passed a new land law in 1820 that reduced the minimum price on land in the West and the minimum size of plots available. It also eliminated the credit provisions of the earlier 1800 act.

22. D

In 1824, Chief Justice Marshall ruled that Robert Fulton's monopoly of steamboat traffic on the Hudson was unconstitutional. He wrote that the federal government has the power to control whatever impacts interstate commerce. This further defined the role of the national government in the area of business and transportation.

23. A

President Lincoln's primary concern was the preservation of the Union. Although he did end up issuing the Emancipation Proclamation of 1863, abolishing slavery wasn't his original objective.

24. B

As a result of the *Brown* case, schools across the country were ordered to integrate. The court found that even if separate and equal facilities *did* exist for students, the psychological impact of separating people by race would give rise to feelings of superiority and inferiority.

25. E

There was much opposition to the war in the North, especially by the anti-slavery interests who believed that Texas might become another southern slave state. President Polk was criticized for sending troops into disputed territory and creating incidents that could lead to war.

26. C

The 19th Amendment gave women the right to vote and support for it did not diminish after ratification. In contrast, support for the 18th Amendment (Prohibition) declined after enactment. It was in force from 1920 to 1933, when it was repealed by the 21st Amendment.

27. C

Free African Americans in the South were able to own property. In fact, some slaves owned property as well.

28. D

A candidate must get over 50 percent of the Electoral votes to become president. If this does not happen, as in 1800 and 1824, then the House of Representatives chooses among the top three candidates.

29. A

The Spanish government was willing to discuss a peaceful solution prior to the Spanish-American War—in early April 1898 it unilaterally offered to stop fighting. Spain even offered to grant Cuba some autonomy if the United States agreed to arbitration. However, McKinley had already given Congress his "war message."

30. D

Railroads needed government regulation to protect the consumer and farmer when railroads had a monopoly on carrying freight. By the early 1930s, the railroads were subject to greater government regulation that had eliminated most discriminatory practices. In addition, the railroads had lost some of their market share to trucks and pipelines. Thus a more diverse transportation system led to lower prices and more competition for services.

31. C

The U.S.S.R. never agreed to stop or even slow the construction of the Berlin Wall. All of the other steps were taken by both countries to ease tensions during the Cold War.

32. E

After the War of 1812, there was a new nationalism which encouraged a less sectional view. Clay saw the need for better roads and canals that would bind the country together and benefit business.

33. B

John Steinbeck's novel *The Grapes of Wrath* describes the lives of Dust Bowl migrants to California. The book raised public awareness of the plight of these people.

KAPLAN
Test Prep and Admissions

34. D

While the 1st Amendment protects the rights of speech, religion, and the press it does not deal with economics or business. Although business is much valued in the U.S., there is no mention of 'freedom of enterprise' in the Constitution.

35. D

There was no interest at the time in increasing immigration to the United States from China—on the contrary, many felt there were too many Chinese immigrants already. Though the government probably favored the work of American missionaries in China, and certainly was interested in increasing American naval presence in the Pacific region, the Open Door Policy was concerned only with furthering and protecting American business interests in China.

36. B

The act required that southern state governments be replaced through new elections where former slaves would be able to vote for the first time. This would guarantee a Republican majority since they had pushed for emancipation and fought the war against the Southern whites. This kept the party of Lincoln in power as it reconfigured southern politics on its terms.

37. E

Many wealthy Americans had supported the British during the period of the revolution, and had their property seized as a result. After the revolution, the new American government decided that it would be best for the future, politically and financially, if their property was returned.

38. C

Jefferson believed that a weak central government would protect the country from the evils of minority rule. He said, "The government is best when it governs least." Jacksonian democracy brought a more active role to the federal government and asserted the power of the federal government over the states.

39. D

The War Powers Act was intended to limit the powers of the president. Congress was concerned that Nixon's actions in Vietnam were extreme, and they wished to limit his ability to take independent action. The goal of the War Powers Act was to make it impossible for presidents to use their power as the commander in chief to involve American forces in wars without Congressional approval.

40. D

Shay's Rebellion was carried out by angry farmers who wanted the state government to issue cheap money so debts could be more easily paid. They armed themselves and stormed courthouses to disrupt bankruptcy cases involving farmers who could not pay their debts.

41. C

The depression of the 1890s affected agriculture more than most other areas of the economy.

42. D

The Fed's rate of interest for member banks is called the discount rate. As the Fed raises the rate, money becomes more expensive to borrow. As loans become more expensive, people borrow less. Thus, the discount rate is used to influence the availability of credit in the U.S.

43. D

Carter's effort to rescue the American hostages in Teheran failed, and he made no effort to restore relations with Cuba. American diplomatic relations with Taiwan had never been severed. Carter didn't sign free-trade agreements with Communist countries. However, he did succeed in negotiating a peace agreement between Egypt and Israel at Camp David.

44. C

Fines, adverse publicity, appeals to patriotism, and the pressure of public opinion during a war which had 18 million Americans in uniform were sufficient deterrents against higher pricing by producers.

45. C

Supporters of Zionism urged President Truman to give their new state of Israel official recognition. In the aftermath of the Holocaust in Europe there was more sympathy for the Zionist goals. Truman recognized the state of Israel shortly after it was proclaimed.

46. C

After the building of the transcontinental railroad which had brought many Chinese laborers to the U.S., there were job shortages in the West. The depression of the 1870s caused much joblessness. Poor whites, especially the Irish, resented the competition they faced from the hard-working and oddly-dressed Chinese. This was a time when Chinese men had to wear a braided length of hair so they stood out from other Americans. Congress passed a series of bills that first limited and then excluded entirely Chinese from immigrating to the U.S.

47. B

President Johnson had a moderate view of Reconstruction and did not intend to grant full rights to freed slaves. He vetoed the Civil Rights Act to show his disapproval of radical Reconstruction, which pushed for full rights for freed slaves including voting and citizenship.

48. E

The State of Israel was created in 1948 and the U.S. has supported Israel politically and militarily ever since. The creation of Israel brought immediate war between the Arabs and Israelis and this warfare has continued sporadically to the present. Many refugee camps in the area still house Arabs who lost their land to the Israelis in 1948. Much of the anti-American sentiment in the Arab world can be traced to the U.S. decision to ally itself with Israel beginning in 1948.

49. D

The improving relations between the U.S. and the USSR led to a number of joint agreements. The most significant was the pact to limit parts of the nuclear arsenals that both nations possessed. This was the SALT I agreement signed by Nixon and Brezhnev.

50. C

The president, as commander in chief of the U.S. military, can deploy U.S. forces to protect the security of the United States. He did so in 1950 so that there would be a military response to Communist aggression in Korea while the UN passed resolutions to organize its own military command.

51. B

The Republican party was founded in 1854 and gathered a number of political elements that all wanted to keep slavery from expanding westward. The party attracted free-soilers and abolitionists.

52. A

Holden Caulfield, the main character in Salinger's novel, chose to rebel against the strong forces demanding conformity around him. This novel was one of the most popular novels for American youth in the 1950s and 1960s.

53. B

While the Populists who were mostly farmers had worked for 'free silver,' the Progressives were more interested in other reforms. They urged the direct election of U.S. Senators, governmental restrictions on big business, prohibition, and new laws that protected children from the work place.

54. A

Article IV, Section 3 of the Constitution states that new states may be admitted by Congress into the Union.

55. D

Jackson could not have dealt with the issue of California statehood because this arose after the Gold Rush of 1849, long after he was out of the White House.

56. D

The *Plessy v. Ferguson* decision was used to justify racial segregation in southern schools and on public transportation until the 1950s.

57. C

Roosevelt believed that the government needed to work actively to end the economic crisis of the early 1930s. The Works Progress Administration was an example of one of his programs and introduced a number of measures to alleviate unemployment during the Depression.

KAPLAN
Test Prep and Admissions

58. D

Both Greenback policies and a lowering of the discount rate at which the Federal Reserve loans money to banks would tend to increase the money supply and cause inflation. Inflation occurs when money becomes less valuable and buys less. The Greenback party of the 1870s called for an issuance of more paper money, which would have made currency more plentiful and less valuable. By lowering the rate it charges member banks for loans, the Federal Reserve encourages more borrowing. With more money in circulation, the value of money declines and inflation results.

59. D

Most of the Japanese Americans who were relocated in 1942 on the west coast were native born and thus U.S. citizens. The young men were also liable to be drafted and many served in the military. The Army regiment made up of these men became famous for its bravery and fighting spirit.

60. C

The WPA provided jobs on public projects for the unemployed during the Great Depression. This gave people more money to spend and encouraged the economy to grow. In a recession, Keynes believed in deficit spending by the government to "prime the pump" of the economy.

61. B

Lodge led the other Senators who had grave reservations about the League of Nations and blocked the ratification of the Versailles Treaty. They feared that the U.S. would lose some of its control over their own destiny as a member of a world body.

62. D

Roosevelt was a strong believer in the use of American power and influence. He was an energetic president who used aggressive diplomacy to get what he thought America needed. His 'big stick' philosophy and his fame as a war hero in 1898 made him a popular president. He supported the imperialistic expansionism popular in America in the early 20th century.

63. A

George Kennan believed that the U.S. should do all it could to stop Communist expansion around the globe. This led to the Truman Doctrine, the Marshall Plan, and NATO, among other things. The idea that Americans should be investigated to determine their loyalty was not part of the policy of containment, although both containment and the Red Scare developed from a fear of the Soviet Union and Communism.

64. D

The Platt Amendment, the Ostend Manifesto, and the Roosevelt Corollary were all developed as a result of an American desire to extend the influence of the United States to the south. In particular, Cuba was eyed by southerners eager to admit more slave states to the United States. Both the Ostend Manifesto (which advocated an American takeover of Cuba) and the Platt Amendment (which prohibited the annexation of Cuba) dealt specifically with Cuba, while the Roosevelt Corollary related to Latin America in general.

65. B

Many of the immigrants who came to the U.S. in the late 1800s were from poor regions in Russia, Italy, Scandinavia, and China. Many were functional illiterates when they arrived and learned what English they could in the workplace.

66. D

Both in 1811 and in 1916, the U.S. claimed that its rights were violated on the high seas when its ships were attacked or otherwise interfered with. The impressments of American sailors into the Royal Navy helped bring about the War of 1812 and German submarine attacks in the Atlantic were a primary cause of U.S. entry into World War I.

67. E

The Scopes Trial was widely covered by the media and many of the statements by Bryan were illogical and simplistic. Many Americans were church-going Christians but were not fundamentalists who believed that every word of the Bible was true. Scopes served no jail sentence and his fine was very modest. This led many to see the conviction as rather meaningless and the teaching of evolution continued to gain ground in U.S. schools.

68. B

When the Confederacy went to war it hoped to receive aid and recognition from Great Britain. Before the war, Britain had close trading ties to the South and British factories bought much of the South's cotton. But the British remained neutral and declined to recognize the South as a legal government. After the Emancipation Proclamation (1863) changed the focus of the war, it became even more unlikely that Britain, with its strong antislavery sentiment, would support the South.

69. D

The story behind the *Marbury v. Madison* case is a complex political tug of war between the Federalists and the Jeffersonians. In the end, it is important because it set the precedent for Congressional acts to be reviewed by the Supreme Court.

70. E

The Constitution prohibits the passing of an *ex post facto* law in Article I, Section 9. Under the U.S. Constitution a person can only be arrested for a crime that was illegal when the act was committed.

71. A

The South had an agriculturally based economy that consisted of few factories. As the war progressed, this became a crucial disadvantage and the South had difficulty supplying its military with everything from shoes to munitions. The North possessed all the cannon factories in the nation, for example.

72. C

The election of the House of Burgesses in 1619 in Virginia marked the beginning of representative government in America. Other colonial legislatures were formed in each colony as they were organized. This experience of local democracy led to the formation of the first Continental Congress in 1774.

73. E

England followed the economic theory of mercantilism, which stated that nations became wealthy by importing raw goods from within an empire. This saved them from having to purchase the materials from other nations. Successful colonies also served the mother country as markets for its manufactured goods. Under mercantilism, the colony existed for the good of the mother country.

74. E

Differences in language and customs made it difficult to recruit immigrants into American unions. Many immigrants were unskilled, making a union less effective since replacement workers could be easily found. Labor unions had their greatest successes in establishing unions in specific trades, such as among miners and machinists.

75. E

For most of American history, the U.S. has kept a small peacetime military. When war has come suddenly, the U.S. military has often been undersupplied and untrained. The year 1812 was no exception and the war went very badly for the U.S. in the first year of the fighting.

76. D

In *Lochner v. New York*, the Supreme Court in 1905 struck down a law that limited bakers from working more than a 10-hour day. Using the 14th Amendment the Court said that it was a violation of the rights of the employer to set the terms of employment. Other laws which had sought to mandate shorter work hours were also undone in this way. It was not until the 30s that the Federal judiciary was more supportive of labor goals.

77. D

The population of Natives in North America and the Pacific was decimated by diseases brought by white men in the 15th and 16th centuries. This so weakened the resistance of the Natives that they were unable to fight in many cases when the Europeans settled on their lands.

78. D

There was a growing realization during the 1960s that the nation's natural resources had taken a severe beating. Books by Rachel Carson explained about the use of chemicals that were poisoning the food chain and other people began to promote a greater awareness of how the Earth should be cared for. This led to the organization of the first Earth Day in 1970 and the beginning of high-profile

KAPLAN
Test Prep and Admissions

political protest relating to the environment. Reacting to the public's growing interest in preserving the nation's environment, President Nixon created the Environmental Protection Agency a few years later.

79. B

Bryan was a champion of the Populists who were largely rural Americans who struggled as farmers. They wanted "cheap" money to pay their debts and felt that using the silver supply to back U.S. currency would help them economically. Bryan gave his famous Cross of Gold speech which supported the idea of "free" silver.

80. C

The right of self determination is the right of a people to determine their own future, free of the control of other nations. After World War I, this principle was applied by the League of Nations and Treaty of Versailles to Central and Eastern Europe, where nationalities formerly part of the Russian, German, and Austro-Hungarian empires were given the right to establish their own nations and determine their own future. New nations that emerged after World War II include Czechoslovakia, Yugoslavia, Poland, Estonia, Latvia, and Lithuania. After World War II, this principle was embodied in the United Nations Charter and used to support the struggle for independence of Africans and Asians seeking to free themselves from European colonial control. During the following years, numerous new nations emerged from the colonial empires, embodying the principle of self determination.

ANALYSES OF THE FREE-RESPONSE QUESTIONS

Part A: Document-based Question (DBQ)

It is often claimed that the major American wars of the last 150 years have resulted in the most important social and political gains of minorities and women. Evaluate this statement with regard to the experience of minorities and women during World War II.

Use evidence from the documents **and** your knowledge of the period from 1941 to 1945 to compose your answer.

Use of the Documents

Each of the documents offers a perspective on the experience of women and minorities during the Second World War and how society as a whole was impacted.

Document A shows a government poster celebrating an African American sailor who won the Navy Cross at Pearl Harbor—this clearly showed that medals could be earned by minorities even though they were largely segregated in their own units.

Document B is a memo by the first African American general officer in American military history.

Documents C, D, and E are all related to the attitude towards the Japanese after Pearl Harbor which led to the evacuation of Japanese living in the West coast to remote detention camps.

Documents F and H are both by FDR. His fireside chats were a well-known means of communicating with the people.

Document G is a wartime photo of women welders—a clear example of a type of job usually held by men, but which women had learned through working in the war industries.

Key Points from Outside Information

- The attack on Pearl Harbor created tremendous national unity after 1941
- Total war meant that ALL Americans, regardless of sex or race, would be called on to serve their country

- Nearly 15 million Americans, men and women, served in the military until 1945
  - Women played a greater role than ever before in the Armed Services
  - Millions were transported to different parts of the nation and around the world
- More than 6 million women took jobs outside the home, many of them in industry
- While the Japanese were sent to remote camps many young men of Japanese descent served in the military
  - Two regiments made up of Japanese Americans were highly decorated for their bravery
- Jobs in California, Washington and Texas attracted thousands of workers
  - Many of these workers were African Americans from the South

Examples of impacts on women and minorities during the war

- Professional sports opened up for some women, i.e. women's baseball
- Native Americans became less marginalized on the reservations because many served in the military
- Women served in thousands of non-combat roles in the military
- The military trained millions and gave them new skills
- Wartime separations were hard on marriages and the divorce rate increased
- Children were encouraged to participate in rationing, recycling and helping to pay for the war
  - War stamps and metal drives
- The government sponsored housing projects and child care for workers
- Increased mixing of the races caused riots in some locales (Los Angeles and Detroit)
- Discrimination against African Americans and the custom of segregation was beginning to be challenged
  - NAACP membership skyrocketed

Students can make the case that minorities and women were given new roles in the war effort which showed they were loyal Americans and capable of many accomplishments. The strongest students will notice the date on Document H, which predates Pearl Harbor. This shows that the government was already encouraging the hiring of women and minorities before the war began.

Connections that can be made in the essay

The documents show that women and other minorities did have new opportunities because of the war. But the three documents highlighting the treatment of Japanese Americans show an example of sanctioned discrimination that argues some minorities were robbed of their civil rights because of the war.

DBQ Scoring Rubric

There are five scoring ranges:

Excellent (8–9)

Argument: The essay must have a strong, clear thesis. The student should take a clear position either in support of or against the proposition stated in the question. The essay should also indicate a grasp of the complexity of the issue, referring to pros and cons of entrepreneurial behavior in this time period.

Critical Thought: The student should explain how each document supports or undermines the thesis. The student should address conflicts and contradictions in the evidence. Any outside information must be relevant to the argument.

Evidence: The student should use documents and outside information (see lists above) throughout the essay. Most of the documents must be used, and students might address the relationship between the sources.

Writing Style: The essay must be well organized and well written; it must make sense throughout.

Very Good (6–7)

Argument: The thesis must be consistent with the question, but it may not be sufficiently focused.

Critical Thought: The answer must include an analysis of several of the documents and must incorporate outside information.

Evidence: The student should make use of the documents and outside information (see lists above) that support the position being argued. Discussion of relationships between the sources used may be limited.

Writing Style: The essay should be well organized and clearly written; it must be logical, but some points may be unclear.

Adequate (4–5)

Argument: The thesis is only partially developed. It may address the question, but it does so in a way that doesn't acknowledge the question's complexity. The essay will most likely fail to prioritize the arguments.

Critical Thought: The essay is primarily descriptive or narrative, and doesn't provide an analysis of the question or of the evidence provided. It will not address all the relevant issues, and will ignore the opposing position.

Evidence: The student may paraphrase the documents and may misinterpret a document to better fit the argument. The student will use only a little outside information and may refer to some but not all of the documents. The answer may contain errors.

Writing Style: The writing and organization is unclear, but acceptable.

Flawed (2–3)

Argument: The thesis will be unclear and will not be supported in the body of the essay. Use of evidence will be unclear, and the argument will be poorly developed.

Critical Thought: The essay will show only a limited understanding of the question, and will offer little or no analysis. What little analysis there is will be inaccurate. The student will show little understanding of the issue of industrialization.

Evidence: The student will not make use of the documents appropriate to their argument, and may use documents that actually support the opposing position. The use of documents will be haphazard, with references only to brief excerpts or paraphrases. There will be little outside information. The argument may contain errors.

Writing Style: The answer will be weakly organized and the writing will be unclear.

Severely Flawed (0–1)

Argument:: The student provides no thesis, or provides one that is not relevant to the question.

Critical Thought: The student demonstrates little or no understanding of the question.

Evidence: The student makes almost no use of the documents provided, and makes little or no use of outside information. The answer contains major errors.

Writing Style: The answer is disorganized and poorly written.

Part B: Question Two

Compare the relationships of TWO of the following colonial powers with the Native Americans up to 1770.

- French
- British
- Spanish

Key Points

European colonial policies

- The French approach was to maximize trade opportunities and also spread Christianity (Roman Catholicism)
- Had the smallest population of settlers of the three nations
- The Spanish came as conquerors and subjugated the Native peoples
- They also wished to spread Roman Catholicism

- The British came more as settlers but also traded some with the Natives
- All European kingdoms subscribed to the mercantilistic theory which held that material wealth needed to be kept under imperial control

Differences among European contacts with Natives

- Because the French did not come to settle in large numbers, they enjoyed the best relations with the Natives of North America
- The Spanish were the most heavy handed and were responsible for more Native deaths than the British or French
- British relations with the Natives ranged from the cordial to the violent from the mid-1600s into the 1700s
- All European peoples brought new diseases that killed many of the Native groups they came in contact with
- European weapons technology transferred in part to the Natives after the 1600s
- Some Europeans immersed themselves in the Native culture and became members of Native tribes

Scoring Rubric

There are five scoring ranges:

Excellent (8–9)

The answer must have a strong, clear thesis that compares two of the three nations mentioned in the question and their relations with the Natives of the Americas. The quality of the writing should be excellent, the answer must show logical patterns, and the student should include many of the major points in the above list (though they may go beyond the list). The organization should be clear. The answer may contain minor errors.

Very Good (6–7)

The answer must have a thesis that makes a clear comparison of how two European kingdoms related to the Natives they encountered in the New World. Organization of the answer must show logical patterns, and the student should include many of the specific points from the above list.

Adequate (4–5)

The answer must try to make some argument and must include at least some of the points listed above. There may be flaws in the thesis argument.

Flawed (2–3)

The answer will demonstrate serious weaknesses. It may have no thesis argument at all, and it will include few of the points listed above. The answer may show little understanding of how even one of the nations related to the Natives of the New World.

Severely Flawed (0–1)

The answer will demonstrate almost no attempt to answer the question, and will include very few, if any, of the points listed above.

Part B: Question Three

Discuss the impact of TWO of the following wars on the domestic politics in the United States.

- War of 1812
- Mexican War
- Spanish-American War

Key Points

- The War of 1812 was supported by some regions and not others
- The West was in favor while New England opposed the war
- The Mexican War was supported by the expansionists but opposed by other Americans
- The educated in the East (Emerson and Thoreau) tended to oppose the war while the frontier peoples supported it

- The Mexican War was also wrapped up with the slavery issue as new territories might become slave states later on
- The Spanish-American War was supported by the imperialists of the day (T. Roosevelt) and opposed by others who rejected the idea of an American empire (Carnegie)

Political impacts of the wars

War of 1812

- The Hartford Convention was proof that New England was unsupportive even to the point of secession
- While the war did not resolve the issues that started it, the ability to fight Britain to a draw was a further acknowledgement that America was able to defend itself against a large European power
- Tensions with Natives in the Northwest and South (including battles with Tecumseh, and with the Seminoles and the Creeks)
- The war produced two war heroes who would later become presidents (Harrison and Jackson)

The Mexican War

- The tensions between the North and the South were increased by the war
- New England abolitionists opposed the war
- New territories added by the war meant more space for settlement
- This gave the West more potential political power in U.S. politics at the expense of the South
- Opposition to the war may be the first example of an American peace movement
- The war produced war heroes, one of whom became president (Zachary Taylor)
- The treaty was ratified by Congress and added millions of acres to U.S. territory

The Spanish-American War

- Waning Spanish imperialism in Cuba was the cause of the war

- For the first time, the media was very involved in promoting the war

- Yellow journalism described Spanish cruelty and barbarism

- Hearst and Pulitzer competed for newspaper sales which fanned the flames of U.S.-Spanish tensions, especially after the *Maine* explosion

- The American public proved easy to manipulate by the press and some politicians

- The war produced a number of war heroes, one of whom became president (T. Roosevelt)

- The Treaty of Paris to end the war was narrowly ratified by the Senate, which showed how ambivalent many Americans were about foreign expansionism

Scoring Rubric

There are five scoring ranges:

Excellent (8–9)

The answer must have a strong, clear thesis that discusses the political impact of the two wars chosen. The essay should focus on the war's impact on domestic politics. The quality of the writing should be excellent, the answer must show logical patterns, and the student should include many of the major points in the above list (though they may go beyond these points). The organization should be clear. The answer may contain minor errors.

Very Good (6–7)

The answer must have a thesis that gives a balanced overview of how American politics were affected by the two wars chosen. The answer must be logically organized, and the student should include many of the specific points from the above list.

Adequate (4–5)

The answer must try to make some argument and must include at least some of the points listed above. There may be flaws in the thesis argument.

Flawed (2–3)

The answer will demonstrate serious weaknesses. It may have no thesis argument at all, and it will include few of the points listed above. The answer may show little understanding of how wars impact national politics or policies.

Severely Flawed (0–1)

The answer will demonstrate almost no attempt to answer the question, and will include very few, if any, of the points listed above.

Part C: Question Four

Discuss the impact of the second 'Red Scare' on American politics in the 1950s.

Key Points

- There were a number of important events in 1949 that shaped U.S. views and fear of Communism
  - The Communist victory in the Chinese Civil War
  - The explosion of the atomic bomb by the Soviet Union
  - The formation of NATO against Communism in Europe

- The Korean War also led to worsening Cold War tensions

- Discovery of Communist spy rings in the U.S. led to more paranoia about the 'red' threat—the Rosenberg trial and execution

- Some American politicians were able to make careers by leading searches for Communist agents or sympathizers

Features of the Red Scare of the 1950s

- The U.S. Congress was very involved in investigating Communist activity in the U.S.

- The First Amendment right to free speech was compromised by the fear of Communism

- Some Americans in academia and the entertainment industry had their reputations ruined when accused of being sympathetic to Communism

KAPLAN
Test Prep and Admissions

- One U.S. Senator from Wisconsin, McCarthy, became very powerful as he accused some people in the U.S. government of being Communists
- Lies and accusations were used
- The word 'witch hunt' was used, referring to the colonial trials in Salem
- The television was used for the first time as a political tool to alter public opinion

Scoring Rubric

There are five scoring ranges:

Excellent (8–9)

The answer must have a strong, clear thesis that gives an assessment of how the 'Red Scare' influenced politics in the 1950s only. The essay should focus on how the deepening Cold War impacted local and national American politics and cover the McCarthy phenomena. The quality of the writing should be excellent, the answer must show logical patterns, and the student should include many of the major points in the above list (though they may go beyond these points). The organization should be clear. The answer may contain minor errors.

Very Good (6–7)

The answer must have a thesis that details the impact of anti-Communism on the political scene in the U.S. in the 50s. The answer must be logically organized, and the student should include many of the specific points from the above list.

Adequate (4–5)

The answer must try to make some argument and must include at least some of the points listed above. There may be flaws in the thesis argument.

Flawed (2–3)

The answer will demonstrate serious weaknesses. It may have no thesis argument at all, and it will include few of the points listed above. The answer may show little understanding of the Cold War or how the fear of Communism shaped American political thinking and policies.

Severely Flawed (0–1)

The answer will demonstrate almost no attempt to answer the question, and will include very few, if any, of the points listed above.

Part C: Question Five

Discuss TWO cultural and societal changes that America experienced during the late 1960s and early 1970s.

Key Points

- The Civil Rights Movement of the 1950s continued into the 60s and produced great changes in race relations in the U.S.
- The maturing 'baby boomers' (those born after 1946) had a different perspective on America than their parents
- The Vietnam War became a polarizing event that created great political and social tension
- The 'counterculture' was born out of a rejection of middle class values and promoted communal lifestyles
- Fashion and social mores were impacted
- Sex was celebrated and discussed more openly in American society
- Homosexuality was also politicized as the Gay Rights Movement was launched by the Stonewall Riots of 1969
- The Women's Movement entered a new phase highlighting issues such as abortion rights, equal pay for equal work, and child care
- A new 'radicalism' permeated politics and mass protests were evidence of this
- A 'youth' culture also came into being that celebrated some utopian ideals and the popular music of the day
- Native Americans organized the American Indian Movement (AIM) to fight for their rights
- A distrust of the government was deepened by U.S. failures in Vietnam and the later political fallout with the Watergate scandal

Key events of the period

- Political assassinations in 1963 (JFK), 1965 (Malcolm X) and 1968 (King and RFK)
- NOW (National Organization for Women) founded in 1966
- The British Invasion of pop music in 1964
- 1968 Tet Offensive in Vietnam creates doubt of an American victory
- AIM occupies Alcatraz in 1969
- Woodstock Rock Fest draws hundreds of thousands of young people in 1969
- Playboy magazine champions the sexual revolution
- Police raid the Stonewall Inn in New York in 1969 sparking gay rights activism
- Anti-war protests peak in 1970 after U.S. invades Cambodia; students killed at Kent State University
- U.S. pulls out of Vietnam in 1973
- Nixon resigns as president in 1974

Scoring Rubric

There are five scoring ranges:

Excellent (8–9)

The answer must have a strong, clear thesis that highlights two major societal changes in the U.S. between 1965 and 1975. The essay should focus on cultural movements during this period. The quality of the writing should be excellent, the answer must show logical patterns, and the student should include many of the major points in the above list (though they may go beyond these points). The organization should be clear. The answer may contain minor errors.

Very Good (6–7)

The answer must have a thesis that gives a clear overview of two changes observed in the latter half of the 60s and early 70s. The answer must be logically organized, and the student should include many of the specific points from the above list.

Adequate (4–5)

The answer must try to make some argument and must include at least some of the points listed above. There may be flaws in the thesis argument.

Flawed (2–3)

The answer will demonstrate serious weaknesses. It may have no thesis argument at all, and it will include few of the points listed above. The answer may show little understanding of the time period or the great changes that took place at the time.

Severely Flawed (0–1)

The answer will demonstrate almost no attempt to answer the question, and will include very few, if any, of the points listed above.

AP U.S. History
Practice Test Two Answer Sheet

1. Ⓐ Ⓑ Ⓒ Ⓓ Ⓔ
2. Ⓐ Ⓑ Ⓒ Ⓓ Ⓔ
3. Ⓐ Ⓑ Ⓒ Ⓓ Ⓔ
4. Ⓐ Ⓑ Ⓒ Ⓓ Ⓔ
5. Ⓐ Ⓑ Ⓒ Ⓓ Ⓔ
6. Ⓐ Ⓑ Ⓒ Ⓓ Ⓔ
7. Ⓐ Ⓑ Ⓒ Ⓓ Ⓔ
8. Ⓐ Ⓑ Ⓒ Ⓓ Ⓔ
9. Ⓐ Ⓑ Ⓒ Ⓓ Ⓔ
10. Ⓐ Ⓑ Ⓒ Ⓓ Ⓔ
11. Ⓐ Ⓑ Ⓒ Ⓓ Ⓔ
12. Ⓐ Ⓑ Ⓒ Ⓓ Ⓔ
13. Ⓐ Ⓑ Ⓒ Ⓓ Ⓔ
14. Ⓐ Ⓑ Ⓒ Ⓓ Ⓔ
15. Ⓐ Ⓑ Ⓒ Ⓓ Ⓔ
16. Ⓐ Ⓑ Ⓒ Ⓓ Ⓔ
17. Ⓐ Ⓑ Ⓒ Ⓓ Ⓔ
18. Ⓐ Ⓑ Ⓒ Ⓓ Ⓔ
19. Ⓐ Ⓑ Ⓒ Ⓓ Ⓔ
20. Ⓐ Ⓑ Ⓒ Ⓓ Ⓔ

21. Ⓐ Ⓑ Ⓒ Ⓓ Ⓔ
22. Ⓐ Ⓑ Ⓒ Ⓓ Ⓔ
23. Ⓐ Ⓑ Ⓒ Ⓓ Ⓔ
24. Ⓐ Ⓑ Ⓒ Ⓓ Ⓔ
25. Ⓐ Ⓑ Ⓒ Ⓓ Ⓔ
26. Ⓐ Ⓑ Ⓒ Ⓓ Ⓔ
27. Ⓐ Ⓑ Ⓒ Ⓓ Ⓔ
28. Ⓐ Ⓑ Ⓒ Ⓓ Ⓔ
29. Ⓐ Ⓑ Ⓒ Ⓓ Ⓔ
30. Ⓐ Ⓑ Ⓒ Ⓓ Ⓔ
31. Ⓐ Ⓑ Ⓒ Ⓓ Ⓔ
32. Ⓐ Ⓑ Ⓒ Ⓓ Ⓔ
33. Ⓐ Ⓑ Ⓒ Ⓓ Ⓔ
34. Ⓐ Ⓑ Ⓒ Ⓓ Ⓔ
35. Ⓐ Ⓑ Ⓒ Ⓓ Ⓔ
36. Ⓐ Ⓑ Ⓒ Ⓓ Ⓔ
37. Ⓐ Ⓑ Ⓒ Ⓓ Ⓔ
38. Ⓐ Ⓑ Ⓒ Ⓓ Ⓔ
39. Ⓐ Ⓑ Ⓒ Ⓓ Ⓔ
40. Ⓐ Ⓑ Ⓒ Ⓓ Ⓔ

41. Ⓐ Ⓑ Ⓒ Ⓓ Ⓔ
42. Ⓐ Ⓑ Ⓒ Ⓓ Ⓔ
43. Ⓐ Ⓑ Ⓒ Ⓓ Ⓔ
44. Ⓐ Ⓑ Ⓒ Ⓓ Ⓔ
45. Ⓐ Ⓑ Ⓒ Ⓓ Ⓔ
46. Ⓐ Ⓑ Ⓒ Ⓓ Ⓔ
47. Ⓐ Ⓑ Ⓒ Ⓓ Ⓔ
48. Ⓐ Ⓑ Ⓒ Ⓓ Ⓔ
49. Ⓐ Ⓑ Ⓒ Ⓓ Ⓔ
50. Ⓐ Ⓑ Ⓒ Ⓓ Ⓔ
51. Ⓐ Ⓑ Ⓒ Ⓓ Ⓔ
52. Ⓐ Ⓑ Ⓒ Ⓓ Ⓔ
53. Ⓐ Ⓑ Ⓒ Ⓓ Ⓔ
54. Ⓐ Ⓑ Ⓒ Ⓓ Ⓔ
55. Ⓐ Ⓑ Ⓒ Ⓓ Ⓔ
56. Ⓐ Ⓑ Ⓒ Ⓓ Ⓔ
57. Ⓐ Ⓑ Ⓒ Ⓓ Ⓔ
58. Ⓐ Ⓑ Ⓒ Ⓓ Ⓔ
59. Ⓐ Ⓑ Ⓒ Ⓓ Ⓔ
60. Ⓐ Ⓑ Ⓒ Ⓓ Ⓔ

61. Ⓐ Ⓑ Ⓒ Ⓓ Ⓔ
62. Ⓐ Ⓑ Ⓒ Ⓓ Ⓔ
63. Ⓐ Ⓑ Ⓒ Ⓓ Ⓔ
64. Ⓐ Ⓑ Ⓒ Ⓓ Ⓔ
65. Ⓐ Ⓑ Ⓒ Ⓓ Ⓔ
66. Ⓐ Ⓑ Ⓒ Ⓓ Ⓔ
67. Ⓐ Ⓑ Ⓒ Ⓓ Ⓔ
68. Ⓐ Ⓑ Ⓒ Ⓓ Ⓔ
69. Ⓐ Ⓑ Ⓒ Ⓓ Ⓔ
70. Ⓐ Ⓑ Ⓒ Ⓓ Ⓔ
71. Ⓐ Ⓑ Ⓒ Ⓓ Ⓔ
72. Ⓐ Ⓑ Ⓒ Ⓓ Ⓔ
73. Ⓐ Ⓑ Ⓒ Ⓓ Ⓔ
74. Ⓐ Ⓑ Ⓒ Ⓓ Ⓔ
75. Ⓐ Ⓑ Ⓒ Ⓓ Ⓔ
76. Ⓐ Ⓑ Ⓒ Ⓓ Ⓔ
77. Ⓐ Ⓑ Ⓒ Ⓓ Ⓔ
78. Ⓐ Ⓑ Ⓒ Ⓓ Ⓔ
79. Ⓐ Ⓑ Ⓒ Ⓓ Ⓔ
80. Ⓐ Ⓑ Ⓒ Ⓓ Ⓔ

Practice Test Two

Section I: Multiple-Choice Questions

Time: 55 Minutes

80 Questions

Directions: Each of the questions or incomplete statements below is followed by five suggested answers or completions. Select the one that is best in each case and then fill in the corresponding oval on the answer sheet.

1. President Jackson resolved the nullification crisis in South Carolina through a combination of:

   (A) threats of force and gradual tariff reductions.

   (B) assimilation of Native American lands and federal interventions.

   (C) threats of federal intervention in the internal affairs of the state and social pressures.

   (D) promises of future tariff reductions and a more heavily enforced fugitive slave law.

   (E) Pressuring the Supreme Court.

2. The most radical of all the initiatives that followed the Second Great Awakening was the movement to abolish slavery. William Lloyd Garrison's vehicle was:

   (A) *Uncle Tom's Cabin*

   (B) *Our Hearts Fell to the Ground*

   (C) *The Liberator*

   (D) *Appeal to the Colored Citizens of the World*

   (E) *My Life As a Slave*

3. The motivations for establishing new settlements in the New World included all of the following EXCEPT:

   (A) religious persecution

   (B) the plague

   (C) wars

   (D) economic opportunity

   (E) criminal records

4. Many colonies were founded as a vision of one man or a small group. Identify which of the following is INCORRECTLY matched.

   (A) William Penn–Pennsylvania

   (B) James Oglethorpe–South Carolina

   (C) Anne Hutchinson–Rhode Island

   (D) Lord John Berkeley and Sir George Carteret–New Jersey

   (E) John Winthrop–Massachusetts

GO ON TO THE NEXT PAGE

5. The triangle trade routes carried merchandise in a roughly triangular pattern from North America to West Africa to the West Indies and back to New England. The merchandise carried included:

   (A) fish, sugar cane, slaves.

   (B) molasses, Africans captives, sugar cane.

   (C) rum, sugar cane, slaves.

   (D) rum, African captives, molasses.

   (E) sugar cane, African captives, lumber.

6. Although the colonies developed along many different lines, there were some commonalities. By the mid-18th century every colony exhibited all of the following characteristics EXCEPT:

   (A) self-government

   (B) religious toleration

   (C) a hereditary aristocracy

   (D) social mobility

   (E) indentured servants

7. The Great Awakening began in New England, and was spread throughout the colonies largely through the efforts of:

   (A) Rev. George Whitefield

   (B) Rev. Jonathan Edwards

   (C) Rev. Cotton Mather

   (D) William Penn

   (E) Rev. Samuel Jones

8. American resistance to British rule following the conclusion of the French and Indian War could be characterized as:

   (A) more militant.

   (B) more philosophical.

   (C) more economically motivated.

   (D) more politically motivated.

   (E) more socially accepted.

9. The American Revolution was not supposed to be won by the Americans because they were fighting a superior force. All of the following contributed to the American victory EXCEPT:

   (A) the distance from the mother country.

   (B) fighting on home turf.

   (C) having much popular support.

   (D) the French alliance and assistance.

   (E) having less Native American interference.

10. The Articles of Confederation were a modification of John Dickinson's first planned Constitution. At issue were large tracts of land to the west, the structures of state governments, and the powers granted to the states. Successes under the Articles include:

    (A) the Northwest Ordinance of 1787.

    (B) the Land Ordinance of 1785.

    (C) the winning of the American Revolution itself.

    (D) all of the above.

    (E) only the ordinances of 1785 and 1787.

11. Thomas Jefferson is the primary author of the Declaration of Independence. He was influenced by the Enlightenment, a movement in literature and philosophy described as leaving "the darkness" through human reason. Jefferson was most influenced by the writings of:

    (A) John Locke

    (B) Benjamin Franklin

    (C) John Hancock

    (D) Sir Thomas Hobbes

    (E) Thomas Paine

GO ON TO THE NEXT PAGE

KAPLAN
Test Prep and Admissions

12. In their attempt to stop colonists from moving westward into the Ohio River Valley, the Proclamation of 1763 was:

    (A) completely successful.

    (B) marginally successful.

    (C) successful at first, but it gradually lost its effect.

    (D) a dismal failure, ignored from the start because the colonists knew it was unenforceable.

    (E) really unnecessary, as the colonists had already moved too far west.

13. Which of the following was one of the major differences between the Virginia Plan and the New Jersey Plan at the Constitutional Convention?

    (A) Whether the national government would have the authority to levy taxes directly on the people

    (B) Whether representation in the new Congress would be apportioned by population or by state

    (C) Whether the national or the state governments would control western lands

    (D) Whether the national government would have the power to raise an army and navy

    (E) Whether the new Congress would be given the power to regulate commerce between the states

14. Publius, in 1788, wrote: "A republic, by which I mean a government in which the scheme of representation takes place, opens a different prospect, and promises the cure for which we are seeking. Let us examine the points in which it varies from pure democracy, and we shall comprehend both the nature of the cure, and the efficacy which it must derive from the union. The two great differences between a democracy and a republic, are first, the delegation of the government, in the latter, to a small number of citizens elected by the rest; secondly, the greater number of citizens, and greater sphere of country, over which the latter may be extended." This fundamental difference was described by:

    (A) Alexander Hamilton

    (B) James Monroe

    (C) Thomas Jefferson

    (D) James Madison

    (E) John Jay

15. In the latter part of the 18th century, the western territories of the United States were fraught with problems. The most pressing issue was:

    (A) paying off overseas debts.

    (B) paying off the debt of states after the Revolution.

    (C) the surveying and selling of land.

    (D) statehood for territories after 1800.

    (E) deciding the issue of slavery.

GO ON TO THE NEXT PAGE

16. "Let us then, fellow-citizens, unite with one heart and one mind. Let us restore to social intercourse that harmony and affection without which liberty and even life itself are but dreary things…But every difference of opinion is not a difference of principle. We have called by different names brethren of the same principle. We are all Republicans, we are all Federalists." The source and author is:

(A) James Madison, Federalist #51

(B) George Washington, Farewell Address, 1796

(C) Alexander Hamilton, Federalist #78

(D) Thomas Jefferson, First Inaugural Address, 1801

(E) George Mason, Virginia Declaration of Rights, 1776

17. The Constitution made no provision for the acquisition of land. Jefferson justified the purchase of Louisiana through his interpretation of:

(A) the commerce clause.

(B) presidential power to negotiate treaties.

(C) congressional approval.

(D) judicial review.

(E) Interstate commerce laws.

18. *Marbury v. Madison* (1803) was the first of the landmark decisions of John Marshall. In his decision, Marshall established the Supreme Court's power of:

(A) judicial review.

(B) impeachment.

(C) contract law review.

(D) state court decision review.

(E) original jurisdiction in mandamus proceedings.

19. All of the following are results of the War of 1812 EXCEPT:

(A) the Federalist Party regained power

(B) the loss of British influence in North America

(C) praise for General Jackson

(D) a victory over Native Americans in the western lands

(E) the Whigs gained political power

20. "…As a principle in which the rights and interests of the United States are involved, that the American continents, by the free and independent condition which they have assumed and maintain, are henceforth not to be considered as subjects for future colonization by any European powers." This is an excerpt of the:

(A) Treaty of 1818

(B) Rush-Bagot Agreement

(C) Monroe Doctrine

(D) Missouri Compromise

(E) The Treaty of Ghent

21. The Missouri Compromise contained all of the following conditions EXCEPT:

(A) Slavery would not be permitted in Maine.

(B) Slavery would be permitted in Missouri.

(C) Slavery in lands in the Louisiana Purchase territory north of 36° 30' would be banned.

(D) Nullification would be allowed south of 36° 30' in lands of the Louisiana Purchase.

(E) All of the above.

GO ON TO THE NEXT PAGE

22. President Monroe issued a declaration of U.S. policy towards Europe and Latin America into his annual message to Congress on December 2, 1823. The "Monroe Doctrine," as it came to be called, contained all of the following EXCEPT:

   (A) a closing of the Americas to further European colonization.

   (B) a provision addressing the fear that Great Britain would seize Cuba.

   (C) a policy of noninterference by the U.S. in other countries in the Americas.

   (D) a policy of noninterference by the U.S. in European internal affairs.

   (E) all of the above.

23. The most important reason the election of Andrew Jackson in 1828 was a departure from previous elections was that:

   (A) Jackson was "a man of the people."

   (B) Jackson was a war hero and veteran fighter.

   (C) Jackson was born in Tennessee and not from Virginia or Massachusetts.

   (D) Jackson was a diplomat ready to represent the United States in negotiations with Great Britain and Spain.

   (E) Jackson was an avowed defender of Native American rights.

24. In response to the Supreme Court's ruling in *Worcester v. Georgia*, President Jackson:

   (A) supported the decision with the backing of the U.S. Army.

   (B) supported the removal of the Cherokee to open Georgia lands to mining and settlement.

   (C) supported the decision but was reluctant to commit troops.

   (D) supported the removal of the Cherokee to preserve their culture.

   (E) supported the Chief Justice but not the decision.

25. The "spoils system" came to fruition during the Jackson administration. Jackson supported the system, saying:

   (A) it ensured that the best qualified would be placed in responsible positions.

   (B) it made sense, the duties of public office were simple enough for any intelligent man to complete.

   (C) it would replace one of three federal office-holders.

   (D) it would make it possible for policies to be carried out with greater continuity between administrations.

   (E) It would prove to be a cost saver.

26. The theory of nullification, as advanced by John C. Calhoun, suggested that:

   (A) there was strong feeling against Jackson in the South.

   (B) there was acceptance of the supremacy of federal law in the South.

   (C) the South would not accept any federal policies that challenged the utilization of slavery.

   (D) states, regardless of their geographic location, would cooperate in areas of tariffs.

   (E) There would be no support for the federal government in South Carolina.

27. Using the ideology of the Declaration of Independence as a starting point, the delegates declared that "all men and women are created equal" but that "the history of mankind is a history of repeated injuries and usurpations on the part of man toward woman, having in direct object the establishment of an absolute tyranny over her." This came from:

   (A) Oneida Community, 1848

   (B) Panic of 1837

   (C) Brook Farm, 1841

   (D) Seneca Falls Convention, 1848

   (E) Compromise of 1850

GO ON TO THE NEXT PAGE

28. Abolitionists were galvanized by the writings of Harriet Beecher Stowe, William Lloyd Garrison, Theodore Dwight Weld, and Elijah Lovejoy. Which of the following is not the correct pairing of the author and his/her work?

    (A) Harriet Beecher Stowe, *Uncle Tom's Cabin*

    (B) William Lloyd Garrison, *The Liberator*

    (C) Theodore Dwight Weld, *American Slavery as It Is: Testimony of a Thousand Witnesses*

    (D) Elijah Lovejoy, *The Sins of Slavery*

    (E) all of the above

29. Between 1800 and 1860, there were changes in society that could be described as:

    (A) a relatively even distribution of wealth throughout the country.

    (B) a gradual decrease in the number of destitute people.

    (C) a gradual increase in the standard of living for most workers.

    (D) an increasingly mobile working class was becoming less politically significant.

    (E) a gradual decrease in the standard of living for agricultural workers.

30. During the 1840s and 1850s, the economy of the country changed in that:

    (A) agriculture in the North became less focused on self-sufficient farming and more geared to supplying food for cities.

    (B) an industrial area developed in the Northwest.

    (C) the South began to manufacture agricultural machinery.

    (D) the Southwest began to develop a transportation system that would become the model for the country.

    (E) the mill towns in the North found it difficult to keep workers.

31. After Mexico became independent from Spain, many American settlers began moving to the Mexican province of California, where cattle ranching was creating a new society and economy. This would eventually lead to:

    (A) manifest destiny.

    (B) annexation of California.

    (C) annexation of Texas.

    (D) the opening of the frontier.

    (E) the closing of the frontier.

32. Contrary to the abolitionists' views, the influential planters of the South:

    (A) added to their profits by selling the children of their slaves.

    (B) often sold slaves to increase their wealth.

    (C) were never close or friendly with the slaves.

    (D) found it was in their own self-interest to give their slaves at least a minimum standard of living so that they would be fit enough to work.

    (E) found it necessary to import more slaves.

33. The Compromise of 1850 was a masterstroke for professional politicians. Henry Clay put together the compromise package that included:

    (A) California as a free state and free settlement in Texas.

    (B) California as a free state, a prohibition on the slave trade in Washington, D.C., and free settlement in New Mexico.

    (C) California as a free state, a prohibition on the slave trade in the District of Columbia, and a stricter fugitive slave law.

    (D) California as a free state, a prohibition on the slave trade in the District of Columbia, a stricter fugitive slave law, and settlement open to slavery in New Mexico.

    (E) California as a free state, settlement in Arizona and New Mexico, and a prohibition on slavery in the District of Columbia.

GO ON TO THE NEXT PAGE ⇨

34. Some historians claim that the breakup of the United States was inevitable. Which of the following conditions best supports that contention?

   (A) The fundamental differences between the South and the North

   (B) The Protestant leanings of the North versus the paternalistic view of the South

   (C) The Northern contention to ensure the eventual extinction of the institution of slavery versus Southern contention of the righteous morality of the question

   (D) The Republicans nominated Abraham Lincoln while the Democrats ran Stephen Douglas and John Breckinridge

   (E) The writings of Alexis de Tocqueville addressed the issue in the 1830s

35. The Supreme Court's decision in *Dred Scott v. Sandford*:

   (A) gave citizenship to African Americans.

   (B) challenged the constitutionality of the Missouri Compromise.

   (C) allowed Congress to control slavery in the territories.

   (D) was received positively in the North.

   (E) was written to condone "popular sovereignty."

36. "I was strong and thought I might go to the rescue of the men who fell…. What could I do but go to them, or work for them and my country? The patriot blood of my father was warm in my veins. The country which he had fought for, I might at least work for…." These are the words of:

   (A) Lucy Breckinridge

   (B) Susan B. Anthony

   (C) Clara Barton

   (D) Mary Chesnut

   (E) Sarah Grimke

37. The Civil War has been referred to as a "total war." Keeping with the context of the time, what did that mean for the North and the South?

   (A) The North put volunteers into the field and the South quickly resorted to conscription to fill their rolls.

   (B) The North could restore the Union only by destroying the southern will to resist, so the conflict was all-inclusive.

   (C) The South's advantages made it almost impossible for the North not to make the struggle one for the freedom of the African Americans.

   (D) Over 200,000 African Americans were involved in the war effort; their contributions encouraged Lincoln to push harder for their rights and the 13th Amendment was passed in January, 1865.

   (E) The South would petition both Great Britain and France for recognition that would scare the North into a peace treaty.

38. The effects of the Civil War on the nation were far-reaching. Which of the following is the most fundamental description?

   (A) The Union had been saved, even though five days after Lee surrendered the Southern Army Lincoln was assassinated.

   (B) The total number of deaths, over 618,000 men, left a generational gap and forced many women to seek roles other than the traditional wife and mother.

   (C) The war gave the federal government predominance over the states, but the states retained primary responsibility for many of the functions of the government.

   (D) The war organized the American people and moved them from a society of individuals and small producers to the beginnings of a modern, bureaucratic state.

   (E) Four million African Americans were free, but not equal.

GO ON TO THE NEXT PAGE

39. "I may state to all our friends, and to all our enemies, that we has a right to the land where we are
located. For why? I tell you. Our wives, our children, our husbands, has been sold over and over
again to purchase the lands we now locate upon;
for that reason we have a divine right to the
land…." These are the words of:

   (A) a slave.

   (B) a white land owner.

   (C) a freedman.

   (D) a carpetbagger.

   (E) a religious leader in Georgia.

40. The 14th Amendment to the Constitution:

   (A) prohibited slavery in the United States.

   (B) extended the protections of the due process
   clause to citizens and their state governments.

   (C) restored governments to the slave states after
   the congressional requirements were met.

   (D) provided the right to vote regardless of race,
   color, creed, or condition of past servitude.

   (E) made the Freedman's Bureau the agency for
   Native Americans and African Americans.

41. Andrew Johnson's adversarial relationship with
the Congress culminated in his impeachment,
which was set off by Johnson's:

   (A) refusal to punish the southern states.

   (B) campaigning for support for the Freedman's
   Bureau.

   (C) firing of the Secretary of War.

   (D) support of a civil rights bill for African
   Americans.

   (E) establishment of a federal agency for war
   veterans.

42. Identify the author of the following: "Up to our
own day American history has been in a large
degree the history of the colonization of the Great
West. The existence of an area of free land, con-
tinuous recession, and the advance of American
settlements westward, explain American development."

   (A) W. E. B. DuBois

   (B) Frederick Jackson Turner

   (C) Abraham Lincoln

   (D) Horace Greeley

   (E) Sojourner Truth

43. The Dawes Act of 1887 made every attempt to disrupt the Native American culture by doing all of
the following EXCEPT:

   (A) increase the power of the tribal councils.

   (B) establish Native American controlled and
   funded educational institutions.

   (C) separating the civilized from the uncivilized
   tribes.

   (D) eliminating the communal ownership of land
   and encouraging Christianity.

   (E) Supporting Native Americans who informed
   on their fellows.

44. The area of the United States whose population
increased by the largest percentage during the last
half of the 19th century was:

   (A) the Northeast.

   (B) the Far West.

   (C) the Old South.

   (D) The Great Plains.

   (E) Texas and New Mexico.

GO ON TO THE NEXT PAGE

45. "This, then, is held to be the duty of the man of wealth: To set an example of modest, unostentatious living, shunning display or extravagance; to provide moderately for the legitimate wants of those dependent upon him; and, after doing so, to consider all surplus revenues which come to him simply as trust funds, which he is called upon to administer, and strictly bound as a matter of duty to administer in a manner which, in his judgment, is best calculated to produce the most beneficial results for the community—the man of wealth thus becoming the mere trustee and agent for his poorer brethren, bringing to their service his superior wisdom, experience, and ability to administer, doing for them better than they would or could do for themselves…." This reflects the philosophy of:

 (A) John D. Rockefeller

 (B) Andrew Carnegie

 (C) Cornelius Vanderbilt

 (D) John P. Morgan

 (E) James P. Hill

46. The theory of natural selection in biology, when combined with theories of the market, resulted in a philosophy that would come to be known as:

 (A) Social Darwinism.

 (B) Laissez-faire capitalism.

 (C) The Gospel of Wealth.

 (D) Acres of Diamonds.

 (E) The Second Great Awakening.

47. The union movement grew in response to all of the following EXCEPT:

 (A) dangerous working conditions.

 (B) an appreciation of a artisan's skill in producing a finished product.

 (C) the performance of monotonous semiskilled tasks.

 (D) an unstable and mobile immigrant workforce.

 (E) mill owners who wanted complete control of the workers.

48. *Machine politics* refers to the consolidation of political power by a select few who, in return for money or votes, provide for the needs of their supporters. One of the most notorious of the urban political machines was:

 (A) Tammany Hall.

 (B) the Knights of Labor.

 (C) Rockefeller Foundation.

 (D) American Protective Association.

 (E) The Free Masons.

49. American imperialism is best exemplified by:

 (A) the War of 1812.

 (B) the Monroe Doctrine.

 (C) the Pan-American Conference.

 (D) the Spanish-American-Cuban War.

 (E) the closing of the frontier.

50. The primary cause of the Spanish-American-Cuban War was:

 (A) the Philippines refusal to allow Spanish ships into Manila harbor.

 (B) the murder of two U.S. diplomats in Madrid.

 (C) the sinking of the battleship *Maine* in Havana harbor.

 (D) American support for Cuban nationalism and independence.

 (E) American intervention in Manila Harbor.

GO ON TO THE NEXT PAGE ▷

KAPLAN
Test Prep and Admissions

51. The Progressives differed from the Populists in that they:

(A) were primarily from the middle class and lived in urban areas.

(B) were independent farmers from the Midwest and small producers from the east coast who championed free silver and the elimination of political machines.

(C) were primarily from New England and willing to take on a host of social evils including civil right violations and the growing gap between workers and owners of big business.

(D) were primarily dedicated to the reform of politics and changes to the immigration laws.

(E) were primarily from the middle class with excess funds and a desire to change society.

52. Theodore Roosevelt's greatest contributions to modern American life are probably:

(A) the creation of the national park system and the Roosevelt Corollary.

(B) the passage of railroad legislation and the creation of the Interstate Commerce Commission.

(C) the passage of the Pure Food and Drug Act and the Meat Inspection Act.

(D) the passage of the Square Deal for labor and closing of the Chicago stockyards.

(E) The exploration of Rio Theodoro in Brazil and the charge up San Juan Hill.

53. "His programme of industrial education, conciliation of the South, and submission and silence as to civil and political rights was not wholly original…. [He] represents in Negro thought the old attitude of adjustment and submission; …[his] programme practically accepts the alleged inferiority of the Negro races…." The speaker is referring to the philosophical differences between himself and:

(A) W. E. B. DuBois.

(B) Booker T. Washington.

(C) George Washington Carver.

(D) Ida Wells Barnett.

(E) Ida Tarbell.

54. Upon asking for a declaration of war at the beginning of American involvement in World War I, President Wilson said that Americans should:

(A) seek to enlarge their sphere of influence around the globe.

(B) stay out of the alliances so prevalent in Europe.

(C) strive to make the world safe for democracy.

(D) continue to remain primarily concerned with domestic issues and only serve in a supportive role in international affairs.

(E) remember that the United States was ready to serve as a guide for all European nations.

55. After the First World War was over, American involvement in European affairs could be described as:

(A) imperialistic.

(B) isolationist.

(C) progressive.

(D) capitalistic.

(E) chauvinistic.

GO ON TO THE NEXT PAGE ⟶

KAPLAN
Test Prep and Admissions

56. The Harding administration can best be characterized as:

   (A) a time of social and political reform after World War I.

   (B) a time of high tariffs, low taxes, and less spending by the federal government.

   (C) a time when the President's friends abused their power.

   (D) a time when the Teapot Dome scandal was exposed and the perpetrators punished.

   (E) a time of peace before the Second World War.

57. The 19th Amendment:

   (A) allowed for the direct election of Senators.

   (B) made Prohibition the law of the land.

   (C) changed the date of the inauguration of the president and vice president.

   (D) gave women the right to vote.

   (E) repealed the poll tax.

58. The philosophical dilemma of Herbert Hoover that paralyzed the speed of his reaction to the impending Depression was:

   (A) the federal government should help only businesses affected by the drought.

   (B) the federal government should remain outside the business realm but could offer support to the larger cities of New York, Los Angeles, and Chicago.

   (C) the federal government should only assist states in providing welfare for the poor and those who were not helped by private charities and other voluntary actions.

   (D) the federal government should not get involved at all in the business affairs of the country.

   (E) the federal government should provide any and all assistance to its people.

59. The First One Hundred Days of the Franklin Roosevelt administration were a whirlwind of activity. FDR's goal was to:

   (A) provide opportunities for recovery through the elimination of labor strikes.

   (B) restore the economy.

   (C) nationalize the economy.

   (D) provide price supports for agriculture through subsidies.

   (E) provide social security.

60. Although "the Supreme Court is never wrong," according to one commentator, the holding issued in *Plessy v. Ferguson* was overturned in:

   (A) *Schenck v. U.S.*

   (B) *Muller v. Oregon.*

   (C) *Brown v. Board of Education.*

   (D) *Schechter v. U.S.*

   (E) *Gibbons v. Ogden.*

61. As nations in Europe began to slide inexorably towards another world war, the United States remained removed from the action. FDR, in an attempt to prepare Americans for what he saw as the "inevitable conflict," instituted a program to assist Great Britain; it was known as the:

   (A) Neutrality Act of 1939.

   (B) Lend-Lease Act.

   (C) Atlantic Charter.

   (D) National Defense Advisory Commission.

   (E) The Yalta Conference.

GO ON TO THE NEXT PAGE

62. "In the future days, which we seek to make secure, we look forward to a world founded upon four essential human freedoms. The first is freedom of speech and expression everywhere in the world. The second is freedom of every person to worship God in his own way everywhere in the world. The third is freedom from want, which, translated into world terms, means economic understandings which will secure to every nation a healthy peace-time life for its inhabitants everywhere in the world. The fourth is freedom from fear—which, translated into world terms, means a world-wide reduction of armaments to such a point and in such a thorough fashion that no nation will be in a position to commit an act of physical aggression against any neighbor-anywhere in the world." The speaker:

   (A) Winston Churchill
   (B) Joseph Stalin
   (C) Franklin Roosevelt
   (D) Harry Truman
   (E) Earl Warren

63. During the Second World War, Japanese Americans, particularly in the West, were:

   (A) allowed to fight with other American troops.
   (B) treated as badly as Jews were treated in Germany.
   (C) deprived of their rights as Americans.
   (D) treated differently than other minorities
   (E) arrested and imprisoned.

64. The Truman Doctrine advocated:

   I.   Support for European nations seeking to rebuild after World War II.
   II. Military support for Greece and Turkey to head off the rising threat of Communism.
   III. Support for the domino theory.
   IV. Support of a military nature to combat Soviet influence in the Middle East.

   (A) I and II only.
   (B) II and III only.
   (C) I, II, and IV only.
   (D) II and IV only.
   (E) all of the above.

65. The Cold War was further escalated when the North Koreans invaded South Korea. Truman made the war a United Nations effort because:

   (A) the war would be finished quickly.
   (B) he knew Americans would not support another war so soon after 1945.
   (C) he knew Americans still blamed the Japanese and saw Korea as an extension of it.
   (D) Truman believed that the Russians ordered the invasion and he could not let that succeed.
   (E) The United Nations had more influence in Korea.

66. Which person below would make the "witch-hunt" for Communists the focus of his re-election campaign and go on to spread fear via unsubstantiated accusation throughout the government?

   (A) Joseph McCarthy
   (B) Klaus Fuchs
   (C) Alger Hiss
   (D) J. Strom Thurmond
   (E) Richard Nixon

GO ON TO THE NEXT PAGE ⇨

67. The French asked for American aid after their defeat at Dien Bien Phu in Vietnam. President Eisenhower refused because:

    (A) he knew that the American people would not support another war.

    (B) he did not think the Communists would be able to sustain an attack.

    (C) he secretly thought the French deserved to lose their colonies.

    (D) he wanted to abide by the Geneva conference rules.

    (E) he wanted Americans to remain neutral.

68. Communism was and is closest to U.S. shores in:

    (A) Venezuela.

    (B) Cuba.

    (C) Chile.

    (D) Nicaragua.

    (E) St. Pierre and Miquelon.

69. The Civil Rights Movement utilized a number of political actions to gain rights for African Americans. The best terms to describe the methods used by the Civil Rights Movement are:

    (A) passive resistance and civil disobedience.

    (B) boycotts and marches.

    (C) violent protest and the use of federal troops.

    (D) legal challenges and freedom rides.

    (E) letter writing campaigns to local newspapers.

70. John F. Kennedy encountered several Cold War tests early in his administration. Although the crises were difficult and extremely risky both politically and militarily, he did succeed in facing down the Russians during the:

    I. military coup in Vietnam

    II. Crisis in Berlin

    III. Cuban Missile Crisis

    IV. Bay of Pigs

    (A) I and II only

    (B) II and III only

    (C) III and IV only

    (D) II, III and IV only

    (E) I, II, III, and IV

71. Television in the 1950s reflected the changing face of American society with an ethnically mixed couple on:

    (A) *All in the Family.*

    (B) *Maude.*

    (C) *I Love Lucy.*

    (D) *Leave It to Beaver.*

    (E) *The Ozzie Nelson Show.*

72. President Johnson's "Great Society" contained all of the following programs EXCEPT:

    (A) federal aid to schools.

    (B) an equal rights amendment to guarantee equality for women.

    (C) federal health insurance and medical care for the poor and disabled.

    (D) passage of civil rights laws to ensure and promote equal opportunity for all Americans.

    (E) aid to Native Americans in Oklahoma.

GO ON TO THE NEXT PAGE

73. Richard Nixon won the presidency in 1968. The circumstances that contributed to the Democratic defeat included:

   (A) the publication of *The Feminine Mystique* and the women's movement.

   (B) the Tet Offensive and the *Pentagon Papers*.

   (C) the Gulf of Tonkin resolutions and the Equal Rights Amendment.

   (D) Johnson's failure to win a victory in Vietnam, and a lack of support for the war.

   (E) all of the above.

74. The Watergate scandal reshaped the relationship between politicians and the media. Richard Nixon's cover-up of his own involvement in the scandal resulted in:

   (A) his impeachment.

   (B) his resignation.

   (C) a demonstration of how the three branches of government work together for the same political goal.

   (D) the loss of the trust of the American people and a Democratic landslide in the next general elections.

   (E) all of the above.

75. The greatest achievement of the Carter administration, in the field of foreign policy, was his mediation of the Arab-Israeli conflict after the Yom Kippur War between Egypt and Israel. The Camp David Accords ushered in:

   (A) the establishment of a Palestinian homeland.

   (B) an Israeli-Egyptian peace treaty and a period of relative calm in the Middle East.

   (C) Egyptian supremacy in the Suez.

   (D) Israeli dominance of the West Bank.

   (E) none of the above.

76. Supply-side economics was a Reagan administration strategy meaning that:

   (A) the federal government should increase spending.

   (B) both federal spending and taxes should be cut in order to release private revenue for future investments.

   (C) the federal government should increase taxes and decrease spending to help eliminate the budget deficit.

   (D) funding for entitlement programs should be increased to make more money available to put into the economy.

   (E) all of the above.

77. A divisive issue of the 1970s was the implementation of affirmative action. Mandated on federal projects, the procedures were imposed to:

   (A) permit whites to experience discrimination in employment and education.

   (B) make more than "token" changes in the workplace.

   (C) allocate for non-whites and women compensation if they were not hired.

   (D) redress a history of discrimination against non-whites and women in employment and education.

   (E) insure Native Americans had access to jobs.

78. Which of the following cases involved the right to privacy?

   (A) *Massachusetts General v. Kelley*

   (B) *Griswold v. Connecticut*

   (C) *Miranda v. Arizona*

   (D) *Brandenberg v. Ohio*

   (E) *Engel v. Vitale*

GO ON TO THE NEXT PAGE

79. The rights of criminal suspects have been addressed on several occasions by the Supreme Court, most notably in:

   (A) *Gideon v. Wainright.*
   (B) *Engel v. Vitale.*
   (C) *Loving v. Virginia.*
   (D) *Roe v. Wade.*
   (E) All of the above

80. Rachel Carson is most closely connected to:

   (A) nuclear power.
   (B) pesticides.
   (C) global warming.
   (D) women's rights.
   (E) strip mining.

IF YOU FINISH BEFORE TIME IS CALLED, YOU MAY CHECK YOUR WORK ON THIS SECTION ONLY. DO NOT TURN TO ANY OTHER SECTION IN THE TEST.
STOP

KAPLAN

Test Prep and Admissions

Section II: Free-Response Questions

Time: 130 Minutes

Directions: This section contains five free-response questions. Answer the document-based question in Part A, one of the essay questions in Part B, and one of the essay questions in Part C. The first 15 minutes of the 130 minutes allocated for Section II is a reading period. During this period you should read the document-based question and plan what you will write, including making any notes. However, you cannot begin to write your essay until the 15-minute reading period has ended.

Part A: Document-Based Question

Suggested writing time: 45 minutes

The following question requires you to write a coherent essay incorporating your interpretation of the documents and your knowledge of the period specified in the question. To earn a high score you are required to cite key pieces of evidence from the documents and draw on your knowledge of the period.

1. The Constitution guarantees fundamental rights to all citizens and makes no exceptions for times of war. Using the documents, construct an argument either for or against the suspension of civil liberties in a time of war.

Document A

Source: Introduction Ex Parte Milligan

A democracy, even at war, must retain its basic democratic character, or else it loses that for which its citizens fight. War, however, places great strains on the body politic, and occasionally individual liberties and the needs of the state come into conflict. The Civil War had its share of overbearing governmental action, including Lincoln's questionable suspension of habeas corpus—the "great writ" of Anglo-American law that provided for the release of people wrongfully imprisoned. Few of the government's actions came under the scrutiny of the courts during the war, but once the Union had achieved victory, the Supreme Court proved willing to hear some cases arising out of the conflict.

Lambden P. Milligan had been sentenced to death by an army court in Indiana for allegedly disloyal activities. Lincoln delayed his execution, but after Lincoln's assassination, the new president, Andrew Johnson, approved the sentence. Milligan's attorney appealed for his release under the 1863 Habeas Corpus Act, and the federal circuit court split on the question of whether civilian courts had jurisdiction over appeals from military tribunals. Although this seems only a technical matter, the case gave the Supreme Court a chance—now that fighting was over—to comment on the limits of the government's war powers.

Document B

Source: Circuit Court D Maryland, April Term, 1861

The case, then, is simply this: a military officer, residing in Pennsylvania, issues an order to arrest a citizen of Maryland, upon vague and indefinite charges, without any proof, so far as appears; under this order, his house is entered in the night, he is seized as a prisoner, and conveyed to Fort Henry, and there kept in close confinement; and when a habeas corpus is served on the commanding officer, requiring him to produce the prisoner before a justice of the Supreme Court, is that he may examine into the legality of the imprisonment, the answer of the officer, is that he is authorized by the president to suspend the writ of habeas corpus at his discretion, and in the exercise of that discretion, suspends it in this case, and on the ground refuses obedience to the writ.

As the case comes before me, therefore, I understand that the president not only claims the right to suspend the writ of habeas corpus himself, at his discretion, but to delegate that discretionary power to a military officer, and to leave it to determine whether he will or will not obey judicial process that may be served upon him. No official notice has been given to the courts of justice, or to the public, by proclamation or otherwise, that the president claimed power, and had exercised it in the manner stated in the return. And I certainly listened to it with some surprise, for I had supposed it to be one of those points of constitutional law upon which there was no difference of opinion, and that it was admitted on all hands, that the privilege of the writ could not be suspended, except by act of Congress.

Document C

Source: Ex Parte Milligan, 1866

It is essential to the safety of every government that, in a great crisis, like the one we have just passed through, there should be a power somewhere of suspending the writ of habeas corpus. In every war, there are men of previously good character, wicked enough to counsel their fellow citizens to resist the measures deemed necessary by a good government to sustain its just authority and overthrow its enemies; and their influence may lead to dangerous combinations. In the emergency of the times, an immediate public investigation according to law may not be possible; and yet, the peril to the country may be too imminent to suffer such persons to go at large.

KAPLAN
Test Prep and Admissions

Document D

Source: Ex Parte Merryman Maryland Circuit Court, 1861

The case, then, is simply this: A military officer, residing in Pennsylvania, issues an order to arrest a citizen of Maryland, upon vague and indefinite charges, without any proof, so far as it appears. Under this order his house is entered in the night, he is seized as a prisoner, conveyed to Fort Henry, and there kept in close confinement. And when a habeas corpus is served on the commanding officer, requiring him to produce the prisoner before a Justice of the Supreme Court, in order that he may examine into the legality of the imprisonment, the answer of the officer is, that he is authorized by the president to suspend the writ of habeas corpus at his discretion, and, in the exercise of that discretion suspends it in this case, and on that ground refuses obedience to the writ.

Document E

Source: April Term, 1861, Circuit Court, d. Maryland

The only power, therefore, which the president possesses, where the "life, liberty or property" of a private citizen is concerned, is the power and duty prescribed in the third section of the second article, which requires "that he shall take care that the laws shall be faithfully executed." He is not authorized to execute them himself, or through agents or officers, civil or military, appointed by himself, but he is to take care that they be faithfully carried into execution, as they are expounded and adjudged by the coordinate branch of the government to which that duty is assigned by the Constitution. It is thus made his duty to come in aid of the judicial authority, if it shall be resisted by a force too strong to be overcome without the assistance of the executive arm; but in exercising this power he acts in subordination to judicial authority, assisting it to execute its process and enforce its judgments. With such provisions in the Constitution, expressed in language too clear to be misunderstood by any one, I can see no ground whatever for supposing that the president, in any emergency, or in any state of things, can authorize the suspension of the privileges of the writ of habeas corpus, or the arrest of a citizen, except in aid of the judicial power. He certainly does not faithfully execute the laws, if he takes upon himself legislative power, by suspending the writ of habeas corpus, and the judicial power also, by arresting and imprisoning a person without due process of law.

Document F

Source: American Patriot Network

Among the 13,000 people arrested under martial law was a Maryland Secessionist, John Merryman. Immediately, Hon. Roger B. Taney, Chief Justice of the Supreme Court of the United States issued a writ of habeas corpus commanding the military to bring Merryman before him. The military refused to follow the writ. Justice Taney, in Ex parte Merryman, then ruled the suspension of habeas corpus unconstitutional because the writ could not be suspended without an Act of Congress. President Lincoln and the military ignored Justice Taney's ruling.

Finally, in 1866, after the war, the Supreme Court officially restored habeas corpus in Ex-parte Milligan, ruling that military trials in areas where the civil courts were capable of functioning were illegal.

Document G

Source: Constitutional Problems Under Abraham Lincoln

"....As a war time president, Lincoln immediately appreciated the importance of having a united country behind him. The difficulty was that residents of the North were significantly divided not only over how the war should be pursued but over whether it was necessary at all. Many so called Peace Democrats, individuals who desired an immediate end to the conflict, lived in the North. In addition, Northern States had strong pockets of Southern sympathizers who, if they could not stop the war, tried to aid the Confederate cause..... To maintain Union dominance, Lincoln sought to suppress disloyal sentiment by suspending the writ of habeas corpus.... Lincoln's action meant that individuals could be arrested and held without formal charges being lodged against them... troublesome individuals were arrested for the revolutionary ideas that they were advocating—meaning separation from the Union and adherence to the Confederacy....

"....Taney ordered Merryman released and denounced the president for undercutting a basic right of the American people. By suspending habeas corpus, the president could arrest and hold anyone indefinitely without trail—an action that Taney thought subverted the constitutional process. Lincoln ignored the 85-year-old jurist's order. The case never reached the Supreme Court; Merryman was eventually released and never heard from again...."

KAPLAN
Test Prep and Admissions

Document H

Source: The Insiders Guide to Civil War Sites

John Merryman was a farmer from Cockeysville, a village north of Baltimore. A Southern sympathizer, Merryman was a lieutenant in the local militia, and he allegedly took part in a gang's plot to burn several railroad bridges west of Baltimore. In May 1861, U.S. troops surrounded Merryman's farm, arrested him and put him in confinement at Fort McHenry without informing him of the charges against him.

The day after the incident, Chief Justice Roger B. Taney—a Marylander himself—issued a writ of habeas corpus and had it served on the commander at the Fort McHenry, USA, Gen. George Cadwalader. Habeas corpus is an age-old common-law writ that is issued by a court to direct one who holds another in custody to produce the individual in person for a specific purpose—usually to correct a violation of the individual's personal liberty or to determine the legality of the detention.

Document I

Source: Civil Liberty and the Civil War: The Indianapolis Treason Trials
Remarks of the Chief Justice of the United States, William Rehnquist:

To those of you who may be asking yourselves, "Why, on the verge of the twenty-first century, should we look back at events that happened during the Civil War nearly a century and a half ago?" I would offer several replies. In the first place, the political events of the Civil War are of considerable interest in their own right. The cast of characters on the stage at that time— Abraham Lincoln; William H. Seward, Lincoln's rival for the Presidential nomination in 1860 whom Lincoln later appointed Secretary of State; Edwin M. Stanton, a remarkably able Secretary of War, and others—make it a lively story.

But the subject of Civil War is of more than just historical interest. The Civil War was the first time that the United States government mobilized for a major war effort, and a major war effort necessarily results in the curtailment of some civil liberties. The Civil War era produced the first important civil liberties decision from the Supreme Court of the United States—the case of Ex parte Milligan, decided in 1866. The ramifications of the Milligan case are with us to this day. And, the case is of particular interest here in Indiana, because it arose out of what historians call the Indianapolis treason trials, which took place in your state capital in the fall of 1864.

Continued on the next page.

Document I, continued

Several weeks later, federal troops arrested a man named Merryman, whom authorities suspected of being a major actor in the dynamiting of the railroad bridges. No sooner was he confined in Fort McHenry than he sued out a writ of habeas corpus. The following day, Chief Justice Roger Taney, sitting as a circuit judge in Baltimore, ordered the government to show cause why Merryman should not be released. A representative of the commandant appeared in court for the government to advise Taney that the writ of habeas corpus had been suspended, and asked for time to consult with the government in Washington. Taney refused, and issued an attachment—a form of arrest—for the commandant of Fort McHenry. The next day, the marshal reported that in his effort to serve the writ he had been denied admission to the fort. Taney then issued an opinion in the case declaring that the President alone did not have the authority to suspend the writ of habeas corpus—only Congress could do that—and holding that Merryman's confinement was illegal. The Chief Justice, knowing that he could not enforce his order, sent a copy of it to Lincoln.

Lincoln ignored the order, but in his address to the special session of Congress which he called to meet on July 4, 1861, he adverted to it in these words:

Must [the laws] be allowed to finally fail of execution even had it been perfectly clear that by the use of the means necessary to their execution some single law, made in such extreme tenderness of the citizens' liberty that practically it relieves more of the guilty than of the innocent, should to a very limited extent be violated? To state the question more directly, are all the laws but one to go unexecuted, and then government itself go to pieces less that one be violated.

Lincoln, with his usual incisiveness, put his finger on the debate that inevitably surrounds issues of civil liberties in war time.

KAPLAN
Test Prep and Admissions

Part B

Suggested time: 35 minutes

Directions: Choose ONE question from this part. You are advised to spend five minutes planning and 30 minutes writing your answer.

2. Historiography suggests that the record of American existence contains numerous examples of recurring themes. Assess the validity of the following:

    > After reviewing John Winthrop's view of the Puritans and his "City Upon a Hill," the ideas of Manifest Destiny, and the Turner Thesis, American history contains few surprises.

3. The 20th century saw a revival of the conservative movement. What factors contributed to that resurgence?

Part C

Suggested time: 35 minutes

Directions: Choose ONE question from this part. You are advised to spend five minutes planning and 30 minutes writing your answer.

4. Explain how TWO of the following helped to facilitate the shift from an agrarian to an industrial economy in the early 1800s.

    - Commercial farming
    - Factory system
    - Inventions
    - Labor
    - Transportation
    - Entrepreneurs

5. Constitutional scholars will suggest that the Supreme Court is never wrong. In light of this argument, explain the ruling in *Brown v. Board of Education* and the "separate but equal" doctrine.

Practice Test Two: **Answer Key**

1. A	21. D	41. C	61. B
2. C	22. C	42. B	62. C
3. B	23. A	43. A	63. C
4. B	24. B	44. D	64. D
5. D	25. B	45. B	65. B
6. C	26. C	46. A	66. A
7. A	27. D	47. B	67. D
8. A	28. D	48. A	68. B
9. C	29. C	49. D	69. A
10. D	30. A	50. D	70. B
11. A	31. B	51. A	71. C
12. C	32. D	52. C	72. B
13. B	33. D	53. B	73. D
14. D	34. A	54. C	74. B
15. C	35. B	55. B	75. B
16. D	36. C	56. C	76. B
17. B	37. B	57. D	77. D
18. A	38. D	58. D	78. B
19. A	39. C	59. B	79. A
20. C	40. B	60. C	80. B

Answers and Explanations

1. A

President Jackson did threaten South Carolina with force, but sweetened the deal with gradual tariff reductions in order to head off the nullification crisis.

2. C

Garrison founded *The Liberator* in 1831 and published weekly for 35 years. His editorials spoke of support for the Declaration of Independence and his plans for ending slavery.

3. B

Exploration and settlement began after 1620; the plagues had taken their greatest tolls in the late 1300s (although the influenza epidemic of 1918 killed as many as died in World War I). Avoidance of disease wasn't a goal that could be accomplished by moving to the New World; in fact, disease was one of the biggest threats to the early settlements.

4. B

James Oglethorpe was instrumental in the founding of Georgia. It was first established as a buffer between the English colonies and the Spanish in Florida, but it would become a haven for debtors wanting to start their lives again the colonies.

5. D

In the triangle trade New England merchants shipped barrels of rum to the west coast of Africa where the rum was traded for captive Africans. If the Africans survived the Middle Passage, they would be worked in the sugar cane fields in the West Indies. The sugar cane would be processed into molasses and shipped back to New England to be made into rum.

6. C

The colonies were dominated by English culture (language and traditions). By the mid-1700s they had all developed at least some degree of religious toleration, self-government, and, with the exception of Africans, social mobility. However, in the colonies, there were no hereditary aristocrats—it was a much different class system, with wealthy landowners at the top and the majority of craftspeople and small farmers.

7. A

Rev. Jonathan Edwards initiated the Great Awakening in New England, but it was Rev. George Whitefield who was instrumental in its spread throughout the colonies when he preached rousing sermons to 10,000 or more. He suggested that ordinary people who had faith and sincerity could understand the Gospels without ministers to lead them.

8. A

The colonists objected to British interference after 1763. The British needed American funds to replenish their treasury after years of fighting the French, but the years of salutary neglect had created an independent lot of colonies, hence the objections to British rule. The colonists probably would have settled for representation in Parliament. However, when King George III refused, the colonial opposition to British rule quickly became more militant.

9. C

At the beginning of the American Revolution and indeed well into the first two years, popular support was minimal. After American victories at Trenton and Saratoga in 1777, many colonists began to believe that an American victory was possible and thus joined in the war effort.

10. D

In spite of the fact that the Articles were weak, there were significant accomplishments while the colonies were governed under them. The American Revolution was won and a peace was negotiated with Great Britain, the Land Ordinance of 1785 was passed to establish a public policy for western lands (including a portion set aside for public education), and the Northwest Ordinance of 1787 was passed, which set new rules for the creation of new states (on an equal basis with all others).

KAPLAN
Test Prep and Admissions

11. A

John Locke wrote that although government is supreme, it followed that there are "natural laws" or rights that people have simply because they are human. He argued that sovereignty ultimately resides with the people rather than the state, and that people have the right to revolt against that government whenever it fails to protect their rights.

12. C

The Proclamation of 1763 was a British effort to appease the Native American tribes of the Ohio River Valley. Successful at first, the Proclamation was soon ignored by the colonists because there was no one to enforce it, and Native Americans did not create a paper trail to protect their holdings.

13. B

The major difference between the Virginia and the New Jersey Plans at the Constitutional Convention was in their method of apportioning representation. The Virginia Plan called for a congress to be divided into two houses, a lower house chosen by population and an upper one chosen by the lower one from nominees of the state legislatures. The New Jersey Plan called for equal representation for all states in a unicameral body.

14. D

James Madison, the author of Federalist #10, is considered the "Father of the Constitution." His encyclopedic knowledge regarding democratic principles was put to the test during the writing of the Constitution, but it is unquestionably his work.

15. C

The Land Ordinances of 1785 and 1787 specified procedures for surveying and selling land, the most pressing issue in the western territories at that time. One reason this was such a pressing issue was that the surveying and subsequent selling of land would generate funds for paying off the government's debts. The Land Ordinances also specified a process by which a territory could become a state once it had enough population and abolished slavery in the territories north of the Ohio River, but these were not pressing issues in the late 18th century.

16. D

This quote is typical of the speeches and inaugural addresses of victorious candidates who seek to put behind them the divisiveness of the election campaign. Thomas Jefferson realized that the election of 1800 had produced strong feelings among the two political parties (the same two that Washington had warned about in his Farewell Address). Jefferson wanted to achieve a smooth transition from the Federalist Party of John Adams to the Republican Party, which he led.

17. B

Jefferson was a strict interpreter of the Constitution, but he saw the great advantages of the Louisiana Purchase and was willing to give up his idealistic position. He persuaded Congress, arguing that although the Constitution did not expressly give a president the power to purchase land (although Alexander Hamilton suggested that some powers were implied), Jefferson could negotiate the purchase under the presidential power to make treaties. Congress quickly ratified the treaty/purchase.

18. A

John Marshall found the Judiciary Act of 1789 unconstitutional because it gave too much power to the Supreme Court. The significance of the decision was the establishment of the doctrine of judicial review. The Supreme Court could decide whether an action of Congress or of the President was unconstitutional.

19. A

The Federalist Party had lost to the Republicans in 1800 and had, for the most part, disbanded. The War of 1812 did not produce a resurgence of the party, but it did result in a victory over the Native Americans in the West. Also, the Whigs gained power, the British never again challenged the Americans in North America, and General Andrew Jackson would ride the wave of popularity after the Battle of New Orleans eventually into the White House.

20. C

The Monroe Doctrine (1823) was part of President Monroe's message to Congress. In it he declared the future United States policy towards Europe and Central America. The message also went on to declare that the

United States would oppose any future attempts by any European power to interfere with the affairs of any nation in the Western Hemisphere. The Rush-Bagot Agreement was a disarmament agreement between the United States and the British regarding the Great Lakes. The Treaty of 1818 resulted in improved relations between the United States and Britain and involved fishing rights off Newfoundland, the joint occupation of the Oregon Territory, and establishing a boundary of the Louisiana Purchase.

21. D

The Missouri Compromise was the culmination of three bills signed into law in 1820 as one piece of legislation. Introduced by Henry Clay, the Compromise set a boundary for slavery in the Louisiana territories at 36° 30′. Maine and Missouri came into the United States within months of each other to preserve the balance of slave and free states. The sectional controversy was thus averted for another 10 years.

22. C

The Monroe doctrine declared that the United States would oppose any attempts by any European nation to create new colonies in the Western Hemisphere (including Cuba). In return the U.S. stated its policy not to get involved in European affairs. The United States did not, however, go so far as to agree not to interfere in the affairs of other nations of the Western Hemisphere. The United States was taking its first steps toward international involvement.

23. A

Andrew Jackson was born to a humble family on the frontier. His election was a departure from previous elections because he was not part of the "establishment" from which previous presidents had been drawn. When Jackson took office, his enthusiastic supporters came back to the White House and celebrated all night, essentially "trashing" the entire building. While he was the first president to come from a state other than Massachusetts or Virginia, this fact is not very important by itself. Jackson's victory at the Battle of New Orleans made him a war hero, but George Washington had been one too.

24. B

The Cherokee removal to the Oklahoma Territory was disguised as an attempt to protect their culture, but the real motivation was to gain access to their land. Even the designation of the Cherokee as a sovereign nation—the ruling in the case—did nothing to stop the removal by U.S. troops. When Chief Justice Marshall handed down the decision, Jackson is reported to have said, "Now that he has made his decision, let him enforce it." Over one quarter of the Native Americans died during the forced march to Oklahoma, the "Trail of Tears" of 1838–39.

25. B

Jackson was one of the first politicians to use the patronage system publicly. He said it was a legitimate example of democratic principles being applied to the "modern" world. Jackson was not given to patience with the world of professional governmental employees; he thought their role could be performed by any intelligent man.

26. C

Nullification was the South's claim that any policy of the federal government that threatened the interests of the South or threatened the use of slavery could be declared "null and void" by southern states. John C. Calhoun was the principal proponent and spoke in the Senate for support of the policy.

27. D

Elizabeth Cady Stanton and Lucretia Mott called the Seneca Falls Convention in upstate New York to outline, for the first time, a program for women's equality. Through the Convention, they repudiated the idea that separate spheres for men and women were the natural order of society. The Convention drew attention and during the 1850s conventions, women at the local, regional, and national level levels worked for reform programs.

28. D

The authors are closely identified with their works which had enormous influence on society. Abraham Lincoln said when meeting Harriet Beecher Stowe, "So this is the little woman who started the war." Elijah Lovejoy was a newspaperman who wrote editorials denouncing slavery, but he did not write *The Sins of Slavery*.

29. C

Workers were able to improve their standards of living through employment in factories and mills. Urban areas were growing in response to the entrepreneurs who invested in water-powered mills located along the banks of the rivers (such as those in Lowell and Lawrence, Massachusetts). Because the West was still open to settlement, there seemed to be little excuse to remain destitute for long. The great American myth was in the making.

30. A

As sectionalism began to grip the country, the North became industrialized, but retained the agriculture necessary to provide food for its cities, as means of distribution were, as yet, relatively undeveloped.

31. B

The movement of American settlers led to the annexation of California after the American victory in the Mexican-American War. Manifest destiny was not a result of the American expansion westward, it was a justification for it. The term *manifest destiny* was created by John L. O'Sullivan in 1845. He said: "Our manifest destiny is to overspread the continent allotted by Providence for the free development of our yearly multiplying millions." The sense of cultural and even racial superiority was thinly disguised as part of the divinely inspired mission to settle from sea to sea. The annexation of California was the goal, particularly after the successful annexation of Texas.

32. D

Southern planters valued their assets, and slaves were an asset. Although there were some sales of slave children, planters found that the continuity of the family contributed to a better working environment. Nurturing the slave families was far more productive and the investment in their care was worth the return.

33. D

The Compromise of 1850 was just that, a compromise. There had to be gains for both the North and the South for the legislation to become law. For the North, entrance into the Union for California as a free state and the prohibition of the slave trade in Washington, D.C., was offset by a stronger fugitive slave law and a chance to settle in an enlarged New Mexico for the South.

34. A

The crisis that precipitated the Civil War was a fundamental conflict between two different ideologies and ways of life that went beyond the slavery issue. The North was inspired by the Protestant view of self-reliance and responsibility; the South continued to see itself as "chivalrous." Slavery was a way of life in the South and considered tyrannical and immoral in the North, but it was only the most visible of many fundamental differences.

35. B

Chief Justice Roger B. Taney, a Southerner, wrote the decision for the Court and found Dred Scott to have no legal standing because he was considered property; thus, there was no case. Taney would go on to conclude that the Missouri Compromise was unconstitutional because Congress could not restrict the right of a slave-owner to take his slaves into a territory.

36. C

Clara Barton was the founder of the Red Cross. She began her career as a nurse on the battlefields, when medical care was often more dangerous than the wounds themselves. She and her "nurses" sought to ease the suffering of the wounded men. She would later approach President Lincoln and ask for assistance in treating the wounded.

37. B

The key to understanding the "total war" description of the Civil War, if there is any understanding to be had, lies in the idea that the North saw the conflict as one kind of argument and the South saw it as another. To the North, the argument was about the union of the states; the South's vision was about their way of life and loss of power and prestige.

38. D

While all of the options have at least some truth, choice (D) states the most fundamental result of the war—the beginnings of a modern bureaucratic nation. The way of life prior to the War would fade as technological advances paved the way for the industrial economy.

39. C

A freedman was a former African American slave. Because the freedmen had no economic resources, they found the purchase of land nearly impossible and were forced to work "shares" which were also enslaving.

40. B

The 14th Amendment did extend the protections of the due process clause (which in the Bill of Rights applied only to the federal government) and extended it to the states. The amendment also defined citizenship as given to all persons born or naturalized in the United States.

41. C

With Lincoln's assassination, Andrew Johnson came into the presidency. The Republicans saw an opportunity to enact legislation that would punish the southern states but Johnson, himself a native of Tennessee, was opposed to such a policy. When Congress passed the Tenure of Office Act that required the President to request permission to fire a Cabinet member, Johnson fired the Secretary of War in spite of it and incurred the wrath of Congress. The impeachment failed by one vote and Johnson served the remainder of his term.

42. B

Frederick Jackson Turner argued what would become known as the Turner Thesis in 1893. He described the character of Americans and suggested that: "…The peculiarity of American institutions is, in fact that they have been compelled to adapt themselves to the changes of an expanding people—to the changes involved in crossing a continent…."

43. A

The Dawes Act made every effort to eradicate Native American culture by eliminating communal ownership of land, decreasing the power of the tribal councils, sending Native American children to white-run schools, and banning the teaching of Native American culture, customs, and language.

44. D

The Great Plains saw the greatest increase because immigrants from Europe and the eastern seaboard were able to access vast acres through the Homestead Act, the expansion of the railroads, and the Dawes Act. That access, coupled with inventions such as the steel plow and mechanized combine, made the plains economically viable.

45. B

Andrew Carnegie came to this country at the age of 12. Through salesmanship, the use of the latest steel producing technology, and a business organization known as vertical integration, he retired in 1900 to devote himself to philanthropic pursuits. The purchase of Carnegie Steel by J. P. Morgan would result in U.S. Steel, the nation's first billion-dollar company. Carnegie believed successful businessmen should use their accumulated wealth to benefit society.

46. A

Although the idea offended many, the natural selection theories of biology, when combined with theories of the market, gave rise to Social Darwinism. English philosopher Herbert Spencer argued that the concentration of wealth in the hands of those best able to utilize it would benefit the whole human race.

47. B

Labor unions, the first attempt to combat the power and influence of management, were often portrayed as un-American and anarchistic. Management used the lockout (the closing of a factory to stop a labor movement before it could organize), blacklists (lists of pro-union sympathizers), and yellow-dog contracts (as a condition of employment, workers had to sign a contract not to join a union) to control their workers. As artisans were replaced by machines, there was diminishing appreciation of their skills.

48. A

Tammany Hall, in New York, was the most notorious. Established as a social club in the 1860s, Boss Tweed and his close associates maneuvered their influence and stole millions from the taxpayers. In return for votes on election day, Tammany Hall created a web of welfare services for millions of immigrants.

49. D

Although the Monroe Doctrine was the first American declaration of international diplomacy, it would be the Spanish-American-Cuban War that would serve notice to the rest of the world that the United States had truly entered the scene. Advocates of American expansion included missionaries, politicians, the press, and the military.

50. D

American support for Cuban nationalism was fueled by economic interests, outrage at the sinking of the *Maine*, and humanitarian concerns. U.S. troops were sent to Cuba in 1898 for a four-month engagement. Theodore Roosevelt would ride to fame and the presidency with the Rough Riders and the Battle of San Juan Hill (actually Kettle Hill).

51. A

The Progressives were from the middle class and primarily urban dwellers who grew concerned with the increasingly large gaps between rich and poor, the conflict between labor and capital, and the influence of political machines. In addition, the Progressives supported women's suffrage and objected to Jim Crow laws in the South that relegated African Americans to a status of second class citizen.

52. C

Roosevelt's legislative triumphs include the Pure Food and Drug Act and the Meat Inspection Act. These acts, which have been expanded over the years, continue to protect Americans on a daily basis. Although Roosevelt did set aside over 55 million acres for environmental and conservation purposes, the national parks system had already been inaugurated before he became president. The Roosevelt Corollary to the Monroe Doctrine, in which Theodore Roosevelt stated that the United States reserved the right to intervene in Latin American affairs, has little effect on the daily lives of Americans today. The Interstate Commerce Commission, established in 1887, was already in existence by the time Roosevelt became president in 1901.

53. B

Booker T. Washington expressed the view that the Negro should learn vocational trades and not involve himself in the political arena. W. E. B. DuBois, the speaker, accuses Washington of asking African Americans to give up their political power, civil rights, and higher educational opportunities.

54. C

Wilson was loath to involve the United States in the international war, but circumstances were such that America could no longer remain neutral. Wilson suggested involvement was based on moral principles and making the world safe for democracy.

55. B

Americans, having crossed the sea for moral reasons, came back after the First World War severely disillusioned by war in general. The trench warfare was brutal, and French commanders had wanted to place American troops on the front lines immediately. Having accomplished their mission (that of saving the world for democracy) most Americans were content to let the European nations argue amongst themselves. When Wilson became heavily involved with the peace negotiations at Versailles, the American public seemed to have little interest.

56. C

Warren G. Harding enjoyed the trappings of the office much more than the political power. During his short administration, many abuses of power were concocted, Teapot Dome being the most flagrant. Calvin Coolidge, who became president when Harding died three years into his term, wisely allowed criminal prosecutions to take place to "purge" the ranks.

57. D

Women's suffrage, ratified in 1920, is the 19th Amendment.

58. D

The prevailing philosophy of the country had always been that business and government were two separate entities and the government should not get directly involved in the affairs of business. Calvin Coolidge said, "The man who builds a business builds a temple." Hoover merely continued the practice of keeping government out of business affairs until 1931 when he was persuaded that federal assistance to farmers to head off foreclosures was warranted. By 1932, however, the only entity large enough and with enough resources to begin to pull the country out of the depression was the federal government.

59. B

FDR did not want to nationalize the economy, he wanted to reform and restore it. With the resources of the federal government at hand, he and his administration were responsible for the introduction of 15 bills, some of which have become a permanent part of the American political landscape. The Social Security Act and the Federal Deposit Insurance Corporation are two prime examples.

60. C

Schenck v. United States was the decision of the Supreme Court to uphold the Espionage Act. Justice Oliver Wendell Holmes wrote that free speech could be limited if it presented a "clear and present danger" to society. *Muller v. Oregon* upheld a ten-hour workday for women. *Schechter v. United States* saw the Supreme Court declare the National Recovery Act (NRA) unconstitutional. *Brown v. Board of Education* was the decision that invalidated the *Plessy v. Ferguson* doctrine of "separate but equal" as being "inherently unequal."

61. B

FDR saw Britain's survival directly tied to security in America. He persuaded Congress to pass the Lend-Lease Act authorizing the president to "lend, lease, or dispose of" arms and other equipment to any country whose defense was considered vital to the United States.

62. C

Those are the classic four freedoms of FDR. His speech was meant to inspire Americans, justify the actions of the United States, and unite a country behind a massive war effort. The speech also inspired Norman Rockwell to paint his famous "Four Freedoms," which was used as a recruiting poster during the war.

63. C

In direct reaction to the Japanese bombing of Pearl Harbor and to allay fears of spies and subversives active on the west coast, Roosevelt was persuaded to issue an executive order to collect Japanese Americans, even first and second generation, and deport them to internment camps scattered throughout the West and Arkansas. Deprived of their rights as Americans, many Japanese withstood the upheaval with great difficulty. When they were allowed to return to their homes, many found their properties had been seized and allocated to others.

64. D

Great Britain notified the United States in 1947 that they could no longer afford to help the Greeks. Truman asked Congress for aid, warning that if Greece fell to Communism that the effects would be serious for Turkey and the rest of the Middle East. President Truman would later use the term *domino theory* to refer to the idea that the fall of one nation to Communism would lead to its neighbors falling to Communism as well. The Truman Doctrine focused on military support while the Marshall Plan offered economic aid to European nations after World War II.

65. B

A war cannot be fought successfully without the support of the people. The Korean Conflict was beginning too soon (1950) after the end of World War II (1945); people remembered the horrors and sacrifices of that war. Truman knew that Americans were tired of fighting wars on foreign soil, but he also knew that the containment of Communism was of primary importance. By making the war effort a United Nations effort, it would be easier to justify the war on moral grounds. And since more countries would be involved, the Americans would not have to do all the fighting, even if the U. S. provided the majority of the war effort, men and supplies.

66. A

Senator Joseph McCarthy made the accusations in hearings designed to focus the media on his re-election campaign. When finally challenged by Senator Margaret Chase Smith from Maine, McCarthy responded by hurtling more accusations. Finally the president and the Senate denounced him, and McCarthy's influence waned.

67. D

After the end of World War II, the French returned their attentions to building an empire in French Indochina. However, the French were facing a Communist-led uprising seeking Vietnamese independence, and the French requested American aid. By 1954, the U.S. was providing 80 percent of the material to the French war effort in Indochina. However, after the decisive defeat of the French at Dien Bien Phu, Eisenhower cut off aid in compliance with the agreement reached at Geneva in 1954 which temporarily divided Vietnam into two countries—the north under Communist rule and the south under a regime friendly with the French and Americans. However, in the end, the elections called for in the Geneva Accords were never held to reunite the country because the South Vietnamese government—and its supporters—were fearful that the Communists would win.

KAPLAN
Test Prep and Admissions

68. B

Fidel Castro came to power in Cuba in 1958 and announced his intentions to adopt Communism shortly thereafter. Castro and Communism remain in power in Cuba today. Castro is the longest serving dictator anywhere in the world.

69. A

Passive resistance and civil disobedience are the encompassing terms that describe all the political activities (including boycotts, marches, sit-ins, freedom rides, etc.) utilized by the Civil Rights Movement. Martin Luther King, Jr. encouraged African Americans to sit where laws forbade them from sitting and to boycott services that were discriminatory. After a boycott of almost a year, the bus system in Montgomery was integrated.

70. B

The Cuban Missile Crisis and the Berlin crisis were the two actions in which the United States achieved its goals of containing the Communists. In West Berlin, the Soviets built a wall between the two sections of the city, but access by the U.S. and its allies to West Berlin was not denied. The Cuban Missile Crisis forced the Russians to stop building missile silos in Cuba after the United States blockaded the island. The United States was not successful in the Bay of Pigs invasion of Cuba and the military coup in South Vietnam did not involve confrontation with the Soviet Union.

71. C

I Love Lucy featured a Latino band leader named Ricky, played by Desi Arnaz, and his wife, played by Lucille Ball, as the ethnically mixed couple. The couple was, however, filmed sleeping in separate beds for the viewing audience, and Lucy's pregnancy was carefully hidden.

72. B

Johnson's "Great Society" did not include amendments to the Constitution. Johnson wanted his administration to go down in history as the most caring since Roosevelt, for whom Johnson had great admiration. While not opposed by the Johnson administration, the Equal Rights Amendment would die of its own volition.

73. D

Lyndon Johnson, seeing that he could not win any kind of a decisive victory in Vietnam and facing growing domestic opposition to the war, announced that he would not run again. That opened the door for anti-war candidate Robert Kennedy. Kennedy was assassinated and Hubert Humphrey, who supported Johnson's position on the war, was nominated. The voters as much voted against the Democrats, whom they blamed for the war, as they voted for Richard Nixon. The women's movement did not really support Nixon, the Pentagon Papers were not published until after Nixon was re-elected president in 1974, and the Equal Rights Amendment was not yet a political issue.

74. B

Richard Nixon was never impeached. The House Judiciary Committee was to vote on articles of impeachment the following week; Nixon stopped the process with his resignation on August 9, 1974.

75. B

Although the Camp David Accords would not bring long-term peace to the Middle East, President Carter appealed to the leaders of Israel and Egypt to begin the process of negotiation that resulted in a peace treaty between Egypt and Israel. This has not led to the establishment of a Palestinian homeland, however. Egyptian control of the Suez Canal and Israeli dominance of the West Bank were not changed by the Camp David Accords.

76. B

Supply side economics relies on the logic of the "trickle-down" effect. By cutting government spending and taxes, more private revenue becomes available for new investments. Supporters argued that this in turn would generate more options for taxes, which in turn would generate more opportunities for investment, and everybody would benefit.

77. D

Affirmative action was first introduced under the Johnson administration; it was designed to open up opportunities for African Americans and Latinos. While the number of African Americans enrolled in colleges doubled and Latinos had some similar gains in the next 10 years, there was only marginal improvement overall in the status. Poor and working-class non-whites still took the brunt of job losses and unemployment in the 1970s.

KAPLAN
Test Prep and Admissions

78. B

In *Griswold v. Connecticut* the Supreme Court ruled that a Connecticut statute was unconstitutional in that its prohibitions on the distribution of contraceptives to married couples violated the "right to marital privacy." *Engle v. Vitale* eliminated prayer in public schools. *Brandenberg v. Ohio* pertained to overturning an Ohio statute that banned persons from urging criminal acts as a means of gaining political reform or joining any group that advocated such activities. In *Korematsu v. United States* the Court held that it was not unconstitutional to have legal restrictions on a single racial group. The holding in the *Stanford v. Kentucky* case involved the easing of restrictions on capital punishment.

79. A

In 1963, Clarence Earl Gideon was given a new trial because the Justices said he had been denied the "right to counsel." The decision went even further in that it sent a message to all court systems that the rights of indigent defendants had to be respected and protected by an attorney. *Miranda v. Arizona* went even further and established the "Miranda warnings" (you have the right to remain silent, you have the right to an attorney, and so forth). *Engel v. Vitale* involved school prayer, *Loving v. Virginia* invalidated the Virginia statute that banned interracial marriage, and *Roe v. Wade* banned all state laws making abortion unconstitutional.

80. B

Rachel Carson published *Silent Spring* in the 1960s. It warned about the consequences of the use and misuse of pesticides.

ANALYSES OF THE FREE-RESPONSE QUESTIONS

Part A: Document-Based Question (DBQ)

The Constitution guarantees fundamental rights to all citizens and makes no exceptions for times of war. Using the documents, construct an argument either for or against the suspension of civil liberties in a time of war.

Use evidence from the documents **and** your knowledge of the period 1820–1861 to compose your answer.

Use of the Documents

Document A: The introduction to *Ex Parte Milligan* provides the "setting" for the case within the confines of the practice of democracy. In spite of Abraham Lincoln's esteemed reputation, he did suspend civil liberties during the Civil War, and the student's task is to find reasonable evidence to support or decry the action.

Document B: This excerpt from the Circuit Court, April term, 1861 established Roger B. Taney's viewpoint. Taney was from Maryland, was a southern supporter, and the author of the Dred Scott decision. Taney suggests that Lincoln misunderstands the implications of suspending a writ of habeas corpus.

Document C: This is an excerpt from the 1866 opinion authored by Justice Davis, writing for the Court. He established a foundation for the suspension of liberties during times of conflict. The emergency of the situation would seem to justify the action. Students should be able to extrapolate the circumstances to more modern situations such as the Red Scares of the 1920s and the internment of the Japanese of the 1940s.

Document D: *Ex Parte Merryman* again sets the scene for the other case referenced in the prompt. Taney paints a picture of a nighttime raid upon the house of an unsuspecting citizen and his subsequent confinement. The involvement of the military in the arrest serves to complicate the action. Again, Taney makes his dislike of Lincoln evident through his use of such terms as "vague and indefinite charges…"

Document E: Taney continues in his decision in the April, 1861 term of the circuit court, to take President Lincoln to task for exceeding his authority as a president. Taney: "…he certainly does not faithfully execute the laws…" and states his opposition to the action. Lincoln, according to the decision, has taken on legislative functions thus blurring the separation of powers safeguards of the Constitution.

Document F: The argument revolves around Lincoln and the charges that he suspended the U.S. Constitution and/or his suspension of habeas corpus. The reading makes some distinction and illustrates the relationship between the executive and judicial branches.

Document G: Margaret Blanchard, in "Free Expression and Wartime: Lessons from the Past, Hopes for the Future," frames the Merryman arrest in Lincoln's suspension of habeas corpus. She also describes the vehemence with which Roger B. Taney berates Lincoln for the action, but then suggests that there was more smoke than fire—the case never reached the Supreme Court.

Document H: The facts of the Merryman case are set out by this account. The case differs from Milligan in that it was an action of a local militiaman which set off the legal wrangle.

Document I: Chief Justice William Rehnquist begins his address on the subject of civil liberties by referencing the Milligan case and its importance to the law of today. Here is the first documented connection to the more recent instances of the suspension of habeas corpus in the 20th century.

Analysis of the DBQ

The loss of civil liberties in a time of war is always a sensitive issue. One the one hand, the argument can be made that the threat of the enemy is enough in itself to warrant the intrusion. On the other hand, the cherished civil liberties are valued to such an extent that under no circumstances should they be limited or curtailed in any way. Both the cases from the reading make that point.

Lambden Milligan was sentenced by a military court for alleged disloyal activities. John Merryman was arrested for reasons unknown at the time. Both men were detained without being told of the charges against them, a clear violation of their civil liberties. The DBQ asks the student to construct an argument for or against the suspension of the civil liberties, and students should be able to construct the facts of the Merryman and Milligan cases and the chronology of the events that led up to the decisions.

Abraham Lincoln was a crafty president but he was not a foolish one. He understood the value of habeas corpus, and the pressures of the Civil War. Lincoln could neither allow the border-states to be influenced by southern sympathizers, or permit extended freedom to the naysayers. All this had to be done within the confines of the executive office, which had restrictions on it as well. The other character in the cases is Chief Justice Roger B. Taney, a Marylander and southern sympathizer. It was he who wrote the Dred Scott decision.

A good student response would recognize the predicament that the loss of civil liberties in a time of war creates. Extending that thinking, a student could make the argument that the Alien and Sedition Acts of 1799 set the precedent for such restrictions; the Palmer raids of the 1920s and the internment of the Japanese in the 1940s were simply extensions.

Key Points from Outside Information

- Roger B. Taney was a long-serving jurist.
- The writ of habeas corpus is specifically referred to in the 6th Amendment.
- Wartime brings out extraordinary conditions that would not be tolerated in peacetime.
- Abraham Lincoln, in spite of his status as a "great" president, did commit some actions that were less than stellar.
- Lincoln had pledged, in his inaugural address, that he would not interfere with the institution of slavery.
- Lincoln promised to hold areas that belonged to the federal government and to continue with the business of running the country.
- Lincoln did request regional harmony when he first became president and faced unusual problems in the transition of the government as his Republicans were new to political power.

- Four of Lincoln's Cabinet members were former presidential candidates: William Seward (State Department), Salmon P. Chase (Treasury Department), Simon Cameron (War Department), and Edward Bates (Attorney General).
- Most of them thought themselves to be better leaders than Lincoln but would come to recognize his "greatness."

Scoring Rubric

There are five scoring ranges:

Excellent (8–9)

Argument: The essay should have a strong, clear thesis; the student should clearly support either the position that Lincoln exceeded his authority as president or that he did not. The student should also indicate an understanding of the complexity of the question.

Critical Thought: The student should explain how each document supports or undermines the thesis. The student should address conflicts and contradictions in the evidence. Any outside information must be relevant to the argument.

Evidence: The student should use documents and outside information throughout the essay. The student should make use of all of the documents that support his or her argument. At least seven of the documents should be used. Students might address the relationship between the sources. The student may make an occasional minor error.

Writing Style: The essay must be well organized and well written; it must make sense throughout.

Very Good (6–7)

Argument: The thesis should be consistent with the question, but it may not be sufficiently focused to earn top marks.

Critical Thought: The answer must include an analysis of several of the documents and must incorporate outside information.

Evidence: The student should make use of the documents and outside information that support the position being argued. Discussion of relationships between the sources used may be limited.

Writing Style: The answer should be well organized and clearly written; it must be logical, but some points may be unclear.

Adequate (4–5)

Argument: The thesis is only partially developed. It may address the question, but it does so in a way that does not acknowledge the question's complexity.

Critical Thought: The answer is primarily descriptive or narrative, and doesn't provide an analysis of the question or of the evidence provided. It will not address all the relevant issues, and will ignore the opposing position.

Evidence: The student may paraphrase the documents and may misinterpret a document to better fit the argument. The student will use only a little outside information and may refer to only five or six of the documents. The answer may contain errors.

Writing Style: The writing and organization is unclear, but acceptable.

Flawed (2–3)

Argument: The thesis will be unclear, and won't be supported in the body of the essay. Use of evidence will be unclear, and the argument will be poorly developed.

Critical Thought: The student will show only a limited understanding of the question, and will offer little or no analysis. What little analysis there is will be inaccurate. The student will show little understanding of the possible connections between the cases and the Civil War.

Evidence: The student will not make use of the documents appropriate to their argument and may use documents that actually support the opposing position. The use of documents will be haphazard, with references only to brief excerpts or paraphrases. There will be little outside information. The argument may contain major errors.

Writing Style: The answer will be weakly organized and the writing will be unclear.

Severely Flawed (0–1)

Argument: The student provides no thesis, or provides one that is not relevant to the question.

Critical Thought: The student demonstrates little or no understanding of the question.

Evidence: The student makes almost no use of the documents provided and no use of outside information. The answer contains major errors.

Writing Style: The answer is disorganized and poorly written.

Part B: Question Two

Historiography suggests that the record of American existence contains numerous examples of reoccurring themes. Assess the validity of the following:

After reviewing John Winthrop's view of the Puritans and his "City Upon a Hill," the ideas of Manifest Destiny, and the Turner Thesis, American history contains few surprises.

This question asks first that the student have some understanding of historiography. Historiography refers to the writing of history, the theory and methods of historical scholarship, a body of historical writings. It is in the third definition that the essay gets its beginning. John Winthrop's "City Upon a Hill" refers to Winthrop's grand plan, his vision of life as it should be in the New World, where all the mistakes of the Old World could be carefully avoided because men knew in advance and could eliminate such folly. Manifest destiny was John O'Sullivan's idea that Americans were destined to settle from sea to sea across the Great Plains in spite of any Native Americans living in the way. This was the way it was to be. Frederick Jackson Turner's thesis was published in the last decade of the 19th century. Turner suggested that Americans had developed into an independent group because the frontier had been open and available. With such a wide expanse readily available, Americans could start anew in a different place and escape whatever misdeeds; or the second son could do more than be only the second son, he could go forth and conquer the world on his own. The student must then assess the validity of the statement. Many examples come to mind when arguing either side.

KAPLAN
Test Prep and Admissions

Scoring Rubric

There are five scoring ranges:

Excellent (8–9)

The answer should have a strong, clear thesis that ties "City Upon a Hill" to the premise of manifest destiny and the Turner Thesis. The quality of the writing should be excellent, the answer must show logical patterns, and the student should include most of the major points. The organization should be clear. The answer may contain minor errors.

Very Good (6–7)

The answer should have a thesis that makes an argument that the three are related. Organization of the answer must show logical patterns, and the student should include many of the specific points listed in the above list. The answer may contain some errors.

Adequate (4–5)

The answer must try to make some argument about the extent to which the three are related. There may be flaws in the thesis and argument, and the answer may contain errors.

Flawed (2–3)

The answer will demonstrate serious weaknesses. It may have no thesis or argument, and it will include few of the points.

Severely Flawed (0–1)

The answer will demonstrate almost no attempt to answer the question, and will include very few, if any, of the points listed above.

Part B: Question Three

The 20th century saw a revival of the conservative movement. What factors contributed to that resurgence?

This question asks the student to analyze the factors that led to the resurgence of the conservative faction in government. Certainly Ronald Reagan (1980–1988) was a conservative, and he was the first Republican elected to two terms since Eisenhower (1952). Students would need to reference the growing federal bureaucracy in the Roosevelt administrations

and Truman's continued support of the same proposals. Following Truman was Eisenhower, and those two administrations were fraught with Cold War histrionics. John Kennedy expanded the federal safety net to millions; Lyndon Johnson's Great Society expanded the federal programs to the poor even more. Nixon was more concerned with ending the conflict in Vietnam and getting reelected. Gerald Ford was President for too little time and Jimmy Carter faced the Iranians. Ronald Reagan argued on the campaign trail that the government had gotten out of hand. He exposed the traditional conservative Republican line that businesses were struggling because of the tax bite and the country needed to restrain itself. By changing our structure to a supply side strategy, the benefits would far outweigh the temporary problems. This struck a chord with the voters and the Republicans were swept into office. George H. W. Bush rode in on the last wave of conservatives, by then the trickle down, supply side economic practices were shown to be ineffective. Bill Clinton was elected in 1992 and the rest, as they say, is history.

Scoring Rubric

There are five scoring ranges:

Excellent (8–9)

The answer should have a strong, clear thesis that defines 20th century conservatives. The quality of the writing should be excellent, the answer must show logical patterns, and the student should include many of the points in the above list. The organization should be clear. The answer may contain minor errors.

Very Good (6–7)

The answer should have a thesis that defines 20th century conservatism. Organization of the answer must show logical patterns, and the student should include many of the points listed in the above list. The answer may contain some errors.

Adequate (4–5)

The answer should try to make some argument about conservatism and must include at least some of the points listed above. There may be flaws in the thesis and argument.

KAPLAN
Test Prep and Admissions

Flawed (2–3)

The answer will demonstrate serious weaknesses. It may have no thesis argument at all, and it will include few of the points listed above. The answer may show little understanding of political conservatism, and will not demonstrate knowledge of what changes took place.

Severely Flawed (0–1)

The answer will demonstrate almost no attempt to answer the question, and will include very few, if any, of the points listed above.

Part C: Question Four

Explain how TWO of the following helped to facilitate the shift from an agrarian to an industrial economy in the early 1800s.

- Commercial farming
- Factory system
- Inventions
- Labor
- Transportation
- Entrepreneurs

The shift from the agrarian economy to the industrial economy would have occurred regardless; the reason it proceeded with such speed was that the factors of production were present in Great Britain in the 1750s and the colonists brought those factors and expectations to the Americas. The factors of production are: a ready supply of the natural resources that are going to be needed to make a product. A labor force, funded by the capital investments of entrepreneurs who were willing to take risks, worked those resources. All four factors need to be present in some form for the change to occur. Coming to the Americas, craftsmen brought their skills, and settlers brought their expectations that the products were going to be available. For a hundred years, the products crafted here in the colonies were still considered inferior to those made back in Great Britain. Once the American Revolution began, the supply of goods was cut off, and craftsmen here in the colonies finally got their consumers. It is interesting to note that Southern families continued to buy overseas. This caused some Northerners to suggest that the Southerners were not true Americans.

The other choices in the list—commercial farming, the factory system and inventions—are reasonable and self-explanatory. Commercial farming refers to the growing of crops and the raising of animals for a large market. The factory system was the industrialization of the cotton industry, particularly in Massachusetts. Mill owners would travel afield and solicit workers, often young girls, who were literally sold into employment by their starving families. The girls would live in factory-supplied housing and follow company rules. The inventions that made the industrialization work came into being almost faster than one could conceive. The steel plow made it possible to plow and plant more acres. Then, the mechanized reaper made it possible to harvest those acres cheaply. The resulting product came to market quickly and cheaply. There are a host of other examples the student could cite.

See the next page for the scoring rubric.

Part C: Question Five

Constitutional scholars will suggest that the Supreme Court is never wrong. In light of this argument, explain the ruling in *Brown v. Board of Education* and the "separate but equal" doctrine.

The doctrine of "separate but equal" was a result of the 1896 decision in *Plessy v. Ferguson*. Homer Plessy wanted to sit in the whites-only railroad car and was arrested. The Court upheld the Louisiana law requiring "separate but equal accommodations" for African American and white passengers. The Court also said that the law did not violate the 14th Amendment's guarantee of "equal protection of the laws." This decision paved the way for a string of segregation laws to be adopted in the southern states. Most facilities became segregated. Included in the segregated facilities were schools. By the early 1950s, African Americans were fighting conventional society for their civil rights. Four cases involving school facilities were group together under the umbrella of Brown and were argued by Thurgood Marshall (a later Supreme Court justice). In the 1954 Brown decision, the Court argued that the segregation of African American children in public school was unconstitutional because it violated the 14th Amendment's guarantee of "equal protection of the laws." In his majority decision for the Court, Chief Justice Earl Warren wrote that "separate but equal is inherently unequal."

KAPLAN
Test Prep and Admissions

How can this be? The same logic was used in both cases; what has changed? The time had come to address the societal ills of segregation, said the Court. When society cannot move itself, other means have to be found. The Justices knew that there would be deep-seated resistance to the decision and its ramifications. President Eisenhower privately expressed reservation, but upheld the federal authority by sending federal troops to states which deliberately ignored the decision and its requirement that: "…segregation in the schools should end with all deliberate speed."

Scoring Rubric for Questions Four and Five

There are five scoring ranges:

Excellent (8–9)

The answer should have a strong, clear thesis that makes a case for two of the possible choices. The quality of the writing should be excellent, the answer must show logical patterns, and the student should include many of the major points in the above paragraphs. The organization should be clear. The answer may contain minor errors.

Very Good (6–7)

The answer should have a thesis that makes an argument or takes a position. Organization of the answer must show logical patterns, and the student should include many of the specific points from the above paragraphs. The answer may contain some errors.

Adequate (4–5)

The answer must try to make some argument and must include at least some of the points discussed above. There may be flaws in the thesis and argument. The answer may contain errors.

Flawed (2–3)

The answer will demonstrate serious weaknesses. It may have no thesis argument at all, and it will include few of the points listed above. The answer may show little understanding of agrarian and/or industrial economies and will not be able to demonstrate connections between the two. The answer will contain errors.

Severely Flawed (0–1)

The answer will demonstrate almost no attempt to answer the question, and will include very few, if any, of the points discussed above.

COMPUTING YOUR SCORE

Remember not to take any score on the practice test too literally. There is no way to determine precisely what your AP grade will be because:

- The conditions under which you take the practice test will not exactly mirror real test conditions.
- While the multiple-choice questions are scored by computer, the free-response questions are graded manually by faculty consultants. You will not be able to accurately grade your own essays.

Section I: Multiple Choice

This section accounts for approximately one-half of the test score. Remember there is a guessing penalty on this section of the test: One-fourth of a point is deducted from your score for each incorrect answer, but no points are deducted for a blank answer. Getting 60 percent of the multiple-choice questions correct (a raw score of 48 on this section), would be equivalent to a grade of 3 (although, of course, this might change, depending on your performance on the free-response section).

Number Correct $- (\frac{1}{4} \times 3$ Number Answered Incorrectly) = Multiple-Choice Raw Score

Section II: Free Response

This section accounts for the other half of the test score. Of course, it will be difficult for you to accurately score your own essays. Review the explanation for each essay and assign yourself a grade of 0–9 for how well you think you did.

$(4.5 \times$ _____ $) + (2.75 \times$ _____ $) + (2.75 \times$ _____ $) =$ _____

DBQ points   First essay score   Second essay score   Free-Response Raw Score

(0–9)   (0–9)   (0–9)

Composite Score

Multiple-Choice Raw Score + Free-Response Raw Score = Composite Score

Conversion Chart (approximate)

Composite Score Range	AP Grade
117–170	5
96–116	4
79–95	3
51–78	2
0–50	1

KAPLAN
Test Prep and Admissions

Index

KAPLAN
Test Prep and Admissions

KAPLAN
Test Prep and Admissions

KAPLAN

Test Prep and Admissions